# Curriculum

# CURRICULUM
## *perspectives*
## *and practice*

John P. Miller
The Ontario Institute for Studies in Education

Wayne Seller
The Ontario Institute for Studies in Education

Longman
New York & London

To Our Children
Patrick, Nancy, Lorie, Angela, and Steven

Executive Editor: Ray O'Connell
Developmental Editor: Naomi Silverman
Production Editor: Pamela Nelson
Text Design: Gloria Moyer
Cover Design: Nina Tallarico
Text Art: Vantage Art, Inc.
Production Supervisor: Eduardo Castillo
Compositor: Publishers Phototype International
Printer and Binder: The Alpine Press, Inc.

**Library of Congress Cataloging in Publication Data**

Miller, John P., 1943–
  Curriculum, perspectives and practice.

  Bibliography: p.
  Includes index.
  1. Curriculum planning.   2. Curriculum evaluation.
I. Seller, Wayne.   II. Title.
LB1570.M545     1985     375'.001     84-17086
ISBN 0-582-284759

# Acknowledgments

Grateful acknowledgment is made for permission to reprint the following copyrighted material.

**Chapter 2:** Excerpts from Abraham Kaplan quoted in Bertrand Russell, *The New World of Philosophy* (New York, 1961), reprinted by permission of Random House, Inc.

**Chapter 3:** Excerpts from Allan Ornstein, "Curriculum Contrasts: A Historical Overview," *Phi Delta Kappan, 63* (1982), p. 405, copyright © 1983 by Phi Delta Kappan, reprinted by permission of Allan Ornstein; Mark Holmes, "Forward to the Basics," *Curriculum Inquiry, 10* (New York, 1980), p. 414, copyright © 1980 by John Wiley & Sons, Inc., reprinted by permission of John Wiley & Sons, Inc.

**Chapter 4:** Excerpts from John Dewey, *Experience and Education* (New York: Macmillan, 1938), reprinted by permission of Kappa Delta Pi, West Lafayette, Indiana; Lawrence Kohlberg and Rochelle Mayer, "Development as the Aim of Education," *Harvard Educational Review*, 1972, copyright © 1972 by the President and Fellows of Harvard College, all rights reserved; Lawrence Kohlberg and Carol Gilligan, "The Adolescent as Philosopher," reprinted by permission of *Daedalus*, Journal of the American Academy of Arts and Sciences, vol. 100, 1971, Boston, Massachusetts.

**Chapter 5:** Excerpts from Rosaline Driver and Gaalen Erikson, "Theories in Action: Some Theoretical and Empirical Issues in the Study of Students' Conceptual Frameworks in Science," *Studies in Science Education, 10* (1983), pp. 39–40, 52, reprinted by permission of Rosaline Driver; Joseph Schwab, "The Concept of the Structure of a Discipline," *Educational Record, 43* (July, 1962), pp. 197, 201–202, reprinted by permission of American Council on Education; Rowena Patte, "Intuition, Creativity, and Centering," *ATP Newsletter* (Fall, 1983), p. 12, reprinted by permission of Transpersonal Institute and A.T.P.; Joseph Schwab, "The Practical: The Language for Curriculum," *The School Review* (November, 1969), p. 10, reprinted by permission of The University of Chicago Press.

**Chapter 6:** Excerpts from James Bugental, *Challenges of Humanistic Psychology* (New York, 1967), p. 9, reprinted by permission of McGraw-Hill Book Company; M. Gandhi and K. Kripalani (Eds.), *All Men Are Brothers* (New York, 1980), pp. 62, 63, 72, reprinted by permission of Continuum; Marilyn Ferguson, "Karl Pribram's Changing Reality in the Holographic Paradigm," *Human Behavior, 7*(5), copyright © 1978 by *Human Behavior* magazine, reprinted by permission.

**Chapter 7:** Excerpts from Arthur Combs, "The Personal Approach to Good Teaching." Reprinted in *Humanistic Education Sourcebook, 21*(6), (1975), p. 254, reprinted with permission of the Association for Supervision and Curriculum Development, copyright © 1964 by the Association for Supervision and Curriculum Development, all rights reserved; Michael Apple and Nancy King, "What Do Schools Teach?" reprinted by permission of the publisher from Richard H. Weller: *Humanistic Education*, © 1977 by McCutchan Publishing Corporation, Berkeley, California 94704.

**Chapter 8:** Excerpts from George Posner, "A Cognitive Science Conception of Curriculum and Instruction," *Journal Curriculum Studies, 14* (1982), p. 348, copyright © 1982, *Journal Curriculum Studies*, reprinted by permission; from Lawrence Metcalf and Maurice Hunt, "Relevance and the Curriculum," *Phi Delta Kappan, LI*(7), (March, 1970), p. 360. Copyright © 1970, *Phi Delta Kappan*, reprinted by permission.

**Chapter 9:** Excerpts from Kliebard, "The Tyler Rationale," *The School Review, 78* (February, 1970), p. 267, reprinted by permission of The University of Chicago Press.

**Chapter 12:** Excerpts from Milbrey Wallin McLaughlin and David D. Marsh, "Staff Development and School Change" in Ann Lieberman and Lynne Miller, editors, STAFF DEVELOPMENT: NEW DEMANDS, NEW REALITIES, NEW PERSPECTIVES (New York: Teachers College Press, 1979), pp. 76, 78; from Leonard Burrello and Tim Orbaugh, "Reducing the Discrepancy Between the Known and the Unknown," *In-Service Education, 63*(6), (1982), pp. 385, 386, copyright © 1982 by *Phi Delta Kappan*, reprinted by permission of Leonard Burrello.

**Chapter 13:** Excerpts from Robert Stake, "The Countenance of Educational Evaluation," *Teacher's College Record, 68*(7), (1967), p. 374, copyright © 1967 by *Teacher's College Record*, reprinted by permission.

**Chapter 14:** Excerpts from Robert Stake and Ralph Tyler (Eds.), "Toward a Technology for the Evaluation of Education Programs," *Perspectives on Curriculum Evaluation* (1967), p. 5, copyright © 1967 by *Perspectives on Curriculum Evaluation*, reprinted by permission of the American Educational Research Association; from John Mann, "Curricular Criticism," *Curriculum Theory Network, CTN 2* (Winter, 1968–69), p. 10, copyright © 1968–69 by *Curriculum Theory Network*, reprinted by permission of John Wiley & Sons, Inc.

**Chapter 15:** Excerpts from Michael Apple, "Curriculum in the Year 2000: Tensions and Possibilities," *Phi Delta Kappan* (January, 1983), pp. 321–326, copyright © January 1983 by *Phi Delta Kappan*, reprinted by permission of Michael Apple; from Clive Smith, "Visions of Tomorrow: Life in the Information Age," *New Age Journal, 7*(2), (September, 1981), pp. 22–23, 68–69, reprinted with permission of *New Age Journal*, © 1981, all rights reserved (NAJ, 342 Western Ave., Brighton, MA 02135); from Peggy Taylor and Marc Barasch, "Interview: The World According to John Naisbitt," *New Age Journal* (October, 1983), pp. 30–33, 93–97, reprinted with permission of *New Age Journal*, October 1983, © Rising Star Associates Ltd. (342 Western Ave., Brighton, MA 02135), all rights reserved.

# Contents

# Preface

The purpose of this book is to help educators conduct curriculum practices from an integrated perspective. What we mean by this is a perspective in which theory and practice are integrated to produce an orientation to curriculum that is consistent with one's personal world view. This is not an easy task. Traditionally, curriculum workers' first step in developing curriculum programs has been to state objectives, without considering the underlying beliefs and assumptions that influence the selection of particular objectives. As a result, educators have often carried out curriculum practices in a fragmented manner, as mere technical procedures that are divorced from the belief structures on which they are based. To assist curriculum workers in developing a clearer perspective, we have attempted in this text to draw relationships between theory (the philosophical, psychological, and social underpinnings of curriculum) and practice (development, implementation, and evaluation).

In the first part of the book, we present three basic orientations to curriculum (curriculum positions)—the transmission, transaction, and transformation positions; we describe the underlying theories, beliefs, and assumptions in which these positions are rooted and explain how the positions are manifested in educational programs. The second half of the book focuses on how curriculum development, implementation, and evaluation can be undertaken from each of the curriculum positions.

We devote significant attention to curriculum implementation, in particular, because we believe this area is often overlooked in curriculum texts. Recent research has helped to identify what makes implementation so difficult and how these difficulties can be addressed. We describe some of this research and provide some practical suggestions to facilitate the use in schools of new curriculum programs.

In sum, we examine in this text the philosophical, psychological, and social contexts that shape curriculum practices, in order to clarify the relationship between theory and practice; our goal in doing so is to provide the reader with a useful framework for analyzing his or her own attitudes and beliefs about curriculum and, more importantly, for using the understanding that is gained from such analysis to conduct curriculum practices from an integrated perspective.

The help of several people was instrumental to the writing of this book. Floyd Robinson, John Ross, and Bruce Cassie, our colleagues at The Ontario Institute for Studies in Education, provided helpful comments that were integral to revisions of the book. Ken Zeichner reviewed an earlier draft of the book and also provided several suggestions that we used in the final draft. Finally, George Posner and Leo Anglin, who saw this book develop from its tentative beginnings to its final form, were particularly helpful. Their consistent support and insightful analysis were invaluable.

Several typists helped complete this book. Earlier drafts were completed by Margaret Gerry and Barbara McEwan. Special thanks goes to Joan Graziani and Joan Doyle, who typed the final manuscript with care and efficiency.

We would like to thank our editors at Longman for their support. Nicki Benevento provided the initial inspiration for this book and Lane Akers and Naomi Silverman saw it to completion.

Finally, this book would not have been possible without the patience and support of our wives, Jean and Amy.

John P. Miller
Wayne Seller

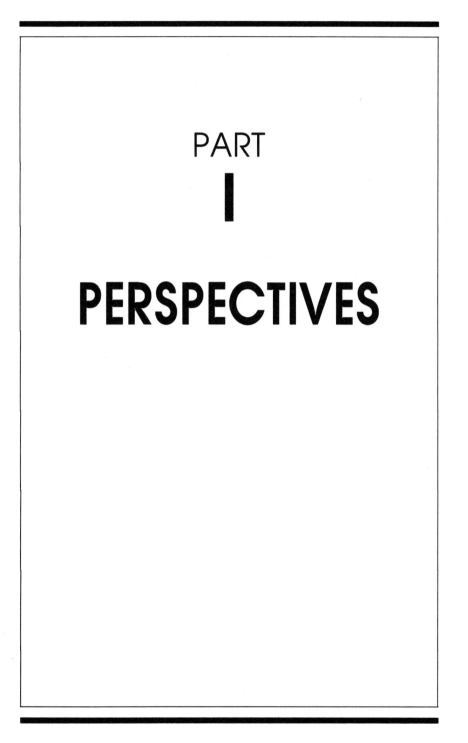

PART

I

# PERSPECTIVES

# CHAPTER 1

# THE CURRICULUM PROCESS

We see the development, implementation, and evaluation of curriculum as a dynamic and complex process that is rooted in personal meaning and in dialogue about what schools should do. This process of interaction among teachers, students, curriculum workers, parents, and others involved with schooling is dynamic because people are continuously developing within a changing and pluralistic society; it is complex because the interrelations and interconnections in a school setting are many. To apply reductionist measures to curriculum is to cut it off from the web of relations that surrounds it; therefore, we believe it is important to look at curriculum from a perspective that acknowledges the interdependence of phenomena.

What do we mean when we use the word *curriculum?* As one would expect, the definitions offered run a spectrum. At one end, curriculum is seen merely as a course of study; at the other end, curriculum is more broadly defined as everything that occurs under the auspices of the school. In the middle of the spectrum, curriculum is viewed as an interaction between students and teachers that is designed to achieve specific educational goals—it has been defined, for example, as "a plan for providing sets of learning opportunities to achieve broad goals and related specific objectives for an identifiable population served by a single school center" (Saylor & Alexander, 1974, p. 6) and as "the reconstruction of knowledge and experience systematically developed under the auspices of the school (or university), to enable the learner to increase his or her control of knowledge and experience" (Tanner & Tanner, 1980, p. 38).

In our view, curriculum is an explicitly and implicitly intentional set of interactions designed to facilitate learning and development and to impose meaning on experience. The explicit intentions usually are expressed in the written curricula and in courses of study; the implicit

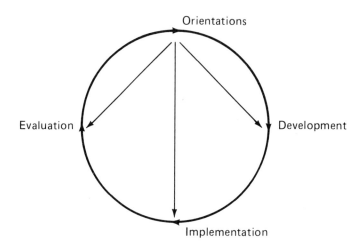

**Figure 1.1**   Curriculum development as an ongoing process.

intentions are found in the "hidden curriculum," by which we mean the roles and norms that underlie interactions in the school. Learning interactions usually occur between teacher and student, but they also occur between student and student, student and subject matter, student and computer, and student and community. These interactions take place at different levels. At the most superficial level, the student merely absorbs factual information from a textbook; at a deeper level, mutual interaction takes place between student and teacher in the course of solving new problems. At the deepest level, the student's encounter with a poem, for example, or a scientific experiment, or music, stimulates new awareness, perceptions, or cognitive understanding; at this level, dialogue between student and teacher becomes Buber's "I–thou" relationship or an open mutuality between student and teacher.

The development of curriculum is an ongoing process, as shown in Figure 1.1. Although, in practice, this cycle can start anywhere, we will describe its components in the following order: orientations, development, implementation, and evaluation.

## ORIENTATIONS

At the root of individual perception is a particular world view or model of reality. Such models of reality shape each educator's personal belief structure about the purposes and methodologies of education. In this book, we refer to these basic beliefs about what schools should do and how students learn as *orientations to curriculum, curriculum positions,* or *metaorientations.*

In *The Educational Spectrum* (1983), Miller describes seven specific orientations to curriculum: behavioral, subject/disciplines, social, developmental, cognitive process, humanistic, and transpersonal. He also articulates the concept that each specific orientation to curriculum expresses a particular point of view in relation to each of the following issues:

- *Educational aims:* Each orientation has certain basic goals that define its overall direction.
- *Conception of the learner:* Each orientation offers a particular view of the learner. In some, the learner is viewed as an active agent; in others, the student is seen as functioning in a more passive (responsive) mode.
- *Conception of the learning process:* Conceptions of the learning process vary with each orientation. For example, a transpersonal orientation emphasizes the inner life of the student, whereas other orientations (e.g., the behavioral orientation) define learning in terms of change in the student's external behavior.
- *Conception of the learning environment:* Each orientation includes a particular view of how the learning environment should be structured and what learning materials are appropriate. Some orientations perceive the ideal environment as one that is loosely structured; others stress the importance of a highly structured environment.
- *Conception of the teacher's role:* Definitions of the role of the teacher differ with the various orientations. Some call for the teacher to take a strong directive role; others see the teacher's role more as a facilitator of learning.
- *Conception of how learning should be evaluated:* Each orientation includes a particular approach to evaluation procedures. Some rely on criterion-referenced tests; others use techniques that are more experimental and open-ended.

As Miller (1983) has pointed out, educators generally adhere to a cluster of two or three orientations to curriculum that form metaorientations (major positions) in curriculum programs. The concept of metaorientation helps one to perceive the linkage between curriculum practices and the philosophical, psychological, and social contexts that shape them. The three major positions presented in this book—the transmission, transaction, and transformation positions—are briefly outlined in the following section and discussed in detail in Chapters 2–7.

## Transmission Position

In the transmission position, the function of education is to transmit facts, skills, and values to students. Specifically, this orientation stresses mastery of traditional school subjects through traditional teaching meth-

**Figure 1.2**  Transmission position.

odologies, particularly textbook learning (subject orientation); acquisition by students of basic skills and certain cultural values and mores that are necessary in order to function in society (cultural transmission orientation); and the application of a mechanistic view of human behavior to curriculum planning, whereby student skills are developed through specific instructional strategies (competency-based learning orientation). In this position, there is primarily one way movement to convey to students certain skills, knowledge, and values. The philosophical–scientific paradigm for this position is an atomistic view of nature in which reality is seen in terms of separate, isolated building blocks. The transmission position is diagrammed in Figure 1.2.

Historically, the transmission position is linked with rote learning methods that have been used in schools since colonial times. The philosophical roots of this position are found in the school of philosophy known as logical positivism, which is concerned with breaking down language into logical components that can be analyzed and verified. This position has its psychological underpinnings in behavioral psychology—particularly in the work of Thorndike and Skinner—where the emphasis is on breaking down human activity into specific responses that can be used to predict and control human behavior. Socially, the transmission position can be linked with various forms of conservative political philosophy that favor traditional values such as the work ethic and patriotism. It is associated with laissez-faire capitalism, a conservative theory of economics that advocates minimum government interference in the economy and sees economic activity as controlled by individual self-interest and competition in the marketplace for goods and services; in a laissez-faire economy the individual is atomized in the marketplace.

**Transaction Position**

In the transaction position, the individual is seen as rational and capable of intelligent problem solving. Education is viewed as a dialogue between the student and the curriculum in which the student reconstructs knowledge through the dialogue process. The central elements in the transaction position are an emphasis on curriculum strategies that facilitate problem solving (cognitive process orientation); application of problem-solving skills within social contexts in general and within the context of the democratic process (democratic citizenship orientation); and development of cognitive skills within the academic disciplines (disciplines orientation). The philosophical–scientific paradigm for the transaction position is the scientific method. Figure 1.3 illustrates the transaction position.

Historically, the transaction position can be traced back to the Enlightenment and its impact on such American thinkers such as Benjamin Franklin and Thomas Jefferson, who did not accept the predominant Calvinist view of education but argued instead for a curriculum that would develop the student's intellectual abilities. During the nineteenth century, educational reformers continued to promote a view of education that called for schools to go beyond their traditional role as conveyors of rote learning. Johann Heinrich Pestalozzi was a central figure in this reform movement; Henry Barnard and Horace Mann were influenced by Pestalozzi's belief that the chief goal of education is the development of intelligence and became important spokesmen for this point of view. The progressive education movement during the early twentieth century, another historical antecedent to the transaction position, was influenced by the educational theories of John Dewey and Lester Ward; this movement focused on developing the student's intelligence through problem solving.

The philosophical roots of the transaction position can be traced to Dewey's pragmatism—his belief that the scientific method can be applied to a broad range of problems. In fact, Gutek (1974) uses the word *transactive* in describing Dewey's philosophy of education. The transaction position has psychological roots in the cognitive developmental theories of Piaget and Kohlberg. Piaget's work advances the view that development results from interaction between the student and a stimulating intellectual environment: Kohlberg argues that cognitive developmental theory is an extension of Dewey's conception of growth. The political ideology linked with the transaction position is small-*l* liberalism, in which there is

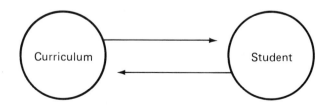

**Figure 1.3**   Transaction position.

general belief that rational intelligence can be used to improve the social environment. This political orientation is characterized by its support for reform efforts to ensure that minority groups have equal opportunity in the society, and is linked with the thinking of economists such as Keynes and Galbraith, who favor systematic economic planning and government intervention to stimulate the economy.

## Transformation Position

The transformation metaorientation focuses on personal and social change. It encompasses three specific orientations: teaching students skills that promote personal and social transformation (humanistic and social change orientations); a vision of social change as movement toward harmony with the environment rather than as an effort to exert control over it, and the attribution of a spiritual dimension to the environment, in which the ecological system is viewed with respect and reverence (transpersonal orientation). The paradigm for the transformation position is an ecologically interdependent conception of nature that emphasizes the interrelatedness of phenomena. As shown in Figure 1.4, in the transformation position the curriculum and the student are seen to interpenetrate each other in a holistic manner.

Historically, the transformation position is linked to two different strands of thought. One is the romantic element, which can be traced to Rousseau's thinking, and is also found in the work of Froebel, Tolstoy, A. S. Neill, and John Holt. These educators have argued that the child is essentially good and that education should allow the inner nature of the child to unfold with minimum interference. Neill's school, Summerhill, represents the classic example of putting this theory into practice. The second strand is found in the social change orientation, which argues that educators must take a more critical view of the role of schools in society so that schools do not just mirror dominant economic interests, and that schools must be on the cutting edge of social and political change. Today, the work of educators such as Michael Apple, and Friere's work in Brazil, reflect this orientation.

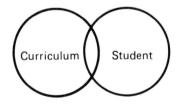

**Figure 1.4**   Transformation position.

Philosophically, the transformation position has its roots in transcendentalism, mysticism, and some forms of existentialism. This position embodies what Huxley (1970) called the "perennial philosophy"—the idea that all phenomenon are part of an interconnected whole. The psychological base of the transformation position is found in humanistic and transpersonal psychology, which emphasize personal fulfillment at the ego (humanistic) and spiritual (transpersonal) levels. Socially, this position is identified with a cultural tendency that advocates decentralized, pluralistic political networks, "small is beautiful" economics, and holistic medicine.

## Curriculum Positions and the Berlak Dilemmas

Berlak and Berlak (1981) view the relationship between educational practices, and the philosophical, psychological, and social assumptions on which they are based, in terms of what they call *dilemmas* about practical issues that teachers and schools face. Their concept of dilemmas overlaps with Miller's list of the issues addressed by each of the three major curriculum positions (see p. 5 in this chapter). In other words, like each of the points listed by Miller, each of the dilemmas identified by Berlak and Berlak is in essence a statement of the range of positions from which it is possible to approach a particular educational issue. At the end of Chapters 3, 5, and 7, in which we discuss the educational practices associated with the transmission, transaction, and transformation positions, respectively, we provide a summary of the stance taken by the orientation under consideration in relation to each of the Berlak dilemmas. Berlak and Berlak identify 16 dilemmas in total; however, for our purposes we have reduced the number to 9:

**1.** *Whole child versus child as student.* At one end of this dilemma is the idea that teachers should be concerned with children's aesthetic, intellectual, physical, social, emotional, and moral development; at the other end is the idea that the teacher should focus only on the child *as student.* In the transformation position, the role of the teacher is generally seen as one in which the teacher works with the whole child; the transmission position is oriented toward seeing the role of the teacher as being confined to working with the child as student.

**2.** *Teacher versus child control.* This dilemma focuses on how much control is retained by the teacher or accorded to the student over a number of dimensions (e.g., time, operations, and standards). For example, in the transmission position control is held by the teacher, whereas in the transformation position the teacher turns over a considerable amount of control to the student.

**3.** *Personal knowledge versus public knowledge.* This dilemma describes the teacher's need to decide how much emphasis to place on knowledge that is part of traditional subject matter and how much to place on knowledge that is rooted in personal meaning. Again, the transmission and transformation positions are at opposite ends of the spectrum, with the transmission position stressing public knowledge and the transformation position emphasizing personal knowledge.

**4.** *Knowledge as content versus knowledge as process.* In the words of Berlak and Berlak (1981), "This dilemma formulates the pull toward viewing public knowledge as organized bodies of information, codified facts, theories, generalizations, on the one hand, or as a process of thinking, reasoning and testing used to establish the truth or adequacy of a body of content or set of propositions, on the other hand" (p. 147). Teachers adhering to the transaction position, for example, can emphasize knowledge as process in various inquiry procedures.

**5.** *Extrinsic versus intrinsic motivation.* In this dilemma the teacher must decide whether motivation comes from without, in which case students must be constantly rewarded or punished, or whether it is primarily initiated and sustained by the learners themselves. In the transmission position, for example, the emphasis is primarily on extrinsic motivation.

**6.** *Learning is holistic versus learning is molecular.* Berlak and Berlak (1981) state, "From the molecular perspective learning is the taking in and the accumulation of discrete parts or pieces; when one has mastered the pieces one knows the whole. From the holistic perspective learning is the active construction of meaning by persons, the understanding of a whole, a process that is in some essential way different from learning a series of parts or elements" (p. 151). This dilemma is central to the three major positions discussed in this book, as the transmission position is basically defined as an atomistic approach to learning whereas the transformation position focuses on interconnections and interdependencies.

**7.** *Each child unique versus children have shared characteristics.* At one end of the spectrum in this dilemma, the teacher views the student as having a unique combination of complex and highly differentiated attributes or, at the other end, the student is seen as having characteristics shared in common with other students. For example, in the latter case, which frequently occurs in the transmission position, the teacher may assume that "everyone in the class can be taught the same material in the same way at the same time" (Berlak & Berlak, 1981, p. 153).

**8.** *Learning is social versus learning is individual.* According to Berlak and Berlak (1981), "From the individual perspective, learning is a private encounter between child and material. The ideal ratio of student to teacher though hardly possible in the real world is one-to-one. From the social perspective learning proceeds best—most efficiently and effectively—if there is interaction among the persons learning" (p. 155). Dewey, for example, whose thinking is central to the transaction position, argued that learning should be a social process.

**9.** *Child as person versus child as client.* In this dilemma, the teacher views the child either as a whole person or, at the other end of the spectrum, as a client with special problems that must be treated. For example, in the transformation position teachers attempt to approach the child as a whole person rather than as someone who requires expert diagnosis and treatment.

## Orientations as a Tool for Curriculum Development, Implementation, and Evaluation

The major positions and specific orientations we have just discussed are important and useful in a number of ways. First, familiarity with the major curriculum positions can help a teacher clarify his or her own approach to teaching and learning. As teachers explore these positions and also the more specific orientations within them, they can identify the aspects of the positions that most closely parallel their own thinking, although, certainly most teachers will find they do not subscribe to any one position in totality.

Second, the three major curriculum positions provide a conceptual framework for curriculum planning. Educators can use their knowledge of the major positions to help them understand the basic approach of a curriculum guideline. Similarly, the positions can be helpful in analyzing specific curriculum materials to determine whether they are appropriate to a particular learning context. If a teacher is basically committed to a transmission position, for example, it is unlikely that materials from a transformation metaorientation will work in that teacher's classroom.

Finally, the curriculum positions can be used as a vehicle for staff development. For example, a study of the metaorientations may be helpful to a school staff seeking to develop an overall school philosophy. Individuals or curriculum committees who have clarified their own stance in relation to the positions can more easily develop aims or goals for a program, which then can be broken down into more specific objectives. The level of specificity, however, will often reflect the particular curriculum position on which a given program is based. In the transmission position, for example, objectives tend to be very specific. In the philosophy, curriculum materials, and evaluation procedures associated with the various orientations, the staff also may find support for programs they have already developed and/or wish to implement.

## DEVELOPMENT

In this phase of the curriculum process, teachers or curriculum workers develop or adapt a guideline or set of learning materials to their school or classroom. Even if they are only adapting preexisting curriculum materials, educators should be aware of the processes that comprise curriculum development:

**1.** *Setting aims and objectives:* Aims and objectives usually will reflect one's overall curriculum position. The transmission position emphasizes objectives that are specific and are sometimes stated in behavioral terms. Lists of objectives within this position can be extensive. In the transaction position, objectives tend to focus on complex intellectual skills or concepts. As Markley et al. (1974) point out, the transformation position stresses holistic, experimental, and open-ended goals based on self-realization and a multidimensional approach to life that does not place undue weight on materialistic goals such as status and consumption.

**2.** *Identifying appropriate content:* Curriculum developers must decide what content is appropriate to the curriculum and identify criteria for selecting it. Philosophical, psychological, and social orientation, student interest, and usefulness are some of the criteria that might be used. What weight these criteria are assigned will reflect one's curriculum orientation. For instance, student interest is a more important criterion in the transformation position than in the transmission position.

**3.** *Choosing teaching–learning strategies:* Teaching–learning strategies can be selected according to several criteria, including orientation, level of complexity, teacher expertise, and student interest. In the transmission position, teaching tends to be structured, repeatable, and specific. The transaction orientation focuses on strategies that facilitate inquiry and thus are somewhat more open-ended than in the transmission position. In the transformation position, teaching strategies are geared toward helping students make connections between their inner and outer worlds; for this reason, techniques such as guided imagery, journal writing, and meditation are employed.

To integrate these components of the curriculum development process, curriculum committees should also examine various models of curriculum development. In Chapter 9, we present a number of these models, such as the Tyler rationale (1949), which, despite its limitations, remains a prototype for many curriculum theorists, and we examine them in terms of the general curriculum positions they reflect. Gagne's system (Gagne & Briggs, 1979), for example, can be linked with the transmission position, whereas models based on the learner (e.g., Weinstein & Fantini, 1970) reflect the transformation position.

## IMPLEMENTATION

Implementation, a major component in the curriculum process, has been neglected by curriculum theorists. In some cases, implementation has been identified with instruction, but this view ignores the multidimensional and complex impact of change as a factor in curriculum implementation. Fullan (1982) identifies three levels on which curriculum change can occur:

1. *Materials:* The use of new or revised instructional materials or technologies.
2. *Teaching approaches:* New strategies, activities, practices, etc., engaged in by the teacher.
3. *Beliefs:* Pedagogical assumptions and theories underlying new politics or programs.

In many cases, curriculum change is confined to changes in materials. However, to be effective it must also involve changes in what teachers do and how they think. Overall, it is important to recognize certain qualities inherent in the change as it relates to curriculum implementation. Fullan and Park (1982, pp. 24–26) summarize these qualities as follows:

1. *Change* is a process not an event.
2. Change happens to *individuals.*
3. Change involves an individual and social process of learning new things with all that entails (or change is developmental in which people develop new meanings, skills, attitudes).
4. The meaning of change varies for people in *different roles* (or change is a multilevel phenomenon).
5. Innovations are *complex* (involving changes in materials, beliefs, and practices and involving multilevel coordination).
6. *Adaptation and variation* in implementation frequently occurs.
7. Implementation is influenced by *many factors* that operate as a system of variables in any given situation.
8. Implementation can be *facilitated.*
9. Implementation involves questions of *values, ethics, and professional responsibility.*
10. The ultimate goal of implementation is not to implement any one particular innovation, but to develop the capacity in school systems, individual schools, and individuals to process all innovations and revisions.

Effective implementation is often difficult because it occurs within a complex environment—the school system—where patterns and structures that have been developed over long periods of time often run counter to the thrust of new programs. It is useful to see the school from an ecological perspective that recognizes the set of interdependent relationships into which new programs are introduced. (This type of perspective is consistent with the transformation position.)

It is our view that implementation is a process, not a product, and thus involves sharing ownership in the new program. This means there is interaction between the teacher and the curriculum worker (e.g., consultant or principal) that will lead to mutual adaptation of the program. Of course, levels of mutual adaptation can range from superficial dialogue about the program to complete examination and revision of it.

A number of models have been developed to facilitate implementation. For example, Hall and Loucks (1978) have developed a model based on teacher concerns and levels of use of a new program. The Hall–Loucks model lets teachers and curriculum workers identify how successfully a program has been implemented. Leithwood (1982) has developed a model that identifies "stages of growth" in implementation. These models are among those described in detail in Chapter 11.

In Chapter 12, we suggest guidelines to facilitate implementation in terms of shared ownership and mutual adaptation and describe the specific elements of an implementation plan, including timelines, tasks, and roles that can assist teachers and curriculum workers in developing a sound basis for introducing a new program.

Although the success of almost any implementation plan depends on adequate professional development, in-service training for the introduction of new programs is often limited to one- or two-day affairs with little follow-up. However, without follow-up, the implementation of most new curriculum programs founders—an outcome that points to the need for an ecological approach to curriculum implementation.

## EVALUATION

The search for an evaluation base is a primary concern in the evaluation phase of the curriculum process. Curriculum evaluation procedures, which have become more inclusive in recent years, now include qualitative procedures that complement more traditional quantitative methods. In Chapter 13, we examine various ideas about the role and purpose of evaluation and how these ideas influence the selection of evaluation bases. We discuss evaluation models in Chapter 14 and analyze each of these models in light of the basic curriculum position it reflects. For example, the discrepancy evaluation model developed by Provus (1972) reflects the transmission orientation, with its emphasis on behavior change, whereas the curriculum criticism approach developed by Eisner (1979) reflects the transformation position, in that it recognizes subjectivity as part of the evaluation process.

## CONCLUDING COMMENTS

It is our view that curriculum is rooted in personal meaning and linked to specific social contexts. In exploring the transmission, transaction, and transformation curriculum positions, we examine the conceptual bases of each of these approaches to schooling. The concept of a personal approach to schooling, which we call metaorientation or general curriculum position, is central to our book, first, because the three metaorientations described in this text provide perspectives on what schools do or what they should be doing, and, second, because it is our contention that the development, implementation, and evaluation of curricula are usually conducted within these overall frameworks.

In analyzing curriculum processes from these three perspectives, we realize that we run the risk of ignoring the nuances of various approaches; for example, it is not always possible to place an approach clearly within one of the metaorientations. Nonetheless, we feel the risk is far outweighed by the advantages of gaining a clearer grasp of the philosophical, psychological, and social contexts of curriculum.

## REFERENCES

Berlak, A., & Berlak, H. (1981). *Dilemmas of schooling.* New York: Methuen.

Eisner, E.W. (1979). *The educational imagination: On the design and evaluation of school programs.* New York: Macmillan.

Fullan, M. (1982). *The meaning of educational change: A synopsis.* Unpublished manuscript.

Fullan, M., & Park, P. (1981). *Curriculum implementation.* Toronto: Ontario Ministry of Education.

Gagne, R.M., & Briggs, L. (1979). *Principles of instructional design.* New York: Holt, Rinehart & Winston.

Gutek, G.L. (1974). *Philosophical alternatives in education.* Columbus, OH, Charles Merrill.

Hall, G.E., & Loucks, S. (1978). Teacher concerns as a basis for facilitating and personalizing staff development. *Teachers College Record, 80,* 36–53.

Huxley, A. (1970). *The perennial philosophy.* New York: Harper Colophon Books.

Leithwood, K.A. (1982). Implementing curriculum innovations. In K.A. Leithwood (Ed.), *Studies in curriculum decision making.* Toronto: Ontario Institute for Studies in Education Press.

Markley, W.W., Campbell, J., Elgin, D., Harman, W., Hasgins, A., Matson, F., O'Regan, B., & Schneider, L. (1974). *Changing images of man.* Menlo Park, CA: Stanford Research Institute.

Miller, J.P. (1983). *The educational spectrum: Orientations to curriculum.* New York: Longman.

Provus, M.M. (1972). The discrepancy evaluation model. In P.A. Taylor & D. M. Cowley (Eds.), *Reading in curriculum evaluation.* Dubuque, IA: Wm. C. Brown.

Saylor, J.G., & Alexander, W.A. (1974). *Planning curriculum for schools.* New York: Holt, Rinehart & Winston.

Tanner, D., & Tanner, L. (1980). *Curriculum development: Theory into practice.* New York: Macmillan.

Tyler, R.W. (1949). *Basic principles of curriculum and instruction.* Chicago: University of Chicago Press.

Weinstein, G. & Fantini, M. (1970). *Toward humanistic education.* New York: Praeger.

# CHAPTER 2

# TRANSMISSION POSITION: The Context

## PHILOSOPHICAL CONTEXT

The empirical philosophies in which the transmission position is rooted can be traced back to Ancient Greece, but this philosophical orientation did not become prominent until it was advanced by philosophers such as Francis Bacon and John Locke. Today, the transmission position can be linked with analytic philosophy.

### Francis Bacon

Bacon (1561–1626), an Englishman, was involved in a variety of activities ranging from philosophy to politics. He argued that our philosophical difficulties arise from dogma and deduction, and that we should turn instead to inductive thinking or scientific inquiry, which enables us to build theory by observing nature: "The true method of experience first lights the candle, and then by means of the candle shows the way; commencing as it does with experience duly ordered and digested, not bungling nor erratic, and from it educing axioms, and from established axioms again need experiments" (quoted in Durant, 1961, p. 133).

By observing nature, then, we can build theory. In Bacon's view, scientific inquiry should be the main method of acquiring new knowledge. Induction, which is central to scientific inquiry, involves more than simple enumeration; inductive thinking must also include methods of classification and ways to assess the validity of a hypothesis.

Bacon's ideas about education and psychology anticipated behaviorism. As Durant (1961) states, "In psychology he [Bacon] is almost a 'behaviorist': he demands a strict study of cause and effect in human action, and wishes to eliminate the word 'chance' from the vocabulary of

science" (p. 122). Bacon's vision of a scientific study of humans was fulfilled in the twentieth century by B.F. Skinner and the behaviorists. Like
Bacon, Skinner argues that all human behavior can be understood in
terms of cause and effect.

## John Locke

Locke, who further developed the empirical view of philosophy, is best
known for his conception of the mind as a tabula rasa (blank slate). In
Locke's (1889) view, the mind is basically passive: "In the reception of
simple ideas, the understanding is for the most part passive. . . . As the
bodies that surround do diversely affect our organs, the mind is forced
to receive the impressions and cannot avoid the perception of those ideas
that are annexed to them" (p. 70). Although Locke acknowledged the human capacity for reflection, he did not adequately reconcile it with his
theory that the mind is passive in the way it receives sensations.

Locke (1889) applies his concept of the mind as a tabula rasa to
teaching and learning in *Some Thoughts Concerning Education*, where he
states that sensation arises first and is followed by ideas coming to the
mind; ideas give rise to actions; actions lead to habits; habits form a person's character. In other words, education is essentially a process of habit
formation.

> But pray remember, children are not to be taught by rules which
> will be always slipping out of their memories. What you think nec-
> essary for them to do, settle in them by an indispensable practice,
> as often as the occasion returns; and if it be possible, make occa-
> sions. This will beget habits in them, which being once establish'd,
> operate of themselves easily and naturally, without the assistance of
> the memory. But here let me give two cautions.
> 1. The one is, that you keep them to the practice of what you would
>    have grow into a habit in them, by kind words, and gentle ad-
>    monitions, rather as minding them of what they forget, than by
>    harsh rebukes and chiding, as if they were wilfully guilty.
> 2. Another thing you are to take care of, is, not to endeavour to
>    settle too many habits at once, lest by variety you confound them,
>    and so perfect none. When custome has made any one thing easy
>    and natural to 'em, and they practise it without reflection, you
>    may then go on to another. (p. 39)

Locke's view of education as habit formation is congruent with the
atomistic paradigm in that he sees habit formation as the putting together
of small behavioral components.

His contention, that to develop habits in students the teacher must focus on repetition and drill, anticipated Thorndike's educational psychology (which stresses the principle of repetitive exercise and the concept of use and disuse) (see p. 23 in this chapter).

## Analytic Philosophy/Logical Atomism

Today, the empiricist orientation can be found in analytic philosophy, a philosophical movement that, in its different forms, has also been called *logical atomism*, *logical positivism*, and *scientific empiricism*. One scholar has summarized the core of analytic philosophy as "a kind of philosophical analysis that proceeds by the piecemeal decomposition of any complex subject into its logically ultimate components" (Barrett, 1979, p. 36).

Ludwig Wittgenstein (1921/1961) played a crucial role in the development of analytic philosophy. He sees the universe as made of isolated facts, or atoms, that may or may not be related to each other; there is no inherent link or bond between them. He gets to the root of empiricism and the atomistic paradigm when he asserts that "each item can either be the case or not the case, while everything else remains the same" (p. 7).

Analytic philosophy focuses on language, which it attempts to break down into small components, so that clarity and verification can be achieved. The thrust to atomize language and, ultimately, reality is at the heart of both the atomistic paradigm and the transmission position. In Wittgenstein's view, the philosophical problems that arise when "our language has gone on vacation" can be resolved by clear and precise language. In other words, confusion in traditional philosophic discourse has often arisen as a result of functional disorders of language but it can be overcome by analyzing language.

Barrett, who has analyzed Wittgenstein's early work, shows how it is tied to the thought of Bertrand Russell and Alfred North Whitehead, particularly Russell's concept of logical atomism. It is Russell's contention that not only language, but reality itself, is composed of "logical atoms"; the components into which language breaks down mirror the "logical atoms that make up the world" (1979, p. 39).

> Hence, in line with our picture theory of language, the world must ultimately be made up of atomic facts that correspond to the atomic statements with which logical analysis terminates. And the various groupings of these atomic facts make up the complex facts that constitute our experience. We thus arrive at the full-fledged doctrine of Logical Atomism. (Barrett, 1979, p. 39).

A fundamental premise in analytic philosophy is that it abandons metaphysical questions and becomes a servant of science. In the words of

Wittgenstein, "Whereof one cannot speak, one must be silent" (1921). In empirical philosophy, one's world view is not a question of choice, or speculation, or personal taste. The only accurate answer to the question, "What is reality?" is the one that is derived from applying the scientific method of this ultimate philosophical question. Kaplan (1961) offers a cogent description of this point of view:

> Traditionally, philosophy presented the appearance of a number of world views, each essentially complete in itself, and impossible to assess in terms of some other philosophy without begging the fundamental questions. One is either a Platonist or Aristotelian, Spinozist or Thomist, Cartesian or Kantian, and so for the rest. And the choice between the great systems seemed to be a matter of taste or temperament; no wonder the controversies were endless. . . . Now, says the analytic philosopher, the time has come to put an end to such pointless disputation. When a philosophic thesis is formulated in sufficiently exact language, there is no longer room for debate—the thing can be settled one way or the other, and once for all. Philosophy could make progress if only the philosopher would rather be definitely wrong than vaguely right. (p. 59)

In the empiricists' view, attempts to theorize (synthesize) should not be undertaken until the basic elements of a problem have been identified and analyzed. Philosophy should use the scientific method as a model for attacking specific problems on a piecemeal basis; through such analysis small, cumulative gains can be made. Analytic philosophy first attempts to identify which questions are worth pursuing. Once the appropriate questions have been identified, science then takes over to confirm whether statements are true or false. The basis for identifying appropriate questions in analytical philosophy is called the "verifiability theory of meaning" (the use of this method of verifying statements on an empirical basis is the reason that analytic philosophy has also been called *scientific empiricism*).

Analytic philosophers argue that metaphysical propositions in traditional philosophies are nonsense because they cannot be verified:

> For analytic philosophy the questions raised in traditional metaphysics are unanswerable because they are not genuine questions. Philosophical arguments have been interminable because in principle there is no way to establish that one side is right and the other wrong. . . . What is crucial, from the standpoint of analytic philosophy, is that metaphysical questions are unanswerable because of defects in their formulation, and not because of any alleged limitations of the human mind. (Kaplan, 1961, pp. 66–67)

In its most radical form, empiricism is seen in the principle of phys-icalism, where sciences can be reworked in the language of physics. From this point of view, psychology is reduced to observations of physical be-havior. Physicalism is the link between the philosophical and the psycho-logical concepts within the transmission position.

The analytic philosopher views the self as no more than a collection of mental states:

> Schematically, we may say that a self is the set of all and only those mental states which either remember or are remembered by a given state—with a sufficiently generous interpretation of the relation of remembering. I am justified in saying that a particular experience is one of mine and not one of yours, because I remember it and you only know of it second hand; and that "I" remember it means only that it is related in a distinctive way to this experience—that is, to the one I can most conveniently, but not irreducibly, convey by re-ferring to it as the experience of now standing before you. On these terms, the possibility presents itself of constructing the whole world out of the materials of only my experience. (Kaplan, 1961, p. 85)

Analytic philosophers contend that humans are connected only through the rational use of language. They reduce human experience (in the same way they reduce philosophical propositions) to that which can be logically verified. Again we are left with Wittgenstein's two statements: "Any fact can be the case or not be the case, and everything else remains the same" and "Whereof one cannot speak, therefore one must be silent."

In analytic philosophy, there is no connection between philosophy and one's personal values. In Kaplan's (1961) words, "What [the analytic philosopher] identifies as philosophy is not something that he lives by, but a purely intellectual pursuit, like the study of mathematics or physics with which it is so intimately associated" (p. 88).

Because the world view of the analytic philosopher is made up of isolated segments that may or may not be related to each other, these phi-losophers focus on science, observations, inference, clarity, and preci-sion; art, beauty, ethics, and spirituality are separate and unrelated realms. This separation between rational and intuitive modes of thought, of course, is not confined to analytic philosophy; it has tended to domi-nate most of academia and has permeated educational philosophy and psychology throughout most of this century, whereas other currents, such as existentialism and humanistic psychology, have generally been isolated from the academic mainstream. In short, analytic philosophy has reinforced the schizoid split that separates head from heart in our cul-ture.

This same dichotomy is apparent in the present-day back-to-basics movement—an approach to curriculum that exemplifies the transmission position. This movement advocates reducing the curriculum to basic elements (e.g., the three Rs), each of which is taught separately. Of course, there are different strands of thought within the back-to-basics movement, but generally it is consistent with the transmission position in that it breaks down the curriculum into small segments that are unrelated and cut off from the affective and spiritual dimensions of life.

## PSYCHOLOGICAL CONTEXT

In the field of psychology, the roots of the transmission position can be found in the work of Thorndike and, more recently, in the work of B.F. Skinner, both of whom developed a behavioral orientation to learning.

### Edward L. Thorndike

Thorndike's dissertation, *Animal Intelligence* (1911), reflects the influence that his study of animals had upon his view of human nature. Thorndike depicts human behavior in terms of stimulus and response (S→R). The situation (S) stimulates the nervous system, which in turn triggers a particular muscle or gland response (R): "A man's intellect, character and skill is the sum of his tendencies to respond to situations and elements of situations. This number of different situation–response connections that make up this sum would, in an educated adult, run well up into the millions" (Thorndike, 1913, vol. 2, p. 4).

Thorndike (1911) states that the bridge between the stimulus and the response (sensory and motor "neurones") is the synapses in the brain, "whereby the disturbance, or neural current, arising in the former is conducted from the former to the latter rather than to some other place. The strength or weakness of the connection is condition of the synapses" (pp. 246–247). He also contends that people are born with certain tendencies that in his view result from inborn connections between stimuli and responses:

> An original bond between a situation and response in human behavior has as its physiological basis an original ease of conduction of the physiological action aroused in certain neurones toward a certain final path rather than toward any other. The original arrangement of the neurones . . . is the main determinant of what responses of sensation and movement the given situation will provoke. (Thorndike, 1913, p. 221)

Although Thorndike (1913) views people as essentially passive beings who simply *respond* to situations (stimuli), he acknowledges that these responses are not uniform in all situations:

> Save in early infancy and amongst the feeble-minded . . . any situation will most probably act unevenly. Some of its elements will produce only the response of neglect; others will be bound to only a mild awareness of them; others will connect with some energetic response of thought, feeling or action, and become positive determiners of the man's future. (p. 27)

However, in the final analysis, Thorndike reduces learning to a physiological mechanism. According to Thorndike (1912), "The physiological basis for education is the modifiability of synapses between neurones" (p. 64). Education, for Thorndike, is above all a matter of facilitating the connections between "neurones."

Thorndike developed a number of laws based on this physiological view of learning. One of these, the law of use and disuse, states that connections between "neurones" are enhanced through exercise and diminish when not in use. Thus, repetition is important to learning. Another Thorndike principle is the law of effect, which anticipated Skinner's law of reinforcement (see p. 25 in this chapter): "When a modifiable connection between a situation (stimulus) and a response is made and is accompanied or followed by a satisfying state of affairs, that connection's strength is increased: when made and accompanied or followed by an annoying state of affairs: its strength is decreased" (1913, vol. 2, p. 4).

Problem solving, for Thorndike, involves trial and error: "A person whose general aim is to solve a mechanical puzzle may hit upon the solution, or some part of it, in the course of random fumbling, may hit upon it sooner in the next trial, and so progress in the learning—all with little help from ideas about the puzzle or his own movements" (1913, p. 131).

Unlike those who subscribe to the transaction position, which states that problem solving is characterized by rational assessment of alternatives, Thorndike (whose theory of education falls squarely into the transmission orientation) sees problem solving as a process of random fumbling by people who, because they are passive by nature, can solve problems only through trial and error.

Thorndike (1916) argues that "teaching is the arrangement of situations which will lead to desirable bonds and make them satisfying" (p. 174). This definition is similar to Skinner's (1968) definition of teaching as "the arrangement of contingencies under which students learn" (p. 64). In Thorndike's (1916) view, then, the teacher is the active determiner of the learning environment and the student is the passive receptor.

Using psychological terms, the art of teaching may be defined as the art of giving and withholding stimuli with the result of producing or preventing certain response. . . . The aim of the teacher is to produce desirable and prevent undesirable changes in human beings by producing and preventing certain responses. (pp. 60–61)

Even if one agrees that the goal of education is to produce desirable student responses, it is still necessary to determine what criteria should be used in selecting the appropriate responses.

## Franklin Bobbitt

Bobbitt, whose thinking was influenced by Thorndike, responded to this question by proposing a set of criteria based on the assumption that the purpose of education is to prepare students for their adult lives; more specifically, education, in his opinion, should prepare students "for the activities of every kind which make up, or ought to make up, well-rounded adult life" (Bobbitt, 1924, p. 7). Furthermore, according to Bobbitt, education should not include any activities that are not specifically intended to serve this purpose. The selection of educational activities should be based on knowledge of "the things for which [students] should be trained" (1924, p. 8). Thus, in choosing criteria for educational programs, "the first task is to discover the activities which ought to make up the lives of men and women; and along with these, the abilities and personal qualities necessary for proper performance. These are the educational objectives" (1924, p. 8).

Bobbitt (1924) identified a number of activities that people perform in daily life. His list reflected Thorndike's work in *The Teacher's Word Book* (1921), a list of 30,000 words developed from counting the number of times certain words appear in magazines, newspapers, and other popular material; these words were arranged so that teachers could identify those most frequently used. Bobbitt (1924) divided his own master list of daily activities into 10 categories:

1. Language activities; social intercommunication.
2. Health activities.
3. Citizenship activities.
4. General social activities—meeting and mingling with others.
5. Spare-time activities, amusements, recreations.
6. Keeping one's self mentally fit—analogous to the health activities of keeping one's self physically fit.
7. Religious activities.
8. Parental activities, the upbringing of children, the maintenance of a proper home life.

**9.** Unspecialized or non-vocational practical activities.
**10.** The labors of one's calling. (pp. 8–9)

According to Bobbitt (1924), these activities must be broken down into specific objectives.

> General unanalyzed objectives are to be avoided. For the ten major divisions of human action, it would be possible to state ten corresponding abilities. These would be so general as to be practically useless for curriculum-making. "Ability to care for one's health," for example, is too general to be useful. It must be reduced to particularity: ability to manage the ventilation of one's sleeping-room, ability to protect one's self against microorganisms, ability to care for the teeth, and so on. (p. 32)

Bobbitt was influenced by Thorndike not only in his belief that schooling should focus on producing desirable responses, but also in his proposition that responses are strengthened through use. According to Bobbitt (1924), "Whether we appeal to science or common sense, the dominant principle of educational method appears to be this: The mind grows as it is exercised" (p. 51).

Thorndike also had an immediate impact on Bobbitt's ideas about curriculum. Bobbitt's work in this area is a good example of how the transmission position is manifested in curriculum. His conception of curriculum is that it reflects the social context; in other words, the school curriculum is a mirror of society. There is little room in the Bobbitt scheme for critical analysis of society or for schools to promote social change. The status quo is accepted.

## B.F. Skinner

Skinner is best known for his theory of operant conditioning, which states that behavior can be controlled through conditioning: "If the occurence of an operant [a behavior that can be controlled through reinforcement] is followed by a presentation of a reinforcing stimulus, the strength is increased" (Skinner, 1968, p. 4).

Although he does not consider himself to be an educational psychologist, Skinner has written extensively on education. In *The Technology of Teaching* (1968), he asserts that "recent improvements in the conditions which control behavior in the field of learning are of two principal sorts" (1968, p. 10), both of which result from recognition and applications of the law of effect. First, we can use this law to shape "the behavior of an organism almost at will" (1968, p. 10); and, second, we can use it to "maintain behavior in given states of strength for long periods of time" (1968,

p. 10). Skinner is referring here to the use of reinforcers, which is the central component in his theory of operant conditioning. Education, in Skinner's view, is a matter of choosing and using reinforcement techniques; teaching is "the arrangement of contingencies of reinforcement under which students learn" (1968, p. 64). By arranging reinforcers in specific ways, the teacher can increase certain desired behaviors. Skinner distinguishes between negative and positive reinforcers. Positive reinforcers, when added to a situation, will increase the desired behavior, whereas, negative reinforcers work in reverse; they increase the frequency of behavior when they are removed.

Punishment involves either presenting a negative reinforcer or removing a positive reinforcer. Skinner does not favor punishment. Although it may appear successful at first, the effects are not permanent and the undesirable behavior can reoccur. In addition, the emotional side effects of punishment are negative and may produce behavior that is both unpredictable and unreliable: "Replacing misbehavior with crying or anger is seldom a good solution" (Skinner, quoted in Hill, 1971, p. 69). In general, Skinner supports the use of positive reinforcers. In his opinion, aversive education, which relies on negative reinforcers, leads to "maladaptive or neurotic" behavior.

Skinner suggests that natural reinforcers occurring within the environment are too slow to bring about change. It is his opinion that if the teacher relies on the environment for reinforcement, he or she actually abandons the role of teacher. Instead, the teacher must intervene to manipulate the environment. One technique Skinner (1968) recommends is programmed learning.

> Programmed instruction is primarily a scheme for making an effective use of reinforcers, not only in shaping new kinds of behavior but in maintaining behavior in strength. A program does not specify a particular kind of reinforcer (the student may work under aversive control or for money, food, prestige, or love), but it is designed to make weak reinforcers or small measures of strong ones effective. (p. 156)

Skinner suggests that students starting a learning task be rewarded immediately. For example, steps in programmed learning should be small to minimize errors. Eventually, however, the student may become saturated with rewards. For example, if the student has been reinforced with chocolates, he or she may become tired of them and they will lose their effect. When this happens, the ratio of reinforcers may have to be stretched. This technique, known as intermittent reinforcement, works on the principle that if reinforcers are administered only occasionally, the desired behavior can be maintained by a smaller number of reinforcers. In other words, intermittent reinforcement is a technique by which the teacher attempts to increase the number of responses per reinforcement without losing student interest in the activity.

Skinner differentiates between two types of intermittent reinforcement: ratio reinforcement and interval reinforcement. In ratio reinforcement, the reinforcer is given after a certain number of responses, whereas interval reinforcements are ones that are administered at specific time intervals. Research suggests that ratio reinforcement is more effective than interval reinforcement, which seems logical because ratio reinforcement is related to how the individual is responding whereas interval reinforcement is not.

Although well-designed reinforcement programs should keep students busy at work, Skinner admits that it is difficult to design effective reinforcement schedules to deal with complex skills. For example, reading the Great Books is something that usually happens as the result of an unusual reinforcement schedule that is difficult to duplicate. Still, Skinner (1968) goes as far as suggesting that great artists are in large part the products of variable-ratio schedules:

> A dedicated person is one who remains active for long periods of time without reinforcement. He does so because, either in the hands of a skillful teacher or by accident, he has been exposed to a gradually lengthening variable-ratio schedule. At first, what he did "paid off" quickly, but he then moved on the things less readily reinforced. It is perhaps presumptuous to compare a Faraday, Mozart, Rembrandt, or Tolstoy with a pigeon pecking a key or with a pathological gambler, but variable-ratio schedules are nevertheless conspicuous features of the biographies of scientists, composers, artists, and writers. (p. 11)

Even if Skinner's argument about artists seems to stretch the point, the application of operant conditioning to various special education programs has been effective. For example, Skinner describes a situation in which the behavior of a boy who was born blind with cataracts became unmanageable. After an operation that removed the cataracts, he refused to wear glasses, even though his refusal to do so meant that he would soon become permanently blind. His tantrums were uncontrollable and he was admitted to a hospital with a diagnosis of "child schizophrenia." In this case, two principles of operant conditioning were used. First, the temper tantrums were extinguished by not rewarding them in any way. Second, a program of reinforcement was used to shape the desired behavior of wearing glasses. At first, wearing the frames alone, without the lenses inserted, reinforced with food. After the boy accepted the frames, the lenses were inserted in them. Eventually, he was conditioned to wear the glasses about 12 hours a day.

Skinner developed a number of techniques for implementing programmed learning. In one, the student is given a sequence of questions that proceeds from the simplest to the most difficult, and is reinforced every time a correct answer is given. Other programs developed by Skinner focus on discrimination—the ability to tell the difference between colors, shapes, patterns, sounds, tempos, and the like. One such program, designed to be used in teaching machines, instructs preschool children in matching shapes, colors, etc. Another program for teaching discrimination is based on operant conditioning. This type of program was used with a retarded 40-year-old who was said to have a mental age of about 18 months. Using chocolates as reinforcers, the subject was taught to discriminate between different types of shapes (e.g., circles, ellipses) and also to use a pencil appropriately in tracing letters.

Although programmed learning has had some impact on educational practice, the teaching machines that Skinner suggested be used with it never got off the ground. (The principle of the teaching machine is that a program is set within the machine and the student turns a knob that moves the program along only when he or she answers correctly.) Generally, the teaching machine has been relegated to the basement of the school along with out-of-date textbooks:

> The trouble was that the devices—no matter how noble their aims— were, in the end, just somebody's old slide show, put together in a time remote from the pupil's, and whose basic lack of intelligence was only too swiftly exposed. To make matters worse they were almost always unreliable, being of such notoriously touchy components as tape recorders and slide projectors, and by the same token not cheap. (Evans, 1979, p. 117)

Turning now to the question of how Skinner's theories of education are manifested in the transmission position, it is clear that Skinner's psychology is atomistic: His programmed learning techniques break down behavior into small bits that can be manipulated; small identifiable components are used to organize student progress by means of sequential steps. However, some wonder how these pieces fit together. For many critics they do not. These critics particularly dislike Skinner's utopian visions such as Walden II. Typical of such criticism, which has been abundant, is this comment made by Becker (1967):

> A vision of the future in which man is controlled by science, made happy by technique, rendered well-adjusted by the manipulation of

others. Emerson's vision? Only the hubris of science could take Theoreau's Walden, and dare to appropriate a world with such noble connotations, for such a vile vision." (pp. 243–244)

Problems with the behavioral orientation arise when Skinner and others, in their zeal, build their view of a new society on such a narrow theoretical base. It is one thing to develop a reinforcement program for a retarded child, quite another to talk about the radical restructuring of society based on the principle of operant conditioning. In Skinner's vision, atomistic technique becomes ideology.

## ECONOMIC/SOCIAL CONTEXT

Among the many varieties of conservatism are religious fundamentalism, Tory conservatism, laissez-faire conservatism, Social Darwinism, and technological conservatism. The particular type of conservatism discussed here in relation to the transmission position is laissez-faire conservatism—it is the one closest to the atomistic paradigm and, also, the predominant conservative viewpoint in North America.

### Laissez-Faire Conservatism

***Adam Smith.*** Laissez-faire conservatism can be traced to Adam Smith, whose *Inquiry into the Nature and Cause of Wealth of Nations,* published in 1776, attacked the dominant economic system of the day—mercantilism—and argued for the free market system. Smith's vision of the free market is based on individual self-interest and competition: individual self-interest creates competitive markets that produce those goods and services society wants. Self-interest drives people to work for whatever society is willing to pay and competition acts as a restraint to self-interest. These two factors—individual self-interest and competition—act as checks on each other to provide the best possible goods at the lowest possible price. For instance, if consumers start to demand one particular good (e.g., microcomputers), initial prices will probably start to rise. However, higher prices will encourage other producers to enter the market and this competition will serve to reduce prices. Just as prices are regulated by the market so are incomes. Wages usually will be uniform within one industry because competition will act as a check to keep wages at a level that allows producers to compete. The market is where self-interest and competition meet; it is a self-regulating mechanism that holds individual freedom in check.

Heilbroner's (1980) description of Smith's vision as "atomistic" highlights its correspondence with the transmission paradigm.

The world of Adam Smith has been called a world of atomistic competition; a world in which no agent of the productive mechanism,
on the side of labor or capital, was powerful enough to interfere
with or to resist the pressures of competition. It was a world in which
each agent was forced to scurry after its self-interest in a vast social
free-for-all. (p. 56)

Although Smith's basic argument is that government or monopolies
should not interfere with the natural laws of the market, he does not oppose some types of government intervention, for example, government
intervention to prevent the stultifying effects of mass production. However, he is opposed to controls on imports and exports and to laws that
would shelter industry from competition. Smith also opposes domination
of the marketplace by monopolies and is critical of industrialists who
"have an interest to deceive and even oppress the public." Somewhat
ironically, capitalists have ignored this aspect of Smith's work and have
focused on his dictum: *Let the market alone.*

***Milton Friedman.***    Today, one of the strongest advocates of laissez-
faire capitalism is Friedman, who argues that government has intervened
too far into the social and economic life of the country, thus reducing the
freedom of the individual. Friedman (1962) asserts that economic and
political freedom are intertwined:

Economic arrangements play a dual role in the promotion of a free
society. On the one hand, freedom in economic arrangements is itself a component of freedom broadly understood, so economic
freedom is an end in itself. In the second place, economic freedom
is also an indispensable means toward the achievement of political
freedom. (p. 8)

Friedman's (1962) argument, derived from Smith, that "capitalism
is a necessary condition for political freedom" leads to a stark view of economic alternatives:

Fundamentally, there are only two ways of co-ordinating the economic activities of millions. One is central direction involving the
use of coercion—the technique of the army and of the modern to-
talitarian state. The other is voluntary co-operation of individuals—
the technique of the marketplace. (p. 13)

Friedman (1962) also adopts Smith's atomistic view of the individual
in the marketplace: "In its simplest form, such a society consists of a number of independent households—a collection of Robinson Crusoes, as it

were" (p. 13). This vision of society as a collection of Robinson Crusoes is revealing: the only link between individuals is through the marketplace. Government, in Friedman's view, should act as an umpire to make sure that one individual or group of individuals does not take over the marketplace. In this way, economic freedom is maintained.

Friedman (Friedman & Friedman, 1980), who makes frequent reference to Smith to support his argument for the free market, argues that "the key insight of Adam Smith's *Wealth of Nations* is misleadingly simple: if an exchange between two parties is voluntary, it will not take place unless both believe they will benefit from it" (p. 13). He suggests that problems develop when government attempts to regulate this exchange. For example, Friedman contends that in 1974 and 1979, when the Organization of Petroleum Exporting Countries (OPEC) limited the amount of oil flowing into the United States, the imbalance of demand and supply that occurred was due to government intervention, whereas in Germany and Japan, where the price system was allowed to work freely, gas shortages did not occur.

Friedman also cites Smith (1930) to support his argument that government should limit its role to very specific areas:

> According to the system of natural liberty, the sovereign has only three duties to attend to; three duties of great importance, indeed, but plain and intelligible to common understandings: first the duty of protecting the society from the violence and invasion of other independent societies; secondly, the duty of protecting, as far as possible, every member of the society from the injustice or oppression of every other member of it, or the duty establishing an exact administration of justice; and, thirdly, the duty of erecting and maintaining certain public works and certain public institutions. (Smith, 1930, vol. 2, pp. 184–185)

Friedman adds a fourth duty of government—the duty to protect members of the community who cannot be regarded as responsible individuals (for instance, children who are severely abused by their parents). Friedman (1980) cites Hong Kong as the best current example of the form of limited government advocated by Smith.

> Hong Kong has no tariffs or other restraints on international trade (except for a few "voluntary" restraints imposed by the United States and some other major countries). It has no government direction of economic activity, no minimum wage laws, no fixing of prices. The residents are free to buy from whom they want, to sell to whom they want, to invest however they want, to hire whom they want, to work for whom they want.

Government plays an important role that is limited primarily to our four duties interpreted rather narrowly. It enforces law and order, provides a means for formulating the rules of conduct, adjudicates disputes, facilitates transportation and communication, and supervises the issuance of currency. It has provided public housing for arriving refugees from China. Though government spending has grown as the economy has grown, it remains among the lowest in the world as a fraction of the income of the people. As a result, low taxes preserve incentives. Businessmen can reap the benefits of their success but must also bear the costs of their mistakes. (p. 34)

Friedman also has something to say about education. In brief, he applies free market theory to education, arguing that parents should be able to choose and pay directly for the kind of education they prefer. He suggests that this was the case in the United States before 1840, until which time schools were financed by fees paid by parents. Since schooling was taken over by the government in 1840, most children in the United States have attended government schools. As government took on a larger role, the focus of schooling changed. Friedman argues that schools "are still expected to teach the three Rs and to transmit common values" (a classic statement of the transmission position) and is critical of schools becoming involved in issues, such as racial integration, that he feels are only "distantly related to their fundamental task."

To restore the health of education, Friedman advocates a voucher system whereby parents would receive a voucher for a designated sum of money (e.g., $2,000) that would only be redeemable if used to pay the cost of schooling. Parents would thus be allowed to choose the type of school they want their child to attend.

Friedman argues that compulsory attendance laws should be repealed, citing the fact that education was universal in both the United States and England before the advent of compulsory attendance. Friedman once again refers to Smith (1930) to support his case:

No discipline is ever requisite to force attendance upon lecturers which are really worth the attending. . . . Force and restraint may, no doubt, be in some degree requisite in order to oblige children . . . to attend to those parts of education which it is thought necessary for them to acquire during that early period of life; but after twelve or thirteen years of age, provided the master does his duty, force or restraint can scarce ever be necessary to carry on any part of education. . . . Those parts of education, it is to be observed, for the teaching of which there are not public institutions, are generally the best taught. (Smith, 1930, vol. 2, p. 253)

In Friedman's model, the voucher is the medium of exchange in the same way that money is the medium of exchange in the commercial marketplace; vouchers allows parents to choose (purchase) the type of schooling (product) they want for their children.

The voucher system does not appeal to all conservatives. Some, whose concerns focus more on achieving a close fit between society and education, object to the pluralism the voucher system might create. However, it is the logical extension of both Smith's laissez-faire capitalism and the atomistic orientation to educational practice.

## CONCLUDING COMMENTS

The atomistic world view in which the transmission position is rooted has made some significant contributions to our culture. The analytic philosophers' focus on logical, precise use of language has forced thinkers in every discipline to define their terms more exactly. The behaviorists' emphasis on specificity also has contributed to clearer and more precise articulation of objectives. As a result of these efforts to define things clearly, people can communicate more readily. Bertrand Russell has summarized the main achievements of analytic philosophy.

> In the welter of conflicting fanaticisms, one of the few unifying forces is scientific truthfulness, by which I mean the habit of basing our beliefs upon observations and inferences as impersonal, and as much divested of local and temperamental bias, as is possible for human beings. To have insisted upon the introduction of this virtue into philosophy, and to have invented a powerful method by which it can be rendered fruitful, are the chief merits of the philosophical school of which I am a member. (Russell, quoted in Kaplan, 1961, p. 89)

Empiricism has had some positive influences. Our scientific knowledge, of course, has grown exponentially through the use of empirical methods. Also, empiricism has led to a healthy skepticism, reflecting the influence of such philosophers as Bacon and Locke, who were part of a movement that encouraged people to question entrenched assumptions and untested dogma.

In the economic sphere, the freedom of an individual to buy and sell goods in an open marketplace is, at first glance, an appealing vision; the problems of centralized planning in Communist countries are well known. Yet, we are also well aware of the excesses of unregulated capitalism. Today, our fragile environment, scarred by industries more concerned with profits than ecology, is one example. Even Adam Smith, the "father" of laissez-faire economics, objected to exploitative capitalism, but present-day conservatives ignore his warnings and tend to focus solely on the importance of the free market.

The atomistic position has made it easier for human beings, including industrialists, to compartmentalize life into segments that are unrelated. When working, the analytic philosopher focuses on analysis and verification; however, this work is unrelated to the philosopher's personal life. The philosopher's values, spirituality, and aesthetic sense do not enter into the well-defined world of analytic philosophy, just as an ecological perspective is remote to the industrialist.

The behaviorist, like the analytic philosopher, tends to work in a segmented world, wherein the pure behaviorist disconnects inner consciousness from behavior and is interested only in the external world. The concern of the behaviorist is to be able to describe and predict behavior; the internal world of thoughts and images is considered irrelevant. The separation in behavioral psychology between inner and outer worlds is similar to the dichotomy that exists between the personal and professional work of the analytic philosopher.

The atomistic paradigm may be at the root of alienation. In a social world where individual self-interest is prominent, we end up isolated and cut off from each other. In the words of Philip Slater (1970):

> It is easy to produce examples of the many ways in which Americans attempt to minimize, circumvent, or deny the interdependence upon which all human societies are based. We seek a private house, a private laundry, self-service stores, and do-it-yourself skills of every kind. An enormous technology seems to have set itself the task of making it unnecessary for one human being ever to ask anything of another in the course of going about his daily business. Even within the family, Americans are unique in their feeling that each member should have a separate room, and even a separate telephone, television, and car, when economically possible. We seek more and more privacy, and feel more and more alienated and lonely when we get it. (p. 7)

In Chapter 3 we discuss more fully how the atomistic paradigm has been translated into educational practices. However, we quote here from Miller's (1981) *The Compassionate Teacher* to demonstrate how the separation between our inner and outer worlds is upheld in schools.

> Schools reinforce this separation. To succeed in school it is important that an individual succeed in conceptual terms. The individual must gain technical skills and abstract knowledge, but there is little emphasis on empathy or compassion. In fact, compassion is nega-

tively reinforced in favor of "playing it cool." Competition and quick-wittedness are stressed over cooperation and warmth.

We detach the head from the heart because we want to hide behind the illusion that we may have created for ourselves. A current illusion is the "back-to-basics movement." By suggesting that we must focus solely on the 3 Rs, we are continuing to perpetuate the split between the heart and head. By stressing cognitive skills over affective and spiritual integration, we reinforce the schizoid culture. (pp. 15–16)

When we break down the world into isolated segments we can feel cut off from spirituality. We move from the I–thou relationship to the I–it position. At the extreme end point of the atomistic viewpoint is the survivalist—one who is prepared for the breakdown of society and perceives almost everyone as a potential enemy. The survivalist is prepared to defend his or her home with a shotgun. In the survivalist's world, Crusoe's household has become an armed camp.

# REFERENCES

Barrett, W. (1979). *The illusion of technique.* New York: Anchor.

Becker, E. (1967). *Beyond alienation.* New York: George Braziller.

Bobbitt, F. (1924). *How to make a curriculum.* Boston: Houghton Mifflin.

Durant, W. (1961). *The story of philosophy.* New York: Simon & Schuster.

Evans, C. (1979). *The micro millennium.* New York: Viking.

Friedman, M. (1962). *Capitalism and freedom.* Chicago: University of Chicago Press.

Friedman, M., & Friedman, R. (1980). *Free to choose.* San Diego, CA: Harcourt Brace Jovanovich.

Heilbroner, R.L. (1980). *The worldly philosophers.* New York: Touchstone Books.

Hill, W. (1971). *Learning: A survey of psychological interpretation.* New York: Thomas Y. Crowell.

Kaplan, A. (1961). *The new world of philosophy.* New York: Random House.

Locke, J. (1889). *Some thoughts concerning education* (2nd ed.). Cambridge: The University Press.

Miller, J. (1981). *The compassionate teacher.* Englewood Cliffs, NJ: Prentice-Hall.

Skinner, B.F. (1968). *The technology of teaching.* East Norwalk, CT: Appleton-Century-Crofts.

Slater, P. (1970). *The pursuit of loneliness.* Boston: Beacon.

Smith, A. (1930). *Inquiry in the nature and causes of the wealth of nations.* Cannon, E. (Ed.). London: Methuen.

Thorndike, E.L. (1911). *Animal intelligence.* New York: Macmillan.

———. (1912). *Education.* New York: Macmillan.

———. (1913). *Education psychology* (Vols. 1–3). New York: Teachers College Press.

_____. (1916). *Educational psychology: Briefer course.* New York: Teachers' College Press.

_____. (1921). *The teacher's word book.* New York: Teachers College Press.

Wittgenstein, L. (1961). *Tractatus-logico philosophicus.* London: Routledge & Kegan Paul. (Originally published in 1921).

# CHAPTER 3 TRANSMISSION POSITION: Educational Practice

## HISTORICAL BACKGROUND

The transmission position can be traced in North America to colonial times. In the Calvinist creed that was predominant in New England at that time, the student was seen to exist within the context of original sin and thus strict discipline was the order of the day. Teachers were not reluctant to use corporal punishment to control student behavior. Reading and religious instruction were the principal areas of instruction and students learned to read through the alphabet method. According to this method of teaching—one that reflects that atomistic paradigm—students first learned their letters, then words. Often one teacher had to work with over 80 students. As a result of the onerous demands placed upon them, teachers often relied on rote learning and recitation (Burton, 1969), where groups of three or four students would be asked to recite what they had memorized from a book. Arithmetic was learned by copying rules into a notebook.

### The Monitor System

A feature of nineteenth-century education was the monitor system developed by Joseph Lancaster, in which "bright" pupils were selected to teach groups of students. The teacher instructed the monitor and the monitor instructed a row of students. This method was influenced by faculty psychology, a theory of education based on the assumption that the child's faculties of mind should be developed; for example, schools should focus on developing the faculty of memory. However, children were *not* expected to engage in independent thinking or analysis. Tanner and Tanner (1980) argue that present-day programmed instruction is similar in many ways to the monitor system of teaching.

> A century and a half later, advocates of programmed instruction are extolling the virtues of mechanized instruction for educating disadvantaged children. Once again "mechanics" (rote learning by reading, writing, and arithmetic) is the whole of schooling for many urban youngsters. Education is seldom valued as a potent social force for the poor. In a climate of retrenchment, the concern is with a few narrow outcomes that can be taught economically by rote and drill, and can be easily measured. In many respects, the situation today parallels that of the early nineteenth century. (p. 210)

History shows that the transmission position becomes more dominant during difficult economic times, when politicians and educators opt for inexpensive solutions to difficult educational dilemmas.

## William T. Harris

Harris, one nineteenth-century educator who articulated the transmission position, wrote an article in 1880 entitled "Textbooks and Their Uses," in which he said the textbook was the center of curriculum and instruction and should reflect "what has been tested and found essential to civilization" (p. 9). This is a classic statement of the transmission position. Harris argued, for example, that in the science classroom, the textbook should be used as the foundation of instruction instead of the laboratory, where a more experimental approach was employed.

Harris was concerned that widely-circulated newspapers dominated public thought. In an argument similar to one used by Neil Postman (1979) today (see pp. 44–45 in this chapter), he stated that education should counter negative trends in society. Postman (1979) argues that television is the "first curriculum" and must be countered by the more formal curriculum of the school. Harris, in his time, argued that the influences of newspapers must be countered through the use of textbooks. As Cremin (1961) points out, Harris was clearly a conservative: "His emphasis is on order rather than freedom, on work rather than play, on effort rather than interest, on prescription rather than election, on the regularity, silence, and industry that preserve and save our civil order" (p. 200).

Harris's emphasis on traditional academic subjects taught through traditional methodologies constitutes one main strand of thought (e.g., textbook learning) within the transmission position. Another major strand is seen in the work of Franklin Bobbitt, who anticipated the competency-based education movement's narrow focus on specific behavioral objectives and breaking the curriculum into small components that can be easily mastered by the student.

## Franklin Bobbitt

In the 1920s and 1930s, some of the ideas in the transmission position were advocated by Bobbitt (who was previously discussed in relation to Thorndike—see Chapter 2, p. 24). Bobbitt thought that the "backward" institution of education could be improved by employing the "scientific management" techniques used in industry. Bobbitt (1912) reflects the transmission position when he says "Education is a shaping process as much as the manufacture of steel rails" (p. 11). He compares the process of teaching to the making of industrial products; therefore, in his opinion, education must focus on creating a product—the student's mind—which should be shaped according to uniform standards. What was needed was to develop and introduce appropriate standards. In fact, Bobbitt suggested that business and industry set these standards for education. Tanner and Tanner (1980) contend that "the trend of education catering to the demands of business has been a continuing trend in American education" (p. 329). An example of this phenomenon in recent times can be found in the 1960s, when school systems turned to businesses to develop "performance contracts" in order to improve pupil performance in the schools.

In *How to Make a Curriculum* (1924), Bobbitt argued (as we have already seen in Chapter 2) that the curriculum should prepare students for all the activities they may encounter in daily life and that the curriculum should consist of activities that can readily be identified and measured. This mechanistic view of teaching, derived from the field of science, dominated education in the 1920s. In Cremin's (1961) words,

> The scientific movement exerted its greatest influence on education at a time when the study of education was making rapid headway as a university discipline. One need only check the dissertation lists at Columbia, Chicago, and Stanford after World War I to see the vast enthusiasm for scientific topics. Here was no dabbling with the tricks of the trade that had been the earmarks of the normal school; here was Wissenschaft with a vengeance. (p. 200)

Bobbitt's theory of education, based as it is on breaking down subject matter into small components that can be measured and verified, reflects the atomistic paradigm that is central to the transmission position.

## Henry Clifton Morrison

Morrison (1871–1945), one of the strongest spokesmen for the transmission position, believed that education involves adjustment:

> Learning how to get on in the world is adjustment, and so we speak
> of the adjustment theory of Education as contrasted with the eru-
> ditional theory or with theories in which it is held that Education is
> a matter of organic development of some sort. It ought, however,
> to be borne in mind that the adjustment theory is not to be under-
> stood as meaning that the individual has literally to learn some-
> where every adjustment he must make. On the contrary, both in the
> race and in the individual the prize is not adjustment but adapta-
> bility, that is, the capacity to meet a very wide range of adjustments
> as the need arises. Hence, it has been said, with great penetration
> as I think, that "we do not learn what to do, but rather become the
> kind of people who will know what to do." (Morrison, 1940, p. 1)

From Morrison's perspective, learning is an essentially passive process in
which students adapt or respond to a situation.

He draws a distinction between curriculum and instruction. *Instruction,* the "social process by which the community seeks to guarantee that
education of the rising generation shall be right education, of which the
citizen and not the criminal or insane is the outcome" (1940, p. 3), is Morrison's term for cultural transmission in schools as a socializing process.
For Morrison, *curriculum*—the basic framework for planning instruction—is based on the assumption that "human nature is at bottom the
same world over." Thus, in most schools, curriculum is the same in its
essentials.

Morrison argued that literacy skills are the most essential element
in the elementary school curriculum and that the elementary school
should therefore focus on teaching the three Rs. According to Morrison,
the reason for making reading the basis for the school curriculum is that
it allows access to the rest of the curriculum. The second most important
curriculum element is the development of computational skills; the main
task of mathematics education is to teach elementary concepts of number
and the ability to deal with basic mathematical relationships. After mathematics, handwriting is the next essential aspect of the curriculum; Morrison claimed that writing encourages students to organize their ideas in
a clear and precise manner.

For the secondary school level, Morrison developed a unit approach
to learning in which material is organized into units students must master
in order to progress to the next level. This concept is similar in some ways
to the current concept of mastery learning. Morrison's unit method involves the following sequential steps: "(1) pretest, (2) teaching, (3) testing

the result of instruction, (4) changing the instruction procedure, and (5) teaching and testing again until the unit has been completely mastered by the student" (Gutek, 1974, p. 90).

In developing the concept of mastery learning, Morrison distinguished between learning and performance. First, the student focuses on learning a skill and acquiring a fundamental grasp of subject matter; this is what Morrison calls *mastery*. Once the student has achieved a certain level of learning, he or she attempts to apply the skill; this application of learning after mastery is called *performance*. The next step after performance is achieved is *adaptation*, the stage at which students become able to apply their learning to any situation. Adaptation is unitary and permanent: one either masters a skill or does not, and once a skill is mastered it does not fade away. There are three different types of adaptation: special skills such as bicycle riding; "understandings," or cognitive abilities; and "attitudes of appreciation." Morrison's unit model encourages the use by teachers of worksheets (called "guidesheets") to assess whether students have achieved mastery. Once an adaptation or skill has been achieved, it is simply checked off on the teacher's worksheet. Because mastery is permanent, the teacher can forget about the skill once the initial adaptation has been achieved.

In addition to his emphasis on student mastery of traditional subject matter, Morrison also saw the school as a vehicle for transmitting cultural values. His views are a good example of how the subject/disciplines and the cultural transmission positions often combine to form a metaorientation. In Morrison's opinion, the most important values to be transmitted by schools are the abilities to get along with others and to accept the teacher's authority in the classroom. Other important values for Morrison include "a willingness to accept the consequences of one's actions; a sense of altruism and fair play; respect for property rights; a willingness to accept criticism; a recognition of the social values of cooperation; fidelity to promises; obedience to legitimate authority; sustained application; a capacity for hard work; a sense of duty, fortitude, and punctuality" (Morrison, quoted in Gutek, 1974, p. 90). Morrison believed that the school could teach these values through the study of biographies of great men and women and could serve as a "moral censor" by eliminating negative influences.

## Arthur Bestor

During the 1950s, Bestor promoted the traditionalist emphasis on academic disciplines. Bestor wrote two books—*Educational Wastelands* (1953) and *The Restoration of Learning* (1955)—that were critical of progressive education and argued for a curriculum based on the intellectual disciplines.

Bestor stated that the main activities in elementary schools should be reading, writing, and arithmetic, with some emphasis on science, geography, and history. In junior high school, study should progress to more rigorous work in algebra, biology, and history, and in high school, the curriculum should be most specialized and rigorous. At the high school level, the mathematics curriculum should include advanced algebra, plane geometry, trigonometry, analytical geometry, and calculus and the study of science should include chemistry, physics, and biology. Other essential subjects in secondary school should be history, English, and a second language. Because, for Bestor, training in the intellectual disciplines was a prerequisite for either a college or vocational education, he argued that all secondary students, even slow learners, should be exposed to the intellectual disciplines.

Bestor believed that the school curriculum should be developed by scholars within the separate disciplines, and that teacher training should focus more on a specific academic discipline than on courses in education. Bestor did not support an interdisciplinary approach and was critical of social studies and language arts programs.

## TRANSMISSION POSITION
## IN CONTEMPORARY EDUCATION

Three specific orientations—subject/discipline, competency-based education, and cultural transmission—make up the present-day transmission metaorientation to education. In the center of this position is the subject orientation, which emphasizes student mastery of subject content. Postman (1979), an advocate of the subject orientation, places a particular emphasis on the teaching of history and language. Closely related is the cultural transmission orientation, the focus of which is to inculcate in students certain behaviors and values. Durkheim (1961), a French sociologist, presented the classic argument of why schools should play a major role in instructing students in certain habits and duties. The third component in the transmission position, the competency-based education/ mastery learning orientation, focuses on breaking down school subjects into small units so that the student can master specific skills and content; this emphasis on dissecting the curriculum into its smallest parts reflects the atomistic paradigm in an education context.

### Subject/Content Orientation

Traditionally, curriculum organization has centered on specific subjects and academic disciplines. The focus in elementary schools is on the three Rs, whereas secondary schools concentrate on subjects such as science, math, English, history, and foreign languages.

Educators adhering to the subject orientation organize curriculum according to how knowledge is developed in a given subject area. Because areas of specialization within the various fields have become so numerous, curricula in some subject areas can become extremely complex. The subject of English, for example, encompasses grammar, literature, creative writing, oral expression, linguistics, reading, spelling, and other subdivisions as well. Common features of subject-oriented curricula have been described by Smith, Stanley, and Shores (1957).

First, there is an emphasis on direct instructional techniques such as lecture and recitation. Lectures explain a subject in a logical fashion, usually proceeding from simple to more complex ideas. In chemistry, for example, an explanation usually begins with basic elements and proceeds to more complex molecules. Some disciplines, such as history, present material in chronological order. Although other teaching procedures in addition to lectures and recitation may be used, including discussion, written exercises, oral reports, and debates, use is rarely made of experimental techniques such as role playing, simulation games, and movement activities.

Second, the subject-oriented curriculum divides subjects into two categories: required ("core") courses and electives. In the late 1960s and early 1970s, there was a trend in secondary schools and universities toward more electives and fewer requirements. In the 1980s, however, there is a general return to curricula having more required and fewer elective subjects. Requiring all students to enroll in core subjects, however, does not necessarily mean that all students receive the same learning experiences. Usually a portion of any course allows teachers a choice in what they will emphasize, and, furthermore, different teachers favor different teaching methods.

Third, the subject curriculum is based on a plan specifying what courses will be required at different levels. Therefore, prerequisites must be decided in accordance with the sequence of course offerings. In other words, curriculum organizers must decide what learning experiences are necessary at the different grade levels.

Fourth, the length of the class period is organized around the subject. At the university level, classes are organized to accommodate both lecture and somewhat longer laboratory periods.

Proponents of the subject curriculum suggest that despite its focus on regimentation and uniformity, it does make allowances for individual differences: electives are provided to suit different interests; instructors of required courses can make some accommodations to different student needs; guidance and special education programs attend to individual needs within the subject matter orientation; extracurricular activities offered after school or during breaks also present students with opportunities to pursue individual interests.

Teacher-education programs geared to the subject-oriented curriculum usually require teachers to attain a level of mastery in one subject area. For instance, to teach science at the secondary school level the teacher often will be required to have a university degree in that discipline. Although teachers are not expected to be scholars in their fields, each should have broad knowledge of his or her discipline so that he or she can articulate its concepts to secondary school students.

**Back-to-Basics Movement.**   Today, the subject orientation is reflected in the back-to-basics movement, which some people believe is a backlash against the relaxation of academic standards during the 1960s and 1970s. People calling for a return to basics include some parent groups, individuals in the media, religious fundamentalists, and university academics. They have expressed concern about schools offering too many electives, automatic promotion, and grade inflation. In Gallup poll surveys done since 1975, respondents have ranked "devoting more attention to teaching the basics" anywhere between first and third in importance as a primary educational concern. In response to this trend, most states have developed some sort of minimum-competency standards for elementary and secondary students.

In some respects, the back-to-basic movement is an extension of the position articulated at an earlier time by Morrison and others:

> Although the back-to-basics movement means different things to different people, it usually connotes an Essentialist curriculum with heavy emphasis on reading, writing, and mathematics. Solid subjects—English, history, science, mathematics—are taught in all grades. History means U.S. and European history and perhaps Asian and African history, but not Afro-American history or ethnic studies. English means traditional grammar, not linguistics or nonstandard English; it means Shakespeare and Wordsworth, not *Catcher in the Rye* or *Lolita.* Creative writing is frowned upon. Science means biology, chemistry, and physics—not ecology. Mathematics means old math, not new math. Furthermore, these subjects are required. Proponents of the basics consider elective courses in such areas as scuba diving, transcendental meditation, and hiking as nonsense. Some even consider humanities or integrated social science courses too "soft." They may grudgingly admit music and art into the program—but only for half credit. (Ornstein, 1982, p. 405)

**Neil Postman/Content Mastery.**   The subject orientation has a number of defenders today. Although he does not consider himself part of the back-to-basics movement, Postman (1979) has become an advocate of the subject orientation. As mentioned previously, he believes the schools must counter the negative influence of today's media, which Postman calls "the first curriculum." Postman argues that schools, which he calls the "second curriculum," should have a conserving function and should not duplicate the "first curriculum." Because television tends to focus on images that are concrete and unique, school should emphasize words and print that are abstract and conceptual. Postman's (1979) opinion that curriculum should be transmission-oriented is reflected when he says, "For what is a curriculum but a design for controlling and shaping the minds of the young?" (p. 88).

Postman's (1979) approach to curriculum encompasses subjects, content, and ideas. He argues that schools should center their curricula around the teaching of history, or what he calls the "ascent of humanity"—the development of man's achievements—and that this theme can easily be integrated into the traditional curriculum:

> But best of all, the theme of the ascent of humanity provides us with a nontechnical, noncommercial definition of education. . . . You will note that such a definition is not child-centered, not training-centered, not skill-centered, not even problem-centered. It is idea-centered and coherence-centered. It is also otherworldly, in the sense that it does not assume that what one learns in school must be directly and urgently related to a problem of today. In other words, it is an education that stresses history, the scientific mode of thinking, the disciplined use of language, a wide-ranging knowledge of the arts and religion, and the continuity of human enterprise. (pp. 135–136)

Postman (1979) contends that history should be a central theme in many subjects. For example, science can be taught from a historical point of view by having students examine the record of scientific achievements. He also suggests that students study the philosophy of science: "Such a course should include a consideration of the language of science, the nature of scientific proof, the source of scientific hypotheses, the role of imagination, the conditions of experimentation, and especially the value of error and disproof" (p. 141).

The use of language is central in Postman's (1979) curriculum. He asserts that "language learning becomes the central preoccupation of a conserving education, wherein every teacher, regardless of level or subject, must be a language educator" (p. 153). In Postman's opinion, the study of semantics should be included in language curricula; courses in semantics, by focusing on improving reading and writing skills and interpreting the meaning of language, would help students discover the underlying assumptions of what they read and hear. Teachers would focus on how questions can be asked, the process of definition, and the role of metaphor. Postman argues that literature, music, art, and comparative religion also must be included in the curriculum.

Postman's approach to curriculum is based essentially on content mastery. He is disenchanted with inquiry methods of teaching, which, in his view, "bypass the teaching of systematic content" and often are reduced to "a set of mechanical procedures" (1979, p. 214). Postman's concept of curriculum, then, is within the transmission position, particularly the strands within this position that focus on mastery of academic subject matter and the inculcation of values.

## Cultural Transmission Orientation

*Emile Durkheim.*   The French sociologist Emile Durkheim (1961) argues that "the schools must be the guardians par excellence of our national character" (p. 4). He calls the method by which schools should inculcate in students the cultural mores of the society *rational moral education.* Durkheim's concept of moral education is based on the rationalist premise that "there is nothing in reality that one is justified in considering as fundamentally beyond the scope of human reason" (p. 4). The model for this concept of moral education is the empirically-based scientific method.

> Once physics and chemistry were established, it was thought that science had to stop there. The biological world seemed to depend upon mysterious principles, which escaped the grasp of scientific thought. Yet biological sciences presently came into their own. Next, the founding of psychology demonstrated the applicability of reason to mental phenomena. Nothing, then, authorizes us to suppose that it is different with moral phenomena. (Durkheim, 1961, p. 5)

Durkheim (1961) claims that the schools' role in moral education is more critical than the family's role, even though this view runs "contrary to the all too popular notion that moral education falls chiefly within the jurisdiction of the family" (p. 18). The schools must "train the child in terms of the demands of society" (p. 19).

What does Durkheim mean by the word *morality?* He argues that morality is connected with duty, by which he means prescribed behavior, a set of rules that predetermine conduct. Some of these rules are specific and focus on interpersonal relations, whereas others determine relations between people and property. Although many rules are fixed in the law, others exist only as part of the public conscience.

> Morality is a totality of definite rules; it is like so many molds with limiting boundaries, into which we must pour out behavior. We do not have to construct these rules at the moment of action by de-

ducing them from some general principles; they already exist, they are already made, they live and operate around us. (Durkheim, 1961, p. 26)

Morality, then, does not derive from within the individual but is an external context into which we fit our behavior; rules determine our behavior and not the converse:

It is in some measure—and to the same extent that it is a rule—beyond personal preference. There is in it something that resists us, is beyond us. We do not determine its existence or its nature. It is independent of what we are. Rather than expressing us, it dominates us. (Durkheim, 1961, p. 28)

Clearly this is a transmission view of morality. Durkheim (1961) suggests that science and rationality control our behavior in a way that is similar to the way morality influences our behavior:

For example, we adopt a given mode of life because it carries the authority of science; the authority of science legitimates it. It is to the science that we defer, in our behavior, and not to ourselves. It is to science that we bend our will. (p. 29)

Two concepts—regularity and authority—are central in Durkheim's view of morality. What he means by *regularity* is that rules enforce regularities of behavior that in turn develop personal habits and character. *Authority* refers to the idea that we act morally not because of some internal principle "but because there is some compelling influence in the authority dictating it." In other words, we obey moral rules because they do not leave room for equivocation; authority demands that we obey them.

Regularity and authority are aspects of *discipline,* which is a more comprehensive concept: "Discipline in effect regularizes conduct. It implies repetitive behavior under determinate conditions. But discipline does not emerge without authority—a regulating authority. Therefore, to summarize this chapter we can say that the fundamental element of morality is the spirit of discipline" (Durkheim, 1961, p. 31).

Durkheim (1961) believes that the most essential aspect of morality is the capacity for restraint or "inhibition which allows us to contain our passions, our desires, our habits, and subject them to law" (p. 46). Education should teach children to restrain and control themselves. External discipline is a cornerstone of the cultural transmission position.

The individual's relationship to social groups is another important element in Durkheim's conception of moral education. He argues that people are not complete unless they are attached to a social group; morality is linked with one's social obligations.

The final element in Durkheim's theory of morality is what he calls *autonomy*. Durkheim's definition of autonomy, however, is not the same as Piaget's or Maslow's. For Durkheim, autonomy comes from a rational understanding of society's rules, which, in turn, leads to respect for authority and discipline and to obedience. What is most important in Durkheim's vision of morality is that people are drawn toward morality on the basis of rationality rather than coercion.

How does Durkheim's theory of rational morality translate into educational practice? First, it relies on discipline in the school. By attending school, the child learns obedience and develops moral behavior.

> In fact, there is a whole system of rules in the school that predetermine the child's conduct. He must come to class regularly, he must arrive at a specified time and with appropriate bearing and attitude. He must not disrupt things in class. He must have learned his lessons, done his homework, and have done so reasonably well, etc. There are, therefore, a host of obligations that the child is required to shoulder. Together, they constitute the discipline of the school. It is through the practice of school discipline that we can inculcate the spirit of discipline in the child. (Durkheim, 1961, p. 48)

Durkheim states that the school initiates the child into "the authority of duty," because the classroom is a small society where each student has a particular place and function. Central to effective school discipline is the teacher's respect for his or her own role as an authority figure, which is then "transmitted" to the student through "word and gesture" and thereby "imprinted on the child's mind." Such authority is impersonal and is not associated with teachers' personal characteristics.

Durkheim states that punishment, also, has a role in maintaining discipline, although it is not as central as the impersonal authority of the teacher. The function of punishment is to show reproach and disapproval for breaking the rules of the school. The essence of punishment is to create a feeling of blame, which strengthens the student's sense of duty. Durkheim is strongly opposed to corporal punishment because there are better means through which a student can be made to sense blame and disapproval. For example, a child who has misbehaved might be excluded from games at playtime. Copywork as a punishment should be avoided in Durkheim's opinion. Punishment should be graduated, proceeding from individual reprimands, to public disapproval before the whole class, to disapproval communicated to parents, and, finally, to suspension. Graduated punishment ensures that each punishment has maximum impact. Once the teacher has decided upon a punishment, it must be administered irrevocably so that the student "develops the habit of seeing duty" imposed directly on the will. Durkheim asserts that rewards should play a lesser role in moral education than punishment and that they should be used to stimulate academic achievement rather than to build moral character.

Another important function in Durkheim's conception of moral education programs is to develop empathy, or altruism, through imitation of adult behavior and through fostering social identifications or attachments within the school setting. Teachers can facilitate social group attachments by emphasizing the "spirit of the class." According to Durkheim, teachers should take every opportunity to develop a feeling of common bonds ("moral unity") within the class. They can use collective rewards and punishments to develop this group sense and can deny collective rewards to the class as a punishment for an anonymous offense. In other words, teachers should develop a sense of cohesion within each class to further strengthen students' sense of a bond with each other and with the school.

### Neil Postman/Discipline as a Tool for Socializing Students.

Durkheim's theory of moral education remains popular with educational conservatives, who argue that one of the main functions of schooling is to integrate the student into the existing social framework. Today, this position has been taken up by Postman. He states that the school plays a key role in developing "a tolerance for delayed gratification, a certain measure of respect for and fear of authority, and a willingness to accommodate one's individual desires to the interests of group cohesion and purpose" (1979, p. 200).

According to Postman, disorder has become more common in the classroom in recent years and this is due to a dissolving family structure that produces children "unfit" for the social climate of the classroom and, also, to the prevalence of an information environment that runs counter to the atmosphere of school. Schools, in Postman's (1979) view, must "devote attention to the immediate consequences of disorder as to its abstract causes." In short, school authorities should run a "tight ship."

Postman (1979) closely follows Durkheim's position when he says that schools have a "special environment which requires the enforcement of traditional rules of controlled group interaction" (p. 205). He argues that in order to maintain this environment, students who cannot accommodate themselves to the rules should be punished. The school, for Postman, is the only public institution in which rules still have any meaning. For example, in Postman's opinion, schools should enforce a dress code because such codes signify that school is a special place that requires certain types of behavior. He argues that a person would not wear jeans and a tee shirt decorated with the words "Feel Me" to a church wedding because this would be considered an outrage against the "tone and meaning of the situation," and, in the same vein, schools have the right to demand similar consideration from students. Postman (1979) believes that schools should require students to subordinate their own interests and wishes to those of the group and that "manners education" is one way to accomplish this goal: "As a rule, elementary school teachers will exert considerable effort in teaching manners. I believe they refer to this effort as socializing the child" (p. 209). He offers an example of a civilized high school class:

> I hesitate to offer the following example since you will think me, for giving it, hopelessly romantic, but the most civilized high school class I have ever seen was one in which both students and teacher said good morning to each other (because the teacher always said it to his students) and in which the students actually stood up when they had something to say. The teacher, moreover, thanked each student for any contribution made to the class, did not sit with his feet on the desk, and did not interrupt a student unless he had asked permission to do so. The students, in turn, did not interrupt each other, or chew gum, or read comic books when they were bored. To avoid being a burden to others when one is bored is the essence of civilized behavior. (p. 210)

### Pursuit of Individual Excellence versus Conforming to Common Social Norms.

It is important to conservatives that the emphasis on obeying rules does not override academic achievement and individual excellence. Holmes (1980) has drawn a careful distinction between individual excellence and the need to be a part of a social group:

> The conservative cannot accept the substitution of group production and group cooperation for excellence and the major objectives of understanding and thinking, objectives that are individual rather than group traits. On the other hand, the conservative recognizes the importance of individuals making contributions to the community. Thus, while the wholesale substitution of group norms, usually characterized by mediocrity for excellence in the cognitive field, is entirely unacceptable, the proposition that some school activities be directed toward social service and cooperation is entirely compatible with principles of truth, excellence, and community. Choirs and bands are obvious examples of cases where the good of the group requires strong discipline and the subordination of individual interests. Similarly, outdoor activities (wilderness camping, winter excursions, canoeing) provide splendid opportunities to combine an emphasis on self-reliance with highly disciplined interdependence. (p. 414)

The conservative faces a conflict between his atomistic concern for the individual and the need to transmit common values. Holmes, for example, attempts to resolve this conflict by distinguishing between academic activities and certain social endeavors. Friedman's voucher plan, discussed previously (see pp. 32–33), presents a more difficult dilemma because this plan allows parents to choose schools that may differ widely in their philosophies. The pluralism that would result from the voucher system is antithetical to the position taken by Holmes and Durkheim. There is, then, a basic tension in the conservative transmission position between the focus on individual freedom and the focus on inculcation of common social values.

## Competency-based Education/Mastery Learning Orientation

*Competency-based Education.* The goal of competency-based education (C.B.E.) is to develop student competencies through specific instructional strategies. C.B.E. focuses on identifying measurable objectives, finding an appropriate instructional plan, and assessing by means of criterion-referenced tests how well students achieve the specified competencies. As McAshan (1979) points out, C.B.E. is based on behavioral learning theory:

> Learning theory indicates that learning begins when stimuli (either internal or external) and their reinforcement cause an organism to react. Learning occurs through this process, and the more complex cognitive, psychomotor, and affective motivational systems develop. Thus, all learning can be said to begin when the learner is sensitized to the existence of stimuli. These stimuli may be thought of as occurring from the result of teaching strategies (or enabling activities) that are part of the instructional delivery system in C.B.E. programs. (p. 51)

C.B.E. reflects the atomisic paradigm in that C.B.E. curricula are broken down into small segments. In America, C.B.E. is an extension of the philosophy of education that is grounded in the work of Thorndike, Bobbitt, Skinner, and Morrison, rooted as it is in a view of the learner as passive and in an atomistic conception of curriculum. A more complete description of C.B.E. is found in *The Educational Spectrum* (Miller, 1983).

*Mastery Learning.* Mastery learning is similar to C.B.E.; however, in mastery learning there is more emphasis on instruction, whereas C.B.E. tends to focus on objectives and assessment. According to Ryan and Schmidt (1979), "Mastery learning, in contrast [to C.B.E.], is an integrated system of instruction that includes not only procedures for identifying desired learning outcomes and for evaluation, but also (and most importantly), the process of instruction that will enhance student learning of those outcomes" (p. 17).

Bloom, the most prominent advocate of mastery learning, draws a sharp distinction between curriculum and instruction. For Bloom, the curriculum specialist focuses on identifying goals and objectives for a program, selecting curriculum materials, and developing learning experiences and should focus also on defining the appropriate relationships between goals, objectives, materials, and learning experiences. In Bloom's (1981) view, curriculum programs are complex and require long-term planning. Bloom sees instruction, on the other hand, as the implementation of teaching–learning activities. People concerned with instructional activities are involved in selecting appropriate teaching–learning strategies and sequencing these activities. Instructional activities not only can be planned more quickly than curriculum projects, they can be undertaken without making curricular alterations (Bloom, 1981).

THE RATIONALE FOR MASTERY LEARNING    Basing his argument on his contention that individual differences are "man made and accidental rather than fixed in the individual," Bloom (1981) reaches the following conclusion about learning: "What any person in the world can learn, almost all persons can learn if provided with appropriate prior and current conditions of learning" (p. 136). He claims that this statement applies to 95 percent of a given school population. According to Bloom, mastery learning can help so-called slow learners to achieve at the same level as others, if slow learners are given more time and extra help. Citing research (Block, 1974; Block & Anderson, 1975) to support his claim that almost all learners can master complex tasks equally well, Bloom states that "80% of students in a mastery class reach the same final criterion of achievement (usually at the A or B + level) as approximately 20% of the class under conventional group instruction" (Bloom, 1981, p. 34).

The students in the mastery class usually need about 10 or 15 percent more time to master tasks than students in the conventional class. This is so, Bloom suggests, because students in the mastery class are usually more cooperative in their behavior, whereas students in conventional classes are more competitive due to the fact that in such classes only a few students receive As and must compete for the few high marks that are allocated. Bloom (1981) contends that if students learn under mastery-learning conditions in which they are given feedback and corrective individualized help, the difference between fast and slow students will disappear: "Most students become very similar with regard to learning ability, rate of learning and motivation for further learning when provided with favorable learning conditions" (p. 135). Bloom argues further that mastery learning leads not only to gains in student achievement but also to student gains in the "elusive quality termed learning to learn" (p. 137), and that mastery learning also leads naturally to increases in student self-esteem as the student gains confidence through achievement (Bloom, 1976; Kifer, 1973). Mastery learning also can have a positive impact on the student's ability to withstand stress and anxiety because, unlike conventional learning situations in which teachers' marks and judgments traditionally have had a strong impact on the student's mental health, in mastery learning classrooms, 80 percent of the students achieve, and this will have a positive impact.

Bloom acknowledges that mastery learning is derived from the work of Morrison (1940), Bruner (1966), Skinner (1954), Suppes (1966), Goodlad and Anderson (1959), Glaser (1968), and Carroll (1963). Carroll, whose work has been particularly influential, asserts that if the time and quality of instruction are made available to students in terms of their needs and characteristics, most students will achieve mastery of the subject. According to Carroll (1963), "Aptitude is the amount of time required by the learner to attain mastery of a learning task" (p. 157). To support this claim, which he agrees is a key assumption in mastery learning, Bloom (1981) cites studies assessing the effects of students learning at their own rate (Glaser, 1968).

Another important principle in mastery learning, also derived from Carroll (1963), is his definition of *quality of instruction* "in terms of the degree to which the presentation, explanation, and ordering of elements of the task to be learned, approach the optimum for a given learner" (p. 159). According to this view, learning situations vary for different students, some of whom may need highly structured learning environments whereas less structured situations are required by others. In other words, mastery learning strategies must be aimed toward the individual learner rather than toward the group.

Carroll argues, as we have shown, that the time spent on a learning task is the key to mastery and that if enough time is available learning will occur. A corollary to his argument is that the length of time required by each student to learn a subject is related to the student's verbal ability, the quality of instruction, and other variables such as teacher feedback. Therefore, mastery learning should attempt to organize these variables so that learning is maximized for each student.

A STRATEGY FOR MASTERY LEARNING  Although there are many strategies that can be employed in mastery learning, Bloom (1981) describes the essence of the approach.

**1.** *Preconditions.* The first step is to identify what is meant by mastery in a specific subject, so that learning can be assessed. In order to establish evaluation procedures, not only objectives but also the content of instruction must be specified. Bloom draws a firm line between the teaching–learning process and evaluation. Furthermore, he believes that evaluation should not encourage competition; instead, "absolute standards" to determine individual mastery should be set for each subject. Also, students should be certain they are being evaluated according to their level of performance and not according to a normal curve or some other relative set of standards.

**2.** *Operating procedures.* One key aspect of mastery learning is the breaking of course material into small units of learning (this procedure in mastery learning parallels Morrison's unit method). A learning unit, which can correspond to a chapter in a textbook or to a specific content topic, usually is designed to be taught in time periods of approximately one to two weeks. These larger units are then broken down into smaller elements that consist of specific facts, concepts, and ideas, as well as units dealing with application of principles and the analysis of complex theoretical statements. Influenced by Gagne (1965), Bloom believes that these elements form a hierarchy of learning tasks.

Another major element in the mastery learning process is the use of diagnostic progress tests, which, as their name implies are used to assess whether the student has mastered the unit. These tests, also referred to as formative evaluation tests, motivate students to approach the unit in a serious manner. Most important, they assist teachers and students in identifying areas in which students still need to work. The tests are most effective when they are accompanied by very specific instructional strategies to deal with the topic at hand. Evaluation tests should not be graded; Bloom claims that grading can condition the student to low expectations and performance. Formative evaluation tests can also help the teacher identify particular points in instruction that need to be modified. If teachers find students need additional work, Bloom (1981) states that "the best procedure we have found thus far is to have small groups of students (two or three) meet regularly for as much as an hour per week to review the results of their formative evaluation tests and to help each overcome the difficulties on these tests" (p. 171).

**3.** *Learning materials.* Bloom states that workbooks and programmed instruction are appropriate for students who cannot grasp a subject as presented in a textbook. Although Bloom believes textbooks are appropriate for many learning situations, other learning materials such as audio-visual material and simulation games can also be helpful. According to Bloom, such materials are appropriate to students who need concrete illustrations and experiences. Knowing that a variety of learning materials and procedures is available reassures students who are having difficulty with one method that an alternative is available. Appropriate learning materials and feedback from the teacher can reduce the time needed to accomplish a learning task as well as reduce the need for student perseverance.

OUTCOMES OF MASTERY LEARNING What are the outcomes of mastery learning? According to Bloom, mastery learning has led to significant gains in both cognitive and affective measures. Ryan and Schmidt (1979), in a review of 15 studies of mastery learning at the elementary and secondary levels, come to the following conclusions:

- Achievement. The evidence definitely favors the mastery learning approach in the acquisition of cognitive skills in the subject areas examined.
- Variability. Mastery learning has proven to be effective in reducing the amount of variability in achievement and retention within a group of students.
- Retention and Transfer of Learning. Although only a few studies examine these outcomes, the evidence favors mastery approaches.
- Student Attitudes. Studies of affective outcomes, while few in number, favor mastery approaches.
- Time Consequences. Mastery strategies seem to require much greater student study time, but there is some evidence to suggest that slower learners tend to learn more quickly as they progress through a series of mastery-taught units. Moreover, students have been found to spend a larger proportion of time in active learning when required to study to mastery.
- Individual Differences in Entry Characteristics. In a few studies, mastery strategies have been shown to *minimize* the effects of student entry characteristics on subsequent learning. Very little has been done to explore the effects of measured I.Q. on a student's achievement under mastery strategies, but the evidence is favorable—i.e., mastery approaches tend to reduce the usual relationship between intelligence and achievement.
- Mastery or Criterion Levels. The unit mastery requirement has been shown to have the strongest impact on student learning of any of the components of the strategy. When this requirement is not imposed or is set at a level lower than normally required for an A, the poorer and less similarly have students studied and learned. A 90 percent level is the recommended optimum. (p 56).

## CONCLUDING COMMENTS

The transmission position contains the following characteristics in relation to the components identified by Miller (1983) as comprising an orientation to curriculum.

*Context.*   This position reflects an atomistic paradigm in which reality is broken down into distinct, separate elements. It is philosophically allied with an empiricist world view, psychologically allied with behaviorism, and politically allied with the conservative economic theory, laissez-faire capitalism, which is characterized by an atomistic view of economic and social activity.

*Aims.*   Mastery of school subjects and inculcation of students in social norms are the major goals of this position.

*Learning Experiences.*   Students are expected to learn facts and concepts associated with the subject and to master certain key skills. The learner is viewed as acting in a passive mode in which he or she merely responds to a structured learning situation. They also are expected to adapt to the school's academic, social, and disciplinary framework, and in this way to absorb the norms that are predominant in the culture.

*Role of the Teacher.*   Teachers in this position tend to play a directive role in the learning process. Instruction in this position is often didactic with students responding to teacher initiatives. In C.B.E. and mastery learning, the teacher plans and sequences the material so that the student can proceed through the units at his or her own pace. In mastery learning, the teacher must also be involved in diagnosis and feedback to students so that learning is facilitated.

*Evaluation.*   Evaluation often focuses on traditional achievement tests to indicate how a student has mastered a particular subject. However, in mastery learning, formative evaluation plays a major role, which allows deficiencies in student learning to be corrected.

## The Transmission Position and the Berlak Dilemmas

*Whole Child versus Child as Student.*   The child is seen not as a whole person but only in his or her role as a student; most advocates of the transmission position do not feel that the school should "tamper" with the emotional life of the student. The basic objective of schools is to teach academic content and literacy and computational skills.

*Teacher Control versus Child Control.*   The teacher retains control of both learning and behavioral standards. Usually the teacher plays a strong directive role in students' learning and in determining how students spend their time. Mastery learning, however, allows some individualization, as the child can proceed at his or her own rate. In both the subject orientation and mastery learning, the teacher or curriculum agent determines the standards.

**Personal Knowledge versus Public Knowledge.** Little room is allowed for exploration or pursuit of personal knowledge. Transmission-oriented educators consider an examination of personal knowledge to be an invasion of privacy.

**Knowledge as Content versus Knowledge as Process.** Knowledge is viewed as content. Knowledge is also seen as something that is relatively "fixed" and thus can easily be organized into subjects and textbooks.

**Intrinsic versus Extrinsic Motivation.** Extrinsic motivation is clearly the dominant mode. Both traditional and behaviorally based programs place a strong emphasis on external rewards such as grades and external reinforcers. In mastery learning, however, there is some room for intrinsic motivation, because the student can determine his or her own pace in moving through the individual units.

**Learning is Holistic versus Learning is Molecular.** Learning is broken down into small elements (e.g., programmed learning units or facts in textbooks). Students are viewed as competent when they have mastered the individual pieces of the curriculum. This view of learning reflects the atomistic paradigm.

**Each Child Unique versus Each Child Has Shared Characteristics.** Students are seen as having shared characteristics. In traditional textbook learning situations, for example, all students are expected to master the same material. There is little room for individual differences. Mastery learning situations allow some room for individuality; however, this allowance is based strictly on the importance mastery learning educators attach to the fact that different students require different amounts of time to move through the same material. Even in mastery learning all students are expected to master the same material.

**Learning Is Social versus Learning Is Individual.** The student is seen as an individual, particularly in the competency-based education and mastery learning orientations. Learning is viewed in a more social context in the cultural transmission orientation. However, the goal is not to encourage students to work collaboratively or collectively; but only to inculcate in them the traditional mores of society.

**Child as Person versus Child as Client.** The child is viewed primarily as client, not as someone having an inner life with individual needs and concerns; the child is seen as an object whose task is to master a prescribed curriculum.

## Arguments for and against the Transmission Position

One argument used to support the subject orientation is that it organizes the curriculum in an efficient way. It has also been suggested that this type of approach to curriculum is easy to administer. Scheduling can be easily built around subjects and the time slots for classes can be uniform (e.g., 40 to 50 minutes).

Tradition provides a large part of the case for the subject matter orientation. Because high schools and colleges usually have been designed around the subject matter, the transmission orientation allows teachers to continue working within a framework with which they are familiar, and in which they are comfortable. Parents also are familiar with this orientation and resist changes to it. Thus, it continues as the principal organizing framework in most secondary schools.

Textbooks and learning materials also are organized around subject matter. Thus, most curriculum materials support the subject orientation and few learning materials have been developed to support an interdisciplinary or integrated approach to learning.

Although it is possible to refute tradition on logical and empirical grounds, the power of tradition has been acknowledged by those who study the problems of implementing innovations in the classroom. In *The Culture of School and The Problem of Change*, Sarason (1971/1982) suggests that the subject matter orientation is one of the "programmatic regularities" that dominate life at school.

Despite the argument that organizing courses and learning materials around subject matter is logical, evidence presented by learning theorists suggests that the structure of subject matter does not correlate with how children learn and develop. For example, much subject matter is presented in an abstract manner that is contrary to what we know about how children learn. In elementary school it is clear most children need concrete experiences to assist learning and development. Furthermore, the breakdown of subject matter into separate subjects has led to the establishment of arbitrary distinctions that make it difficult to explore relationships between ideas and concepts in different subjects.

There is also the danger that this orientation can become divorced from social concerns. As Smith, Stanley, and Shores (1957) state, subject matter specialists can lose themselves in an area of study and ignore problems of poverty, racism, and economic decay:

The products of the subject curriculum know more about the crusades than they know about the management of modern industry;

more about the structure of the earthworm than about their own bodies and the status of public provisions for their health; more about the exploits of Napoleon than about the nature and workings of their own economic and political systems. (p. 248)

Another criticism is that the subject matter orientation traditionally has been related to lower levels of learning, that is, the focus has been on information recall and basic skills with little opportunity to develop high-order analytic and conceptual skills. Similarly, the affective domain has often been ignored. Other orientations have been developed in response to this difficulty, particularly the humanistic and developmental orientations. The humanistic orientation, which gained strength in the late-1960s, focuses on developing curriculum in harmony with student interests, whereas the developmental position focuses on constructing programs in accordance with the appropriate student level of development.

Criticisms have been raised about the implications of the cultural transmission orientation for a democratic society. Clearly, some inculcation is inevitable in schools, even in the most open and democratic schools. However, critics of this position argue that inculcation should not override respect for the student's basic autonomy. The greatest weakness of the transmission position may be its rigidity in the face of cultural pluralism. Although it posits that among adherents to this position certain values must be upheld in a society, there is little consensus on specific issues such as the role of government in the economy. Society at one time may have been more monolithic in its structure and values; however, the pluralism that runs so deep in today's society undercuts the cultural transmission orientation, whereas the social orientation in the transaction position relates the school curriculum to democratic citizenship and is more in keeping with the school's role in a pluralistic society.

C.B.E. and mastery learning, which, along with the cultural transmission orientation, comprise the major components in the transmission position, have made definite contributions to the educational scene. Their emphasis on specific objectives has encouraged educators to be more clear and precise in their work and has generally enhanced curriculum planning in many areas. The focus on individualization is another positive aspect, particularly in the case of mastery learning. Mastery learning is designed to enhance individualized student achievement in a noncompetitive atmosphere—a laudable goal no matter what orientation a person is working from. The research on mastery learning is also impressive; a considerable amount of empirical evidence has been gathered to support its effectiveness.

Despite these achievements, however, definite concerns can be raised about C.B.E. and mastery learning. The emphasis in C.B.E. on breaking down the curriculum material into small segments is appropriate for some subjects; however, subjects such as art and drama do not lend themselves to the unit approach. Thus, mastery learning clearly should be limited to subjects, such as math, where the unit approach can be adapted more readily. However, there is a tendency in the C.B.E., and mastery approaches for the "medium to become the message"; if creativity, divergent thinking, and moral reasoning cannot be reduced to mastery learning units, then they are excluded from the curriculum. The programmed nature of C.B.E. and mastery learning can also reduce the teacher's flexibility. Sometimes, it is important that teachers "move" with student interests in a way that takes the teacher beyond stated objectives. This is particularly important in the context of an ecological or interdependent perspective, where the ability to synthesize is essential.

## REFERENCES

Bestor, A.E. (1953). *Educational wastelands: Retreat from learning in our public schools.* Urbana: University of Illinois Press.

_____. (1955). *The restoration of learning.* New York: Knopf.

Block, J.H. (Ed.). (1974). *Schools, society and mastery learning.* New York: Holt, Rinehart & Winston.

Block, J.H., & Anderson, L.W. (1975). *Mastery learning in classroom instruction.* New York: Macmillan.

Bloom, B.S. (1976). *Human characteristics and school learning.* New York: McGraw-Hill.

_____. (1981) *All our children learning.* New York: McGraw-Hill.

Bobbitt, F. (1912). Elimination of waste in education. *The Elementary School Teacher, 12,* 269.

_____. (1924). *How to make a curriculum.* Boston: Houghton Mifflin.

Bruner, J. (1966). *Toward a theory of instruction.* Cambridge, MA: Harvard University Press.

Burton, W. (1969). *The district school as it was.* New York: Arno Press & *The New York Times.*

Carroll, J. (1963). A model of school learning. *Teachers College Record, 64,* 723–733.

Cremin, L. (1961). *The transformation of the school.* New York: Random House.

Durkheim, E. (1961). *Moral education: A study in theory and application of the sociology of education.* New York: Free Press.

Gagne, R.M. (1965). *The conditions of learning.* New York: Holt, Rinehart & Winston.

Glaser, R. (1968). Adapting the elementary school curriculum to individual performance. In *Proceedings of the 1967 Invitational Conference on Testing Problems.* Princeton, NJ: Educational Testing Service.

Goodlad, J.I., & Anderson, R.H. (1959). *The nongraded elementary schools.* New York: Harcourt, Brace & World.

Gutek, G.L. (1974). *Philosophical alternatives in education.* Columbus, OH: Charles E. Merrill.

Harris, W.T. (1880). Textbooks and their uses. *Education, 1* (9).

Holmes, M. (1980). Forward to the basics: A radical conservative reconstruction. *Curriculum Inquiry, 10,* 383–418.

Kifer, E. (1973). The effects of school achievement on the affective traits of the learner. Unpublished doctoral dissertation, University of Chicago.

McAshan, H.H. (1979). *Competency-based education and behavioral objectives.* Englewood Cliffs, NJ: Educational Technology Publishers.

Miller, J. (1983). *The educational spectrum.* New York: Longman.

Morrison, H.C. (1940). *The curriculum of the common school.* Chicago: University of Chicago Press.

Ornstein, A.C. (1982). Curriculum contrasts: A historical overview. *Phi Delta Kappan, 63,* 404–407.

Postman, N. (1979). *Teaching as a conserving activity.* New York: Dell Books.

Ryan, D.W., & Schmidt, M. (1979). *Mastery learning: Theory, research and implementation.* Toronto, Ontario: Ministry of Education.

Sarason, S. (1982). *The culture of the school and the problems of change.* Boston: Allyn and Bacon. (Originally published in 1971)

Skinner, B.F. (1954). The science of learning and the art of teaching. *Harvard Educational Review. 24,* 86–97.

Smith, P.O., Stanley, W.O., & Shores, J.H. (1957). *Fundamentals of curriculum development.* New York: Harcourt, Brace & World.

Suppes, P. (1966). The uses of computers in education. *Scientific American. 215,* 206–221.

Tanner, D. & Tanner, L.N. (1980). *Curriculum development: Theory into practices.* New York: Macmillan.

# CHAPTER 4 TRANSACTION POSITION: The Context

## PHILOSOPHICAL CONTEXT

### John Dewey

The transaction position has its philosophical roots in experimental pragmatism, particularly in the work of John Dewey, whose work provides the philosophical underpinnings of inquiry approaches to curriculum. Dewey's thought can also be linked with liberal political philosophies that advocate facilitation of social and economic growth through active government intervention. Dewey's childhood experiences in a small, rural community, and especially his experiences in New England town meetings, influenced his conception of the democratic process. He felt that people should be able to discuss, debate, and make decisions about problems in an open and public forum. Dewey directed a laboratory school at the University of Chicago from 1896–1904; this school emphasized cooperative interaction between students and teachers and was intended to be a microcosm of the democratic process applied to education.

Dewey (1938/1969) rejected the mechanistic thinking of the behavioral psychologists; instead, he developed the concept of interaction, or transaction:

> If what is designated by such terms as doubt, belief, idea, conception, is to have any objective meaning, to say nothing of public verifiability, it must be located and described as behavior in which organism and environment act together, or inter-act. . . .
>
> Unfortunately, however, a special philosophical interpretation may be unconsciously read (by others, including certain critics) into the common sense distinction. It will then be supposed that or-

ganism and environment are "given" as independent things and interaction is a third independent thing which finally intervenes. In
fact, the distinction is a practical and temporal one, arising out of
the state of tension in which the organism at a given time, in a given
phase of life-activity, is set over against the environment as it then
and there exists. There is, of course, a natural world that exists independently of the organism, but this world is environment only as
it enters directly and indirectly into life-functions. The organism is
itself a part of the larger world and exists as organism only in active
connections with its environment. (pp. 33–34)

Dewey moves beyond the atomistic conception of behavior developed by Locke and Thorndike in his particular concern with cognitive
interaction and mental processes.

**Democracy and Education.**   In one of Dewey's main works, *Democracy
and Education* (1916/1966), he carefully describes the relationship between society and education. Education, in Dewey's view, has both a conservative and a reconstructive function. On the one hand, he recognizes
that education has an inculcative function in that schools should pass on
to students the mores and language of the culture. On the other hand,
however, he does not see the role of schools as limited to this conserving
function; instead, he views education as a dynamic process that can help
the student participate in the democratic process. Education, by employing the scientific method, can help direct the course of social change in a
positive direction.

Growth, for Dewey (1916/1966) is the overriding aim of education:

Since life means growth, a living creature lives as truly and positively
at one stage as at another, with the same intrinsic fullness and the
same absolute claims. Hence education means the enterprise of supplying the conditions which insure growth, or adequacy of life, ir-
respective of age. We first look with impatience upon immaturity,
regarding it as something to be got over as rapidly as possible. Then
the adult formed by such educative methods looks back with im-
patient regret upon childhood and youth as a scene of lost opportunities and wasted powers. This ironical situation will endure till it
is recognized that living has its own intrinsic quality and that the
business of education is with that quality. (p. 51)

In *Democracy and Education,* Dewey claims that schools have a three-
fold function—to simplify, purify, and balance the cultural heritage. *Sim-
plification* means that the school identifies key elements of the culture that

students should study. *Purification* means that schools should stress those elements of the culture that facilitate positive growth and eliminate those that retard it. *Balance* refers to the integration of the various aspects of experience into a harmonious whole. Schools, then, simplify, purify, and balance experience to facilitate growth.

Dewey claimed that schools should focus on cooperation and sharing. His vision of schools as miniature communities where teachers and students develop shared goals and solve mutual problems is clearly different from the atomistic vision that is at the center of the transmission position. Dewey criticized laissez-faire capitalism because he believed that in this system a few individuals exploit the majority of workers; in other words, he felt that laissez-faire capitalism is based too much on individual self-interest and competition and thus is antithetical to his own social vision of group cooperation.

### *Growth as an Aim of Education.*

As mentioned earlier, Dewey believed that the aim of education is growth. In his view, growth involves the reconstruction of experience and knowledge, which helps in refining and controlling future experience, and educational experiences are judged on their ability to promote growth; positive experiences facilitate growth whereas negative experiences arrest or retard it.

> Some experiences are miseducative. Any experience is miseducative that has the effect of arresting or distorting the growth of further experience. . . . An experience may be immediately enjoyable and yet promote the formation of a slack and careless attitude . . . [which] operates to modify the quality of subsequent experiences so as to prevent a person from getting out of them what they have to give. . . . Just as no man lives or dies to himself, so no experience lives or dies to itself. Wholly independent of desire or intent, every experience lives on in further experiences. Hence the central problem of an education based on experience is to select the kind of present experiences that live fruitfully and creatively is subsequent experience. (Dewey, 1938/1969, pp. 25–28)

Dewey rejected the idea that education is preparation for work, believing, instead, that schools should focus on the present lives of children. However, he did not believe in romanticizing childhood:

> Realization that life is growth protects us from that so-called idealizing of childhood which in effect is nothing but lazy indulgence. Life is not to be identified with every superficial act and interest. Even though it is not always easy to tell whether what appears to be

mere surface fooling is a sign of some nascent as yet untrained power, we must remember that manifestations are not to be accepted as ends in themselves. They are signs of positive growth. They are to be turned into means of development, of carrying power forward, not indulged or cultivated for their own sake. (Dewey, 1916/1966, pp. 51–52)

***Problem Solving.*** According to Dewey, intelligence is developed through the individual's interaction with the social environment, particularly through solving problems. Ideally, this problem solving should occur in a cooperative social context where people can work collaboratively. Problem solving, both as an individual and a group process, plays a central role in Dewey's overall concept of education. He believed that problem-solving activities in the school not only develop intelligence and facilitate growth, but also that the skills developed in problem solving should transfer to society at large.

Dewey's concept of problem solving is rooted in the scientific method. In the first step of the problem-solving process the individual confronts a problematic situation that causes confusion or puzzlement he or she must resolve. In the second step the person must define exactly what the problem is. The third step, clarification of the problem, consists of a careful examination or analysis of the factors contributing to the problem. In the fourth step the person develops hypotheses or "if–then" statements that offer possible solutions to the difficulty; here the person may also generate alternative solutions and consider the possible consequences of each alternative. In the fifth and final step the person selects one hypothesis or alternative and implements it. If the chosen alternative is successful the person continues his or her activity; if the hypothesis does not work out the individual selects another alternative.

In school, students can apply this methodology in solving the variety of personal and social dilemmas with which they are presented. Dewey argued that, instead of organizing school around traditional subjects, topics should be problem-centered. With his focus on problem solving, Dewey laid the theoretical groundwork for many inquiry approaches in curriculum (see Chapter 5).

As we have seen, in the transmission position knowledge is viewed as being static; students master a relatively fixed core curriculum. For Dewey (1916/1966), on the other hand, knowledge is related to experience; it is not something that is passively received by students but, rather, is acted upon by students as they test out ideas and hypotheses:

When education under the influence of a scholastic conception of knowledge which ignores everything but scientifically formulated facts and truths, fails to recognize that primary or initial subject matter of an active doing, involving the use of the body and the handling of material, the subject matter of instruction is isolated from the needs and purposes of the learner, and so becomes just a something to be memorized and reproduced on demand. (p. 184)

Extrinsic aims (which by definition are outside the learner's sphere of interest) should not be a source of educational activity. When they become the focus of educational activity, external rewards and punishments must be employed, which, in Dewey's view, does not facilitate student self-control and self-discipline.

Problems selected for the classroom should be related to the intrinsic interests of students, for the obvious reason that if a student is not motivated by a problem, it is no longer a problem. Learning, then, in Dewey's view, is not dictated by the teacher; rather, the teacher first attempts to help the student identify problems and then acts as a resource.

***Progressive Education.***   Dewey has been identified with the progressive education movement; however, he was critical of certain aspects of this movement. It was his opinion that the debate between traditionalists and progressive educators was in many ways unproductive because much of progressive education was merely a reaction *against* traditionalism. Thus, progressives ignored the past and focused only on the present, leading in many cases to an emphasis on activity for activity's sake. Furthermore, Dewey claimed, rather than emphasizing an interaction between the child and the environment, progressives too often merely romanticized the child and succumbed to the child's impulses and wishes. Dewey (1938/1969) felt that schools should not do this but instead should facilitate inquiry based on the scientific method.

> I see at bottom but two alternatives between which education must choose if it is not to drift aimlessly. One of them is expressed by the attempt to induce educators to return to the intellectual methods and ideals that arose centuries before the scientific method was developed. The appeal may be temporarily successful in a period when general insecurity, emotional and intellectual as well as economic is rife. For under these conditions the desire to lean on fixed authority is active. Nevertheless, it is so out of touch with all the conditions of modern life that I believe it is folly to seek salvation in this direction. The other alternative is systematic utilization of scientific method as the pattern and ideal of intelligent exploration and exploitation of the potentialities inherent in experience. (pp. 85–86)

The scientific method is at the heart of the Dewey/transaction position. In Dewey's (1938/1969) words, it is

> the only authentic means at our command for getting at the signif-
> icance of our everyday experiences of the world in which we live.
> . . . Consequently, whatever the level of experience, we have no
> choice but either to operate in accord with the pattern it provides
> or else to neglect the place of intelligence in the development and
> control of a living and moving experience. (p. 88)

In sum, the scientific method allows the person to examine and control experience; the individual working from the transaction position places his or her faith in analysis and rational intervention.

Dewey's basic position on education was first published in 1897 in *My Pedagogic Creed* and remains a classic statement of the transaction position.

## MY PEDAGOGIC CREED*
### *ARTICLE I—What Education Is*

**I Believe that**
—all education proceeds by the participation of the individual in the social consciousness of the race. This process begins uncon-sciously almost at birth, and is continually shaping the individu-al's powers, saturating his consciousness, forming his habits, training his ideas, and arousing his feelings and emotions. Through this unconscious education the individual gradually comes to share in the intellectual and moral resources which hu-manity has succeeded in getting together. He becomes an inher-itor of the funded capital of civilization. The most formal and technical education in the world cannot safely depart from this general process. It can only organize it or differentiate it in some particular direction.

—the only true education comes through the stimulation of the child's powers by the demands of the social situations in which he finds himself. Through these demands he is stimulated to act as a member of a unity, to emerge from his original narrowness of action and feeling, and to conceive of himself from the stand-point of the welfare of the group to which he belongs. Through the responses which others make to his own activities he comes

*This was published originally as a pamphlet by E.L. Kellogg and Co., 1897.

to know what these mean in social terms. The value which they have is reflected back to them. For instance, through the response which is made to the child's instinctive babblings the child comes to know what those babblings mean; they are transformed into articulate language, and thus the child is introduced into the consolidated wealth of ideas and emotions which are now summed up in language.

—this educational process has two sides—one psychological and one sociological—and that neither can be subordinated to the other, or neglected, without evil results following. Of these two sides, the psychological is the basis. The child's own instincts and powers furnish the material and give the starting-point for all education. Save as the efforts of the educator connect with some activity which the child is carrying on of his own initiative independent of the educator, education becomes reduced to a pressure from without. It may, indeed, give certain external results, but cannot truly be called educative. Without insight into the psychological structure and activities of the individual, the educative process will, therefore, be haphazard and arbitrary. If it chances to coincide with the child's activity it will get a leverage; if it does not, it will result in friction, or disintegration, or arrest of the child nature.

—knowledge of social conditions, of the present state of civilization, is necessary in order properly to interpret the child's powers. The child has his own instincts and tendencies, but we do not know what these mean until we can translate them into their social equivalents. We must be able to carry them back into a social past and see them as the inheritance of previous race activities. We must also be able to project them into the future to see what their outcome and end will be. In the illustration just used, it is the ability to see in the child's babblings the promise and potency of a future social intercourse and conversation which enables one to deal in the proper way with that instinct.

—the psychological and social sides are organically related and that education cannot be regarded as a compromise between the two, or a superimposition of one upon the other. We are told that the psychological definition of education is barren and formal— that it gives us only the idea of a development of all the mental powers without giving us any idea of the use to which these powers are put. On the other hand, it is urged that the social definition of education, as getting adjusted to civilization, makes of it a forced and external process, and results in subordinating the freedom of the individual to a preconceived social and political status.

—each of these objections is true when urged against one side isolated from the other. In order to know what a power really is we must know what its end, use, or function is, and this we cannot know save as we conceive of the individual as active in social relationships. But, on the other hand, the only possible adjustment which we can give to the child under existing conditions is that which arises through putting him in complete possession of all his powers. With the advent of democracy and modern industrial conditions, it is impossible to foretell definitely just what civilization will be twenty years from now. Hence it is impossible to prepare the child for any precise set of conditions. To prepare him for the future life means to give him command of himself; it means so to train him that he will have the full and ready use of all his capacities; that his eye and ear and hand may be tools ready to command, that his judgment may be capable of grasping the conditions under which it has to work, and the executive forces be trained to act economically and efficiently. It is impossible to reach this sort of adjustment save as constant regard is had to the individual's own powers, tastes, and interests—that is, as education is continually converted into psychological terms.

In sum, I believe that the individual who is to be educated is a social individual, and that society is an organic union of individuals. If we eliminate the social factor from the child we are left only with an abstraction; if we eliminate the individual factor from society, we are left only with an inert and lifeless mass. Education, therefore, must begin with a psychological insight into the child's capacities, interests, and habits. It must be controlled at every point by reference to these same considerations. These powers, interests, and habits must be continually interpreted— we must know what they mean. They must be translated into terms of their social equivalents—into terms of what they are capable of in the way of social service.

## ARTICLE II—*What the School Is*

### I Believe that
—the school is primarily a social institution. Education being a social process, the school is simply that form of community life in which all those agencies are concentrated that will be most effective in bringing the child to share in the inherited resources of the race, and to use his own powers for social ends.

—education, therefore, is a process of living and not a preparation for future living.

—the school must represent life—life as real and vital to the child as that which he carries on in the home, in the neighborhood, or on the playground.

—that education which does not occur through forms of life, forms that are worth living for their own sake, is always a poor substitute for the genuine reality, and tends to cramp and to deaden.

—the school, as an institution, should simplify existing social life; should reduce it, as it were, to an embryonic form. Existing life is so complex that the child cannot be brought into contact with it without either confusion or distraction; he is either overwhelmed by the multiplicity of activities which are going on, so that he loses his own power of orderly reaction, or he is so stimulated by these various activities that his powers are prematurely called into play and he becomes either unduly specialized or else disintegrated.

—as such simplified social life, the school life should grow gradually out of the home life; that it should take up and continue the activities with which the child is already familiar in the home.

—it should exhibit these activities to the child, and reproduce them in such ways that the child will gradually learn the meaning of them, and be capable of playing his own part in relation to them.

—this is a psychological necessity, because it is the only way of securing continuity in the child's growth, the only way of giving a background of past experience to the new ideas given in school.

—it is also a social necessity because the home is the form of social life in which the child has been nurtured and in connection with which he has had his moral training. It is the business of the school to deepen and extend his sense of the values bound up in his home life.

—much of present education fails because it neglects this fundamental principle of the school as a form of community life. It conceives the school as a place where certain information is to be given, where certain lessons are to be learned, or where certain habits are to be formed. The value of these is conceived as lying largely in the remote future; the child must do these things for the sake of something else he is to do; they are mere preparations. As a result they do not become a part of the life experience of the child and so are not truly educative.

—the moral education centers upon this conception of the school as a mode of social life, that the best and deepest moral training is precisely that which one gets through having to enter into proper relations with others in a unity of work and thought. The present educational systems, so far as they destroy or neglect this unity, render it difficult or impossible to get any genuine, regular moral training.

—the child should be stimulated and controlled in his work through the life of the community.

—under existing conditions far too much of the stimulus and control proceeds from the teacher, because of neglect of the idea of the school as a form of social life.

—the teacher's place and work in the school is to be interpreted from this same basis. The teacher is not in the school to impose certain ideas or to form certain habits in the child, but is there as a member of the community to select the influences which shall affect the child and to assist him in properly responding to these influences.

—the discipline of the school should proceed from the life of the school as a whole and not directly from the teacher.

—the teacher's business is simply to determine, on the basis of larger experience and riper wisdom, how the discipline of life shall come to the child.

—all questions of the grading of the child and his promotion should be determined by reference to the same standard. Examinations are of use only so far as they test the child's fitness for social life and reveal the place in which he can be of the most service and where he can receive the most help.

### ARTICLE III—The Subject-Matter of Education

**I Believe that**
—the social life of the child is the basis of concentration, or correlation, in all his training or growth. The social life gives the unconscious unity and the background of all his efforts and of all his attainments.

—the subject-matter of the school curriculum should mark a gradual differentiation out of the primitive unconscious unity of social life.

—we violate the child's nature and render difficult the best ethical results by introducing the child too abruptly to a number of special studies, of reading, writing, geography, etc., out of relation to this social life.

—the true center of correlation on the school subjects is not science, nor literature, nor history, nor geography, but the child's own social activities.

—education cannot be unified in the study of science, or so-called nature study, because apart from human activity, nature itself is not a unity; nature in itself is a number of diverse objects in space and time, and to attempt to make it the center of work by itself is to introduce a principle of radiation rather than one of concentration.

—literature is the reflex expression and interpretation of social experience; that hence it must follow upon and not precede such experience. It, therefore, cannot be made the basis, although it may be made the summary of unification.

—once more that history is of educative value in so far as it presents phases of social life and growth. It must be controlled by reference to social life. When taken simply as history it is thrown into the distant past and becomes dead and inert. Taken as the record of man's social life and progress it becomes full of meaning. I believe, however, that it cannot be so taken excepting as the child is also introduced directly into social life.

—the primary basis of education is in the child's powers at work along the same general constructive lines as those which have brought civilization into being.

—the only way to make the child conscious of his social heritage is to enable him to perform those fundamental types of activity which make civilization what it is.

—in the so-called expressive or constructive activities as the center of correlation.

—this gives the standard for the place of cooking, sewing, manual training, etc., in the school.

—they are not special studies which are to be introduced over and above a lot of others in the way of relaxation or relief, or as additional accomplishments. I believe rather that they represent, as types, fundamental forms of social activity; and that it is possible and desirable that the child's introduction into the more formal subjects of the curriculum be through the medium of these activities.

—the study of science is educational in so far as it brings out the materials and processes which make social life what it is.

—one of the greatest difficulties in the present teaching of science is that the material is presented in purely objective form, or is treated as a new peculiar kind of experience which the child can add to that which he has already had. In reality, science is of value because it gives the ability to interpret and control the experience already had. It should be introduced, not as so much new subject-matter, but as showing the factors already involved in previous experience, and as furnishing tools by which that experience can be more easily and effectively regulated.

—at present we lose much of the value of literature and language studies because of our elimination of the social element. Language is almost always treated in the books of pedagogy simply as the expression of thought. It is true that language is a logical instrument, but it is fundamentally and primarily a social instrument. Language is the device for communication; it is the tool through which one individual comes to share the ideas and feelings of others. When treated simply as a way of getting individual information, or as a means of showing off what one has learned, it loses its social motive and end.

—there is, therefore, no succession of studies in the ideal school curriculum. If education is life, all life has, from the outset, a scientific aspect, an aspect of art and culture, and an aspect of communication. It cannot, therefore, be true that the proper studies for one grade are mere reading and writing, and that at a later grade, reading, or literature, or science, may be introduced. The progress is not in the succession of studies, but in the development of new attitudes towards, and new interests in, experience.

—education must be conceived as a continuing reconstruction of experience; that the process and the goal of education are one and the same thing.

—to set up any end outside of education, as furnishing its goal and standard, is to deprive the educational process of much of its meaning, and tends to make us rely upon false and external stimuli in dealing with the child.

## ARTICLE IV—The Nature of Method

**I Believe that**

—the question of method is ultimately reducible to the question of the order of development of the child's powers and interests. The law for presenting and treating material is the law implicit within the child's own nature. Because this is so I believe the following statements are of supreme importance as determining the spirit in which education is carried on:

—the active side precedes the passive in the development of the child-nature; that expression comes before conscious impression; that the muscular development precedes the sensory; that movements come before conscious sensations; I believe that consciousness is essentially motor or impulsive; that conscious states tend to project themselves in action.

—the neglect of this principle is the cause of a large part of the waste of time and strength in school work. The child is thrown into a passive, receptive, or absorbing attitude. The conditions are such that he is not permitted to follow the law of his nature; the result is friction and waste.

—ideas (intellectual and rational processes) also result from action and devolve for the sake of the better control of action. What we term reason is primarily the law of orderly or effective action. To attempt to develop the reasoning powers, the powers of judgment, without reference to the selection and arrangement of means in action, is the fundamental fallacy in our present methods of dealing with this matter. As a result we present the child with arbitrary symbols. Symbols are a necessity in mental development, but they have their place as tools for economizing effort; presented by themselves they are a mass of meaningless and arbitrary ideas imposed from without.

—the image is the great instrument of instruction. What a child gets out of any subject presented to him is simply the images which he himself forms with regard to it.

—if nine-tenths of the energy at present directed towards making the child learn certain things were spent in seeing to it that the child was forming proper images, the work of instruction would be indefinitely facilitated.

—much of the time and attention now given to the preparation and presentation of lessons might be more wisely and profitably expended in training the child's power of imagery and in seeing to it that he was continually forming definite, vivid, and growing images of the various subjects with which he comes in contact in his experience.

—interests are the signs and symptoms of growing power. I believe that they represent dawning capacities. Accordingly the constant and careful observation of interests is of the utmost importance for the educator.

—these interests are to be observed as showing the state of development which the child has reached.

—they prophesy the stage upon which he is about to enter.

—only through the continual and sympathetic observation of childhood's interests can the adult enter into the child's life and see what it is ready for, and upon what material it could work most readily and fruitfully.

—these interests are neither to be humored nor repressed. To repress interest is to substitute the adult for the child, and so to weaken intellectual curiosity and alertness, to suppress initiative, and to deaden interest. To humor the interests is to substitute the transient for the permanent. The interest is always the sign of some power below; the important thing is to discover this power. To humor the interest is to fail to penetrate below the surface, and its sure result is to substitute caprice and whim for genuine interest.

—the emotions are the reflex of actions.

—to endeavor to stimulate or arouse the emotions apart from their corresponding activities is to introduce an unhealthy and morbid state of mind.

—if we can only secure right habits of action and thought, with reference to the good, the true, and the beautiful, the emotions will for the most part take care of themselves.

—next to deadness and dullness, formalism and routine, our education is threatened with no greater evil than sentimentalism.

—this sentimentalism is the necessary result of the attempt to divorce feeling from action.

### ARTICLE V—*The School and Social Progress*

**I Believe that**
—education is the fundamental method of social progress and reform.

—all reforms which rest simply upon the enactment of law, or the threatening of certain penalties, or upon changes in mechanical or outward arrangements, are transitory and futile.

—education is a regulation of the process of coming to share in the social consciousness; and that the adjustment of individual activity on the basis of this social consciousness is the only sure method of social reconstruction.

—this conception has due regard for both the individualistic and socialistic ideals. It is duly individual because it recognizes the formation of a certain character as the only genuine basis of right living. It is socialistic because it recognizes that this right character is not to be formed by merely individual precept, example, or exhortation, but rather by the influence of a certain form of institutional or community life upon the individual, and that the social organism through the school, as its organ, may determine ethical results.

—in the ideal school we have the reconciliation of the individualistic and the institutional ideals.

—the community's duty to education is, therefore, its paramount moral duty. By law and punishment, by social agitation and discussion, society can regulate and form itself in a more or less haphazard and chance way. But through education society can formulate its own purposes, can organize its own means and resources, and thus shape itself with definiteness and economy in the direction in which it wishes to move.

—when society once recognizes the possibilities in this direction, and the obligations which these possibilities impose, it is impossible to conceive of the resources of time, attention, and money which will be put at the disposal of the educator.

—it is the business of every one interested in education to insist upon the school as the primary and most effective interest in social progress and reform in order that society may be awakened to realize what the school stands for, and aroused to the necessity of endowing the educator with sufficient equipment properly to perform his task.

—education thus conceived marks the most perfect and intimate union of science and art conceivable in human experience.

—the art of thus giving shape to human powers and adapting them to social service is the supreme art; one calling into its service the best of artists; that no insight, sympathy, tact, executive power, is too great for such service.

—with the growth of psychological service, giving added insight into individual structure and laws of growth; and with growth of social science, adding to our knowledge of the right organization of individuals, all scientific resources can be utilized for the purposes of education.

—when science and art thus join hands the most commanding motive for human action will be reached, the most genuine springs of human conduct aroused, and the best service that human nature is capable of guaranteed.

—the teacher is engaged, not simply in the training of individuals, but in the formation of the proper social life.

—every teacher should realize the dignity of his calling; that he is a social servant set apart for the maintenance of proper social order and the securing of the right social growth.

—in this way the teacher always is the prophet of the true God and the usherer in of the true kingdom of God.

## PSYCHOLOGICAL CONTEXT

### Lawrence Kohlberg and Jean Piaget: Stages of Growth

The transaction position is strongly linked with the developmental psychologists' view of the life cycle as a series of developmental stages. Piaget (1963) formulated a classification of the stages of growth. Kohlberg and Mayer (1972) use Piaget's work as the starting point for their own theory of moral development. Kohlberg and Mayer (1972) argue that their own work and the developmental theory of Piaget are, in part, the extension of Dewey's thinking into the realm of psychology; whereas Dewey simply stated that growth is a principal aim of education but did not explain precisely how growth occurs, Piaget and Kohlberg define the stages of growth more clearly. At the heart of the Piaget–Kohlberg conception is the interactionist position:

> The child is not a plant or a machine; he is a philosopher or a scientist-poet. The dialectical metaphor of progressive education is supported by a cognitive-developmental or interactional psychological theory. Discarding the dichotomy between maturation and environmentally determined learning, Piaget and Dewey claim that mature thought emerges through a process of development that is neither direct biological maturation nor direct learning, but rather a reorganization of psychological structures resulting from organism-environment interactions. Basic mental structure is the product of the patterning of interaction between the organism and the

environment, rather than a direct reflection of either innate neu-
rological patterns or external environmental patterns. (Kohlberg &
Mayer, 1972, pp. 456–457)

According to Kohlberg, the child's experience is organized through
internal structures that interact with the environment; these "internally
organized wholes or systems of internal relations" are rules for processing information. Development occurs when these internal structures become more comprehensive in the way they are able to deal with cognitive
conflict. In the words of Kohlberg and Mayer (1972), "The core of development is cognitive change in distinctively human, general patterns of
thinking about the self and the world" (p. 457).

The concept of life stages is central to the Piaget–Kohlberg theory.
Stages have the following characteristics:

1. Stages imply distinct or qualitative differences in children's
   modes of thinking or of solving the same problem.
2. These different modes of thought form an invariant sequence,
   order, or succession in individual development. While cultural
   factors may speed up, slow down, or stop development, they do
   not change its sequence.
3. Each of these different and sequential modes of thought forms
   a "structural whole." A given stage-response on a task does not
   just represent a specific response determined by knowledge and
   familiarity with that task or tasks similar to it; rather, it represents an underlying thought-organization.
4. Cognitive stages are hierarchical integrations. Stages form an order of increasingly differentiated and integrated structures to
   fulfill a common function. (Kohlberg & Mayer, 1972, p. 458)

Experience is the intermediary between the person and environment and
is essential to facilitate movement through the stages. The brief description that follows of the stages of growth outlines five periods—infancy,
early childhood, middle childhood, adolescence, and adulthood. Piaget's
cognitive stages are described first, followed by Kohlberg's stages of
moral development.

### Infancy.

COGNITIVE DEVELOPMENT    Infancy is characterized by immediate
sensory experience. Piaget calls this the *sensori-motor stage* (age 0–2), as the
learning that occurs during this stage of development takes place within
a physical orientation. For example, during this stage one of the infant's
principal learnings is visual projection—the ability to follow the path of
a moving object. If you drop a ball in front of a 4-month-old baby, the

infant will continue to look at the hand that held the ball. However, at the end of the sensori-motor period the child is able to follow the ball to the ground. The infant also gains an understanding of object permanence—the recognition that when an object disappears from view it still exists. For instance, if you hold a ball in front of an 18-month-old child and then place it behind your back, usually the infant will go behind you to find the ball because he or she knows that the object is not gone; in short, memory is beginning to develop.

### Early Childhood.

COGNITIVE DEVELOPMENT    Piaget calls this period the *preoperational stage* (age 2–7). It is the stage during which elementary reasoning appears. This early reasoning is based on the appearance of objects; for instance, if the child is presented with two rows of five coins and one row is longer, he will usually identify the longer row as having more coins. Judgments are based on appearance because at this stage the child cannot retain his original perspective if appearances are changed.

During this stage children cannot relate individual parts to the whole. They can focus on one element at a time, but cannot master relationships between the elements. For example, when a toy car finishes a race first it is called the fastest car, even if it traveled a shorter distance than the other cars in the race. It is only during middle childhood that a more complete understanding of such relationships develop.

MORAL DEVELOPMENT    Children begin to exhibit moral reasoning toward the end of early childhood. Up to the age of 6 or so, children usually do not exhibit any moral reasoning; instead, their actions become their judgments. *Good* is what they like and want; *bad* is what they do not like or do not want. Around the age of 6 or 7, however, children begin stage 1 moral reasoning. They usually think in terms of the automatic physical consequences of an act. Children reason that behaviors are bad if they lead to punishment and that acts are good if they lead to rewards; for instance, children will assert that it is not good to steal because they will have to go to jail if they are caught, or they might say that cleaning up their room is good because they get a chocolate for doing it.

During early childhood the value of life is seen in terms of physical objects. The child at this stage of development is not able to recognize the interests of others and is unable to relate differing viewpoints. Children will also confuse the perspective of those in authority with their own perspective.

### Middle Childhood.

COGNITIVE DEVELOPMENT    Piaget refers to middle childhood as the period of *concrete operations* (age 7–11), by which he means the ability to understand and conduct various operations on concrete materials. One example of an operation is conservation. This means that the child is no longer fooled by appearances, but has developed the ability to *see* that quantities do not change even if their form changes. For example, a child in the concrete operations stage will not be fooled by the length of the rows of coins; if one row is longer but there is an equal number of coins in each row, he or she will be able to conserve number and realize that each row contains the same number of coins. Children at this stage of development also learn to conserve volume. This means that when water is poured from a low, wide beaker into a tall, narrow one, the child will assert that each beaker contains an equal amount of water, unlike children in the period of early childhood, who usually think that the taller beaker holds more water. During middle childhood children also are able to reverse operations. In other words, if a child is unsure about the water beaker problem he or she will pour the water back and forth between the beakers to reverse the problem to its starting point.

The term *concrete operations* is derived from the fact that children in this stage of development prefer to work with concrete materials. In dealing with the coin or the beaker problem they rely on the physical presence of the coins or the beakers to solve the problem, whereas they will not be able to solve it if the problem is given verbally.

MORAL DEVELOPMENT    With regard to moral development, right action for most children at this stage (stage 2) consists of what satisfies their own needs and, occasionally, the needs of others. This is the point in development when children begin to identify the interests of others. Deals or agreements can be made on an equal-exchange basis—an exchange morality that is sometimes summarized by the saying, "You scratch my back and I'll scratch yours!"

In the middle childhood children see things from the perspective of isolated individuals who value things subjectively, unlike children in the early childhood stage, who are not aware of other individual's perspectives but, rather, respond to experience in terms of automatic, physical responses. Because all values are subjectively defined in middle childhood, children at this stage can develop a relativistic perspective. Some individuals never go beyond this stage. The "playboy philosophy" is one example of this type of morality in operation. Many chronic criminal offenders also function at this moral stage.

### Adolescence.

COGNITIVE DEVELOPMENT    Piaget refers to this stage of development as the period of *formal operations*. By this he means that individuals can conduct operations (e.g., conservation) without reference to concrete materials. The adolescent enters the world of ideas and contemplation and also begins to hypothesize about relationships. He or she can consider "if–then" statements and also the notion that there are any number of possibilities in relation to a particular problem. In brief, the individual takes a logical, systematic approach to problem solving, as the following example shows.

> An example of the shift from concrete to formal operations may be taken from the work of E.A. Peel. Peel asked children what they thought about the following event: "Only brave pilots are allowed to fly over high mountains. A fighter pilot flying over the Alps collided with an aerial cableway, and cut a main cable causing some cars to fall to the glacier below. Several people were killed." A child at the concrete-operational level answered: "I think that the pilot was not very good at flying." A formal-operational child responded: "He was either not informed of the mountain railway on his route or he was flying too low, also his flying compass may have been affected by something before or after take-off, this setting him off course causing collision with the cable."
>
> The concrete-operational child assumes that if there was a collision the pilot was a bad pilot; the formal-operational child considers all the possibilities that might have caused the collision. The concrete-operational child adopts the hypothesis that seems most probable or likely to him. The formal-operational child constructs all possibilities and checks them out one by one. (Kohlberg & Gilligan, 1971, pp. 1061–1062)

Compared with children in the concrete operations stage, individuals in the formal operations stage are no longer satisfied with observation of specific events, but see these events as a point of departure for conceptualizing, hypothesizing, or imagining the consequences of or possible solutions to various problems.

MORAL DEVELOPMENT    This is an important factor in personal and moral development because, at this stage (stage 3), individuals become capable of applying speculations to social problems; in examining moral dilemmas, they can now understand how others see an issue. At this stage the adolescent also begins to reason according to the expectations others hold for him or her and thereby moves toward conventional moral thinking; conformity to and maintenance of the family/group/national social order is now perceived as valuable in its own right and moral judgments are now based on role taking and legitimately perceived expectations.

Stage 3 is the first stage of conventional moral thinking. Individuals at this level of development are concerned about other people and their feelings and are motivated by what others expect of them. They are concerned about being "good" or "nice" and seek to maintain mutual relations with others based on shared feelings and agreements. Thus, praise and blame are important at this stage and mutual expectations become the reference point for moral decision making. Stage 3 reasoning may begin around age 10, is more likely to begin around 11 or 12, and is the dominant stage among high school students, whose focus on peer group approval—being "one of the boys (girls)"—exemplifies the issues that are central to people at this level of development.

At the next level of development the individual becomes concerned with maintenance of the social system and with rules that support it. The central issue in this stage (stage 4) is the development of the concept that the individual exists to serve society and that individual rights are subordinate to the overall needs of society. At this stage, which usually is not fully manifested before age 16–18, the individual has moved beyond an interpersonal to a societal perspective.

### Adulthood.

MORAL DEVELOPMENT    In adulthood, normally reached in the third decade of one's life, the individual is able to fully integrate postconventional moral reasoning. This stage (stage 5) is characterized by a social contract–legalistic orientation in which *right action* tends to be defined in terms of individual, inalienable rights and standards that have been critically examined and agreed upon by the whole society. The individual recognizes that rules can be changed and negotiated through the democratic process; the "official" morality of most democratic governments reflects the type of thinking that emerges at this stage of the individual growth process. At this stage the individual also develops a theoretical and abstract view of society as existing for and organized to serve the individual as well as the general welfare. In other words, in stage 4 moral reasoning, the individual is seen as being subordinate to the welfare of the society at large, whereas at stage 5 the needs of the individual are prior to those of society and the value of life is defined in terms of universal human welfare and human rights.

By approximately age 30 the individual can fully incorporate the sixth and final stage of moral reasoning, wherein *right* is defined by applying self-chosen ethical principles that appeal to universality and consistency. For example, the golden rule should be applied in an abstract sense to individuals in a consistent and universal manner. Only a small percentage of the population (roughly 5%) (Kohlberg & Mayer, 1972) attains this stage of moral development.

## Implications for Education of Developmental Psychology

The developmentalists see human life as a process of movement toward intellectual and moral autonomy through interaction with the environment. Development takes place when the individual builds new structures of thought as a result of this interaction. Piaget suggests that development occurs through maturation, physical interaction, social interaction, and finally, equilibration, which occurs when the individual restructures his or her thinking to accommodate new problems. Kohlberg suggests that moral development occurs through social interactions in which the person grapples with a moral dilemma and is thereby exposed to higher levels of moral reasoning (Kohlberg & Mayer, 1972).

Central to the transaction orientation is the idea derived from developmental psychology, that the student must be given the opportunity to inquire about the physical, moral, and social world. The learning environment, then, although structured, should be rich in materials and ideas and allow for open inquiry into various problems. Application of the developmental orientation to the classroom generally involves the following steps:

1. Sensitivity to developmental differences
2. Presentation of task or dilemma
3. Student interaction with the task or dilemma and teacher follow-up

***Sensitivity to Developmental Differences.*** The first step for the teacher is to be aware of the child's stage of development and to be sensitive to the child's view of the world, in light of the developmental psychologists' emphasis on the importance of these factors. For example, Piaget views the child as a "cognitive alien," because the child has cognitive styles that differ from adult thought. The preoperational child, for instance, believes that nature is conscious and is endowed with purpose, just like himself or herself. Piaget calls this characteristic *animism*. A typical example of animism is when children say the sun follows them to "show them the way." Piaget states that, in order to be effective, the teacher or adult responding to the child must be careful not to impose an adult vision on the child's perspective. Therefore, in responding to children's questions, it is important that the teacher listen and answer within the cognitive framework of the child in a manner that can also stimulate further development.

Kohlberg, like Piaget, recognizes the importance of teacher awareness of developmental stages. The teacher should be a good listener so that he or she can identify the various levels of moral reasoning in the classroom. After identifying the levels, the teacher can then establish student groupings for discussions of morality. This is important because the individual is always in motion toward the next stage of reasoning and will eventually adopt the next stage under appropriate conditions. The student, however, cannot understand reasoning that is two stages or more above his or her own (e.g., stage 4 reasoning cannot be understood by a stage 2 person). The teacher should identify the approximate levels of reasoning in the classroom and then try to match the stages in student groupings so that each student is exposed to one level higher than his or her own.

### Task Presentation and Cognitive Conflict.

After identifying the approximate level of development the teacher should present the student with a task or problem that stimulates cognitive conflict. For Piaget, conflict occurs when the child's thinking is thrown into a state of disequilibrium through exposure to some problem. For example, when a child in the preoperational stage is presented with two pieces of clay equal in size and shape he or she will usually indicate they are the same. After the form of one of the pieces is changed, the preoperational child will indicate they are no longer the same in size or weight. If the child says that the deformed piece contains more clay, a small bit of clay can be added to the nondeformed piece or subtracted from the deformed piece and the child can be asked again for a comparison. Thus, the addition–subtraction operation conflicts with the child's perceptions and the resulting cognitive conflict brings about an attempt at resolution. If approached at the appropriate point in the child's development, the child would subscribe to the idea of conservation as a result of the addition–subtraction operations. In sum, cognitive conflict usually facilitates cognitive growth because it forces the child to develop new mental processes to deal with the problem.

Kohlberg, who agrees with this perspective, has constructed a number of case studies that pose moral-conflict questions. There is no right answer to these moral dilemmas, but the child's attempt to wrestle with them generally facilitates moral development.

### Interaction with the Task or Dilemma.

An important factor in dealing with cognitive conflict is the opportunity to act on the task or dilemma. For example, in Piaget's conservation experiments the likelihood for cognitive growth to occur increased when the child was given the opportunity to actively manipulate the beakers and water, or the clay.

The key to this process is not movement or activity per se, but an environment in which the child can introduce relations between or transformations of objects and discover the effects of such transformations. The active process may not necessarily involve external actions of the learner; Piaget points out that Socrates used an active method with langauge in which the learner was encouraged to actively construct his or her own knowledge and beliefs.

During early and middle childhood, concrete materials can be used to facilitate the active process of acting on the task or dilemma. For instance, the rows of coins or the pieces of clay mentioned previously are valuable aids in the process of gaining an understanding of conservation.

To facilitate growth, it is important that the materials be matched to the child's stage of development. For a 6- or 7-year old child, for example, the materials should be chosen to generate cognitive conflict with respect to conservation problems. Kohlberg suggests that as the student interacts with the problem or dilemma, the teacher should ask questions that help the student to clarify his or her thinking and thus stimulate development. To stimulate moral development, the teacher can generate dilemma discussions with a variety of questions or probes such as the ones that follow:

- *Clarifying probe:* Asks the student to further explain his or her position
- *Universal-consequences probe:* Asks the student to consider what would happen if everyone reasoned or acted in a particular manner
- *Role-switch probe:* Asks the student to assume the perspective of another person in the dilemma
- *Issue-specific probe:* Asks the student to explore a particular moral issue (e.g., justice, authority) that is central to the dilemma. (Hersh, Miller, & Fielding, 1980, pp. 137–147).

The introduction of such probes by the teacher helps the student reflect on his or her position. In sum, teachers who use a developmental orientation do not work in a laissez-faire manner but actively intervene in the learning situation to stimulate interaction leading to growth.

Piaget and Kohlberg are not the only psychologists who articulate a transaction perspective. Ausubel, for example, whose work is discussed in *The Educational Spectrum* (1983), also can be linked with this position. However, Piaget and Kohlberg specifically link their work directly with Dewey, whose thinking is so fundamental to the transaction position.

## ECONOMIC/SOCIAL CONTEXT

The transaction position can be linked with liberal economic and political theory, particularly with the work of two liberal economists—John Maynard Keynes and John Kenneth Galbraith. At the heart of the liberal position is the idea that government should rationally intervene to improve the economic and social welfare of the nation.

### John Maynard Keynes

In his *Treatise on Money* (1930), Keynes, an English economist whose theories became popular in the 1930s, analyzes why capitalist economies regularly fluctuate between prosperity and depression, and generally challenges many of the assumptions of classic economic theory. He develops these ideas in his most influential book, *The General Theory of Employment, Interest, and Money* (1964)—a book that is as important to

economic thinking as Smith's (1930) *Wealth of Nations. The General Theory,*
which first came out in 1936, was in one sense a defense of President
Roosevelt's active intervention to stimulate the United States' economy.
In 1929 private investment had been approximately $15 billion; in 1932
it had fallen 94% to $886 million, a staggering decline in economic activ-
ity. In this book Keynes presents the kernel of his economic theory when
he argues that only through government spending could the economy
recover from this precipitous decline.

Keynes differs from the laissez-faire capitalists in his contention that
some planning and intervention by the government is necessary to keep
the economy running smoothly; unregulated competition and individual
self-interest are not enough.

> I should say that what we want is not no planning, or even less plan-
> ning, indeed I should say we almost certainly want more. But the
> planning should take place in a community in which as many people
> as possible, both leaders and followers, wholly share your own
> moral position. Moderate planning will be safe enough if those car-
> rying it out are rightly oriented in their own minds and hearts to the
> moral issue. (Keynes, quoted in Heilbroner, 1980, p. 276)

Keynes, however, did not feel that government intervention should be
permanent; instead, it should only be applied when private investment
falters: "I see the problem of recovery in the following light: How soon
will normal business enterprise come to the rescue. On what scale, by
which expedients and for how long is abnormal government expenditure
advisable in the meantime?" (Keynes, quoted in Heilbroner, 1980, p. 273)

Keynes's economic theory was viewed when it first appeared as a
tremendous threat by conservative businessmen and laissez-faire economists, many of whom accused him of advocating a "socialist" economy,
and is now under attack once again. However, it should be noted that
Keynes developed his theory to deal with the problems of the Depression,
and in general did not intend for it to grapple with the problem of inflation, which was so prevalent in the 1970s.

## John Kenneth Galbraith

Galbraith has inherited the liberal mantle; just as Milton Friedman is the
principle spokesman today for the laissez-faire position, Galbraith is the
most prominent spokesman for liberal interventionist economic theory.
One of the most complete presentations of his position is in *Economics and
the Public Purpose* (1973). This book has two major parts: Galbraith's analysis of the economy and his theory of reform.

Galbraith claims that one of the main components of the economy
is the large corporations such as Mobil and Esso, which have vast powers

to control prices and even the demand for goods. Each of these firms has a corporate bureaucracy, which Galbraith calls the *technostructure*, whose main concern is survival. Much interaction takes place between the corporate technostructure and government; for example, people frequently move back and forth between government positions and the technostructure. These large firms, in Galbraith's view, act virtually independently of their boards and their shareholders.

In addition to the large corporations, Galbraith identifies a second component in the economy—a market system composed of smaller corporations and businesses, including small stores and restaurants. The functioning of this section of the economy is closer in form to laissez-faire capitalism. Galbraith argues that government should stimulate and support this market system, including the formation of guilds by small businesses, so that the system is not swallowed up by the large corporations.

The third element in Galbraith's economic model is the government. He states that government has an essential role to play in the economy in providing essential services such as education, and that it also must serve as the principal party in combatting inflation by imposing wage and price controls.

Turning now to his proposals for economic reform, Galbraith (1973) argues that reliance on the laissez-faire system leads to "unequal development, inequality, frivolous and erratic innovation, environmental assault, indifference to personality power over the state, inflation, and failure in interindustry coordination." An important aspect of his proposal is his call for government to change so that it serves the market system rather than the needs of the technostructure. Galbraith claims that government now is a servant of the big firms and that voters must stop electing incumbents to Congress so that new members can be elected who will not continue the cosy relationship between government and big business.

In his program for economic reform, Galbraith points to the areas in which he thinks government should actively intervene. He argues that government should not only implement a guaranteed income to people who cannot find work, but also reduce excessive incomes through progressive taxation. Galbraith contends that certain industries should be nationalized and publically owned, including housing, medical services, public transport, and the defense industries; Galbraith's "socialism" is not ideological but more pragmatic in nature, based on his view that these particular industries could function better if they were made public enterprises. In general, Galbraith argues that government expenditures should be for public services rather than, for example, space programs. Public purpose is the main priority for government in the economic system Galbraith proposes. In his opinion, the free market system cannot adequately bring about the changes that he feels are needed. In sum, for Galbraith laissez-faire economics is irrelevant, and the only solution to today's problems is greater planning. Galbraith even advocates that the governments of different countries cooperate to control distribution of capital and to combat inflation.

## CONCLUDING COMMENTS

The transaction position is rooted in pragmatism and liberalism. Kaplan (1961) states that pragmatism can "be described as providing meaning to the old-fashioned and much abused term liberalism" (p. 41). Unlike the conservative position, which posits that the universe is better left alone, the liberal position states that things can be improved. Both pragmatism and liberalism embody an optimistic view that people can improve the social environment through rational intervention, and both encourage active efforts toward reform. Related to this is the positive attitude in both pragmatism and liberalism to social planning; both support the view that social planning can improve the overall welfare of society. However, despite this overall support for government involvement in the economy, pragmatists such as Sidney Hook insist on the importance of individual rights within the political structure. In other words, they believe that economic development must take place in a framework of political freedom wherein civil rights are respected. Finally, pragmatic liberalism is committed to the democratic process as a method for developing policy. In Kaplan's (1961) words, "The method is the application of intelligence to social problems." Pragmatic liberalism insists that rational intelligence in the form of the scientific method can resolve most problems and that education plays a key role in developing this rational intelligence.

Gambs (1975) draws the link between pragmatism and liberalism and, more particularly, the link between Dewey and Galbraith:

> I have long thought of Galbraith as the potential John Dewey of economics—the Dewey particularly of the Reconstruction of Philosophy. In outward things the men are completely different. I used to see Dewey walk into Teachers College at Columbia looking slightly bewildered and countrified, carrying a couple of crates of eggs from his farm for delivery to customers on the faculty. I have not seen Galbraith often, but when I do see him in person or in pictures, he is always well dressed and urbane. Dewey's writing was awkward; Galbraith's prose flows like the body of a gifted ballet dancer. Galbraith makes his vanity bearable by the humourous device of exaggerating it; if Dewey exaggerated anything, it was his humility.
>
> But now for the similarities. Both have been active in reform politics. Both saw that their fields of study—philosophy and economics, respectively—have not really been a search for truth, but

rather a search for myths to explain this curious and unreasonable world: such things as high and low rank, abject poverty and ridiculously great wealth, domination and obedience. Both saw that these myths, though perhaps once serviceable to mankind, are no longer relevant. Dewey invented instrumentalism as a guiding philsophy and Galbraith is (seemingly) an unconscious instrumentalist who, like Moliere's M. Jourdain, had unwittingly been speaking prose for forty years. Even though Galbraith does not have the singleness of purpose that characterized Dewey, he has done pretty well with this left hand—and this is perhaps the tragedy of Galbraith—not for himself, for he seems to be having a good time living out his life in his own way. But for the rest of us it is too bad. (pp. 113–114)

The major contribution of pragmatism and liberalism is their focus on political freedom and their belief in rational intervention. More specifically, pragmatism and liberalism have given rise to numerous improvements including various human rights codes and legal precedents supporting individual rights. In the economic and social welfare field, social security, Medicare in the United States, public health programs in Canada and Great Britian, and a host of social and education programs are part of this tradition. Liberalism has in fact provided the impetus for most political and economic reforms in Western democracies. However, these reforms have now become associated with some undesirable trends. For instance, conservatives argue that certain political reforms (e.g., legal rights for criminal suspects) have led to more crime and that social reforms have contributed to inflation and a stagnant economy.

Pragmatism has specific limitations and drawbacks, the most serious, in our view, being that it gives little recognition to the intuitive, imaginative side of human activity. Pragmatists tend to view science as logical problem solving, but even many scientists acknowledge the importance of imagination in scientific discovery. In the social realm, moral vision and imagination may be more important than the commitment to logic. Certainly, the impact of people such as Mahatma Gandhi and Martin Luther King on the development of human and civil rights stemmed from their moral imagination and spirituality rather than from a commitment to the scientific method.

This same criticism can be applied to the work of Piaget and Kohlberg, who, essentially, present models of development of the rational person. Sullivan (1977) argues that Kohlberg dismisses the imaginative capacity of human beings:

There is something lacking in all the conceptual elegance of both Piaget's and Kohlberg's structuralisms. One significant gap is in the area of the "aesthetic imagination" and the potential role it may play in the development of intellectual and moral understanding. It can be said of Kohlberg, as it is said of Piaget, that his theory is confined to an analysis of "decentring" in logical and moral structures. The imagination is the thorn in the rosy development of most theoretical rationalists. . . . Piaget seems to pass off figurative knowledge as simply a lower form of intellectual development. Kohlberg's theory has no systematic place for it. In our everyday life, value synthesis is not a science but probably encompasses, when done well, the virtuosity of an artist. (pp. 23–24)

This emphasis on the rational has extended to the specific orientations that translate the transaction position into educational practice. These orientations—cognitive process, democratic citizenship, disciplines—all stress rational problem-solving procedures.

## REFERENCES

Dewey, J. (1897). *My pedagogic creed.* New York: E.L. Kellogg Co.
_____. (1966). *Democracy and education.* New York: Macmillan/Free Press. (Originally published in 1916)
_____. (1969). *Experience and education.* New York: Macmillan/Collier Books. (Originally published in 1938)
Galbraith, J. (1973). *Economics and the public purpose.* Boston: Houghton Mifflin.
Gambs, J. (1975). *John Kenneth Galbraith.* Boston: Twayne Publishers.
Heilbroner, R.L. (1980). *The wordly philosophers.* New York: Simon & Schuster. (Originally published in 1953)
Hersh, R., Miller, J.P., & Fielding, G. (1980). *Models of moral education.* New York: Longman.
Kaplan, A. (1961). *The new world of philosophy.* New York: Random House.
Keynes, J.M. (1930). *Treatise on money.* New York: Harcourt Brace Jovanovich.
_____. (1964). *The general theory of employment, interest, and money.* New York: Harcourt Brace Jovanovich.
Kohlberg, L., & Gilligan, C. (1971). The adolescent as a philosopher: The discovery of the self in a post-conventional world. *Daedalus, 100,* 1051–1086.
Kohlberg, L.N. & Mayer, R. (1972). Development as an aim of education. *The Harvard Educational Review, 42,* 449–496.
Miller, J. (1983). *The educational spectrum.* New York: Longman.
Piaget, J. (1963). *The origins of intelligence in children.* New York: Norton.
Sullivan, E. (1977). *Kohlberg's structuralism: A critical appraisal.* Toronto: Ontario Institute for Studies in Education.

# CHAPTER 5 TRANSACTION POSITION: Educational Practice

## HISTORICAL BACKGROUND

The transaction position views the student as capable of intelligent interaction with the environment. Even in colonial times, when most educators subscribed to the Calvinistic view of the child, there were some, such as Benjamin Franklin in the United States, who developed a broader vision of education. He proposed, for example, that education at the secondary level should offer study in handwriting, drawing, arithmetic, "accounts" geometry, astronomy, English grammar, oral reading, history, natural history or science, "the history of commerce" (Franklin, quoted in Bayles & Hood, 1966, p. 69), and mechanics. In essence, Franklin believed that the role of the academy should be to help prepare the student for life, whereas most academies in colonial times saw their role to be the narrower one of preparing students for college (Bayles & Hood, 1966, p. 72).

### Johann Heinrich Pestalozzi

In the early-nineteenth century, many educational reformers in the United States were influenced by Pestalozzi, an important Swiss educator. Pestalozzi, who argued that teachers should be able to understand the needs and wishes of the child, developed a curriculum based on "the Art of Sense Impressionism." He claimed that students learn through observation of nature, wherein they are presented with opportunities to analyze and to make inferences about experience. In a contribution to a biography of Pestalozzi (de Guimps, 1889), Moif sums up Pestalozzi's pedagogical principles:

1. Intuition is the basis of instruction.
2. Language should be linked with intuition.
3. The time for learning is not the time for judgment and criticism.
4. In every branch, teaching should begin with the simplest elements and proceed gradually according to the development of the child, that is, in psychologically connected order.
5. Sufficient time should be devoted to each point of the teaching in order to ensure the complete mastery of it by the pupil.
6. Teaching should aim at development and not dogmatic exposition.
7. The educator should respect the individuality of the pupil.
8. The chief end of elementary teaching is not to impart knowledge and talent to the learner, but to develop and increase the powers of his intelligence.
9. Power must be linked to knowledge; and skill to learning.
10. The relations between the master and the pupil, especially as to discipline, should be based upon and ruled by love.
11. Instruction should be subordinated to the higher aim of education. (p. 108)

***Pestalozzi's Influence on American Education.*** Pestalozzi's ideas about schooling influenced a number of educators in the United States. His idea that language should be linked with intuition can be seen in Horace Mann's theory that students should learn to read by learning whole words first rather than the letters of the alphabet, and also in Mann's opposition to corporal punishment for students. Henry Barnard, another educator who promoted Pestalozzi's work in the United States, was involved in writing, editing, and publishing *The American Journal of Education,* first published in 1855, in which there were articles on Pestalozzi and his influence on American education.

Pestalozzi's influence was also present in the so-called object-teaching method that was promoted by William Sheldon and became popular in the United States in the 1860s. In the object-teaching method, which is similar to Pestalozzi's "sense impressionism," the child would observe an object and then develop concepts about the object that he or she would then translate into words. Tanner and Tanner (1980) argue that object teaching was a "tremendously important reform because direct experience concerning an object was substituted for teacher verbalism" (p. 215). They view object teaching as a forerunner of inquiry learning.

In the late-nineteenth century, Pestalozzi's ideas influenced Francis Parker, to whom Dewey referred as the father of progressive education. In Quincy, Massachusetts, where he became superintendent of schools in 1875, Parker introduced a number of innovations. He advocated the whole-word method of reading and introduced the discussion method into the classroom so that children would move away from rote recitation; writing activities in the classroom focused on having children describe their own activities; arithmetic was taught through induction rather than by rote memorization; field trips were used to teach geography. Tanner and Tanner assert that Parker, "like Dewey. . . . saw the child as part of a unified evolutionary process" (p. 250).

Lester Ward was another educator in the late-nineteenth century who helped usher in progressivism. Unlike Parker, Ward was a Social Darwinist or, more accurately, a Reform Darwinist. In his book *Dynamic Sociology* (1903), he criticized laissez-faire economics and instead proposed a planned society in which education would have an important role, in that it would inform the student about his or her relationship to society. Ward argued that the social sciences should play a significant part in the education process, as they would allow the student to participate in public affairs in an informed manner—an idea that is consistent with the transaction position's focus on development of the student as an individual who can intelligently participate in social and political life and resolve social problems. In the early-twentieth century, John Dewey (see Chapter 4, pp. 62–77) was a major spokesman for this current of thought in progressivism. His laboratory school remains the classic example of the transaction position put into practice. In Dewey's words, the purpose of the school was "to discover in administration, selection of subject-matter, methods of learning, teaching, and discipline, how a school could become a cooperative community while developing in individuals their own capacities and satisfying their own needs" (Mayhew & Edwards, 1936, p. xiv).

At the same time Dewey was promoting his theory of education, another current of thought in progressive education focused on the role of the school as a social-change agent (e.g., Counts, *Dare the School Build a New Social Order?*, 1932); this position is more representative of the transformation position (see Chapters 6 & 7).


## TRANSACTION POSITION
## IN CONTEMPORARY EDUCATION

During the last two decades, the transaction position has been represented by the cognitive-process orientation, certain elements of the discipline orientation, and the democratic-citizenship orientation. The work of Piaget and Kohlberg can also be seen as an extension of Dewey's interactionist philosophy. The three orientations comprising the transaction position are now discussed in more detail.

## Disciplines Orientation

*Joseph Schwab.*   The disciplines orientation focuses on development of student inquiry skills within a specific academic discipline. Schwab (1974), a central figure within this orientation, argues that the disciplines are important in two ways:

> In brief, the structures of the disciplines are twice important to education. First, they are necessary to teachers and educators: they must be taken into account as we plan curriculum and prepare our teaching materials; otherwise, our plans are likely to miscarry and our materials, to misteach. Second, they are necessary in some part and degree within the curriculum, as elements of what we teach. Otherwise, there will be failure of learning or gross mislearning by our students. (p. 163)

For Schwab, disciplines center mainly around conceptual and syntactical structures. Schwab defines *conceptual structures* as the general conceptions that guide inquiry and determine what will be studied in a discipline.

The general conceptions in a discipline can change. For example, the classical physics in the early part of this century, based on a Newtonian world view, gave way to the new physics, whose relativistic view of space and time changed the way in which scientists approach problems.

In Schwab's (1974) view, general conceptions lead to emphasis on the study of pattern and process rather than the cataloging of information.

> This shift from catalogues to patterns in the disciplines means, in turn, that teaching and learning take on a new dimension. Instead of focusing on one thing or idea at a time, clarifying each and going on to the next, teaching becomes a process of focusing on points of contact and connection among things and ideas, of clarifying the effect of each thing on the others, of conveying the way in which each connection modifies the participants in the connection—in brief, the task of portraying phenomena and ideas not as things in themselves but as fulfillments of a pattern. (p. 163)

Schwab suggests that this interconnectedness within a discipline increases its complexity. In the study of light, for example, its interdependence with electricity and magnetism must be acknowledged.

Schwab (1974) defines *syntactical structures* as the "operations that distinguish the true, the verified, and the warranted in that discipline from the unverified and unwarranted" (p. 173). Each discipline has its own syntactical structure—its own methods of verification.

Schwab moved away from a narrow conception and toward an acknowledgment of the relationships among disciplines. He began to talk about the importance of what he calls the "practical" mode of inquiry, a second mode in addition to the disciplines mode. The practical mode aims "to discover the relations which exist or which can be induced among various subject areas—the arts which make possible recognition and repair of divorces" (Schwab, 1972). Schwab (1972) even argues that eclecticism must be accepted:

> A curriculum grounded in by one or a few subsubjects of the social sciences is indefensible; contributions from all are required. There is no foreseeable hope of a unified theory in the immediate or middle future, nor of a metatheory which will tell us how to put those subsubjects together or order them in a fixed hierarchy of importance to the problems of curriculum. What remains as a viable alternative is the unsystematic, uneasy, pragmatic, and uncertain unions and connections which can be effected in an eclectic. And I must add, anticipating our discussion of the practical, that *changing* connections and *differing* orderings at different times of these separate theories, will characterize a sound eclectic. (p. 87)

**Curriculum Projects.**   The disciplines orientation found its realization in various curriculum projects, many of which began in the early 1960s and some of which are still in use today. One such project, the Biological Sciences Curriculum Study (BSCS), was designed to teach students skills similar to the methods of scientific investigation and inquiry used by biologists in the laboratory. The BSCS argued that the focus of study should be on inquiry. Schwab was a supervisor in the BSCS and his name is associated with one BSCS teachers' handbook in which the emphasis is on how biologists carry out their investigations. The BSCS was critical of many texts in biology that focused solely on exposition of scientific conclusions, arguing that these texts give students the impression that science consists of unalterable, fixed truths and that science is complete. Thus, the student is not made aware that generalizations change and science is dynamic. The BSCS attempted to show students how knowledge is developed from raw data, in contrast to most texts, which ignore the scientific process and also the fact that scientists do much of their work by trial and error.

> The essence, then, of a teaching of science as inquiry, would be to show some of the conclusions of science in the framework of the way they arise and are tested. This would mean to tell the student about the ideas posed, and the experiments performed, to indicate the data thus found, and to follow the interpretation by which these data were converted into scientific knowledge. (Schwab, 1965, p. 40)

Brandwein, Metzner, Mucholt, Roe, and Rosen, other educators associated with the BSCS, argue that the total school environment should contribute to encouraging and facilitating student investigation. In a book entitled *Teaching High School Biology: A Guide to Working with Potential Biologists* (1962), they outline the characteristics of schools that have a reputation for facilitating academic inquiry:

a) At least one teacher in the department was a scholar in the field; he maintained scholarship through advanced university courses, or work toward a degree, or research, or serious reading. He also had the energy and the desire to work with individual students.

b) The guidance program tended to give emphasis to individual interviews and, where possible, to individual testing (after group tests have been given). Also, it was generally true that the homeroom and science teachers would function as counsellors as well, in the specific area of the course of studies.

c) There was clear emphasis on intellectual attainment as the prime objective of the school; scholarship did not take second place to sports. But physical fitness was held as one of the prime goals for all.

d) The curriculum was up to date; experimentation with the "newer" curriculums was going on in at least one "experimental" class.

e) In the laboratory the learning was toward individual rather than group work. Demonstrations by the teacher did not rob students of the right to discovery.

f) There was an emphasis on problem-solving in addition to the traditional problem-doing. (Operationally: Problem-solving implies that the solution to the problem is deferred over a relatively long period; it may not be in a readily available reference, or it may not yet be published. Problem-solving implies originality. In problem-doing, the solution is to be experienced within a reasonable, predicted period, say within a laboratory period or perhaps during the period assigned to homework.)

g) The teaching pattern, the curriculum, the kinds of instructional materials all tended to stress conceptual schemes and concepts—rather than memorization and recall-on-demand. Books were chosen for their tendency to organize content around major concepts. The texts that organized their content around an anthology of topics were not in favor. (p. 47)

Their language reflects the disciplines orientation. For example, the terms *scholarship, conceptual schemes,* and *intellectual attainment,* convey an image of a school with a strong commitment to the disciplines.

***Current Research in the Disciplines Orientation.*** Science educators have been leading articulators of the disciplines orientation. Recently, Driver and Erickson (1983) and Posner (1982) have described research that integrates cognitive psychology with student work in a discipline such as science. Driver and Erickson summarize the thrust of this work:

> Empirical Premise One. Many students have constructed from previous physical and linguistic experience frameworks which can be used to interpret some of the natural phenomena which they study formally in school science classes.
>
> Empirical Premise Two. These student frameworks often result in conceptual confusion as they lead to different predictions and explanations from those frameworks sanctioned by school science.
>
> Empirical Premise Three. Well-planned instruction employing teaching strategies which take account of student frameworks will result in the development of frameworks that conform more closely to school science.
>
> Value Premise One. One should conduct research which will lead to a better understanding of school science by students.
>
> Conclusion. We ought to engage in research endeavours which will uncover student frameworks, investigate the ways they interact with instructional experiences and utilize this knowledge in the development of teaching programmes. (pp. 39–40)

Driver and Erickson (1983) claim that, until recently, the emphasis in science curricula has been on the inherent structure of the knowledge to be taught, whereas now it is shifting to the idea that students approach material to be learned with "invented ideas" or conceptual frameworks of their own that are based on sense experience and language. Researchers have found that "invented ideas" influence student investigations in the science classroom and can confuse investigation and lead to inaccurate conclusions.

Some of the recent research in this area has focused on how students develop conceptual frameworks. Strauss (1981) contends that students' common-sense knowledge is "spontaneous and universal," that is, acquired by individuals without formal instruction. Brown (1982) argues that detailed descriptions of these conceptual frameworks, which he calls "novice frameworks," should be developed in a number of areas (e.g., mechanics, energy, evolution) and that, after they have been identified, instructional strategies can be developed that will move students to an understanding of the explanatory systems developed by expert scientists.

Students, then, according to these researchers, do not enter a science experiment with a "blank slate," but with some basic conceptualization about the problems at hand which they have developed through sensory and linguistic experience. For example, when studying science, students usually have "novice frameworks" about subjects such as mechanics, heat, and temperature. When such "novice frameworks" are firmly entrenched, they are more difficult to alter through instruction.

Research is currently underway on how student frameworks interact with instruction. Some of this work is descriptive. For example, Anderson and Smith (1983) conducted studies that describe student conceptions before, during, and after instruction of topics such as light, color, and photosynthesis. Tiberghien (1980) and her associates at the Université de Paris have examined the frameworks students have during instruction about heat.

Finally, research has been done to examine how student conceptual frameworks can be changed through instruction. Some of this research has focused on producing changes in student frameworks through cognitive conflict, a technique that is similar to Piaget's "equilibration" concept and Festinger's concept of "cognitive dissonance." Stavy and Berkovitz (1980), for example, developed strategies that brought children's qualitative–verbal representation systems into conflict with their quantitative–numerical representation systems. They used the subject of temperature change to generate this conflict.

Driver and Erickson (1983) assert that the overall results of this research have been mixed. However, other research has been more encouraging. For example, research by Hewson and Hewson (1981) and by Posner, Strike, Hewson, and Gertzog (1979) that attempts to integrate the philosophy of science with information-processing psychology has also yielded information about altering students' conceptual frameworks. Driver and Erickson (1983) claim that research by Hewson and Hewson (1981) and Hewson (1982) "provided specific instructional prescriptions for changing secondary school students' intuitive notions about the concepts of mass, volume, density and particulate nature of matter" (p. 52) and "for diagnosing and subsequently altering students' 'alternate conceptions' about the concept of speed, using a microcomputer as the means of presenting and pacing the instructional materials" (p. 52).

## Cognitive-Process Orientation

The cognitive-process orientation focuses on how people think and solve problems. Curriculum programs based on this orientation facilitate thinking and problem-solving skills. Although several approaches to problem solving are found within this orientation (see Miller, 1983), each of which reflects a different conception of mental functioning, in the section that follows we present the particular approach that has been developed by Robinson and his associates at O.I.S.E. and described by Ross and Maynes (1982).

***Problem Solving.*** Ross and Maynes (1982) state that several studies indicate that teachers give only a small percentage of time to developing students' thinking skills. For example, in Alberta, Canada, one study (Hughes, 1979) found that 98% of classroom instruction deals with content objectives and only 2% with skill objectives. This is due, in part, to what Ross and Maynes (1982) call the "seduction of the narrative"; teachers can become so involved in presenting interesting topics and ideas that "the method of inquiry disappears from view" (p. 2). Time pressures also make teachers feel that they must cover a certain amount of material in a given time period. As a result, there is little time for students to learn problem-solving skills, particularly complex skills.

Ross and Maynes (1982) claim that problem solving and content mastery do not have to be juxtaposed; the two can be integrated in productive ways. Ross and Maynes (1982) and Robinson, Ross, and White (1985) have demonstrated how this can be done.

One of the problems in teaching problem solving is that people can become confused about the labels associated with the various steps in problem solving. As a result, Ross and Maynes (1982, pp. 5–7) outline an 11-step process that clearly defines the problem-solving sequence.

1. *Defining the problem.* The first step involves "establishing a focus for the inquiry and defining the elements of the problem to be solved or identifying the question to be answered" (p. 5). The skill the student develops in this step is the ability to narrow his or her focus of concern to a definable problem.
2. *Establishing a framework for the inquiry.* The student forms a mental image of the problem and its solution. The goal here is for the student to develop an overall conception of the problem and how the various elements relate to one another. The student begins by developing an internal image of the problem and then conveys the problem in a visible form, for example, a table, graph, or diagram. Ross and Maynes claim that this is the most important skill in problem solving and that the "failure to provide assistance to student in developing competence in this skill is the major factor impeding growth in problem-solving performance" (p. 6).
3. *Determining sources of data.* The student identifies resources (e.g., books, maps) that can help solve the problem.
4. *Obtaining data at source.* The student selects the relevant information from the sources that relate to the problem.
5. *Judging the adequacy of the data.* The student assesses the selected data with regard to its relevance, accuracy, and quantity.
6. *Putting data into a framework.* The student organizes the relevant data. For example, the skill may involve putting the data into a table or graph.

7. *Reducing data to summary form.* The student performs simple calculations, such as averaging or computing percentages, in order to interpret the data within the framework.
8. *Observing relationships in data.* The student looks for trends in the data. This skill may involve establishing or disconfirming a statistical relationship between two or more variables.
9. *Interpreting data.* The student accurately records the relationships observed in Step 8.
10. *Extrapolating the interpretation.* The student generalizes and applies the conclusions he or she draws to different contexts. This skill involves making predictions about new situations.
11. *Communicating an inquiry.* The student reports the results of the problem-solving exercise. This is the final product of problem solving.

Ross and Maynes (1982) claim that teachers can transfer this sequence to a variety of problems and that students should be able to transfer these skills to different contexts (p. 7). They identify four types of problems:

1. *Comparative problems.* Students attempt to find similarities and differences between two or more entities. An example: "How did the political reform movements in 19th century Canada differ from similar movements in the United States? Or, compare the transportation networks of Toronto and Los Angeles, or contrast the characters of Macbeth and Lady Macbeth" (p. 8).
2. *Decision-making problems.* The student must think about the best course of action in a complex situation. For example, "What alternative sources of energy should be used?" is representative of this type of problem.
3. *Correlational problems.* The student investigates relationships between two or more variables. For example, "What factors contribute to high unemployment?" is a correlational problem.
4. *Experimentally oriented problems.* This type of problem is most common in science, where a causal relationship is examined by physically manipulating the variables. One example of this type of problem is the question, "What is the effect of more fertilizer on crop production?"

Although the fourth type of problem is found most often in science, all four problem types can be found in most subjects. Ross and Maynes (1982) state:

It should be emphasized once again that although these problems are extremely important to particular programs, they are not unique to any one subject. This suggests that problem-solving training in one subject can have benefits for other subjects. It is also important to recognize that these situations are analogous to real-life problems that confront students during and after their school experience. Training in solving these problems contributes to the foundation that makes life-long learning a genuine possibility and helps students make connections between school tasks and life tasks. (p. 9)

TEACHING PROBLEM SOLVING  Ross and Maynes (1982) outline a seven-step process for teaching problem solving.

*Step 1: Select an instructional context.* One way to identify an appropriate context is to develop a chart (see Table 5.1) listing the 11 skills and the 4 types of decision making (p. 15). Topics within particular subjects can be placed in each of the blank boxes in Table 5.1. For example, correlational problem solving might be taught in a unit on agriculture, as a component of a geography program. Ross and Maynes (1982) suggest that the most important skills are focusing, frameworking, and filling in the framework (skills 1, 2, and 6) (p. 14).

*Step 2: Develop a growth scheme.* According to Ross and Maynes (1982), "A growth scheme is a multileveled description of cognitive maturation that provides a highly detailed definition of problem-solving performance of students at various stages of growth" (p. 10). In other words, a growth scheme consists of a detailed sequence that indicates how novice problem solvers move to more sophisticated and complex levels of problem solving in a particular area. Ross and Maynes (1982) claim that a growth scheme is not necessarily an invariant hierarchy (p. 20); some students may skip a particular step, whereas others may go through the skills step by step. A sample growth scheme is outlined in Table 5.2.

*Step 3: Set problem-solving goals for students.* This step includes, first, identifying the initial level of student competence and, second, working out a feasible set of goals for the students.

*Step 4: Develop practice materials.* Materials might, for example, consist of student worksheets that would be prepared for each level beyond the students entry level.

*Step 5: Develop teaching strategies to promote growth.* Ross and Maynes (1982) suggest that strategies that stimulate cognitive conflict are helpful in promoting growth. If the tasks are too simple, the students will not be encouraged to develop new problem-solving strategies. However, students should not be stretched too much or they can become frustrated.

**TABLE 5.1   Simple Outcome Organizer**

| | | PROBLEM TYPES | | |
| | | *Decision* | | |
| *Skills* | *Comparative* | *making* | *Correlational* | *Experimental* |
| --- | --- | --- | --- | --- |
| 1. Focus | | | | |
| 2. Framework | | | | |
| 3. Sources of data | | | | |
| 4. Obtaining data | | | | |
| 5. Assessing adequacy | | | | |
| 6. Filling framework | | | | |
| 7. Summarizing data | | | | |
| 8. Observing relationships | | | | |
| 9. Interpreting relationships | | | | |
| 10. Extrapolating | | | | |
| 11. Reporting | | | | |

From Ross, J.A., and Maynes, F.J., *Teaching problem solving,* Toronto: Ontario Institute for Studies in Education, 1982, p. 15. Reprinted with permission.

*Step 6: Develop test instruments.* The test instrument allows the teacher to diagnose deficiencies in student performance and to determine the effectiveness of instruction. Ross and Maynes (1982) acknowledge that problem-solving skills are difficult to measure.

*Step 7: Develop a sequence of instructional events in lesson plans.* Ross and Maynes (1982) state that the overall sequence of problem-solving skills might take the following course:

Preliminary experience suggests to us that . . . an optimal arrangement might involve developing competence in comparative problem-solving (beginning in the primary division), followed by decision-making (beginning in the junior division), leading to experimental and correlational thinking (beginning in the intermediate division). Realizing an optimal sequence would require the allocation of responsibility for various types of problem-solving skills to particular grades and subjects, a plan that would require the cooperation of curriculum planners beyond the individual classrooms. (p. 32)

Several studies (Ross, 1981; Ross & Maynes, 1983a, 1983b) demonstrate the effectiveness of Ross and Maynes's instructional program.

## Democratic-Citizenship Orientation

In this orientation the student learns basic inquiry and decision-making skills that facilitate his or her participation in the democratic process. Many social studies educators have presented models within this orientation. For example, Oliver and Shaver (1966) developed an approach that teaches students to analyze complex disputes and then to develop a defensible position about a particular issue. Bourne and Eisenberg (1978) have developed an approach that teaches students to do the following:

- Read and discuss a case with sensitivity and open-mindedness toward the various positions taken.
- Take a stand, if only tentatively, on the issue under consideration.
- Defend their positions by giving reasons, invoking principles, and presenting evidence.
- Argue against opposing views in the same open and rational manner.
- Modify their positions in light of their dialogue with others. (p. 12)

Massialas and his associates (Massialas, Sprague, & Hurst, 1975) have developed an approach to citizenship education that focuses on decision-making inquiry. The goal of instruction in Massialas's approach is "to clarify the issue and to offer different hypotheses or positions related to it, and then to resolve conflicts that arise and to determine defensible solutions to them" (p. 24). Massialas states that after the person has developed a solution, there may then be individual or group action to implement it.

Figure 5.1 (p. 109) illustrates the contrast between Massialas's inquiry model for teaching and traditional teaching. In this diagram, the traditional and the reflective social studies processes also can be viewed as models of the transmission and transaction positions respectively.

**TABLE 5.2  Growth Scheme for the Skill of Establishing a Framework for Solving a Correlational Problem Question: Why is it colder in some places than others?**

| Performance level | Operations in strategy | Spatial representation |
|---|---|---|
| 1 | 1. Make a list of factors relevant to the problem | List of important things<br>—weather<br>—how far north it is<br>—prevailing winds<br>—kind of thermometer used<br>—whether there is water nearby |
| 2 | 2. Select two factors from the list | |
| | 3. Select a few cases for which information is available on each factor | |
| | 4. Make a chart with 3 columns: one column for identifying the cases; one column for the first factor; and one column for the second factor | |

| Place | How far north it is | How cold it is |
|---|---|---|
| First place | ? | ? |
| Second place | ? | ? |
| Third place | ? | ? |

104

3

5. Define the two variables and their measurement scale more precisely

6. Increase the number of cases from a few to a dozen or more, including a broad range of values on one of the variables

7. Order the cases on one of the variables (i.e., list the cases from lowest to highest)

4

8. Expand the chart by adding a new column for every variable listed in step 1 for which there is data for the dozen or more cases

| Cities | Latitude (in °N) | Temperature (in °C) |
|---|---|---|
| 1st city | ?(lowest) | ? |
| . | . | . |
| . | . | . |
| . | . | . |
| 12th city | ?(high-est) | ? |

| Cities | Tempera-ture (in °C) | Latitude (in °N) | Elevation (in m) | Nearness to water (in km) | Longitude (in mer E) |
|---|---|---|---|---|---|
| 1st city | ?(lowest) | ? | ? | ? | ? |
| . | . | . | . | . | . |
| . | . | . | . | . | . |
| 12th city | ?(high-est) | ? | ? | ? | ? |

**TABLE 5.2** Continued.

| Performance level | Operations in strategy | Cities with elevation below 2,000 metres | Latitude (in °N) | Temperature (in °C) | Spatial representation |
|---|---|---|---|---|---|
| 5 | 9. Select one control variable that might affect the relationship between the main variable in the 2nd and 3rd columns | 1st city | ?(lowest) | ? | |
| | 10. Group the cases into 2–3 categories in terms of their values on the control variable | · | · | · | |
| | 11. Select one of the value ranges | · | · | · | |
| | 12. Make a new chart with 3 columns; the 1st column identifying all the cases within the designated range of the control variable and one column for each of the main variables | 12th city | ?(highest) | ? | |

6    13. Expand the chart by adding groups of cases that fall into the other value ranges of the control variable (using the

14. Increase the number of cases in each group to at least six

| Elevation | Cities | Latitude (in °N) | Tempera-ture (in °C) |
|---|---|---|---|
| below 2,000 m | 1st city | ?(lowest) | ? |
| 2,001–4,000 m | 8th city | ?(highest) | ? |
| | 9th city | ?(lowest) | ? |
| over 4,000 m | 14th city | ?(highest) | ? |
| | 15th city | ?(lowest) | ? |
| | 23rd city | ?(highest) | ? |

From Ross, J.A., and Maynes, F.J., *Teaching problem solving*, Toronto: Ontario Institute for Studies in Education, 1982, pp. 18–19. Reprinted with permission.

Massialas's (1975) inquiry model includes six sequences:

1. Defining and categorizing concepts and distinguishing between ideas.
2. Clarifying values underlying positions.
3. Collecting and analyzing evidence.
4. Using evidence to validate or evaluate hypotheses or positions.
5. Exploring logical consequences of positions.
6. Generalizing.


In the following sequence, students are discussing alternatives to the property tax. At this juncture the class is trying to decide whether the property tax or the income tax is the more fair form of taxation.


TEACHER: Don, which do you think is the fairer form of taxation?

DON: The income tax because how much tax you can afford to pay depends on your income. People can have a house but not be able to afford to pay taxes.

CAROL: But what about those rich people who have big mansions. They should pay taxes. The property tax is the most fair.

TEACHER: Why is the property tax more fair than the income tax? You said the property tax is most fair. Why?

CAROL: Because I read that a lot of rich people get out of paying income tax. They have big houses though and have to pay property tax.

TEACHER: Jack.

JACK: But Don is right. My grandfather is retired and doesn't have too much money. He said that he might have to sell his house because he can't pay the property taxes. It doesn't seem fair because he has lived in his house for 40 years or something like that.

SUE: Can he pay his income taxes?

JACK: I think so, at least he hasn't complained about them. Of course he doesn't get too much money every month.

CAROL: I still say the property tax is best. You might be right for your grandfather, but my father complains about his income tax. He wouldn't like it if he had to pay more income tax. Also with property

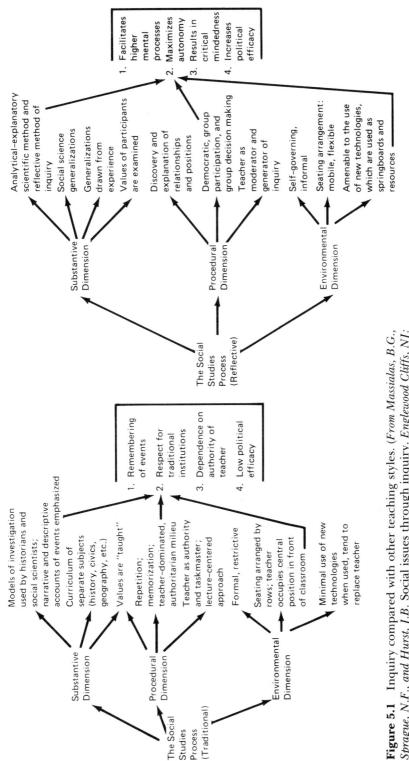

**Figure 5.1** Inquiry compared with other teaching styles. *(From Massialas, B.G., Sprague, N.F., and Hurst, J.B. Social issues through inquiry. Englewood Cliffs, NJ: Prentice-Hall, 1975. Reprinted with permission.)*

|              | tax, you don't have to buy a home. You can rent and not have to pay property tax. |
|--------------|--------------|
| TEACHER:     | Don. |
| DON:         | But if a tax is fair everyone should pay taxes based on his ability to pay. Everyone has an income so everyone has to pay an income tax based on his income . . . well, except for the really poor. With property tax, not everyone has property so not everyone pays. |
| CAROL:       | That's right. So property tax is more fair. You have a choice of buying a house or not. |
| TEACHER:     | It seems to me that we have to decide what we mean by fair. Carol, what do you mean by a "fair" tax? (pp. 31–32) |

In this sequence, students are developing positions on what is "fair" taxation. The teacher sometimes "probes" the discussion to ask students (e.g., Carol) to clarify and define their position. According to Massialas, teachers should also stimulate students to ask each other questions; through this process the student learns to ground his or her position rather than to offer spontaneous opinions.

## CONCLUDING COMMENTS

*Context.* The transaction position is most clearly represented in the work of John Dewey, whose thinking about interaction between the person and the social environment is central to this position. In the field of psychology, Kohlberg has claimed that the work of Piaget and other cognitive developmentalists is an extension of Dewey's thinking. In the social realm, liberalism, with its emphasis on rational intervention to facilitate social and economic development, can be linked with the transaction position.

*Aims.* The goal of curricula based on the transaction position is the development of rational intelligence in general and complex problem-solving skills in particular.

*Learning Experiences.* The transaction position tends to stress inquiry and problem-solving skills. Learning experiences may occur within the framework of an academic discipline, with students pursuing inquiry as would an academic within a particular discipline. It is also possible in this position to pursue inquiry within an interdisciplinary framework or a social context. In a social context, the emphasis is on developing inquiry skills that facilitate democratic decision making.

***Role of the Teacher.***   The teacher working from this position attempts to facilitate the development of student inquiry skills. He or she must be familiar with the appropriate resources and be able to stimulate inquiry with questions and probes. The teacher also should be interested in how children think and how they approach problems, and be able to listen to their reasons and thinking processes.

***Evaluation.***   Transaction-oriented evaluation focuses on the student's acquisition of complex intellectual frameworks and skills (e.g., analysis, synthesis) and on social skills that are important in a democratic context.

## The Transaction Position and the Berlak Dilemmas

***Whole Child versus Child as Student.***   In the transaction position, most educators tend to take a limited view of the child, seeing him or her as student or as someone attempting to develop conceptual frameworks and problem-solving skills within a specific discipline. In the social realm, however, there is tendency to see the child in a somewhat broader context.

***Teacher Control versus Child Control.***   Both the teacher and the child share control of learning tasks. To encourage the student to develop new frameworks, there are usually opportunities to experiment and try out various solutions to problems, and the teacher must allow the child to control a portion of the learning process in order to complete these tasks. However, the teacher is generally in control of identifying tasks and the student's entry into these tasks. The teacher attempts to provide learning activities that are appropriate to the student's initial level of development (framework level). Teachers also generally are in control of the standards; they identify the general level of intellectual competence they expect students to attain. Students can begin to set their own standards only when they have reached higher levels of thinking.

***Personal Knowledge versus Public Knowledge.***   In the transaction position, the emphasis is on public knowledge. This public knowledge, however, is not necessarily seen as fixed and immutable, as in the transmission position. Instead, knowledge is viewed in relation to the knower and, particularly, in relation to the *procedures* the knower uses to explore and verify knowledge.

***Knowledge as Content versus Knowledge as Process.***   Knowledge is generally viewed as process, that is, it is related to various modes of inquiry and to the scientific method. Recently, there has been a tendency to interrelate cognitive psychology and various disciplines (e.g., science) into a conception of student learning and instructional activities. In this more recent work, knowledge developed by experts is viewed in relation to the "novice frameworks" that students develop.

***Intrinsic versus Extrinsic Motivation.***   The transaction position is oriented toward intrinsic motivation. Cognitive process models tend to rely on the need of individuals to resolve problems. For example, Piaget's equilibration concept is based on the inner need to develop new reasoning structures (schema). However, transaction educators avoid idealizing intrinsic motivation and are concerned with providing an environment that supports problem solving. Again, the emphasis is on the interaction, or transaction, between the student and the environment.

***Learning Is Holistic versus Learning Is Molecular.***   Transaction educators do not view learning either holistically or atomistically. Although subject matter is broken down for the purpose of analysis, the main emphasis is on the process of analysis and other related skills, such as frameworking.

***Each Child Unique versus Child Has Shared Characteristics.***   The transaction position presents a middle position between these two extremes. Children are viewed as having shared characteristics in terms of mental processes, because problem-solving sequences are linear and sequential. However, the transaction educator also focuses on the uniqueness of the individual student. There is a concern for the student's level of development (e.g., Piaget) and for the "invented ideas" that students bring to a problem or task. Learning activities, then, must be related to the individual student framework.

***Learning Is Social versus Learning Is Individual.***   There is no clear overall position regarding this dilemma. Followers of Dewey are clearly oriented toward social learning. Thelen's group-investigation model (Joyce & Weil, 1980) also reflects this thrust within the transaction position. However, some of the inquiry models are more individually oriented; Piaget's theories, for example, have been applied to programs, to justify an individualized approach to learning.

***Child as Person versus Child as Client.***   The tendency in the transaction position is to view the child as client. After the child's framework has been diagnosed, instructional strategies are designed to overcome the child's "invented ideas" that conflict with knowledge systems developed by experts.

## Arguments for and against the Transaction Position

The transaction position has been the main source of educational innovation for the past 25 years. After Sputnik was launched in 1957, causing
the American public to become preoccupied with "catching up with the
Russians" in science and technology, the disciplines orientation became
the predominant source of educational reform. Bruner (1960) outlines
this thrust in *The Process of Education.* The disciplines orientation led to a
number of curriculum-development projects in biology, physics, math,
and social studies. Tanner and Tanner (1980) argue that these projects
were too narrow in focus, as they were essentially geared to those bound
for university, and that most general students found the new math and
curriculum projects such as the BSCS too abstract.

In recent years, the cognitive-process orientation and the disciplines
orientation have become interrelated. Cognitive psychology has provided analyses of problem solving (e.g., novice–expert studies by Larkin,
McDermott, Simon, & Simon, 1980; Champagne, Klopfer, & Anderson,
1980), children's thinking in specific content domains (e.g., Driver &
Erickson, 1983) such as science, schemata function, conceptual change
(e.g., Hewson & Hewson, 1981; Posner, 1982), and classroom interaction.
This research has given us a clearer conception of how children think.
As researchers examine how individuals process information, solve problems, and make decisions, we get a clearer image of how children learn,
and thus we are better able to design instructional procedures that facilitate student growth in specific intellectual competencies.

Despite these gains, the cognitive-process orientation can lead to
certain problems related to the narrowness of some of the academics
working within this orientation. Basically, most of these individuals focus
on left-brain, logical, analytical problem solving and ignore right-brain,
intuitive, synthetic problem solving. Because most of the inquiry models,
therefore, are related to the scientific method, we do not get a sense of
how problem solving occurs in the aesthetic domain. Even in scientific
discovery there is an intuitive element, which is often dismissed in various
curriculum projects. In aesthetic and creative problem solving, one is not
attempting to identify a clear set of alternatives and then logically reduce
the set of alternatives to one best solution. Instead, one is seeking something novel, which involves a leap outside of an existing framework. Patte
(1983) defines a conception of creative problem solving:

1. RECEPTIVITY, or opening with a calm unbiased mind what the
   current situation of "problem" is.
2. INTUITION, or flashes of insight and inspiration that are fu-
   gitive but can be prolonged.

**3.** CONCENTRATION of the mind so as to bring "vertical" energy and focus into the "horizontal" situation or "problem."
**4.** IMAGINATION or generation of possible creative solutions.
**5.** MEMORY as a structuring and deep correlative reserve.
**6.** ENERGY or the power of synthesis and seeing wholeness or interrelations of all aspects in balance; and
**7.** MANIFESTATION or the power to actualize what is discovered or seen (in daily life or in tangible form). (p. 12)

There are also limitations to the democratic-citizenship orientation. Although this orientation would seem to represent an acceptable middle ground between the transmission and the transformation positions, we should recognize the limitations of programs that focus solely on cognitive analysis. Students can clearly differentiate when they are "playing school" and when they are dealing directly with real social problems. It is not enough to discuss a social problem, even in the most intelligent manner; at some point the student must be able to act on those concerns so that problem solving is integrated at a deeper, more holistic level.

## REFERENCES

Anderson, C.W., & Smith, E.L. (1983). Children's preconceptions and content area textbooks. In Duffy, G., Roehler, L., and Mason, J. (Eds.). *Comprehension instruction: Perspectives and suggestions*. New York: Longman.

Bayles, E., & Hood, B. L. (1966). *Growth of American educational thought and practice*. New York: Harper & Row.

Bourne, P., & Eisenberg, J. (1978). *Social issues in the curriculum*. Toronto: Ontario Institute for Studies in Education.

Brandwein, P. F., Metzner, J., Mucholt, E., Roe, A., & Rosen, W. (1962). *Teaching high school biology: A guide to working with potential biologists*. Washington, DC: American Institute of Biological Sciences.

Brown, A. (1982). Learning and development: The problems of compatibility, access and induction. *Human Development, 25,* 89–115.

Bruner, J. (1960). *The process of education*. Cambridge, MA: Harvard University.

Champagne, A., Klopfer, L., & Anderson J. (1980). Factors influencing learning of classical mechanics. *American Journal of Physics, 48,* 1074–1079.

Counts, G. (1932). *Dare the school build a new social order?* New York: Day.

de Guimps, R. (1889). *Pestalozzi: His aim and work*. Syracuse: C.W. Bardeen.

Driver, R. and Erickson, G. (1983). Theories-in-action: Some theoretical and empirical issues in the study of students' conceptual framework. *Studies in Science Education 10,* 37–60.

Hewson, M. (1982). Students' existing knowledge as a factor influencing the acquisition of scientific knowledge. Unpublished Ph.D. dissertation, University of Witwatersrand, Johannesburg.

Hewson, M., & Hewson, P. (1981, April). *Effect of instruction using students' prior knowledge and conceptual change strategies on science learning.* Paper presented to meeting of NARST.

Hughes, A.S. (1979). Curricular knowledge organization and variations in motivational emphases. *Alberta Journal of Education, 25*(1), 4–19.

Joyce, B., & Weil, M. (1980). *Models of teaching.* Englewood Cliffs, NJ: Prentice-Hall.

Larkin, J., McDermott, J., Simon, D., & Simon, H. (1980). Expert and novice performance in solving physics problems. *Science, 208,* 1335–1342.

Massialas, B.G., Sprague, N.F., & Hurst, J.B. (1975). *Social issues through inquiry.* Englewood Cliffs, NJ: Prentice-Hall.

Mayhew, K.C., & Edwards, A.C. (1936). *The Dewey school.* New York: Appleton-Century.

Miller, J.P. (1983). *The educational spectrum.* New York: Longman.

Oliver, D.W., & Shaver, J.P. (1966). *Teaching public issues in the high school.* New York: Houghton Mifflin.

Patte, R. (1983, Fall). Intuition, creativity and centering. *Association for Transpersonal Psychology Newsletter, 12.*

Posner, G. (1982). A cognitive science conception of curriculum and instruction. *J. Curriculum Studies, 14,* 343–351.

Posner, G., Strike, K., Hewson, P., & Gertzog, W. (1979). *Learning special relativity: A study of intellectual problems faced by college students.* Paper presented at the International Einstein Conference, Hofstra University, Hempstead, NY.

Robinson, F., Ross, J., & White, F. (1985). *Curriculum development for improved instruction.* Toronto: Ontario Institute for Studies in Education.

Ross, J.A. (1981). The measurement of student progress in a decision-making approach to values education. *Alberta Journal of Educational Research, 27,* 1–15.

Ross, J.A., & Maynes, F.J. (1982). *Teaching problem solving.* Toronto: Ontario Institute for Studies in Education.

Ross, J.A., & Maynes, F.J. (1983a). Teaching problem solving: An instructional design strategy. *Canadian Journal of Education, 8*(2), 155–173.

Ross, J.A., & Maynes, F.J. (1983b). The development of a test of experimental problem-solving skills. *Journal of Research in Science Teaching, 20*(1), 63–75.

Schwab, J. (Ed.). (1965). Biological science curriculum study. In *Biology teachers' handbook.* New York: Wiley.

———. (1972). The practical: A language for curriculum. In Purpel, D., & Belanger, M. (Eds.). *Curriculum and the cultural revolution.* Berkeley, CA: McCutchan.

———. (1974). The concept of the structure of a discipline. In Eisner, E., and Vallance, E. (Eds.). *Conflicting Conceptions of Curriculum.* Berkeley, CA: McCutchan.

Stavy, R., & Berkovitz, B. (1980). Cognitive conflict as a basis for teaching quantitative aspects of the concept of temperature. *Science Education, 64*(5), 679–692.

Strauss, S. (1981). Cognitive development in school and out. *Cognition, 10,* 295–300.

Tanner, D., & Tanner, L., (1980). *Curriculum development: Theory into practice*. New York: Macmillan.

Tiberghien, A. (1980). Modes and conditions of learning—An example: The learning of some aspects of the concept of heat. In Archenhold, W.F., Driver, R.H., Orton, A., & Wood-Robinson, C. (Eds.). *Cognitive development research in science and mathematics*. Leeds: University of Leeds.

Ward, L. (1903). *Dynamic sociology*. New York: Macmillan.

# CHAPTER 6 TRANSFORMATION POSITION: The Context

## PHILOSOPHICAL CONTEXT

Fritjof Capra (1982) argues that the "new physics" provides an interesting metaphor for clarifying the transformation position. According to Capra, the Western world view since about 1750 has focused on "belief in the scientific method as the only valid approach to knowledge; the view of the universe as a mechanical system composed of elementary building blocks, the view of life in society as a competitive struggle for existence; and the belief in unlimited material progress to be achieved through economic and technological growth" (p. 31). However, the new physics has made discoveries of subatomic processes that reveal a different view of reality than that offered by the Newtonian world view.

> Subatomic particles . . . , are not "things" but are interconnections between "things," and these "things," in turn, are interconnections between other "things," and so on. In quantum theory you never end up with "things"; you always deal with interconnections.
>
> This is how modern physics reveals the basic oneness of the universe. It shows that we cannot decompose the world into independently existing smallest units. As we penetrate into matter, nature does not show us any isolated basic building blocks, but rather appears as a complicated web of relations between the various parts of a unified whole. (pp. 80–81)

What Capra describes here is a system, or ecological view of life.

> Systems theory looks at the world in terms of the interrelatedness and interdependence of all phenomena, and in this framework an

integrated whole whose properties cannot be reduced to those of its parts is called a system. Living organisms, societies and ecosystems are all systems. (p. 43)

This ecological or interdependent view provides the philosophical core of the transformation position.

## The "Perennial Philosophy"

A world view that Huxley (1970) has named the "perennial philosophy" corresponds to Capra's vision of the universe. At the center of the "perennial philosophy" is the view that all phenomena are interconnected and part of a unified whole and that the individual is also part of this unity. The main principles of the "perennial philosophy" are as follows:

- The interconnectedness of reality and the fundamental unity of the universe
- The intimate connection between the individual's inner or higher self and this unity
- The cultivation of intuition and insight through contemplation and meditation in order to "see" this unity more clearly
- The realization of this unity among human beings leads to social action designed to counter injustice and human suffering

These principles have been articulated in different spiritual and intellectual traditions in both the East and the West. In the West, the "perennial philosophy" can be traced to early Greek times. For example, Pythagoras, a Greek philosopher, made the connection between the inner person and the universe; he designated the word *psyche* to represent the "inner self," which corresponds to the highest principles of the universe. Jaboc Needleman (1982) points out that in Pythagoras' view, "the cosmos, the deep order of nature, is knowledgeable through self-knowledge—man is a microcosm" (p. 59). Thus, according to Pythagoras, the individual must contemplate or meditate to gain access to the connection between the psyche and the highest principles of the cosmos. He suggested that certain techniques be used in the search of self-knowledge, including "the use of parable and symbol, of meditation, of the discipline of silence, of the study of music and sacred dance" (Needleman, 1982, p. 45).

In the nineteenth century, transcendentalists including Emerson, Walt Whitman, Bronson Alcott, and Henry Thoreau, articulated many of the principles of the "perennial philosophy." Emerson argued that within each person there is a "moral sentiment" that is connected to the unity of the universe, or "the oversoul," as Emerson called it.

Thoreau had a strong influence on Gandhi, particularly on Gandhi's thinking about nonviolent action. Gandhi was able to integrate his spirituality (Hinduism, in his case) with social action (as did Martin Luther King who integrated spirituality in this century in the United States). Gandhi's work represents the "perennial philosophy" in Eastern terms.

Teilhard de Chardin, a Jesuit priest who made major contributions as scientist to the study of geology and paleontology, represents a Christian perspective on the "perennial philosophy." Teilhard integrated into an evolutionary world view his scientific thinking with mystical insight. His conception of evolution is different from Darwin's in that he focuses on spiritual development. He developed the "law of complexity—consciousness" which states that evolution moves in a direction of increasing complexity that is accompanied by a corresponding heightening of consciousness. Teilhard believes that this evolution will culminate in a widespread enlightenment he calls the "Omega Point."

The German philosopher Martin Heidegger is often classified as an existentialist philosopher, but his ideas also have been linked with Eastern thought (Barrett, 1962; Von Eckartsberg & Valle, 1981).

It should be noted that there are differences among these four thinkers. For example, each views contemplation and meditation differently. However, they all articulate some of the principles of the "perennial philosophy." We proceed now to a discussion of the four basic principles of the "perennial philosophy" in relation to the different traditions represented by Ralph Waldo Emerson, Mahatma Gandhi, Pierre Teilhard de Chardin, and Martin Heidegger.

### The Interconnectedness of Reality and the Fundamental Unity of the Universe.
Emerson (1903) argues that the universe reveals this unity in a number of forms:

> There is one animal, one plant, one matter and one force (that is, energy). The laws of light and of heat translate into each other,— so do the laws of sound and of color; and so galvanism, electricity and magnetism are varied forms of the selfsame energy. While the student ponders this immense unity, he observes that all things in Nature, the animals, the mountain, the river, the seasons, wood, iron, stone, vapor, have a mysterious relation to his thoughts and his life; their growths, decays, quality and use to curiously resemble himself, in parts and in wholes, that he is compelled to speak by means of them. (p. 4)

Emerson's thinking is similar to Capra's (1975) idea that "new physics" reveals "a basic interconnection of matter showing that energy of motion can be transferred into mass, and suggesting that particles are processes rather than objects" (p. 275).

For Gandhi (1980), this unity both reveals itself in the immediacy of daily life and lies behind all religions:

> The forms are many, but the informing spirit is one. How can there be room for distinctions of high and low where there is this all-embracing fundamental unity underlying the outward diversity? For that is a fact meeting you at every step in daily life. The final goal of all religions is to realize this essential oneness. (p. 63)

Gandhi's position that this unity is evident in everyday life reflects the notion that the interconnectedness of reality should not be relegated to remote forms of mysticism.

Heidegger (1971) states that the interconnectedness of reality is found in what he calls *the fourfold:* the earth, the sky, the divinities, and the mortal. These four elements constitute a basic oneness:

> Earth is the building bearer, nourishing with its fruits, tending water and rock, plant and animal. When we say earth, we are already thinking of the other three along with it by way of the simple oneness of the four.
>
> The sky is the sun's path, the course of the moon, the glitter of the stars, the year's seasons, the light and dusk of day, the gloom and glow of night, the clemency and inclemency of the weather, the drifting clouds and blue depth of the ether. When we say sky, we are already thinking of the other three along with it by way of the simple oneness of the four.
>
> The divinities are the beckoning messengers of the godhead. Out of the hidden sway of the divinities the god emerges as what he is, which removes him from any comparison with beings that are present. When we speak of the divinities, we are already thinking of the other three along with them by way of the simple oneness of the four.
>
> The mortals are human beings. They are called mortals because they can die. To die means to be capable of death as death. Only man dies. The animal perishes. It has death neither ahead of itself nor behind it. Death is the shrine of Nothing, that is, of that which in every respect is never something that merely exists, but which nevertheless presences, even as the mystery of Being itself. As the shrine of Nothing, death harbors within itself the presencing of Being. As the shrine of Nothing, death is the shelter of Being. . . . When we say mortals, we are then thinking of the other three along with them by way of the simple oneness of the four. (pp. 178–179)

Teilhard de Chardin (1965) also recognized the interconnectedness of the universe and expressed this principle in these terms:

> The farther and more deeply we penetrate into matter, by means of increasingly powerful methods, the more we are confounded by the interdependence of its parts. Each element of the cosmos is positively woven from all others. . . . It is impossible to cut into this network, to isolate a portion without it becoming frayed and unravelled at all its edges. All around us, as far as the eye can see, the universe holds together, and only one way of considering it is really possible, that is, to take it as a whole, in one piece. (pp. 43–44)

*The Intimate Connection between the Individual's Inner or Higher Self and the Fundamental Unity of the Universe.* Many different names in many different contexts have been given to the higher self. For example, Carl Jung, the Swiss psychologist, calls it *the Self*, while the Hindus name the higher self the *Atman*.

Emerson (1965) refers frequently in his work to the connectedness between the inner self and the fundamental unity:

> In the woods, we return to reason and faith. There I feel that nothing can befall me in life,—no disgrace, no calamity (leaving me my eyes), which nature cannot repair. Standing on the bare ground,—my head bathed by the blithe air, and uplifted into infinite space,—all mean egotism vanishes. I become a transparent eyeball; I am nothing; I see all; the currents of the Universal Being circulate through me; I am part or particle of God. (p. 189)

> We live in succession, in division, in parts, in particles. Meantime within man is the soul of the whole; the wise silence; the universal beauty, to which every part and particle is equally related; the eternal ONE. And this deep power in which we exist, and whose beatitude is all accessible to us, is not only self-sufficing and perfect in every hour, but the act of seeing and the thing seen, the seer and the spectacle, the subject and the object, are one. We see the world piece by piece, as the sun, the moon, the animal, the tree; but the whole of which these are the shining parts, is the soul. (p. 28)

Gandhi (1980) observes the same interconnectedness between the individual and the universe:

> I believe in the absolute oneness of God and, therefore, of humanity. What though we have many bodies? We have but one soul. The rays of the sun are many through refraction. But they have the same

source. I cannot, therefore, detach myself from the wickedest soul
nor may I be denied identity with the most virtuous. (p. 72)

Gandhi continually made the link between the interconnectedness of all
things and his interrelatedness with all other human beings. As mentioned, for him it is important that one does not use spirituality as a way
to escape from humanity but as a means to renew one's encounter with
others.

For a Westerner, Martin Heidegger had a unique vision of the human being. He did not see the person as a skin-encapsulated ego, but as
a "force field," or what he called *Dasein*. *Dasein*, then, is intimately connected with the surrounding environment. Barrett (1962) comments:

> Existence itself, according to Heidegger, means to stand outside
> oneself, to be beyond oneself. My Being is not something that takes
> place inside my skin (or inside an immaterial substance inside that
> skin); my Being, rather, is spread over a field or region which is the
> world of its care and concern. Heidegger's theory of man (and of
> Being) might be called the Field Theory of Man (or the Field The-
> ory of Matter), provided we take this purely as an analogy; for Hei-
> degger would hold it a spurious and inauthentic way to
> philosophize to derive one's philosophic conclusions from the
> highly abstract theories of physics. But in the way that Einstein took
> matter to be a field (a magnetic field, say)—in opposition to the
> Newtonian conception of a body as existing inside its surface
> boundaries—so Heidegger takes man to be a field or region of
> Being. (pp. 217–218)

Heidegger's view of the individual stands in contrast to the atomistic view
in the transmission position of the individual as a "Robinson Crusoe."

### The Cultivation of Intuition and Insight through Contemplation and
### Meditation.    How is one to perceive the interconnectedness of reality
and fundamental unity of things? A consistent idea within the "perennial
philosophy" is the need to cultivate intuition so one can "see" clearly how
things are. Emerson (1965), for example, refers to intuition as "primary
wisdom":

> The inquiry leads us to that source, at once the essence of genius,
> of virtue, and of life, which we call Spontaneity or Instinct. We de-
> note this primary wisdom as Intuition, whilst all later teachings are
> tuitions. In that deep force, the last fact behind which analysis can-
> not go, all things find their common origin. For, the sense of being
> which in calm hours rises, we know not how, in the soul, is not di-

verse from things, from space, from light, from time, from man, but one with them, and proceeds obviously from the same source whence their life and being also proceed. (p. 267)

Gandhi (1980) refers to intuition as that "still small voice within" that prods him to social action: "There are moments in your life when you must act, even though you cannot carry your best friends with you. The 'still small voice' within you must always be the final arbiter when there is a conflict of duty" (p. 62).

Whereas Gandhi claims that intuition can stimulate social consciousness, Teilhard de Chardin (1968) states that it leads to personal transformation:

Deeper still: a transformation had taken place for me in the very perception of being. Thenceforward being had become, in some way, tangible and savorous to me; and as it came to dominate all the forms which it assumed being itself began to draw me and intoxicate me. (p. 129)

Heidegger distinguishes between two modes of thinking—rational, calculative thinking and intuitive, meditative thinking. The rational mode predominates in Western technological society; it attempts to objectify things so that they can be classified and controlled. In contrast, intuitive thinking is based on an openness to "Being"; it allows for a direct intuitive encounter with what is.

Within the "perennial philosophy," specific approaches to the cultivation of intuition have been advocated, such as contemplation and meditation. These methods have been developed to help one to "see." This "seeing" is not flash of blinding light but a gradual awakening to the interconnectedness of things. Emerson, for example, suggests that it is helpful to be quiet and to listen. In this quiet state, one can begin to see one's relationship with the environment more clearly than when one is frantically attempting to manipulate the environment according to one's own ends. Gandhi (1980) also believed that silence is helpful in seeking God:

It [silence] has now become both a physical and spiritual necessity for me. Originally it was taken to relieve the sense of pressure. Then I wanted time for writing. After, however, I had practised it for some time, I saw the spiritual value of it. It suddenly flashed across my mind that that was the time when I could best hold communion with God. And now I feel as though I was naturally built for silence. (p. 101)

Heidegger, too, felt that contemplation is useful in realizing "Being." He himself spent much time in his Black Forest retreat hut, where he could contemplate and reflect. The type of contemplation advocated by Heidegger and Emerson, however, is different from Gandhi's form of meditation. Gandhi's meditation followed Eastern practices in which meditation tends to be more focused (e.g., repeating a mantra, counting one's breath).

***Social Action as a Means to Relieving Human Suffering.*** This principle of the "perennial philosophy" is a logical extension of the interconnectedness perspective: If, indeed, I am intimately related to all other beings, then I cannot ignore injustice to others. Gandhi (1980) frequently made this point:

> Man's ultimate aim is the realization of God, and all his activities, political, social and religious, have to be guided by the ultimate aim of the vision of God. The immediate service of all human beings becomes a necessary part of the endeavour simply because the only way to find God is to see Him in His creation and be one with it. This can only be done by service of all. And this cannot be done except through one's country. I am a part and parcel of the whole, and I cannot find Him apart from the rest of the humanity. My countrymen are my nearest neighbours. They have become so helpless, so resourceless, so inert that I must concentrate on serving them. If I could persuade myself that I should find Him in a Himalayan cave I would proceed there immediately. But I know that I cannot find Him apart from humanity." (p. 57)

Like Gandhi, Mother Theresa in Calcutta is another person who has applied this principle in her work in India.

What are the implications for education of these principles which provide the philosophical base of the transformation position? Unlike the other metaorientations, the transformation position cannot ignore the wholeness of the child. To do so would be to deny the interdependent nature of reality. Gandhi (1980) states this idea in these words:

> I hold that true education of the intellect can only come through a proper exercise and training of the bodily organs, e.g., hands, feet, eyes, ears, nose, etc. In other words an intelligent use of the bodily organs in a child provides the best and quickest way of developing his intellect. But unless the development of the mind and body goes hand in hand with a corresponding awakening of the soul, the former alone would prove to be a poor lopsided affair. By spiritual training I mean education of the heart. A proper and allround de-

velopment of the mind, therefore, can take place only when it proceeds *pari passu* with the education of the physical and spiritual faculties of the child. They constitute an indivisible whole. According to this theory, therefore, it would be a gross fallacy to suppose that they can be developed piecemeal or independently of one another. (p. 138)

## PSYCHOLOGICAL CONTEXT

### Humanistic Psychology

Humanistic psychology emerged in the late 1950s as an alternative to the dominant psychologies of behaviorism and the Freudian school. Bugental (1967) summarizes the basic assumptions of humanistic psychology:

The humanistic psychologist:
1. Disavows as *inadequate* and even misleading, descriptions of human functioning and experience based wholly or in large part on subhuman species.
2. Insists that *meaning* is more important than method in choosing problems for study, in designing and executing the studies, and in interpreting their results.
3. Gives primary concern to man's *subjective experience* and secondary concern to his actions, insisting that this primacy of the subjective is fundamental in any human endeavor.
4. Sees a constant interaction between "science" and "application" such that each constantly contributes to the other and the attempt rigidly to separate them is recognized as handicapping to both.
5. Is concerned with the *individual,* the exceptional, and the unpredicted rather than seeking only to study the regular, the universal, and the conforming.
6. Seeks that which may expand or enrich man's experience and rejects the paralyzing perspective of nothing-but thinking. (p. 9)

Abraham Maslow and Carl Rogers are two of the most influential humanistic psychologists. Maslow developed the concept of self-actualization; Rogers focuses on how people in the helping professions can facilitate learning and personal growth.

*Abraham Maslow.*   Maslow, like other humanistic psychologists, argues that psychology had focused too much on neurosis and pathology and that, therefore, very little research had been done on how humans move to higher levels of functioning. He states this idea in the preface to the revised edition of *Motivation and Personality* (1970):

> If I had had to condense the thesis of this book into a single sentence, I would have said that, in *addition* to what the psychologies of the time had to say about human nature, man also had a higher nature and that this was instinctoid, i.e., part of his essence. And if I could have had a second sentence, I would have stressed the profoundly holistic nature of human nature in contradiction to the analytic-dissecting-atomistic-Newtonian approach of the behaviorisms and of Freudian psychoanalysis. (p. ix)

One important aspect of Maslow's theory is his view of human motivation. According to Maslow human needs can be placed within a hierarchy at the bottom of which are lower-level needs that must be satisfied before a person can move on to fulfill higher-level needs.

The first level of need consists of physiological needs, including the need for food, water, warmth, and sex. After these needs have been met, another set of needs arises, which have to do with physical and emotional safety. Safety needs include "security, stability, dependency, protection, freedom from fear, from anxiety and chaos" (Maslow, 1970, p. 39). Unless the individual feels safe and secure, the higher needs will not arise. In some sectors of society (e.g., the inner city) safety needs are not met and, thus, there is little opportunity to move to higher-level needs.

The third level of needs centers on belongingness and love. If physiological and safety needs are met, the person "will hunger for affectionate relations with people in general, namely for a place in his group or family. . . . Now he will feel sharply the pangs of loneliness, of ostracism, of rejection, of friendlessness, of rootlessness" (Maslow, 1970, p. 43). If the belongingness needs have been met, the person will then begin to focus on the need for esteem, which involves the desire for achievement, mastery, and competency as well as the need for recognition, appreciation, and status. If these needs are not met, the person will not become self-confident, but, instead, can be overcome with feelings of inferiority.

At the top of the Maslow hierarchy is the need for self-actualization. At this level, the person seeks the actualization of his or her deepest potentials: "What a man can be, he must be. He must be true to his own nature. This need we call self-actualization" (Maslow, 1970, p. 46).

Although Kurt Goldstein (1939) coined the term *self-actualization*, the concept was developed fully by Maslow (1970, pp. 153–174), who studied self-actualized adults and developed a list of characteristics that are associated with self-actualization:

• Acceptance of self, others, and nature
• Spontaneity, simplicity, naturalness

- Problem-centered, that is, these individuals customarily have some mission in life, some task to fulfill
- Openness to mystic experience and the peak experience
- Identification and sympathy with other human beings and the human race in general
- Deeper and more profound interpersonal relations
- Democratic character structure
- Philosophical sense of humor

Maslow suggests that self-actualization usually is not attained in young adulthood, but arrives sometime after age 35 or 40. However, the lower-level needs, which are present in childhood, have been applied to teaching and learning situations by some educators, who argue that it is important that student physiological, safety, and belongingness needs be met if the student is to master much of the work that is expected of him or her in the classroom.

Toward the latter part of his life, Maslow (1971) wrote about transcendence as a stage beyond self-actualization. Transcendence "refers to the very highest and most inclusive or holistic levels of human consciousness, behaving and relating, as ends rather than as means, to oneself, to significant others, to human beings in general, to other species, to nature and to the cosmos" (p. 279). This concern of Maslow's was part of a thrust toward transpersonal psychology and education that appeared in the late 1960s and early 1970s.

**Carl Rogers.** Although Rogers' work has been wide-ranging, one important area of it is his description of facilitative conditions that are crucial to a helping or teaching relationship. Rogers has mentioned, in particular, qualities in teachers and counselors that are generally facilitative of healthy human relations, notably genuineness, regard, and empathy.

*Genuineness* is the capacity to be in tune with or congruent with one's own feelings and concerns. It means not putting on a facade, but accepting feelings and dealing with them at a conscious level. As an example of genuineness, Rogers (1969) cites the behavior of a teacher who made art materials available to her students for creative work, was bothered by the chaos of the room, and was able to express this feeling honestly. This teacher said:

> I find it maddening to live with the mess—with a capital M! No one seems to care except me. Finally, one day I told the children . . . that I am a neat, orderly person by nature and that the mess was driving me to distraction. Did they have a solution? It was suggested there were some volunteers who could clean up. . . . I said it didn't seem fair to me to have the same people clean up all the time for others—

but it would solve it for me. "Well, some people like to clean," they replied. So that's the way it is. (p. 108)

*Regard* is the teacher's ability to convey respect for the individual student and his or her potential for growth, including respect for the student's right to make decisions affecting his or her growth. Expressing regard does not involve relinquishing authority, but means that the teacher conveys a sense of respect for the student's concerns, feelings, and values.

*Empathy* is the teacher's ability to understand the student's perceptions and to convey that understanding. It means trying to put oneself in the student's shoes. If the teacher is not aware of the child's perspective, the child's growth may be thwarted.

Another important aspect of Rogers' work is his development of the concept of self-directed learning. This approach to learning often is associated with the humanistic orientation.

- It seems to me that anything that can be taught to another is relatively inconsequential, and has little or no significant influence on behavior. . . .
- I realize increasingly that I am only interested in learning which significantly influences behavior. . . .
- I have come to feel that the only learning which significantly influences behavior is self-discovered, self-appropriated learning. . . .
- Such self-discovered learning, truth that has been personally appropriated and assimilated in experience, cannot be directly communicated to another. . . .
- As a consequence of the above, I realize that I have lost interest in being a teacher.
- I realize that I am only interested in being a learner, preferably learning things that matter, that have some significant influence on my own behavior. (Rogers, 1961, p. 276)

Rogers (1980) states that self-directed learning is based on the hypothesis that "individuals have within themselves vast resources for self-understanding and for altering their self-concepts, basic attitudes, and self-directed behavior; these resources can be tapped if a definable climate of facilitative psychological attitudes can be provided" (p. 115). Again, these facilitative attitudes include genuineness, empathy, and respect. According to Rogers (1962), if these attitudes are present, the individual will naturally develop toward what he calls a "fully functioning person"—one who is in touch in an immediate and open way with his or her feelings and inner being.

Such a person experiences in the present with immediacy. He is able to live in his feelings and reactions of the moment. He is not bound by the structure of his past learnings but these are a present resource for him insofar as they relate to the experience of the moment. He lives freely, subjectively, in an existential confrontation with this moment of life. (p. 31)

## Transpersonal Psychology

Transpersonal psychology emerged in the late 1960s, as some people sensed an inadequacy in certain aspects of humanistic psychology. In particular, some individuals felt there was too much stress on self or ego in humanistic psychology; this emphasis on self-fulfillment left the person in a spiritual vacuum. Transpersonal psychology is different from other psychologies because it acknowledges human spiritual needs.

*Ken Wilber.*   One of the most prolific writers in the field is Ken Wilber, who, in his writings, continues to define new perspectives in the field. In a recent work, Wilber (1983) integrates a broad spectrum of thinking to construct a developmental model of human existence in which there are seven levels. Figure 6.1 compares Wilber's model of development with the models developed by Maslow, Kohlberg, and Piaget.

ARCHAIC LEVEL   At the base of development is what Wilber calls the *archaic* level. The focus of this stage is on physical sensation and emotional, sexual energy. According to Wilber, people operating at this level are dominated by their physical needs. The archaic level is parallel to Maslow's physiological-need level and Kohlberg's stage-one morality level that is organized around punishment and obedience.

MAGICAL LEVEL   At this stage of development, the person begins to think instead of just reacting to physical needs. This stage parallels Piaget's preoperational stage, Maslow's safety-needs stage, and Kohlberg's stage-two morality level that is based on egocentric needs.

MYTHIC LEVEL   At this level, the person begins what Piaget calls concrete operational thinking; that is, he or she can figure things out without being deceived by appearances. However, the child at this level cannot reason abstractly (hypothetico-deductive reasoning). This stage corresponds to Maslow's belongingness-needs stage and Kohlberg's convential morality stage (stages 3 & 4). In general, the person at this level is oriented toward conformity in his or her personal relations.

RATIONAL LEVEL   Here the person is capable of abstract thinking and also can hypothesize and then rationally examine the variables which may or may not support the hypothesis. Thus, the person at the rational

| WILBER | MASLOW | KOHLBERG | PIAGET |
|--------|--------|----------|--------|
| Causal | | | |
| Subtle | Self-tran-scendence | | |
| Psychic | Self-actualiza-tion | Self-chosen ethi-cal principles | |
| Rational | Self-esteem | Social-contract position | Formal opera-tions |
| Mythic | Belongingness | Conventional morality stages 3-4 | Concrete op-erations |
| Magical | Safety needs | Egocentric orien-tation | Pre-operations |
| Archaic | Physiological needs | Punishment ori-entation | Sensori-motor |

**Figure 6.1**   Comparison of Wilber's, Maslow's, Kohlberg's and Piaget's development models.

stage has entered Piaget's stage of formal operations. This stage correlates with Kohlberg's post-conventional morality stage and Maslow's self-esteem-needs stage.

Many hierarchies of development end at this point. However, transpersonal psychologists suggest that the individual is capable of higher levels of consciousness. Wilber (1983) believes that it is reasonable to speculate in this way about the evolution of human consciousness:

> The point is that the general concept of evolution continuing beyond its present stage into some legitimately trans-rational structures is not a totally outrageous notion. Look at the course of evolution to date: from amoebas to humans! Now what if that ratio, amoeba-to-human, were applied to future evolution? That is, amoebas are to humans as humans are to—what? Is it ridiculous to suggest that the "what" might indeed be omega, geist, supermind, spirit? (p. 24)

Based on his study of mystical psychologies, Wilber has developed three stages beyond the rational.

PSYCHIC LEVEL    This is the first stage beyond the rational level. The psychic level goes beyond the rational level by forming networks of conceptual relationships. At this level, the person moves toward a higher order synthesizing ability and makes "connections, relates truths, coordinates ideas, integrating concepts" (Wilber, 1983, p. 27). This stage culminates in what Aurobindo (n.d.) calls the "higher mind." This level "can freely express itself in single ideas, but its most characteristic movement is a mass ideation, a system of totality of truth-seeing at a single view; the relations of idea with idea, of truth with truth, self-seen in the integral whole" (Aurobindo, quoted in Wilber, 1983, p. 27). This stage is parallel to Maslow's self-actualization stage. Wilber (1983) suggests persons at this stage can also experience insight and even illumination—"a type of vision, noetic, numinous, inspiring, often enstatic, occasionally ecstatic" (p. 29).

SUBTLE LEVEL    At this level, the person experiences what Maslow calls *self-transcendence*. According to Wilber, the disciplines and insights of the great saints reflect this level of development. At this level, the person experiences the highest level of intuition, that which is not emotionalism or some form of hunch, but direct spiritual insight.

CAUSAL LEVEL    This is the highest level of transpersonal development. Wilber (1983) states: "Passing full through the state of cessation or unmanifest absorption, consciousness is said finally to re-awaken to its absolutely prior and eternal abode as spirit, radiant and all-pervading, one and many, only and all" (pp. 30–31). Here the person becomes identified with Tillich's "Ground of Being" or Spinoza's "Eternal Substance." At this level, one does not have a particular set of experiences, but transcends his or her identity as the "experiencer." Thus, subject–object duality is transcended. Wilber (1983) labels individuals at this level as *sages,* drawing a distinction between *saints* and *sages:*

> As an example of the distinction between subtle saints and causal sages, we may take the Mosaic and Christic epiphanies. The Mosaic revelation on Mt. Sinai has all the standard features of a subtle level apprehension: a numinous Other that is Light, Fire, Insight, and Sound (shabd). Nowhere, however, does Moses claim to be one with or identical with that Being. . . . Christ, on the other hand, does claim that "I and the Father are one," a perfect Atmic or causal level apprehension. (pp. 31–32)

Wilber argues that the form of education should match the level of the learner's development. Thus, for children operating at the archaic stage there should be a good deal of physical experience and the opportunity to move about. At the magical stage, play is crucial to the child's development, as it allows children to experiment with their growing conceptions of the world and to learn to get along with others. At the mythic level, the student's thinking can be developed more fully. Students can be presented with problems that stimulate their thinking. The problems are best presented with concrete materials that enable students to test their logic. Students at the rational level should focus on developing abstract thinking skills. Because self-esteem needs are important at this stage of personal development, educational approaches designed to facilitate self-concept are appropriate, including various humanistic education curricula such as Purkey's (Purkey & Novak, 1983) "invitational teaching" and Weinstein's (Weinstein, Hardin, & Weinstein, 1976) "self-science education."

At the psychic level, where the individual is capable of genuine spiritual insight, he or she can work with various transpersonal techniques such as visualization, dreamwork, and yogic disciplines. At the subtle and causal levels, the individual may work with various forms of meditation; at the subtle level the meditative experience allows insight, whereas at the causal level the personal merges with the "one."

**The Holographic Model.** Wilber's concept of development is broadly conceived and integrates a number of perspectives. It should be noted, however, that other individuals have proposed other models of consciousness/reality. For example, Wilber has engaged with others in a dialogue about the holographic paradigm that has been developed by two scientists, Pribram (1976) and Bohm (1980). Karl Pribram, a neuroscientist, suggests that the brain operates in a manner that is similar to a hologram, which is a kind of three-dimensional picture produced by lensless photography. A hologram is formed on a photographic plate by light that is reflected from an object and a reference beam. The reference beam is formed by light deflecting into the mirror and then onto the plate. The plate then becomes a series of scribbles that do not resemble the object; however, the three-dimensional image of the object will appear if a light source such as a laser beam is made to shine through the plate. If part of the hologram is broken, any piece of it will reconstitute the entire image. Pribram argues that the hologram is an appropriate model for the way brain stores memory. Ferguson (1982) provides a clear description of how this process corresponds to the working of the human brain:

> In taking a hologram, light waves are encoded and the resulting hologram that's projected then decodes, or deblurs, the image. The brain may similarly decode its stored memory traces. (p. 19)

David Bohm (1980), a physicist, has explored the possibility that the universe is holographic. He suggests that the unfolded universe, or everyday reality, is not the stable day-to-day world that we encounter but, instead, is dynamic and changing. Below what Bohm calls the *explicit,* or unfolded, reality is what he calls the *implicate,* or enfolded, order. According to Ferguson (1982), "The enfolded order harbors the reality, much as the DNA in the nucleus of the cell harbors potential life and directs the nature of unfolding" (p. 21). Intuitive or transcendent experiences may, then, reveal the enfolded order. Marilyn Ferguson (1982) summarizes the work of Pribram and Bohm: "The theory, in a nutshell, is that our brains construct reality by interpreting frequencies from another dimension, a realm of meaningful primary reality that transcends time and space. The brain is a hologram, interpreting a holographic universe" (p. 5).

Bohm indicates that scientific methods have focused on separate entities, but, instead, it is more appropriate to focus on objects in movement. Suggesting that the model of the holograph is too static, he recently has developed the concept of holomovement. Ferguson (1982) articulates this concept:

> Our very act of objectifying, as in an electron microscope, alters that which we hope to see. We want to find its edges, to make it sit still for a moment, when its true nature is in another order of reality, another dimension, where there are no *things.* It is as if we are bringing the "observed" into focus, as you would bring a picture into resolution, but the *blur* is a more accurate representation. The blur itself is the basic reality. (pp. 21–22)

There is no consensus among transpersonal thinkers about the new paradigm(s) for consciousness/reality. For example, Wilber (1983) has been critical of the holographic model, because he views consciousness/reality as a hierarchy moving from the lower, fragmentary realms to the highest, most unified realms. Wilber argues that the holographic model reduces reality to two levels—implicate and explicit—when there are, in fact, many more levels. However, despite these differences, we are witnessing a fascinating dialogue about the nature of consciousness/reality, and, whatever perspective is taken within this debate, it has certain implications for educators.

The main thrust of this thinking is that we do not have to limit ourselves to one way of looking at the world. If we limit ourselves, we are reducing ways of interacting with what is going on around us. Looking at Wilber's work, we can also acknowledge that different students will be operating at different levels of consciousness. To be most effective, teachers should try to take these different levels into account. Thus, if a student is working at Wilber's mythic level, the teacher should attempt to fully develop the child's abilities at that level, (Maslow's belongingness-needs level); this means the child would fully develop operational thinking, conventional moral reasoning, and the ability to get along with others. By being aware of the different levels and working with them, the teacher's effectiveness can be enhanced.

## ECONOMIC/SOCIAL CONTEXT

### Ethical Principles

Mark Satin (1979) suggests, in his book *New Age Politics*, that there are four principles or "ethics" that underlie the social thrust of the transformation position: 1) self-development, 2) ecology, 3) self-reliance/cooperation, and 4) nonviolence.

***Self-development Ethic.***   This ethic suggests that it is valid for persons to seek growth and fulfillment and assumes that it is natural, even lawful, for individuals to move toward higher, integrative states, such as the transpersonal levels of consciousness described by Wilber. To facilitate self-development, various forms of discrimination based on race, sex, and age must be eliminated. Instead, there should be a maximization of cultural, intellectual, and spiritual freedom.

***Ecology Ethic.***   As individuals move toward higher stages of functioning and become more aware of the interconnectedness of life, they perceive that personal, social, and economic behavior are not isolated events but are interdependent. Accordingly to Willis Harman, the self-development and ecology ethics are closely related: "These two ethics, one emphasizing the total community of [people] in nature and the oneness of the human race, and the other placing the highest value on developing one's own self, are not conflicting but complementary—two sides of the same coin. . . . Each is corrective against excesses of misapplication of the other" (quoted in Satin, 1979, p. 103).

***Self-reliance/Cooperation Ethic.***   The transformation orientation focuses on the connection between one's inner life and the community. It emphasizes the possibility of being in touch with one's inner self and, at the same time, communicating with others. According to Satin (1979), "We need maximization of self-reliance of communities, regions, and nation-states, and maximization of the cooperative potential of communities, regions, and states" (p. 105).

***Nonviolence Ethic.***   At the heart of the transformation position is reverence for life. Thoreau, Tolstoy, Gandhi, and Martin Luther King extend this reverence to nonviolent political action; no matter how valid the cause, violence is not condoned in pursuit of social and political goals.

These four basic ethics are at the center of the transformation orientation. Satin (1979) suggests that these ethical principles are reflected in more specific values:

- *Enoughness:* The transformation orientation argues that more is not necessarily better. Instead, there is a focus on appropriate technology. Bender, author of *Sharing Smaller Pies,* says "We are learning that too much of a good thing is not a good thing and that we would often be wiser to determine what is enough rather than how much is possible. . . . The fewer our wants, the greater our freedom from having to serve them" (quoted in Satin, 1979, p. 106).
- *Stewardship:* The transformation orientation focuses on a concern for the present environment. Earth and its resources are not to be used in an unconscious manner; rather, they should be cared for and nurtured.
- *Diversity/pluralism:* The transformation orientation places value in pluralism and diversity, through which people are more able to realize wholeness. If the culture moves towards a monolothic ethic, conformity tends to override diversity. Satin suggests that diversity also can occur within ourselves; thus, we can acknowledge the different parts of ourselves—masculine and feminine, young and old, active and passive, independent and interdependent. In this sense, we are multidimensional persons.
- *Voluntary simplicity:* Duane Elgin (1981) explores this concept in a book by the same name. There is a tendency in the transformation position to follow Thoreau's dictum: "Simplify, simplify, simplify." In other words, people should attempt to simplify their lives so that their wants and their lifestyles are not excessive.
- *Quality:* In general, there is an emphasis in the transformation orientation on the qualitative aspect of life over the quantitative. Pirsig (1974) discusses the concept of quality in his book, *Zen and the Art of Motorcycle Maintenance,* where he states that fixing a motorcycle can be a higher-quality activity than attending the University of Chicago.

The ethics and values outlined by Satin have been translated into many domains of action. In the following sections, we discuss them in relation to economics, politics, and health.

## Economics

In the transformation position, economics cannot be separated from social realities. Economic well-being, then, is not defined in terms of the gross national product (GNP). Gary Synder (1977) argues that GNP fails to measure what he calls the "real values" of "nature, family and mind." He suggests that accounting measures instead should consist of "what is the natural spiritual price we pay for this particular piece of affluence, comfort, or labor saving" (Synder, quoted in Satin, 1979, p. 175). In other words, transformation economics attempts to grapple with the personal, social, and ecological costs of economic activity. Economics from a transformation perspective is based on the following principles:

- *Interrelationship of social purpose and profit:* Although profit is a valid goal in transformation economics, it is not seen as a valid goal in itself; instead, it is connected with right livelihood, which means work that is not exploitative in any way.
- *Appropriate pricing:* Prices are not marked up to highest possible level; instead, goods are priced at a level that allows for reasonable, not excessive, profit.
- *Appropriate consumption:* People consume according to basic needs, not in response to manipulative consumer advertising.
- *Worker participation:* Workers are involved in decision making; hierarchial organizational structures are replaced by small, human-scale organizations.
- *Cooperative economics:* Cooperatives often are used as a way to pool capital and resources; cooperatives are preferred over competitive modes, although competition still has a role in making business less wasteful.
- *Blending of work and play:* Work is not separate from play; in transformation economics, work is seen as rewarding in itself.
- *Integration of economics and spiritual values:* Work is not separated from one's spiritual life; how one does his or her job is as important as any product, thus, ends do not override means.
- *Ecological consciousness:* Economic activity is a part of a larger whole; thus, business endeavors should take into account their relationship with the surrounding environment.
- *Appropriate technology:* Technology is used as an appropriate tool, but does not become extended beyond basic economic requirements; technology remains a tool rather than a master.

Ferguson (1980) describes some examples of transformation economics:

> The new entrepreneurs have moved from a manipulative I–it to an I–Thou philosophy, relating to both consumer and product in immediate, personal ways. . . .
> The Renascence Project in Kansas City, a network of entrepreneurs, demonstrated that alternatives can be both cost effective and profitable. Among its activities: renovation of properties at a key Kansas City location into an eight-million-dollar business complex, the establishment of learning networks, an educational program for the "whole person," a self-supporting alternative high

school, restoration of a historic dance hall, restoration of a large house by a partnership of residents, and development of a master plan for Kansas City calling for block-by-block renovation of neighborhoods along an eleven-mile pedestrian mall. . . .

The new entrepreneurs refuse to separate good-for-business from good-for-people. Mo Siegel, co-founder of the Celestial Tea Company in Boulder, Colorado, has articulated this view for his two hundred and thirty employees: "All department leaders will be held accountable for their people development as well as business results." (p. 355)

## Politics

Politics in the transformation orientation are not tied to traditional ideologies, e.g., socialism or communism; instead there is a search for methods through which people can directly participate in the political process. Transformation politics tend to have the following characteristics:

***Decentralized Political Structures.***   There is a general distrust of large centralized government. Transformation politics encourages decentralized, pluralistic, alternatives; where possible, decisions should be made by local bodies so that people can have direct input into decisions. Huxley comments on the value of decentralized decision making:

> As H.G. Wells once remarked, the mind of the Universe is able to count above two. The dilemmas of the artist-intellectual and of the political theorist have more than two horns. Between ivory towerism on the one hand and direct political action on the other lies the alternative of spirituality. And between the totalitarian fascism and totalitarian socialism lies the alternative of decentralism and cooperative enterprise—the economic-political system most natural to spirituality. (Huxley, quoted in Ferguson, 1980, p. 223)

***Direct Democracy.***   Through new technologies, people may have an opportunity to have a direct say in major issues. Two-way cable and computer-based communication systems could enable people to register their views directly, rather than through representative government.

***Political Networks.***   Networks are flexible structures that form around specific issues and concerns. Gandhi used coalitions, or what he called "grouping unities," to provide a basis for synergistic change in society. The antinuclear movement is an example of a broadly based international network. Ferguson (1980) calls the network that is composed of smaller networks aimed at broad social change the "Aquarian Conspiracy."

*Nonmanipulative Leadership.* In the transformation orientation, leadership is not based on charisma or back-room politics; instead, it is conceived in Gandhian terms, whereby a political action is related to spiritual values. Gandhi's concept of *satyaghrahra* or "soul force" is based on compassion and respect for personal autonomy. In other words, leadership respects individual conscience or, the "still small voice within."

Some examples of transformation politics are described by Sale (1980):

> At the regional level a wide variety of groups has emerged in the last ten years devoted to community organization and rural redevelopment, to citizen activism and consumer resistance, in statewide and multi-state contexts. Some are specifically regional—Save Our Cumberland Mountains, Kentucky Rivers Coalition, Carolina Action, Appalachian Peoples' Organization—and some are narrower—Massachusetts Fair Share, Illinois Public Action Council, California Citizens Action League—some are essentially rural—La Raza Unida in South Texas, ACORN (Association of Community Organizations for Reform Now) in the South and Mississippi River valley—and some more urban—the California Campaign for Economic Democracy, founded by Tom Hayden, which develops reform slates for city and community elections, and Community Jobs Clearinghouse, which is a kind of activists' employment center for the West Coast. In practically every sizeable state it is now possible to find statewide groups working for local control of health care, food-growing and marketing, housing, communcications, alternative technology, energy development, education, and culture, an extraordinary and quite spontaneous development of localism that has taken politicians and pundits, not to mention the professors paid to predict such things, quite by surprise. (p. 440)

## Holistic Medicine

The health field is another area in which the transformation position is evident. Holistic medicine is an approach to healing that respects the interaction of mind, body, and environment. Rather than focusing solely on "treatment," holistic medicine also deals with underlying causes affecting the person. The holistic practitioner does not ignore the person's environment or psychological state. In addition, the holistic approach includes the following characteristics:

• Emphasis on nutrition and physical exercise, as well as conventional medical techniques.
• Focus on achieving maximum wellness, rather than merely overcoming disease.

- Involvement of the patient in the treatment of disease. The patient is not someone who receives a treatment, but who actively participates in understanding and choosing the appropriate form of therapy.
- Mind plays a principle role in all illness. Psychosomatic illness is not a concern of the psychiatrist only, but is the appropriate concern of all health-care professionals.
- Qualitative data (e.g., subjective feelings) are used in addition to quantitative data (e.g., tests, charts) in dealing with health issues.

Two examples of holistic medicine are the work of Gerald Jampolsky and the work of Carl Simonton and Stephanie Matthews-Simonton.

Jampolsky has established the Center for Attitudinal Healing, in Tiburon, California, where he works with children encountering life threatening illnesses such as cancer. He holds meetings in homes with groups of children, in which they can discuss their illnesses and meditate together. Jampolsky's work with the children focuses on helping them identify with their spiritual nature, rather than with their diseased body only.

Carl Simonton and Stephanie Matthews-Simonton have established a cancer clinic in Houston, in which they use guided imagery as a technique to combat cancer. They believe that cancer can be viewed, in part, as a breakdown in one's immune system. The Simontons have the patient visualize the immune system (e.g., the white blood cells) fighting the cancer cells. According to preliminary studies (Simonton, Matthews-Simonton, & Creighton, 1978), the average survival time for cancer patients using this technique is three times the national average in the United States. The quality of life of these individuals also shows marked improvement.

## CONCLUDING COMMENTS

The philosophical and historical roots of the transformation position are not always clear and accessible. The philosophical basis for this position is connected with transcendentalism and with various forms of mysticism—philosophies that have not been at the center of the western intellectual tradition. This remoteness from conventional thinking and the ineffable nature of mystical literature have made it difficult to understand the implications of this position.

However, the work of Wilber, Pribram, Bohm, Capra, and others is helping to clarify the transformation paradigm in a way that is intellectually respectable. In particular, Wilber has integrated a vast body of literature into new theories and frameworks that offer a new vision of human existence/consciousness. Pribram and Bohm's work on the holographic theory also presents a new vision of reality that attempts to link mysticism with science. Although much of this work is impressive, there are certain difficulties. For example, Wilber has developed a peculiar jargon that can make his work inaccessible. Terms such as *pleromatic* and *uroboric*, which abound in *The Atman Project* (1980) and other of his works, obscure his thinking. His theory of developmental stages of growth is also open to question. Is human development like an escalator that inevitably moves us along and upward, or is it more fluid and spontaneous? His vision of development beyond the stages outlined in conventional models such as Piaget's or Kohlberg's is useful; however, must we also accept the lock-step nature of the model? There is no question that humans grow and develop, but we question whether this movement occurs in the manner he suggests.

Other transpersonal theorists also have been questioned. For example, some physicists have criticized Capra, arguing that some of his examples from physics are out-of-date.

Despite these limitations, we feel that the transformational thinkers are opening significant areas of investigation that educators should be aware of. Perhaps the most important aspect of this work is its linking our inner experiences with the outer world. The model of a holographic brain interacting with a holographic universe provides us with a new framework for understanding how humans interact with the universe, and along with other transpersonal models, tends to be both intellectually stimulating and spiritually satisfying.

The social thrust of this orientation also holds promise. The various movements working for small, more flexible economic and social structures, as outlined by Satin and others, are appealing, because it is clear that traditional approaches to social and economic change have not worked. High unemployment and inflation are evidence of the failure of both liberal and conservative measures. However, one of the dangers of this movement is a certain messianic tone that comes through in some of the writing. For example, consider the following passage from Ferguson's (1980) *Aquarian Conspiracy:*

> The paradigm of the Aquarian Conspiracy sees humankind embedded in nature. It promotes the autonomous individual in a decentralized society. It sees us as stewards of all our resources, inner and outer. It says that we are not victims, not pawns, not limited by conditions or conditioning. Heirs to evolutionary riches, we are capable of imagination, invention, and experiences we have only glimpsed.
>
> Human nature is neither good nor bad but open to continuous transformation and transcendence. It has only to discover itself. The new perspective respects the ecology of everything: birth, death, learning, health, family, work, science, spirituality, the arts, the community, relationships, politics. (p. 29)

This is too much like a call to arms and, in that sense, it is counter-productive. Instead of fostering linkages between people, a messianic tone leads to a we–they dichotomy. Even the word *conspiracy* suggests some group that is at odds with everyone else. The idea that the people involved in the Aquarian Conspiracy are part of a unique group can also be seen in Satin's (1979) term, the "New Age." This term suggests that social movements such as the Aquarian Conspiracy are without historical links and that people involved in "New Age" activities are divorcing themselves from the past. Admittedly, there is much in the past that we should reject, but words like "New Age" are alienating in their own way.

Despite these problems, the transformation position offers a rich theoretical, psychological, and social base for educational practice. In the next chapter, we examine attempts to translate the transformation position into programs for the classroom.

## REFERENCES

Aurobindo, (n.d.). The life divine and the synthesis of yoga. (Vols. 18–21). Pondicherry: Centenary Library.

Barrett, W. (1962). *Irrational man: A study in existential philosophy*. New York: Doubleday-Anchor.

Bender, T. (1975). *Sharing smaller pies*. Portland, OR: Rain Publishers.

Bohm, D. (1980). *Wholeness and the implicate order*. London: Routledge & Kegan Paul.

Bugental, J. (1967). The challenge that is man. In Bugental, J. (Ed.), *Challenges in humanistic psychology*. New York: McGraw-Hill.

Capra, F. (1975). *The Tao of physics*. Boulder, CO: Shambala.

———. (1982). *The Turning Point*. New York: Simon & Schuster.

Elgin, D. (1981). *Voluntary simplicity*. New York: Morrow.

Emerson, R.W. (1903). *The Complete Works* (Vol. III). Boston: Houghton Mifflin.

———. (1965). *Selected writings*. Gilman, W.H. (Ed.), New York: New American Library.

Ferguson, M. (1980). *The Aquarian conspiracy*. Los Angeles, CA: J.P. Tarcher.

———. (1982). A new perspective on reality. In Ken Wilber (Ed.), *The holographic paradigm and other paradoxes*. Boulder, CO: Shambala.

Gandhi, M. (1980). *All men are brothers: Autobiographical reflections*. Krishna Kripalani (Ed.). New York: Continuum.

Goldstein. K. (1939). *The Organism*. New York: American Books.

Heidegger, M. (1971). *Poetry, language, thought*. New York: Harper & Row.

Huxley, A. (1970). *The perennial philosophy*. New York: Harper Colophon Books.

Maslow, A. (1970). *Motivation and personality*. New York: Harper & Row.

———. (1971). *The farther reaches of human nature*. New York: Viking.

Needleman, J. (1982). *The heart of philosophy*. New York: Knopf.

Pirsig, R. (1974). *Zen and the art of motorcycle maintenance*. New York: Bantam.

Pribram, K. (1976). Languages of the brain. In G. Globus et al. (Eds.). *Consciousness and the brain*. New York: Plenum.

Purkey, W., & Novak, J. (1983). *Inviting school success: A self-concept approach to teaching.* Belmont, CA: Wadsworth.

Rogers, C. (1961). *On becoming a person.* Boston: Houghton Mifflin.

_____. (1962). Toward becoming a fully functioning person. In *Perceiving, behaving, becoming.* (Association for Supervision and Curriculum Development Yearbook). Washington, DC: National Educational Association.

_____. (1969). *Freedom to learn.* Columbus, OH: Charles Merrill.

_____. (1980). *A way of being.* Boston: Houghton Mifflin.

Sale, K. (1980). *Human scale.* New York: G.P. Putman.

Satin, M. (1979). *New age politics.* New York: Delta Books.

Simonton, C., Matthews-Simonton, S., & Creighton, J. (1978). *Getting well again.* Los Angeles: Tarcher.

Synder, G. (1977). *The old ways: Six essays.* New York: City Lights.

Teilhard de Chardin, P. (1965). *The phenomenon of man.* New York: Harper Torch Books.

_____. (1968). *The divine milieu.* New York: Harper & Row.

Von Eckartsberg, R., & Valle, R. (1980). Heideggerian thinking and the Eastern mind. *Revision, 3*(2), 100–110.

Weinstein, G., Hardin, J., & Weinstein, M. (1976). *Education of the self.* Amherst, MA: Mandala.

Wilber, K. (1980). *The Atman Project.* Wheaton, IL: Theosophical Publishing House.

_____. (1983). *A sociable God.* New York: McGraw-Hill.

# 7 TRANSFORMATION POSITION: Educational Practice

## HISTORICAL BACKGROUND

Historically, the transformation position has been represented by two different currents of thought. One is the romantic or humanistic element, which can be traced to Rousseau and is also found in the work of Froebel, Tolstoy, A.S. Neil, and John Holt. The other is the social change position; George Counts, Theodore Brameld, Jonathan Kozol, and Michael Apple are some of the major spokespeople for this orientation.

### Jean Jacques Rousseau

The romantic element of the transformation position can be traced in particular to Rousseau's *Emile* (1911/1955), where he states, "The education of the earliest years should be merely negative. It consists not in teaching virtue or truth, but in preserving the heart from vice and from the spirit of error" (p. 57). Rousseau felt that children in their natural state are good, and that they become corrupted through their contact with society. Education, then, should not attempt to manipulate the child, but simply let the child's inner nature unfold. Education as unfoldment has been a pervasive theme in the romantic element within the transformation position.

### Friedrich Froebel

Froebel (1887) was influenced by both Rousseau and Pestallozzi. However, his mysticism clearly places him within the transformation position. The following statement reflects his belief in the interdependence of all things:

143

In all things there lives and reigns an eternal law. To him whose mind, through disposition and faith, is filled, penetrated, and quickened with the necessity that this can not possibly be otherwise, as well as to him whose clear, calm mental vision beholds the inner in the outer and through the outer, and sees the outer proceeding with logical necessity from the essence of the inner, this law has been and is enounced with equal clearness and distinctness in nature (the external), in the spirit (the internal), and in life which unites the two. This all-controlling law is necessarily based on an all-pervading, energetic, living, self-conscious, and hence eternal Unity. This fact, as well as the Unity itself, is again vividly recognized, either through faith or through insight, with equal clearness and comprehensiveness; therefore, a quietly observant human mind, a thoughtful, clear human intellect, has never failed, and will never fail, to recognize this Unity. (pp. 1–2)

By education, then, the divine essence of man should be unfolded, brought out, lifted into consciousness, and man himself raised into free, conscious obedience to the divine principle that lives in him, and to a free representation of this principle in his life.

Education, in instruction, should lead man to see and know the divine, spiritual, and eternal principle which animates surrounding nature, constitutes the essence of nature, and is permanently manifested in nature. (pp. 4–5)

Froebel is best known for his development of the kindergarten. Froebel's work influenced Horace Mann's sister-in-law, Elizabeth Peabody, to start the kindergarten movement in the United States. She lectured widely in the U.S. on the kindergarten and was instrumental in starting the first training school for kindergarten teachers in Boston.

## Leo Tolstoy

Tolstoy was another mystic who was interested in education. He established a school for the children of peasants who worked on his estate at Yasnaya Polyana in Russia. Influenced by Rousseau, Tolstoy was a firm believer in negative education, which was one of the principles on which his school was based. Students did not attend school unless they wanted to; if they did come, they could pretty much do as they pleased. Troyat (1980) describes the school:

At eight in the morning a child rang the bell. Half an hour later, "through fog, rain, or the slanting rays of the autumn sun," the black silhouettes of little muzhiks appeared by twos and threes, swinging their empty arms. As in the previous years, they brought no books or notebooks with them—nothing at all, save the desire to learn. The classrooms were painted pink and blue. In one, mineral samples, butterflies, dried plants and physics apparatus lined the shelves. But no books. Why books? The pupils came to the class-room as though it were home; they sat where they liked, on the floor, on the windowledge, on a chair or the corner of a table, they listened or did not listen to what the teacher was saying, drew near when he said something that interested them, left the room when work or play called them elsewhere—but were silenced by their fel-low pupils at the slightest sound. Self-imposed discipline. The les-sons—if these casual chats between an adult and some children could be called that—went on from eight-thirty to noon and from three to six in the afternoon, and covered every conceivable subject from grammar to carpentry, by way of religious history, singing, ge-ography, gymnastics, drawing and composition. Those who lived too far away to go home at night slept in the school. In the summer they sat around their teacher outdoors in the grass. Once a week they all went to study plants in the forest. (p. 227)

## A.S. Neill/Summerhill

Perhaps the most famous example of the Rousseauian position in prac-tice is the Summerhill school in Great Britain. Founded in 1921 by A.S. Neill, this school is still in operation. Neill (1960) describes the philosophy of the school in his book, *Summerhill*:

> When my first wife and I began the school, we had one main idea: to make the school fit the child—instead of making the child fit the school. . . .
>
> Well, we set out to make a school in which we should allow chil-dren freedom to be themselves. In order to do this, we had to re-nounce all discipline, all direction, all suggestion, all moral training, all religious instruction. We have been called brave, but it did not require courage. All it required was what we had—a complete belief in the child as a good, not an evil, being. For almost forty years, this belief in the goodness of the child has never wavered; it rather has become a final faith. (p. 4)

By 1969, *Summerhill* was selling at a rate of more than 200,000 copies a year. It influenced a number of writers, such as Paul Goodman, John Holt, and Herbert Kohl, as well as the free-school movement in North America. According to Graubard (1972), the number of free schools reached approximately 500 by 1972 (p. 40). Graubard claims that these schools did away with "all of the public school apparatus of imposed dis-ciplines and punishments, lock-step age gradings and time-period divi-sions, homework, frequent tests and grades and report cards, rigid graded curriculum, standardized classrooms, dominated and com-manded by one teacher with 25 to 35 students under his or her power" (p. 40). However, the average life of these schools was about 18 months, as often there were ideological disputes among the parents and the staff. Sometimes there were splits between the romantics and the political rad-icals.

## Open-Education Movement

In the late 1960s and early 1970s, the romantic orientation in public ed-ucation was manifested in the open-education movement. Silberman's *Crisis in the Classroom* (1970) put open education into the limelight. Rav-itch (1983) claims that this book universalized open education, which be-came a panacea for all educational institutions and age groups.

Another proponent of open education, Rathbone (1971), claims that in open classrooms each child is "a self-activated maker of meaning, an active agent in his own learning process . . . a self-actualizing individ-ual" (p. 100).

Ravitch (1983) argues that the open-education movement failed:

> The open education movement . . . did not survive as a movement because, lacking a definition, it became identified with ideas and practices of its extremely child-centered advocates, those who zeal-ously opposed whatever was traditional in the structure, content, or methods of the classroom. Their ideological tenets stressed the free-dom of the child, the passivity of the teacher, equality between teacher and child, the virtues of play and unstructured activity, and distrust of extrinsic motivation. Open classroom teachers who ex-pected their methods to work as the ideology said it would were in for a rude awakening. Nothing prepared them for criticism from parents and other teachers about the noisiness of their classrooms and the neglect of "basics." They were taken aback when children demanded that teachers take a more active role or asked to learn from a textbook; they did not know how to deal with discipline problems because they were not suppose to have any. (pp. 254–255)

## Social-Change Movement

In his first book, *Death at an Early Age* (1967), Jonathan Kozol, initially a romantic critic of schools, condemned the Boston public school system and its effects on children from the ghettos. However, he quickly moved to the social-change orientation. Critical of free schools, Kozol, in *Children of the Revolution* (1978), argues that Cuban schools are an appropriate model for social change. In these schools, the students are sent into the countryside to teach others basic literacy skills.

Kozol's work represents the second major current of thought within the transformation position—the social-change position. Historically, this position is seen in the work of Counts (1932), who believed that teachers should be actively involved in social change and even run for political office. In his book *Dare the Schools Build a New Social Order?*, he prodded progressive educators to take this stand. Counts argues that educators should collaborate with other groups to effect social change and that educators should clarify their assumptions and values and make them explicit. He also contends that schools cannot be morally neutral. Counts (1932) was particularly critical of progressive educators who espoused a position of value neutrality:

> If Progressive Education is to be genuinely progressive, it must emancipate itself from the influence of this class, face squarely and courageously every social issue, come to grips with life in all of its stark reality, establish an organic relation with the community, develop a realistic and comprehensive theory of welfare, fashion a compelling and challenging vision of human destiny, and become less frightened than it is today at the bogies of *imposition* and *indoctrination*. (pp. 9–10)

Counts's position was taken up by the Social Reconstructionists. Brameld (1956), for example, has called for educators to take a stronger position in promoting social change. Brameld refers to the Chicago community activist Saul Alinsky and the consumer advocate Ralph Nader as models for how teachers should become involved in overcoming injustice and inequities in society. Social Reconstructionism, then, encourages schools and teachers to be at the forefront of social change. Today, the social change orientation is represented by Paulo Freire, Alfred Alschuler, and Michael Apple. This orientation, together with the humanistic and transpersonal orientations, constitutes the transformation position.

The romantic, humanistic orientation and the social-change orientation sometimes have been juxtaposed. However, in programs such as "Social Literary Training" (Alschuler, 1980) they are effectively integrated.

## TRANSFORMATION POSITION
## IN CONTEMPORARY EDUCATION

### Humanistic Orientation

Humanistic education became a dominant force in education in the 1960s. Humanistic educators felt that the focus at that time on academic disciplines ignored the intrinsic needs of the child. These educators turned to the work of Rogers and Maslow (see Chapter 6) and other humanistic psychologists to provide the rationale for their own work. Humanistic programs are based on the following assumptions which, in part, reflect the influence of humanistic psychology:

- Human beings have a tendency to realize their positive inner potential. Although students are capable of a range of behaviors, if the right conditions are provided they will move toward higher levels of functioning.
- Individuals have the capacity to direct their own behavior. Although young children need the teacher's assistance, as they mature they are increasingly able to carry out their own learning.
- Values play an essential role in the learning process. It is important that students understand and develop a coherent value system that gives meaning to their lives and provides inner direction to their actions.
- Self-concept is integral to how a student learns and develops. Humanists cite evidence correlating positive self-concept with student learning and achievement. Thus, they try to develop a classroom climate and curricula that are conducive to developing a positive self-concept.
- Cognitive, affective, and psychomotor learning are interrelated. Humanistic educators emphasize that cognitive learning must be geared to students' affective and psychomotor development levels.
- Teachers should be facilitators of learning. Although, at times, the teachers may be directive, their main task is to develop a trusting and open classroom climate and then to help students achieve their learning goals.
- In the humanistic classroom, the students' concerns are accepted as valid content. Although the teacher may not be able to respond to all of their concerns, at least he or she can create a climate in which these concerns can be acknowledged (Kirschenbaum, 1975).
- Self-evaluation is central to humanistic education. Kirschenbaum (1975) states that "humanistic education tends to move away from teacher-controlled evaluation and shift to the student as he learns to evaluate his own progress toward his goals" (p. 329).

Many programs in humanistic education can be grouped under two general categories: The first has its roots in Maslow's work and focuses on the development of positive self-concept. The second major area of emphasis is related to Rogers' theory and focuses on building interpersonal skills.

***Self-Concept Programs.***    Many humanistic programs are based on research that links positive student self-concept with school achievement.

WILLIAM PURKEY/THE INVITATIONAL TEACHER AND THE INVITATIONAL SCHOOL    Some of this research has been summarized by Purkey in *Self-Concept and School Achievement* (1970) and in *Inviting School Success* (1978).

Purkey (1978) states that a "student's self-concept does not cause the student to misbehave in the classroom. A better explanation is that the disruptive student has learned to see himself or herself as a trouble maker and behaves accordingly" (p. 19). Thus, a student's self-concept does not cause the student to behave in a particular way, but interacts with other variables (e.g., teacher expectations, programming, and classroom environment) to affect how the student behaves and performs in school.

To facilitate a positive self-concept and positive school climate, Purkey (1978) has developed the concepts of the "invitational teacher" and the "invitational school." The invitational teacher is one who intentionally sends invitations to the student to encourage learning. Such "invitations" include listening to students with care, being authentic with students and oneself, and reaching out to students. Purkey (1978) suggests a number of specific invitations teachers can utilize, for instance, using student experts so that individual student expertise is acknowledged, or letting students know they are missed by sending them notes when they are absent.

ARTHUR COMBS   Combs' theory of education, based on what he calls *perceptual psychology,* states that, in order to encourage a positive student self-concept, the teacher should have a positive view of himself or herself. Combs (1975) asserts that the teacher can use his or her own positive self-concept as an instrument in teaching; as the teacher experiences his or her uniqueness as a person, the act of teaching is enhanced:

> The good teacher is no carbon copy but stands out as a unique and effective personality, sometimes for one reason, sometimes for another, but always for something intensely and personally his own. He has found ways of using himself, his talents, and his environment in a fashion that aids both his students and himself to achieve satisfaction—their own and society's too. Artists sometimes refer to "the discovery of one's personal idiom," and the expression seems very apt applied to teaching as well. We may define the effective teacher *as a unique human being who has learned to use his self effectively and efficiently for carrying out his own and society's purpose.* (p. 254)

Combs (1975) has developed a teacher training program that focuses on the development of a positive teacher self-concept.

VALUES CLARIFICATION   Values clarification is another humanistic program that attempts to facilitate a positive self-image. Initially developed by Raths, Merrill, and Simon (1978), this approach attempts to develop positive, purposeful, and consistent behavior and attitudes in students through a process of valuing. Simon and his associates suggest that, as students clarify and identify their values, they become less apathetic, drifting, and conforming. To achieve these goals, the values clarification movement has developed a number of structured exercises published in a variety of books and kits. Teachers' communication skills also are important in this approach. Some academics (Lockwood, 1976) have argued that values clarification lacks an adequate theoretical base and encourages ethical relativism. For example, consider the teacher who raises the problem of whether cheating is acceptable on tests. Some students may indicate that they think it is acceptable to cheat, although this opinion may conflict with the rules the teacher has established for the class. If the teacher opens the cheating issue to discussion, and the students decide it is all right to cheat, then the teacher must either accept that position or resort to the use of power and insist that cheating will not occur within his or her class. If many conflicts arise between the position students arrive at through the open process of valuing and the position of the teacher, students may see the valuing process as a "game" that is unrelated to real issues that can arise in schools. The teacher using values clarification must be careful, then, as to what issues are opened to the valuing process, because if the issues to be addressed in the classroom fundamentally conflict with his of her concept of how things should be run, the teacher will end up having to use authority arbitrarily, which runs counter to the basic ethic of values clarification.

GERALD WEINSTEIN: SELF-SCIENCE EDUCATION    Weinstein's self-science education program is another approach to self-concept education. He first presented this approach in *Toward Humanistic Education* (Weinstein & Fantini, 1970), which became a key text in the field of humanistic education. Since then, he has developed his ideas in *Education of the Self* (1976). According to Weinstein, Hardin, and Weinstein (1976), there are five criteria for developing humanistic programs:

1. The needs of the individual are the central data source for decision making.
2. Humanistic education increases the options of the learners.
3. Personal knowledge gets at least as much priority as public knowledge.
4. No single individual's development is fostered at the expense of anyone else's development.
5. All elements of the program contribute to the sense of significance, value, and worth of each person involved.

Self-science education applies an inquiry method to self-examination. Weinstein suggests that one's self-concept is, in part, a cluster of hypotheses about oneself; his self-science education program consists of examining these hypotheses to see how accurate they are. Sometimes we hold beliefs about ourselves that we have never checked out. Weinstein's program, which is designed to help individuals see their own unique style of relating to the world, is based on his hypothesis that having more accurate perceptions of oneself can have a positive impact on self-concept.

The central tool in self-science education is a method of teaching called the Trumpet: The word *trumpet* is used because the shape of that instrument is such that something goes in the narrow end and becomes expanded when it comes out. According to Weinstein et al. (1976), this also happens in the process of achieving self-knowledge. The Trumpet, which applies problem-solving skills to self-inquiry, consists of the following steps:

1. *Confront the situation.* The individual confronts a situation that elicits some sort of response. In the classroom, structured activities can sometimes be used to initiate such a confrontation.
2. *Take an inventory.* The person lists his or her responses. The inventory process involves thoughts, feelings, and behaviors. Here the individual responds to questions such as these: "How did you respond?" "What is unique and what is common to your response?"
3. *Recognize patterns.* The individual examines any consistent patterns in his or her response. For example, when the teacher asks for an opinion in class, someone might say, "Whenever I'm in one of my academic classes and there is a discussion that calls for our opinions, I begin to experience feelings of nervousness, fright. My heart begins to pound. I say to myself, 'Don't be a fool. Don't take any chances. Even if you have something you'd like to say, cool it. Just listen and make like you understand whatever is happening.' And so I sit, and when I have something to say, I don't. I just clamp down on it and try to look my wisest" (Weinstein et al., 1976, p. 30).
4. *Own patterns.* The person examines what function the pattern serves. This can be done by asking oneself, "What does this pattern do for me? What does it protect me from or help me avoid?" Continuing with the example given in Step 3: "By not talking in class it helps me avoid saying something foolish or stupid. It protects me from being put down by others. I suppose what it gets for me is the feeling that I'm not dumb" (Weinstein et al., 1976, p. 31).
5. *Consider consequences.* The person examines the price or consequences of the behavior pattern. In our example, the response might be as follows: "Well, one way I pay is that by being so quiet I never get a chance to express myself in public. I'm always holding back and that's not a very satisfying feeling. I get particularly annoyed when something I was thinking of saying is mentioned by someone else, and everyone thinks it's great—and I sit there stewing over the fact that I could have said that. I guess, too, that my passivity in that situation carries over to other situations that I'm not even aware of" (Weinstein et al., 1976, pp. 31–32).
6. *Allow alternatives.* At this stage the individual examines alternative patterns of response. "In the example we are using, the person may de-

cide that, during the coming weeks, he or she will try to offer at least one opinion in three different classes. In order to accomplish this, it may be necessary to rehearse all during those classes. Repeating the sentence, 'What I say is good and intelligent so I don't have to prove my smarts to anyone' over and over before venturing the opinion, is a suggested route" (Weinstein et al., 1976, p. 33).

7. *Make evaluations.* After using a new behavior, the person can ask how it worked. Was the new response satisfactory or should another response be tried?

8. *Choose.* In this last step, the person decides whether he or she wants to adopt the new pattern, return to the old pattern, or try another set of responses.

The Trumpet is not meant to be simply another problem-solving technique. Although it uses problem-solving skills, its broader purpose is self-examination. Ideally, the student should learn the method and apply it regularly in his or her life to gain greater self-understanding.

*Interpersonal Skills.*   Some humanistic programs focus on the development of interpersonal skills. Two of these programs are Gordon's (1974) "teacher effectiveness training" and Gazda et al.'s (1973) "human relations development" programs. Both of these programs were influenced by Rogers' work on conditions (e.g., empathy, regard) that facilitate personal growth. Aspy and Roebuck (1977) also have been influenced by Rogers in their research, carried out over a 17-year period, which found that "students learn more and behave better when they receive high levels of understanding, caring and genuineness, than when they are given low levels of them" (Aspy & Roebuck, quoted in Rogers, 1983, p. 202). In one study of 600 teachers and 10,000 students, the teachers had received training to offer higher levels of empathy, congruence, and positive regard; the students of these teachers were compared with a control group consisting of students who were taught by teachers with lower-level interpersonal skills. This study found that students of the teachers who were trained to be facilitative exhibit the following traits:

1. Miss fewer days of school during the year;
2. Have increased scores on self-concept measures, indicating more positive self regard;
3. Make greater gains on academic achievement measures, including both math and reading scores;
4. Present fewer disciplinary problems;
5. Commit fewer acts of vandalism to school property;
6. Increase their scores on I.Q. tests (grades K–5);

7. Make gains in creativity scores from September to May; and
8. Be more spontaneous and use higher levels of thinking. (Aspy & Roebuck, quoted in Rogers, 1983, pp. 202–203)

The study also found that in classrooms of teachers who were more empathic, congruent, and respecting, there was

1. More student talk
2. More student problem solving
3. More verbal initiation
4. More verbal response to teacher
5. More asking of questions
6. More involvement in learning
7. More eye contact with teacher
8. More physical movement
9. Higher levels of cognition
10. Greater creativity (Aspy & Roebuck, quoted in Rogers, 1983, p. 204)

The empirical work of Aspy and Roebuck has documented a number of the claims of humanistic educators.

## Transpersonal Orientation

Transpersonal education is similar to humanistic education in that it focuses on the inner needs of the student. However, it stresses the intuitive and spiritual needs of the child, rather than his or her ego needs. Miller (1981) identifies the basic assumptions of transpersonal education:

- *Intuition is a valid way of knowing.* Split-brain research has helped to describe how we think both analytically and intuitively. The left side of the brain tends to operate in a linear, step-by-step fashion, whereas the right side works in an intuitive, holistic manner as it processes information. Creative thinking employs both types of thought. Transpersonal education attempts to facilitate interaction between the two spheres of the brain.
- *Children are viewed from a holistic perspective.* Transpersonal educators assert that we should not ignore the emotional and spiritual needs of the child and focus on programs that acknowledge the various needs (e.g., intellectual, spiritual, emotional) of the whole child. For example, the arts often are integrated with reading and writing activities.
- *Self-inquiry is central to the learning process.* A primary goal in transpersonal education is the realization of the higher self. This self or center is a source of spiritual awareness. If we are in touch with our center, then we become aware of the deep interconnectedness of life. Individ-

uals attempt to make contact with higher self through methods such as meditation, visualization, and yoga.

- *Individuals are capable of experiencing various levels of consciousness.* Ken Wilber (1983) has described how humans can experience levels of consciousness ranging from lower levels, in which physical and emotional reactions are central, to higher levels, in which deep spiritual insight is realized.
- *Teachers can facilitate learning and development by working with both their own and their students' individual levels of consciousness.* Learning theorists have recognized that students vary in their learning styles. These styles are related to the different levels of consciousness; therefore, teacher awareness of the levels can facilitate both the teacher's self-awareness and intercommunication between teacher and students.

***Transpersonal Programs.*** The small number of programs in transpersonal education include Waldorf education, synectics, superlearning, and confluent education. We will describe Waldorf education in some detail and give a brief overview of the other programs.

WALDORF EDUCATION    Waldorf education is a comprehensive approach to schooling that is based in transpersonal theory. Waldorf education was developed by Rudolph Steiner, an Austrian philosopher and educator. Steiner was heavily influenced by Goethe's belief that the quality of people is determined by their "moral imagination." Steiner's theoretical work synthesized scientific thinking with spiritual inquiry; he used the word *anthroposophy* to identify this synthesis. Steiner was attacked in his later years by right-wing nationalists (Nazis) and orthodox religious groups for his nonconventional thinking.

Steiner (1975) was concerned with the person's inner development, with "reconnecting the inwardness of man with the universe or seeing how man and the universe are part of the common physical spiritual linkage" (p. 6). According to Steiner, "The outer world with all its phenomena is filled with divine splendor, but we must have experienced the divine within ourselves before we can hope to discover it in our environment" (p. 7).

Steiner outlines his approach to education in *Education of the Child in the Light of Anthroposophy* (1975), which begins with an explanation of how the nature of the child forms the basis of Waldorf education: "We shall not set up demands nor programmes, but simply describe the child-nature. From the nature of the growing and evolving human being, the proper point of view for Education will, as it were, spontaneously result" (p. 8). He states that child development occurs in seven-year cycles. At each stage, or during each seven-year period, the child has a different

"body." Steiner calls the first "body," which lasts to about age seven, the
*physical* body. During this period it is important that the physical environment be appropriate, so that the body can develop. Steiner suggests
that toys and games allow for fantasy and imagination, but recommends
that children should not be given commercial toys, only those they can
work with, such as homemade dolls and picture books with movable figures. He also believes that songs, music, and dance are important to the
child's development at this age. Songs and hand-clapping are used in association with learning letters and words. Songs and music also provide
part of the ritual of each day at school. In kindergarten, sometimes the
day is started with the children and teacher sitting in a circle. At the end
of the day the teacher may stand at the door and say goodbye to each
child as he or she leaves.

During the elementary years, which begin around age seven, the
second "body," which Steiner calls the *etheric* body, develops. Education
in the elementary years is not based on the intellect, but imagination and
inner images. Steiner (1975) says, "The formation and growth of the etheric body means the moulding and developing of the inclinations and
habits, of the conscience, the character, the memory and temperament.
The etheric body is worked upon through pictures and examples, i.e., by
carefully guiding the imagination of the child" (p. 29).

Another characteristic of children this age (7–14) is their desire to
love and respect their teachers. According to Steiner, this need is met in
the Waldorf school by having the same teacher work with the child
throughout eight years of elementary school. Although other teachers
work with the children in special subject areas, the benefit of having one
teacher who works with the child over a long period is that this teacher
can clearly identify a child's strengths and needs.

Steiner believes that school work should not be overconceptualized
or overintellectualized during the elementary school years; this can occur
later, during adolescence. He suggests that older elementary students can
benefit from the study of history and biographies of great men and
women and that children in the early elementary school years study fairy
tales, legends, myths. Like Bettleheim (1977), Steiner believes that fairy
tales, myths, and parables can reach the inner child. Steiner also advocates the use of pictures and images, which can attune the inner life of
the student to the subject matter that is to be learned.

With regard to reading and writing, Steiner suggests that children
should write to explain their drawings. Colored pencils and crayons can
be used. After these experiences, reading can begin.

Education in language arts centers on feeling and artistic experience. According to Steiner (1976), "Speech is rooted in human feeling.
In feelings you are linked to the whole world and give whole world

sounds that in some way express these links of feeling" (p. 63). For language education to be grounded in feeling, words must make a connection with the inner life of the student.

Feeling is developed by exposure to the arts. In fact, central to Waldorf education is artistic activity, which involves focusing on how form, color, and rhythm are part of the wholeness of experience and how art and feeling are related to learning.

Movement exercises are also important when seen in this light. Steiner (1976) says:

> To think out gymnastic exercises from this point of view requires more than an intellectual knowledge of human anatomy and physiology. It requires an intimate intuitive knowledge of the connexion of the sense of happiness and ease with the positions and movements of the human—a knowledge that is not merely intellectual, but permeated with feeling. Whoever arranges such exercises must be able to experience in himself how one movement and position of the limbs produces an easy feeling of strength, and another, an inner loss of strength. (p. 44)

Richards (1980) suggests that the development of a sense of connectedness between oneself and the universe is at the heart of Waldorf education:

> I believe the tone of his [Steiner's] meaning is this: in every individual there is an instinctive sense of connection between oneself and the universe. There is a built-in sense of meaning and of identity. There is an inner world of spiritual being and of spiritual beings in which mankind, nature, and universe participate. A sense of connection with this inner spirit is what is ordinarily called religion. It is as natural to people as a sense of self and a feeling for nature. It is a crossing point between inside and outside. (p. 59)

This connection is also at the center of a transpersonal orientation. Although holidays are celebrated, there is no formal religious instruction in Waldorf schools. Instead, simple rituals are performed, such as sitting in a circle and singing. The focus on creative experience attempts to let children and teachers have access to their inner life.

For Steiner, education is an art. The teacher, like the artist, should be in touch with one's inner resources and creative imagination. Education should provide a form for expression of the inner life, so that it becomes perceptible. In elementary school, the "Main Lesson," which is taught in the morning, focuses on language development or mathematics; however, these subjects are integrated with art. In geometry, for example, the children make colored figures and string constructions. Richards (1980) describes the general form of the "Main Lesson":

> Each Main Lesson will call upon the child's powers of listening, of body movement, of thinking, and of feeling. Artistic activity is particularly related to the will: it is an experience of doing, of making. Artwork also invites the child's feeling for expressiveness and encourages a kind of intuitive thinking about how to get things done. In the early grades, some teachers allow the children to copy what has been drawn on the board so that they may learn to draw in ways they would not otherwise know. Other times the children draw freely. Variety exists, according to teacher and grade. (p. 25)

In the afternoon, the children learn other subjects, such as foreign languages, music handwork, gardening, physical education, and eurhythmy, a form of movement education that is usually performed to spoken poetry and attempts to put words into motion.

In high school (ages 14–21), the student moves to the next stage in Steiner's cycle, which he calls the *astral* period. This stage is characterized by independent judgment, abstract thinking, and critical assessment. The high school student works with various teachers, but will often study one subject with the same teacher over four years. High school subjects include math, chemistry, physics, botany, biology, zoology, geometry, foreign languages, handicrafts, music, and painting. Mythology is still part of the curriculum, as it is linked with history. Art continues to be integrated with all other subjects, as it was in elementary school. Richards (1980) describes the benefits that result from this practice: "Mathematics and geometry lead not only to capacities for thinking, but to surveyor's maps and projections of planetary orbits and artistic modeling. Connections between projective geometry and plant growth are rendered in drawings and in watercolor plates" (p. 39).

High school students share in running the school. They raise money for field trips by putting on dinners, bazaars, and plays. The culminating event of each year is a play put on by the seniors. According to Richards (1980), "The production makes use of their talents and skills which are considerable by this time in painting, arts, singing, acting playing, instruments, doing eurythmy, and bringing into their characterizations a depth of human understanding" (p. 40).

SYNECTICS    Gordon's approach to creative thinking, which he calls *synectics*, was initially used in industry, but has been designed for use in the classroom also. The use of metaphor is central to synectics. Gordon (1966) argues that an individual's creative skills can be enhanced by using metaphor. Classroom materials have been developed that encourage the student to use various forms of analogous thought. In general, synectics gets the student to make the kind of "intuitive leaps" that we associate with right-brain thinking.

SUPERLEARNING   Synectics focuses on creative thinking, whereas *superlearning* develops the individual's ability to recall large amounts of factual information. Superlearning, also known as *suggestology,* was developed by the Bulgarian psychologist Georgi Lozanov (1975) and is now being used in North America; it combines relaxation exercises, guided imagery, and music, to help the person absorb large amounts of information. For example, superlearning techniques have been used to learn foreign-language vocabulary. Some studies indicate that students using these methods learn as many as 1,000 words of a new language in a day. In North America, Ostrander and Shroeder (1979) have been spokespersons for the superlearning approach to education.

CONFLUENT EDUCATION   Synectics and superlearning are educational approaches that have a fairly specific focus. Other programs, such as *confluent education,* which combines both humanistic and transpersonal techniques, are more comprehensive in nature. Confluent education, originally developed by Brown (1971), refers to the confluence, or coming together, of the cognitive and the affective domains. The strongest influence on confluent education has been Gestalt psychology. A number of Gestalt techniques, which serve to ground both teacher and student in the "here and now" and to minimize game playing, are used in confluent education.

## Social-Change Orientation

A third current of thought in the transformation position focuses on social change. Some individuals, such as Brameld (1956), have argued that educators cannot ignore the social context of schooling; in fact, these educators contend that teachers should be on the forefront of social change. The major assumptions of the social-change orientation are as follows:

- Schools traditionally tend to reinforce apathy and passivity. Most social change theorists argue that the hidden curriculum of the school promotes conformity and counteracts the development of citizenship skills.
- Schools should embody the democratic process. Instead of reinforcing conformity, schools should be places where students and teachers can collaborate in an environment that promotes autonomy.
- Social-action projects can promote a sense of efficacy. Students' and teachers' participation in activities that promote social change can reduce apathy and help develop a sense that they can affect the social en-

vironment. According to Newmann (1975), social action projects can include the following:

> Telephone conversations, letter writing, participation in meetings, research and study, testifying before public bodies, door-to-door canvassing, fund-raising media production, bargaining and negotiation; and also publicly visible activity associated with the more militant forms. Social action can take place in or out of school and, if out of school, not necessarily in the streets, but in homes, offices, and work places. It might involve movement among several locations or concentration at one. (pp. 54–55)

- Social-change education can facilitate citizen participation in the political process. When citizen participation is low, the democratic process can be manipulated by a few special interest groups; by involving teachers and students in various aspects of the political process, social-change education can ensure a more broadly based democracy.
- Social change tends to rely on an ecological perspective. Problems are seen in terms of roles, structures, and norms that dominate social interaction. Thus, the focus is on changing these roles, structures, and norms rather than on changing a few individuals.
- Personal growth and social development are interrelated. Individual growth should be viewed in relation to the social environment; people cannot merely "do their own thing," but must be aware of the impact on society of their behavior. Conversely, if the individual can develop the ability to affect the environment, he or she will develop a sense of efficacy.

***Social-Change Programs.*** Two programs that focus on social change are Newmann's (1975) Social Action Model and Alschuler's (1980) Social Literacy Training.

FRED W. NEWMANN/SOCIAL ACTION MODEL   Newmann's program attempts to develop environmental competence in students—in other words, the ability to effect certain consequences in the environment. Students in this program study the political process and work in a social action project:

> Students may wish to work for better bicycle trails, improved low-income housing, a "freer" school, the opening of a drug counseling center, the election of a particular official. They might wish to oppose a curfew ordinance, high-rise apartments, credit practices of a particular firm, or a school's dress code. (Newmann, 1975, p. 55)

The Social Action model is described in more detail in *The Educational Spectrum*.

ALFRED ALSCHULER/SOCIAL LITERACY TRAINING  Whereas Newmann's Social Action Model focuses on the student, Alschuler's Social Literacy Training stresses teacher involvement in problems at the school level. Alschuler based his model on the work of Paulo Freire, a Brazilian educator, who has exerted a strong influence on social change educators in the United States. Freire's book, *The Pedagogy of the Oppressed* (1972), outlines an approach to teaching illiterate peasants in Brazil. He developed a method for teaching basic literacy skills to Brazillian students that involves raising their social awareness. Freire describes how individuals can move through different stages, leading ultimately to a stage in which they are able to take action to overcome oppression. In the first stage, the *magical conforming stage*, people are passive and do not see their situations as oppressive. In the next stage, the *naive reforming stage*, individuals assume that problems can be solved without reference to larger social structures. At the third level, the *critical transforming stage*, people begin to analyze their culture and to become active participants in changing their own status through social action that aims at changing the larger social system.

To move toward the critical transforming stage, Freire developed a three-step procedure:

**1.** *Name the important conflicts in the situation.* In Brazil, a team of teachers, social workers, and psychologists working with Freire's program would enter a community and interview the people in that community. Through these discussions, the team would develop a list of key words to represent conflict situations in the society—for example, the word *slum* might be a key word. The teachers would introduce key words to the people in the community, in order to encourage analysis of the concept. They might ask, for example, "What are the causes of poverty? Why is housing inadequate in the slums?" The principle behind this technique is that, by generating interest in these key words, literacy is enhanced.

**2.** *Analyze the systemic causes of conflict.* Here the discussion goes beyond the immediate list of key words to analysis of the system that produces conflict. This analysis often focuses on various social, political, and economic factors that promote social inequality.

**3.** *Encourage collaborative action to resolve conflicts.* In this last step, Freire encourages individuals to work together to solve various social problems and to collaborate to overcome oppression.

Alschuler suggests that each of the three stages Freire identifies can be applied to teachers in schools. From a magical conforming perspective, things appear to be static and unchangeable. Statements such as "there will always be a group of bad kids" reflect this position. Teachers at this stage see their situation as fixed and see little opportunity to change it. These teachers often feel a sense of resignation and helplessness. In Alschuler's (1980) words, this "inaction is a form of passive collusion, though unconscious and unintentional, to maintain oppressive conflict-laden situations" (p. 13).

Alschuler suggests that in the next stage, naive reforming, individuals focus on themselves rather than on the system. At this stage, the individual will try to improve himself or herself; the system is accepted, so the onus for change lies with the individual.

People in the third stage, the critical transforming stage, are able to critically examine the structure in which they are working. The responsibility for change is no longer on the individual, but, instead, on people who work collaboratively to question and to deal with problems.

Alschuler has applied Freire's model for moving toward the critical transforming stage to his model for Social Literacy Training. This training involves working with people in schools to name, analyze, and solve social problems, particularly discipline problems. According to Alschuler (1980), Social Literacy Training can start in school with a small group of students. A Social Literacy group composed of four or five teachers names the "essential systemic causes of widespread problems." After examining causes, the group looks at alternative solutions and proposes some form of action. In one school system in which Alschuler (1980) worked for several years, a Social Literacy group came up with the following solutions to a variety of problems (pp. 40–41):

- The problem at hand was to find ways to reduce referrals to the office. Instead of sending students to the vice principal, teachers in the Social Literacy group made a "mutual aid agreement" based on the idea that disruptive incidents could be defused by sending the student to another teacher's class or by having one of the teachers in the Social Literacy group come into the class with the disruptive problem, to help deal with the problem. Referrals in this school were reduced by 75 percent.
- Some teachers were concerned about new legislation requiring education students to be "mainstreamed" into regular classrooms. The Social Literacy group worked with special-education teachers to develop an in-service program for the regular classroom teacher. During this process, they focused on developing new methods for individualizing instruction.
- The Social Literacy group identified the use of the intercom as a problem in the school, because its use was leading to long disruptions in the

classroom. The teachers met with the principal, who agreed to limit the use of the intercom.

- Teachers set up a "care" room in the school, where a teacher was available to give special help to students who needed it. The room also provided a cooling-down period for students. Teachers who participated in this project were entitled to send students to the room.

Alschuler (1980) comments on these solutions:

> These examples illustrate several unique characteristics of socially literate methods of reducing the discipline problem: (1) Socially Literate solutions do not blame individuals. Individuals cooperate to change the rules and roles of the system. (2) Social Literacy leads to multileveled solutions that win peace in interpersonal, classroom, and school-wide war games. (3) Socially Literate solutions yield a broad range of outcomes related to better discipline—fewer classroom conflicts, more learning of the subject matter discipline, greater disciple-ship and increased personal discipline. (p. 42)

Several techniques are used in Social Literacy groups. One, called the *nuclear problem-solving process,* is best done in a small face-to-face group of five or six teachers. There are four steps to this problem-solving method:

**1.** *Naming the problematic incident.* At the beginning, one teacher poses a problem. He or she has five minutes to do this. The problem can vary from a discipline problem to an interpersonal difficulty. In explaining the problematic incident, the teacher should focus on who was involved and what happened. Next, the teacher should identify what led up to this incident. Finally, the teacher should outline the consequences of the event. In other words, how did the people feel after the incident and what events occurred as a result of the incident?

**2.** *Identifying patterns of conflict.* Social Literacy groups should focus on patterns rather than on specific incidents. Successful solutions do not deal with isolated problems, but, instead, arise from an understanding of the underlying patterns. For example, one teacher who was having discipline problems in his classroom videotaped his classroom in order to identify an underlying pattern to the discipline problem. He discovered a pattern of outside interruptions that was causing the discipline problems. To find a solution to a problem, the brainstorming technique is used to develop as many solutions as possible. There is no limit on the number of alternatives and the group does not evaluate the alternatives as they are being proposed. The group should encourage unusual, creative solutions.

**3.** *Brainstorming alternative solutions.* The group also examines the "rules and roles that govern people's behavior" (Alschuler, 1980). Alschuler provides an example from one middle school in which there were a number of discipline problems. Instead of starting a school-wide "crackdown," the teachers examined the rules and found that they were inconsistent. The Social Literacy group developed a new student handbook, based on suggestions from students, teachers, and support staff.

**4.** *Developing democratic plans for implementing one solution.* The teacher who posed the problem in the first step chooses one of the solutions and discusses an action plan to implement that solution. The group should then agree on a follow-up method to check out how the solution is working.

Alschuler (1980, pp. 115–117) has developed a method for evaluating the nuclear problem-solving process. The process is more effective if the following guidelines are used:

• The problem is identified as a pattern of behavior.
• The analysis focuses on rules and roles rather individuals.
• The brainstorming generates a large number of alternatives.
• The people affected by the change in the rules are involved in providing a solution.
• The solution is developed by a consensus approach that is mutually satisfying to those involved.
• The solution provides a permanent solution to the problem.

The nuclear problem-solving process can also be used with students in the classroom. Alschuler (1980) gives an example of one teacher who used this process after first introducing an inquiry approach in his class to which the students were not responding:

> "It seemed to me that it would be a refreshing break, but didn't turn out that way. There was once a great deal of participation in this class, but it seemed to be breaking down. The same problems that were bothering me, also bothered the students. I decided to try the nuclear problem-solving technique with the class. We went through each step and came up with many solutions which were narrowed down to one which has worked very well. We mutually decided to revert back to the traditional text which was successful at the beginning of the semester. The interest and participation quickly returned. The main point here is that the students had some input in deciding what direction the class was going to take." (p. 152)

Alschuler (1980, p. 154) identifies three critical elements in implementing the problem-solving process in the classroom:

1. Teachers and students engage in dialogue
2. Teachers and students should speak true words about central conflicts
3. The metagoal of specific problem solving, in terms of Freire's stages of consciousness, is to develop critical consciousness, not magical or naive consciousness

These elements reflect Freire's influence on Alschuler's program for Social Literary Training.

NEO-MARXIST PROGRAMS AND THE HIDDEN CURRICULUM   The social change position today also is represented by Neo-Marxists, who see the school in terms of its social/cultural role. In the words of Apple and King (1977), Neo-Marxist educators,

> The curriculum field especially, among other educational areas, has been dominated by a perspective that might best be called "technological" in that the major interest guiding its work has involved finding the one best set of means to reach prechosen educational ends. Against this relatively ameliorative and uncritical background, a number of sociologists and curriculum scholars, influenced strongly by the sociology of knowledge in both its Marxist or "Neo-Marxist" and phenomenological variants, have begun to raise serious questions about this lack of attention to the relationship of school knowledge to extra-school phenomena. A fundamental basis for these investigations has been best articulated by Michael F.D. Young. He notes that there is a "dialectical relationship between access to power and the opportunity to legitimize certain dominant categories, and the process by which the availability of such categories to some group enables them to assert power and control over others." In essence, just as there is a relatively unequal distribution of economic capital in society, so, too, is there a similar system of distribution surrounding cultural capital. In advanced industrial societies, schools become particularly important as distributors of this cultural capital and play a critical role in giving legitimacy to certain categories and forms of knowledge. (p. 30)

The Neo-Marxists argue that schools reinforce the class divisions in society and that tinkering with school reform is not likely to be very productive because small curricular changes will not address the real economic and cultural problems that exist. Instead, society itself must be transformed and schools must be an integral part of this social transformation.

Neo-Marxists such as Michael Apple and Henry Giroux have placed a strong emphasis on analyzing the *hidden curriculum*. Giroux and Purpel's (1983) book, *The Hidden Curriculum*, includes the work of Apple, Anyon, Lundgren, Bowles, and Gintis, and, also, Jackson's (1968) classic description of the hidden curriculum.

Jackson is not a Neo-Marxist. His focus is not on the economic and social context of schooling, but, rather, on how the institutional life of the school affects the psychological life of the child. Jackson discusses three main themes in school life—crowds, praise or evaluation, and power. Students must constantly deal with these aspects of institutional life in order to survive or to succeed. Jackson states that the student "must also develop strategies for dealing with the conflict that frequently arises between his natural desires and interests on the one hand and institutional expectations on the other" (p. 17). The school bell is representative of the emphasis schools place on organizational efficiency as opposed to the pursuit of intrinsic interests. Jackson observes the effect of the school clock: "There seems to be no other way . . . but to stop and start things by the clock, even though this means constantly interrupting the natural flow of interest and desire for at least some students" (p. 16). Jackson also observes that the student knows that the teacher is the person who sets the "wheels of retributive justice" into motion when the behavior of the student does not meet institutional expectations. The teacher is also the person whose function often is to substitute institutional plans for the student's own interests. Although these plans may coincide with some student interests, Jackson concludes that usually the "students must learn to employ their executive powers in the service of the teacher's desires rather than their own. Even if it hurts" (p. 30).

Students employ a variety of strategies to meet teacher expectations, but most are self-alienating. One strategy is compliance—the student becomes a "good worker." In other words, he or she internalizes the school's standards as guidelines for behavior and as a principal source for value-making. Other strategies involve more devious tactics. One method cited by Jackson is the seeking of special favors. At one extreme, this strategy involves the use of false compliments and extreme competitiveness to seek the teacher's favor. Jules Henry (1963), in *Culture Against Man*, gives an example of this strategy in a fifth grade arithmetic lesson that is applicable to many other elementary and secondary school classes as well:

> Boris had trouble reducing 12/16 to the lowest terms, and could only get as far as 6/8. The teacher asked him quietly if that was as far as he could reduce it. She suggested he "think." Much heaving up and down and waving of hands by the other children, all frantic to correct him. Boris pretty unhappy, probably mentally paralyzed. The teacher quiet, patient, ignores the others and concentrates with look and voice on Boris. After a minute or two she turns to the class

and says, "Well, who can tell Boris what the number is?" A forest of
hands appears, and the teacher calls Peggy. Peggy says that four
may be divided into the numerator and the denominator. (p. 295)

Henry comments:

> Boris' failure made it possible for Peggy to succeed; his misery is the
> occasion for her rejoicing. This is a standard condition of the con-
> temporary American elementary school. To a Zuni, Hopi, of Da-
> kota Indian, Peggy's performance would seem cruel beyond belief,
> for competition, the wringing of success from somebody's failure,
> is a form of torture foreign to those non-competitive cultures. . . .
> In school the external nightmare is internalized for life. Boris was
> not learning arithmetic only; he was learning the essential night-
> mare also. To be successful in our culture one must learn to dream
> of failure. (pp. 295–296)

In other words, some students internalize the "nightmare of defeat" in
order to achieve or succeed in school and, in their own way, become self-
alienated by incorporating fear as a springboard to "success."

Jackson (1968) draws the conclusion that students learn to "employ
psychological buffers to protect them from some of the wear and tear of
classroom life" (p. 27). However, he states that detachment is not an
either/or state of affairs: "To anyone who has been in a classroom it is
also evident that some students end up being more insulated than others"
(p. 27). Jackson's observations lead him to the conclusion that "the dominant relationship in the classroom is quite impersonal when compared
with that which goes on in the home" (p. 29). Not only is the teacher–
student relationship often an impersonal one, but institutional pressures
encourage lack of communication among the students. Because the emphasis in many classes is on discipline or control, the students learn to not
communicate with one another, except in the manner prescribed by the
teacher. As Jackson puts it, "In a sense, then, students must try to behave
as if they were in solitude, when in point of fact they are not" (p. 16).

Like Jackson, the Neo-Marxists focus on institutional effects. However, they claim that the institutional life of the school is a microcosm of
the larger economic and social context. In the words of Giroux and
Penna:

> Viewed from the student's perspective, the classroom becomes a
> miniature work place in which time, space, content, and structure
> are fixed by others. Rewards are extrinsic, and all social interaction
> between teachers and students is mediated by hierarchically orga-
> nized structures. The underlying message learned in this context
> points less to schools helping students to think critically about the

world in which they live than it does to schools acting as agents of social control. (Quoted in Giroux and Purpel, 1983, p. 111)

## CONCLUDING COMMENTS

The transformation position consists of the following characteristics

*Context.* This metaorientation is rooted in an ecological paradigm that acknowledges the interdependence of phenomena. This paradigm is linked with various forms of mysticism, transcendentalism, and some forms of existentialism (e.g., Heidegger). Transpersonal psychology, with its stress on spirituality, and humanistic psychology provide the psychological base. Finally, this orientation is linked with social movements such as the Aquarian Conspiracy and other "New Age" activities (e.g., holistic health).

*Aims.* Self-actualization, self-transcendence, and social involvement are the principal goals of this orientation.

*Learning Experiences.* Learning focuses on integration of the physical, cognitive, affective, and spiritual dimensions; the curriculum tends to center around learning experiences that focus on interdisciplinary activities. Connections between disciplines, between one's inner and outer worlds, and between school and community are sought; the curriculum tends to be oriented around projects of a social nature or activities related to self-inquiry.

*Role of the Teacher.* Teachers in this metaorientation must first work on themselves. They tend to see life as a process of being and becoming. Teachers try to be in touch with their inner life, and, at the same time, to work on their communication skills so that they are in touch with their students. Finally, teachers will make links with the community, which will, in turn, facilitate student contact with the community.

*Evaluation.* Evaluation, to some extent, may include conventional modes that focus on skill and subject mastery. However, there is usually a strong emphasis on informal and experimental forms of evaluation, including student self-evaluation, feedback from peers and the teacher, and student interaction with teachers in critiquing the curriculum.

### The Transformational Position and the Berlak Dilemmas

*Whole Child versus Child as Student.* In the transformation position, the emphasis is on the whole child. The teacher acknowledges that intellectual development cannot be isolated from emotional, social, physical, and moral development. However, within the transformation position there are often different emphases; the transpersonal educator focuses on inner development, whereas the social change educator stresses social consciousness.

**Teacher Control versus Child Control.** Educators within this position assert that students should have as much control as possible over their own learning. This assumption is based on a romantic view of the child that has been articulated by Rousseau, Tolstoy, and Neill. Many transformation educators advocate letting students assess their own work or at the least letting them have a role in the determination of standards.

**Personal Knowledge versus Public Knowledge.** Teachers working within the transformation position usually focus on the importance of personal as well as public knowledge. From the transformation perspective, knowledge is always filtered through personal perception and, thus, one of the main tasks of education is to facilitate awareness of these perceptions. The work of Combs (1975), in particular, deals with what he calls *perceptual psychology*.

**Knowledge as Content versus Knowledge as Process.** Because of the emphasis on personal perception within the transformation position, knowledge is viewed more as process than as content. It is rarely seen as something that is "fixed" or separate from the individual; rather, knowledge is viewed as being rooted in personal meaning. Transformation educators have turned to the "new physics" to support their claim that even in the "hardest" science the observed cannot be separated from the observer.

**Intrinsic Motivation versus Extrinsic Motivation.** The transformation educators' view of perception influences their conception of motivation as primarily an intrinsic phenomenon. Therefore, the teacher tries to relate the subject matter to student interests and concerns; learning and development will flow naturally if the proper connection can be made between the external curriculum and the inner life of the student.

**Learning Is Holistic versus Learning Is Molecular.** In the transformation position, the emphasis is on holistic learning. In fact, holistic learning is at the heart of the transformation position. The transformation educator asserts that students should learn to see relationships between themselves and their social environment, and between themselves and all aspects of the curriculum. Connections can be perceived by going within (e.g., meditation) and by acting consciously in the social realm.

***Each Child Unique versus Child Has Shared Characteristics.***
Although the basic emphasis in the transformation position is on seeing
the child as unique, and teachers within this position try to see each child
as an individual and to respond to each individual's needs and concerns,
there is a recognition in this position that all individuals share common
concerns, such as the need for meaning and connectedness.

***Learning Is Social versus Learning Is Individual.*** In the transformation position, learning is seen as both social and individual. For example, the humanistic and transpersonal orientations tend to focus on
the individual, whereas the social change orientation, by definition,
stresses social interaction. Sometimes these different conceptions have
been effectively integrated. At other times they have been dichotomous;
for example, within the progressive education movement, the romantic
and the social thrusts were at opposite ends of the spectrum.

***Child as Person versus Child as Client.*** Teachers within the transformation position try to work with the child as a whole person rather than
as a client. The emphasis in this position is to acknowledge the inner subjectivity of the child and base one's responses on an awareness of this subjectivity.

***Arguments for and against the Transformation Position.*** Teachers
working within the transformation position may emphasize one of the
more specific orientations over the others. Certainly, the most popular of
these orientations has been the humanistic. Although it reached its peak
in the early 1970s, it continues to exert considerable influence. At the
center of the humanistic orientation is a respect for personhood. In the
words of Theodore Rozak (1979):

> The experience of personhood. . . . has the same uncanny feeling of
> a truth always known, but only now called up to remembrance.
> Those who have awakened to the summons of self-discovery, who
> have found their way to the point of saying, *"I matter, I* am *special,*
> there is something *more* in me waiting to be discovered, named, lib-
> erated," will never take back the words. Under the pressure of that
> declaration of uniqueness, the most venerable institutions may be
> shaken to their foundations, the worthiest political movements may
> collapse as they are deserted by people whose sense of personhood
> will not allow them to follow and obey as part of an organized mass.
> (p. 27)

Parents today are asking that their children's needs be respected.
One could argue that special education programs have been developed,

in part, from the humanistic concern that all children, no matter what their disability, should be treated equally and humanely. Mainstreaming has been advocated as a way of ensuring that students with handicaps are not placed in some marginal situation away from other children. Humanistic education has had its strongest impact at this level, where educational systems and other organizations simply cannot override individual needs on an arbitrary basis. Institutions may try and, in some cases, succeed, but there is now a general recognition that people have a right to exercise personal autonomy. Humanistic education has contributed to bringing this about.

Humanistic education has been hindered by certain factors. First, there has been an inadequate theoretical base. Despite the pioneering efforts of Rogers and Maslow, few coherent theoretical frameworks for humanistic programs have been developed. Instead, much of the thinking has consisted of polemical introductory statements to a set of personal growth strategies. Another problem is that these strategies have sometimes been manipulative; when used in the classroom, some of these strategies have been psychologically threatening and have unnecessarily invaded the student's personal privacy; teachers have sometimes used these strategies without thinking through the consequences and then trouble has erupted in the community. The research on many of the humanistic programs has been limited. Admittedly, these programs are very difficult to assess, but there have been few systematic attempts to gather data about the impact of these programs.

Transpersonal education counters one of the deficiencies of humanistic education. As mentioned in Chapter 6, the work of Wilber, Pribram, Capra, and others offers a more demanding and satisfying conceptual picture than those offered by humanistic psychologists. However, the impact of transpersonal psychology has been limited as far as education is concerned. Most transpersonal programs, such as Waldorf education, lie on the edge of the education system. The impact of transpersonal education will probably be related to the fate of the larger cultural movement identified as the Aquarian Conspiracy. If the principles associated with the Aquarian Conspiracy appeal to larger groups of people, then transpersonal education could have a larger impact on schools, However, its growth will be hampered by the separation in the schools between church and state and the reluctance to focus on spirituality in the classroom.

Social change education also has not had a broad impact on schools. However, in our view, Alschuler's "Social Literacy Training" could appeal to teachers. It offers a collaborative approach to countering many of the difficulties teachers face in schools. "Social Literacy Training" does not isolate the teacher, but, rather, fosters collaboration in examining the systemic causes of school problems. This approach, particularly its focus on patterns and relationships, is congruent with the ecological approach advocated in this text.

## REFERENCES

Apple, M.W., & King, N.R. (1977). What do schools teach? In Weller, R.H. (Ed). *Humanistic Education*. Berkeley, CA: McCutchan.

Alschuler, A. (1980). *School discipline: A socially literate solution*. New York: McGraw-Hill.

Aspy, D.N., & Roebuck, F.N. (1977). *Kids don't learn from people they don't like*. Amherst, MA: Human Resource Development Press.

Bettleheim, B. (1977). *The uses of enchantment*. New York: Vintage.

Brameld, T. (1956). *Toward a reconstructed philosophy of education*. New York: Holt, Rinehart and Winston.

Brown, G.I. (1971). *Human teaching for human learning: An introduction to confluent education*. New York: Viking.

Combs, A. (1974). *The professional education of teachers*. Boston: Allyn and Bacon.

————. (1975). The personal approach to good teaching. In Read, D.A., & Simon, S.B. (Eds.). *Humanistic education sourcebook*. Englewood Cliffs, NJ: Prentice-Hall.

Counts, G. (1932). *Dare the schools build a new social order?* New York: Day.

Freire, P. (1972). *The pedagogy of the oppressed*. New York: Herder and Herder.

Froebel, F. (1887). *The education of man*. New York: Appleton-Century-Crofts.

Gazda, G., Asbury, F., Balzer, F., Childers, W., Deselle, R., & Walters, R. (1973). *Human relations development: A manual for educators*. Boston: Allyn and Bacon.

Giroux, H., & Purpel, D. (1983). *The hidden curriculum*. Berkeley, CA: McCutchan.

Gordon, T. (1974). *T.E.T., Teacher effectiveness training*. New York: Peter Wyden.

Gordon, W.J.J. (1966). *The metaphorical way of knowing*. Cambridge, MA: Porpoise Books.

Graubard, A. (1972). *Free the children: Radical reform and the free school movement*. New York: Pantheon.

Henry, J. (1963). *Culture against man*. New York: Vintage.

Jackson, P. (1968). *Life in classrooms*. New York: Holt, Rinehart.

Kirschenbaum, H. (1975). What's humanistic education? In Roberts, T.B. (Ed.). *Four psychologies applied to education*. Cambridge, MA: Schenkman.

Kozol, J. (1967). *Death at an early age*. Boston: Houghton Mifflin.

————. (1978). *Children of the revolution*. New York: Delacorte.

Lockwood, A. (1976). A critical view of values clarification. In Purpel, D., & Kerwin, R. *Moral education: It comes with the territory*. Berkeley, CA: McCutchan.

Lozanov, G. (1975). The nature and history of the suggestopedia system of teaching foreign languages and its experimental prospects. *Suggestology and Suggestopedia Journal*.

Miller, J. (1981). *The compassionate teacher*. Englewood Cliffs, NJ: Prentice-Hall.

Neill, A.S. (1960). *Summerhill: A radical approach to child rearing*. New York: Hart Publishing Co.

Newmann, F. W. (1975). *Education for citizen action: Challenge for secondary curriculum*. Berkeley, CA: McCutchan.

Ostrander, S., & Shroeder, L. (1979). *Superlearning*. New York: Delacorte Press.

Purkey, W.W. (1970). *Self-concept and school achievement*. Englewood Cliffs, NJ: Prentice-Hall.

————. (1978). *Inviting school success: A self-concept approach to teaching and learning*. Belmont, CA: Wadsworth.

Rathbone, C.H. (1971). The implicit rationale of the open education classroom. In Rathbone, C.H. (Ed.). *Open education: The informal classroom*. New York: Citation Press.

Raths, L.E., Merrill, H., & Simon, S.B. (1978). *Values and teaching: Working with values in the classroom*. Columbus, OH: Merrill.

Ravitch, D. (1983). *The troubled crusade: American education 1945–1980*. New York: Basic Books.

Richards, M.C. (1980). *Toward wholenss: Rudolph Steiner education in America*. Middleton, CT: Wesleyan University Press.

Rousseau, J.J. (1955). *Emile*. New York: Everyman's Library. (Original work published 1911).

Rogers, C. (1983). *Freedom to learn for the 1980s*. Columbus, OH: Charles Merrill.

Rozak, T. (1979). *Person/planet: The creative disintegration of industrial society*. Garden City, NY: Anchor Press/Doubleday, 1979.

Silberman, C. (1970). *Crisis in the classroom*. New York: Random House.

Steiner, R. (1975). *Education of the child in the light of anthroposophy*. London: Anthroposophic Press.

————. (1976). *Practical advice to teachers*. London: Rudolph Steiner Press.

Troyat, H. (1980). *Tolstoy*. New York: Crown Publishers, Harmony Books.

Weinstein, G., & Fantini, M. (1970). *Toward humanistic education: A curriculum of affect*. New York: Praeger.

Weinstein, G., Hardin, J., & Weinstein, M. (1976). *Education of the self*. Amherst, MA: Mandala.

Wilber, K. (1983). *A sociable god*. New York: McGraw-Hill.

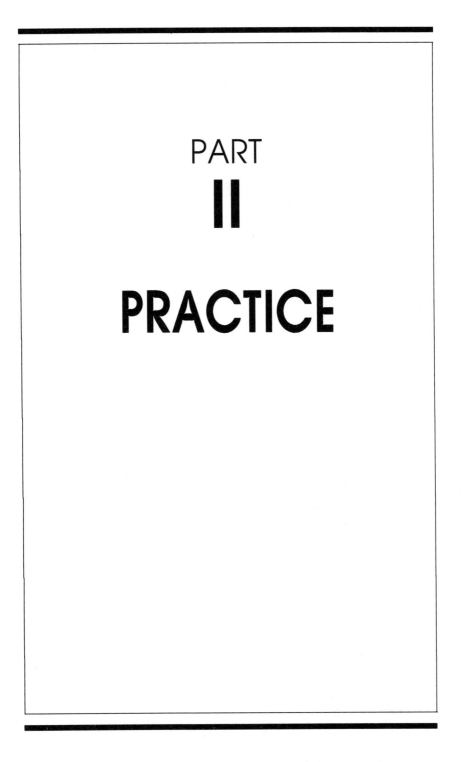

PART

II

PRACTICE

# 8 CURRICULUM COMPONENTS

We turn now from the curriculum orientations to an examination of key elements commonly associated with curriculum development: 1) aims and objectives, 2) content, 3) teaching strategies/learning experiences, and 4) organization of content and teaching strategies. Evaluation is sometimes included in this set of components, but we treat this element of the curriculum process separately in Chapters 13 and 14. The focus in this chapter is on examining curriculum aims and objectives, content, and teaching strategies/learning experiences from the perspective of the three major curriculum positions; in Chapter 9, we examine how curriculum theorists have integrated these curriculum components in various teaching models.

## AIMS/DEVELOPMENTAL GOALS/OBJECTIVES

### Aims

Aims provide overall direction or guiding images for curriculum development. Ideally, a statement of aims should reflect a well-developed position that is rooted in a particular conception of philosophy, psychology, and society. We present here two statements of aims, as examples of the many different kinds of statements that have been formulated (Tables 8.1 and 8.2). The first of these statements (Table 8.1) comes from the Florida Department of Education.

Like the statement issued by the Florida Department of Education, most statements of goals reflect more than one major curriculum position. This statement, for example, reflects both transmission and transaction influences. Statement I(a) is transmission-oriented, as it focuses on

## TABLE 8.1 Florida Department of Education

### Goals for Student Development

**Goal Area I.** *Communication and Learning Skills.* All students shall acquire, to the extent of their individual, physical, mental, and emotional capacities, a mastery of the basic skills required in obtaining and expressing ideas through the effective use of words, numbers, and other symbols.

  a. All students shall achieve a working knowledge of reading, writing, speaking, and arithmetic during the elementary school years, accompanied by gradual progress into the broader fields of mathematics, natural science, language arts, and the humanities.

  b. All students shall develop and use skills in the logical processes of search, analysis, evaluation, and problem-solving, in critical thinking, and in the use of symbolism.

  c. All students shall develop competence and motivation for continuing self-evaluation, self-instruction, and adaptation to a changing environment.

**Goal Area II.** *Citizenship Education.* All students shall acquire and continually improve the habits and attitudes necessary for responsible citizenship.

  a. All students shall acquire knowledge of various political systems with emphasis on democratic institutions, the American heritage, the contributions of our foreign antecedents, and the responsibilities and privileges of citizenship.

  b. All students shall develop the skills required for participation in the processes of public and private political organizations and for influencing decisions made by such organizations, including competence in judging the merits of competing political ideologies and of candidates for public office.

**Goal Area III.** *Occupational Interests.* All students shall acquire a knowledge and understanding of the opportunities open to them for preparing for a productive life, and shall develop those skills and abilities which will enable them to take full advantage of those opportunities—including a positive attitude toward work and respect for the dignity of all honorable occupations.

  a. All students shall acquire knowledge of and develop an understanding of the fundamental economic structure and processes of the American system, together with an understanding of the opportunities and requirements for individual participation and success in the system.

  b. All students shall develop those occupational competencies consistent with their interests, aptitudes, and ability which are prerequisite to entry and advance in the economic system, and/or academic preparation for acquisition of technical or professional skills through post-high school training.

  c. All students shall develop competence in the application of economic knowledge to practical economic functions (such as planning and bud-

**TABLE 8.1** *Continued.*

geting for the investment of personal income, calculating tax obligations, financing major purchases, and obtaining desirable employment).

**Goal Area IV.** *Mental and Physical Health.* All students shall acquire good health habits and an understanding of the conditions necessary for the maintenance of physical and emotional well-being.

    a. All students shall develop an understanding of the requirements of personal hygiene, adequate nutrition, and physical exercise essential to the maintenance of physical health, and a knowledge of the dangers to mental and physical health from addiction and other aversive practices.

    b. All students shall develop skills in sports and other forms of recreation which will permit life-long enjoyment of physical exercise.

    c. All students shall develop competence in recognizing and preventing environmental health problems.

    d. All students shall acquire a knowledge of basic psychological and sociological factors affecting human behavior and mental health, and shall develop competence for adjusting to changes in personal status and social patterns.

**Goal Area V.** *Home and Family Relationships.* All students shall develop an appreciation of the family as a social institution.

    a. All students shall develop an understanding of their roles and the roles of others as members of a family, together with a knowledge of the requirements for successful participation in family living.

    b. All students shall understand the role of the family as a basic unit in the society.

**Goal Area VI.** *Aesthetic and Cultural Appreciations.* All students shall develop understanding and appreciation of human achievement in the natural sciences, the social sciences, the humanities and the arts.

    a. All students shall acquire a knowledge of major arts, music, literary and drama forms, and their place in the cultural heritage.

    b. All students shall be active in one or more fields of creative endeavor, and develop skills in the creative use of leisure time.

    c. All students shall acquire competence in the critical evaluation of cultural offerings and opportunities.

**Goal Area VII.** *Human Relations.* All students shall develop a concern for moral, ethical, and spiritual values and for the application of such values to life situations.

    a. All students shall acquire the greatest possible understanding of and appreciation of themselves as well as of persons belonging to social, cultural, and ethnic groups different from their own, and of the worthiness of all persons as members of society.

    b. All students shall develop skill in interpersonal and group relationships, and shall recognize the importance of and need for ethical and moral standards of behavior.

Source: Florida Department of Education, *Goals for Education in Florida* (Tallahassee, Fla.: State Department of Education, © 1972), pp. 6–9. Reprinted by permission.

basic skill development, whereas I(b), with its emphasis on problem-solving skills, is a transaction-oriented statement. However, most of the aims in this statement are transmission-oriented, because they emphasize basic knowledge in various subject areas; this emphasis is consistent with the competency thrust within the state of Florida.

The second goal statement comes from the Province of Ontario in Canada (Table 8.2).

This statement of aims in Table 8.2 is for the most part transaction-oriented and even includes some transformation-oriented statements. Transaction-oriented statements include statements 1.3.1, 1.3.2, 1.3.8, 1.3.9, and 1.3.13; for example, statement 1.3.1 emphasizes "observing, sensing, inquiring, creating, analysing, synthesizing, evaluating and communicating," and statement 1.3.8 focuses on practical problem solving in a variety of contexts. Transformation-oriented statements include statement 1.3.5, which stresses artistic expression in relation to personal perception and experience, and statement 1.3.6, in which the stress on self-worth reflects a humanistic orientation.

We believe it would be useful if the statements of aims formulated by states or by boards of education were to include preambles stating the assumptions that lie behind the aims. We have composed the short preambles that follow as examples of preambles that reflect the different curriculum positions, although, of course, most preambles would, in reality, reflect a combination of positions and orientations.

***Transmission Position Preamble.***   Our schools should prepare students for their proper role in society. Schools can accomplish this through an emphasis on basic literacy and computational skills and by inculcating in students values that bind our society together. In our elementary schools, the basics should be taught and teachers should use methodologies, such as mastery learning, that have proven effective in teaching basic skills. Although other subjects such as art and music are important, the main emphasis in these formative years should be on mastery of the essential skills. In high school, the basic academic subjects such as English, math, science, history and a second language should make up a core curriculum; electives should be provided, but the basic focus of secondary schools is on mastery of these core subjects. A student graduating from our schools should be competent in basic skills and also be prepared to uphold the values and traditions that are central to our society.

***Transaction Position Preamble.***   Students should be prepared to perform complex tasks in the modern world. Our schools should instruct students in thinking and problem-solving skills. This basic emphasis should begin in the elementary years and continue through secondary school. To achieve this goal, the method by which subjects are taught should focus on processes that are central to problem solving and inquiry within academic disciplines. As students are engaged in these processes, they should learn both the subject matter and a variety of inquiry skills, including identifying assumptions, developing hypotheses, testing one's assumptions and hypotheses through various analytic procedures and empirical methods, and stating one's conclusions. Students should also learn how to apply critical-thinking skills in the social realm, so that they can make intelligent decisions in a democratic context. The basic role of education, then, is to teach our students how to reason, analyze, and make intelligent decisions in a variety of contexts.

***Transformation Position Preamble.*** Our schools should assist students in becoming full human beings. To do this, they must foster in students a positive self-concept, an awareness of the spiritual dimension of life, and a strong social commitment. School should not deny the importance of learning basic skills, but should integrate these tasks with the emotional, physical, social, and spiritual dimensions of life. In fact, it is this interrelatedness that is at the center of our educational system. We feel it is important for students to see the connections and relations between themselves and the world around them, as well as the relationships among the various disciplines that they study. By seeing these connections, we hope to bring into society students who feel a deep sense of responsibility to their ecological and social environment.

## Developmental Goals

After a general statement of aims has been formulated, there is a need to develop more specific goals. This is an intermediate step between general aims and instructional objectives. In this step, aims are broken down into general growth patterns, which may or may not be age-related. The breakdown of a general goal into more specific levels provides the teacher with some conception of student growth that can be used as a framework for achieving that particular goal. For example, consider aim 1.3.13 in the statement of aims for the Province of Ontario: "Develop values related to personal, ethical or religious beliefs and to the common welfare of society." Here one might adopt the Kohlberg scheme of moral development as a guide teachers can use in diagnosing and assessing stages of moral development.

It is also possible to break down skills into levels of complexity. Bloom's (1956) taxonomy of educational objectives is an example of how cognitive goals are broken down into various levels. The levels Bloom identifies are as follows:

1. Knowledge: Recall of basic information
2. Comprehension: Understanding the knowledge

## TABLE 8.2  Province of Ontario: The Goals of Education

The Ministry of Education in Ontario strives to provide in the schools of the province equal opportunity for all. In its contribution to programs, personnel, facilities, and finances, the ministry has the overall purpose of helping individual learners to achieve their potential in physical, intellectual, emotional, social, cultural, and moral development. The goals of education, therefore, consist of *helping each student to:*

**1.  Develop a responsiveness to the dynamic processes of learning**
Processes of learning include observing, sensing, inquiring, creating, analysing, synthesizing, evaluating, and communicating. The dynamic aspect of these processes derives from their source in many instinctive human activities, their application to real-life experiences, and their systematic interrelation within the curriculum.

**2.  Develop resourcefulness, adaptability, and creativity in learning and living**
These attributes apply to modes of study and inquiry, to the management of personal affairs such as career plans and leisure activities, and to the ability to deal effectively with challenge and change.

**3.  Acquire the basic knowledge and skills needed to comprehend and express ideas through words, numbers, and other symbols**
Such knowledge and skills will assist the learner in applying rational and intuitive processes to the identification and solution of problems by:
a)  using language aptly as a means of communication and an instrument of thought;
b)  reading, listening, and viewing with comprehension and insight;
c)  understanding and using mathematical operations and concepts.

**4.  Develop physical fitness and good health**
Factors that contribute to fitness and good health include regular physical activity, an understanding of human biology and nutrition, the avoidance of health hazards, and concern for personal well-being.

**5.  Gain satisfaction from participating and from sharing the participation of others in various forms of artistic expression**
Artistic expression involves the clarification and restructuring of personal perception and experience. It is found in the visual arts, music, drama, and literature, as well as in other areas of the curriculum where both the expressive and receptive capabilities of the learner are being developed.

**6.  Develop a feeling of self-worth**
Self-worth is affected by internal and external influences. Internally it is fostered by realistic self-appraisal, confidence and conviction in the pursuit of excellence, self-discipline, and the satisfaction of achievement. Externally it is reinforced by encouragement, respect, and supportive evaluation.

**TABLE 8.2** *Continued.*

**7. Develop an understanding of the role of the individual within the family and the role of the family within society**
Within the family the individual shares responsibility, develops supportive relationships, and acquires values. Within society the family contributes to the stability and quality of a democratic way of life.

**8. Acquire skills that contribute to self-reliance in solving practical problems in everyday life**
These skills relate to the skilful management of personal resources, effective participation in legal and civic transactions, the art of parenthood, responsible consumerism, the appropriate use of community agencies and services, the application of accident-prevention techniques, and a practical understanding of the basic technology of home maintenance.

**9. Develop a sense of personal responsibility in society at the local, national, and international levels**
Awareness of personal responsibility in society grows out of knowledge and understanding of one's community, one's country, and the rest of the world. It is based on an understanding of social order, a respect for the law and the rights of others, and a concern for the quality of life at home and abroad.

**10. Develop esteem for the customs, cultures, and beliefs of a wide variety of societal groups**
This goal is related to social concord and individual enrichment. In Canada it includes regard for:
a) cultural diversity;
b) national identity and unity.

**11. Acquire skills and attitudes that will lead to satisfaction and productivity in the world of work**
In addition to the appropriate academic, technical, and interpersonal skills, this goal relates to good work habits, flexibility, initiative, leadership, the ability to cope with stress, and regard for the dignity of work.

**12. Develop respect for the environment and a commitment to the wise use of resources**
This goal relates to a knowledgeable concern for the quality of the environment, the careful use of natural resources, and the humane treatment of living things.

**13. Develop values related to personal, ethical, or religious beliefs and to the common welfare of society**
Moral development in the school depends in part on a consideration of ethical principles and religious beliefs, a respect for the ideals held by others, and the identification of personal and societal values.

From *OSIS Ontario Schools: Intermediate and Senior Divisions*, Toronto, Canada: Ontario Ministry of Education, 1983, pp. 3–4. Reprinted with permission.

3. Application: The ability to use generalizations and to apply principles to specific situations
4. Analysis: The ability to break down a concept or idea into its components
5. Synthesis: The ability to combine a number of unorganized elements into a unified whole
6. Evaluation: The ability to assess concepts, theories, and materials according to selected criteria.

Bloom, then, has developed a broad developmental sequence for intellectual growth. However, each of these components can be made more specific in order to apply them to classroom instruction. For example, Bloom also has participated in developing taxonomies for the affective and the psychomotor domains (Krathwohl, Bloom, and Masia, 1964). Another example is the specific scheme of intellectual growth developed by Ross and Maynes (1982), which we described in Chapter 5. Growth schemes such as these explicitly define levels of increasing maturity in different areas (e.g., concepts, skills, affect), so that teachers have a clear conception of student progress.

In summary, developmental goals can range from rather broad developmental sequences (e.g., Piaget, Kohlberg, and Bloom) to much more specific sequences (e.g., Robinson, Ross, and Maynes).

## Instructional Objectives

The next level of objectives, used to define the objectives of a unit or lesson, is the most specific level in objective setting. At this level, we are confronted with the possibility of using behavioral objectives that define explicit student behaviors.

Robert Mager (1962) has been one of the principal proponents of writing behavioral objectives. He suggests that behavioral objectives should contain three components:

1. Expected student behavior
2. The appropriate conditions under which the behavior can be carried out
3. The degree of performance required

Here is one example of a behavioral objective: *The student will type a minimum of 60 words per minute on two different occasions.* The components in this behavioral objective are as follows:

1. Behavior—typing
2. Conditions—typing on a typewriter
3. Degree of performance—60 words per minute on two different occasions (Oliva, 1982, p. 364)

The big push in the 1960s and 1970s for behavioral objectives has diminished, having been absorbed by the competency-based education (C.B.E.)/mastery learning movement, in which the emphasis is on objectives that are related to instructional strategies and evaluation. Nonetheless, it is still worth examining some of the advantages and disadvantages of using behavioral objectives (Saylor, Alexander, & Lewis, 1981, pp. 172–177).

*Advantages*
- Communication is enhanced by making behavioral objectives as specific as possible.
- Behavioral objectives help in planning curriculum. These objectives assist the teacher in knowing what is expected and in designing programs that achieve the stated objectives. Popham (1969) states that "precise objectives stated in terms of measurable learner behavior makes it definitely easier for the teacher to engage in curricular decisions. The clarity of precisely stated goals permits the teacher to make more judicious choices regarding what ought to be included in the curriculum" (p. 40).
- Behavioral objectives assist with individualizing instruction. C.B.E. and mastery learning use behavioral objectives to clarify competency levels and to promote individualized instruction.
- Objectives stated behaviorally improve evaluation procedures. If objectives are too vague or general, evaluation is more difficult.

*Disadvantages*
- The complexity of human activity makes it difficult to reduce all worthwhile activities to behavioral terms. For example, complex thinking skills and some affective objectives cannot be stated in specific observable terms. Thus, the behavioral orientation can force educators into an inappropriate reductionism.
- Another objection arises from the fact that the use of behavioral objectives can cause us to lose sight of fundamental human goals. Because of their complexity, goals such as developing creativity, divergent thinking, and moral autonomy are seldom included in lists of behavioral objectives. Does this mean these goals should be excluded from school programs? Popham (1972) states: "There are more important goals which we have for our children which are currently unassessable. To the extent that such goals are extremely meritorious they are worth the risk of our pursuing them if we cannot reliably discern whether they have been accomplished" (p. 608).
- Although behavioral objectives can help clarify the direction of programs, they can also hinder teacher's flexibility and creativity. Sometimes, it is important that teachers "move" with students' interests in such a way that it takes the teacher beyond stated objectives. If com-

petency-based programs are stated in terms that are too rigid, the teacher may feel that he or she is working in a straitjacket.

- Saylor, et al., (1966/1974/1981) assert that "instruction based on the performance paradigm largely destroys the opportunities for student and teacher to engage in choice making, in probing alternative course of action, in risk-taking activities, in testing out intuitive hunches, and cooperatively selecting and planning activities that are meaningful and significant—in short, in engaging in the sheer joy of just 'growing up' of being oneself" (p. 177). Behavioral objectives remove the chance for children to explore randomly the kinds of divergent activities that are the source of creativity.

- Lists of behavioral objectives can be cumbersome. Specific competencies listed for each part of the curriculum can add up to an extremely long list of objectives. Some programs with behavioral objectives can be so long that the teachers cannot develop a curriculum that covers all of the objectives, given their limited time and resources.

Behavioral objectives generally are used within a transmission framework. They are inappropriate for either transaction- or transformation-oriented curricula, because complex problem-solving skills, personal growth skills, and social action strategies cannot be reduced to behavioral terms. The three curriculum orientations, then, can help the curriculum worker or teacher analyze what type of objectives are appropriate.

Zais (1976) argues that we tend to draw unnecessary dichotomies between behavioral and nonbehavioral objectives, and that a more useful approach is to focus on the concept of behavioral clues. Behavioral clues are probable indices of what might be expected, rather than a stipulation of prescribed behavior.

> To define the issue as a choice between behavioral and nonbehavioral objectives is a fallacy that may have been propagated by the very language inherent in the term "behavioral objectives." The term implies (1) that the observed behavior is equated with (as opposed to a *hypothesized manifestation of*) some level of a learner's attainment, and (2) that the objective (behavior) is an external fixed terminal point at which action is to be directed. This interpretation invites all of the criticisms of behavior objectives raised in the preceding paragraphs. On the other hand, utilizing operationalism as a liberally construed empirical method—i.e., in terms of the generation of behavioral clues—enables curriculum workers to retain the advantages of the empirical method while at the same time escaping the trap of rigid scientism. As curricular dogma, both behavioral and nonbehavioral objectives deserve rejection. (p. 316)

Zais, however, does not include many examples of what he means by a behavioral clue. Thus, it is difficult to get a sense of how practical his concept of a behavioral clue would be in curriculum planning.

Another factor that should be mentioned in a discussion of curriculum objectives is unanticipated outcomes. In defining goals, it is not possible to identify all the outcomes. For example, it is possible to develop a highly structured math program that achieves its stated goals but, as an unanticipated outcome, the students acquire an aversion to math. It is not enough, then, to develop a set of aims, developmental goals, and instructional objectives; the teacher also should be aware of unstated outcomes. After objectives have been selected, teachers and curriculum workers are faced with two basic questions—what will I teach (what will be the *content* of my lessons) and how will I teach this material (what teaching strategies will I use)?

## CONTENT

To answer the first question—What will I teach?—we must first determine what content or knowledge is appropriate. What is content? Saylor et al. (1966/1974/1981), offer the following definition:

> [Content is] those facts, observations, data, perceptions, discernments, sensibilities, designs, and solutions drawn from what the minds of men have comprehended from experience and those constructs of the mind that reorganize and rearrange these products of experience into lore, ideas, concepts, generalizations, principles, plans, and solutions. (p. 160)

This definition, although fairly broad, excludes skills and affect.

The word *content* is used interchangeably with terms such as *subject matter, knowledge, concepts,* and *ideas.* Traditionally, content has been organized into subjects or disciplines. This subject orientation falls within the transmission position; any curriculum that is highly content-oriented tends to be part of the transmission position. However, even transformation educators identify topic areas (e.g., women's studies, nuclear war) they feel are important.

### Criteria for Selecting Content

In selecting content, curriculum workers will emphasize various criteria. Generally, the criteria for choosing content fall into the following categories:

- Psychological criteria
- Social/political criteria

- Student interest criteria
- Student readiness criteria
- Utilitarian/practical criteria
- Philosophical criteria

***Psychological Criteria.*** These criteria focus on how learning theory can be applied to the teaching of subject matter. For example:

- Content should relate to themes or concepts, because this facilitates retention and understanding of new information.
- Content should be organized logically and coherently, so that students can identify relationships within the subject matter.
- Students should learn to apply knowledge to different contexts.
- Content should be integrated with process activities and with the affective dimension.
- Content should be taught in a "spiral" manner, so that ideas are reinforced and developed.
- Advance organizers (concepts) should be presented at the beginning of units, to facilitate understanding of the content.

Specific criteria can reflect an overall curriculum position. For example, the concept of an advance organizer is associated with Ausubel (1963) and with the transaction position generally, whereas integrating content with the affective dimension is a criterion that can be associated with the transformation position.

***Social/Political Criteria.*** Another set of criteria used to select content is political and social criteria. For example, there is a general consensus today that content in the school curriculum should not be sexist or racist; thus, textbooks are reviewed to ensure that they do not present unfavorable stereotypes of women or ethnic groups, such as pictures portraying women in their narrow, traditional role rather than in a range of roles and activities. Social criteria can be categorized within the different curriculum positions:

*Transmission Criteria*
- Content should help maintain a strong national consensus.
- Content should assist in the inculcation of traditional values.
- Content should not be too controversial or include topics that undermine traditional values.

*Transaction Criteria*
- Content should allow students to make decisions about public policy dilemmas that occur in a democratic society.

- Content should include a wide range of social issues and various value positions that are part of a democratic society.
- Content should support democratic values, such as the principle of individual dignity, a belief in individual intelligence, and pluralism, and more specific rights, such as the rights to due process and to freedom of speech.
- Content should promote participation in the democratic process and a sense of democratic community.

*Transformation Criteria*
- Content should foster students' awareness of cultural and economic forces that influence their lives.
- Content should foster students' commitment to working for positive social change.
- Content should be related to pressing social concerns.
- Content should be integrated with social action.

**Student Interest Criteria.**   Another criterion for selecting content is that subject matter should be related to the interests and maturity level of the learner. For example, a model of curriculum development created by Weinstein and Fantini (1970), which we discuss in detail in Chapter 9, uses the concerns and interests of the learner as the main criterion for selecting content. In the 1960s, student interest was strongly emphasized and the word *relevant* was used frequently to justify the inclusion of content based on student interest. This movement led to curriculum as "fashion"; mini-courses were developed in secondary schools that reflected the most recent trends and interests. The excesses of this movement in turn provided the impetus in the late 1970s and early 1980s to stress core curriculum activities.

Dewey (1902) argued that student interests should be only a starting point for curriculum development: "Interests in reality are but attitudes toward possible experiences; they are not achievements, their worth is in the leverage they afford, not in the accomplishment they represent" (pp. 99–100). In Dewey's view, student interests should be integrated with subject matter and problem solving to lead to a reconstruction of experience.

**Student Readiness Criteria.**   Another factor related to selection of content is the student readiness level. These criteria come from developmental psychology. For example:

- Content should be related to the internal frameworks held by students. These frameworks are related to stages of cognitive development.
- The complexity level of the content needs to be articulated, so that student framework can be matched with appropriate content level. The

proper match between content and student readiness level will spur pupil growth; an inappropriate match will lead to ineffective instruction. Therefore, teachers need skills in diagnosing student frameworks and readiness levels.

- Content should be related to the "invented ideas" of students (see Ch. 5, pp. 97–98). Students can develop "ideas" in certain subject areas, such as science, that are different from the "official" body of knowledge and research findings in a given subject area. Thus, the content selected should teach students the generally accepted ideas and knowledge in a subject area.

***Utilitarian/Practical Criteria.***  Utility criteria focus on content that will be socially useful, or, in other words, knowledge that students will need in order to be employed when they become adults. Bobbitt's (1924) study of society, for example, reflects an emphasis on utility as a criterion for selecting curriculum content. The emphasis on utility and job skills is currently undergoing a revival, as schools attempt to bolster their programs for teaching vocational and technical skills. Computer studies also reflect the current focus on providing programs in schools that help students to develop skills that will make them readily employable. The emphasis in curricula on utility can be counterposed to an emphasis on liberal arts studies.

Practicality criteria focus on the feasibility of including specific learning material in the school curriculum. For example, a school might want to provide computer studies but be unable to meet the expenses of doing so. A practicality criterion may run counter to a utility criterion. For instance, the choice to offer computer studies would reflect the utility criterion, whereas the excessive cost of acquiring computer equipment may not be practical.

Practicality criteria can also provide barriers to innovations; for example, a teacher might be interested in pursuing social action projects, but the practical and legal obstacles to such activities may be prohibitive. Practicality is often used as a criterion to support transmission-oriented curricula.

***Philosophical Criteria.***  Philosophical criteria focus on epistemological issues and basic value positions. The following examples of philosophical criteria for selecting content are grouped according to the curriculum position each reflects:

*Transmission*
- Content should be broken down into small, manageable components.
- Because transmission educators tend to view knowledge within various subjects as "fixed" and "objective", the curriculum should contain content that is central to these major subject areas.

- Content should be that which can be organized according to its own inherent logic.

*Transaction*

- Content should be that which can be subjected to various analytic processes.
- The curriculum should contain content that can be used in problem-solving activities.
- Content should not be an end itself, but a means to facilitating cognitive growth in students.

*Transformation*

- Content should place as much priority on personal knowledge as on public knowledge.
- Content should be that which can be personally appropriated by the learner, because personal appropriation of knowledge leads to personal and social transformation.
- Content should be that which can be easily integrated with the various domains (e.g., cognitive, affective, psychomotor) and learning processes.
- Content should help the learner view knowledge in terms of relationships; knowledge is viewed holistically rather than atomistically.

The various kinds of criteria that are used to select content often are applied unconsciously. The three major curriculum orientations provide us with a framework for examining with greater clarity the types of criteria we use to select curriculum content; this enables us to make conscious decisions about curriculum content—decisions that reflect our particular orientation to schooling.

## TEACHING STRATEGIES/LEARNING EXPERIENCES

How does a teaching strategy (instruction) differ from content (curriculum)? In our view, the difference is more one of degree than of kind. We define *curriculum* as an intentional set of interactions that facilitate learning and development. In curriculum, the focus is on the global—or a macro set of interactions; one attempts to develop an overall sense of where the teaching–learning process is leading. In *instruction,* the focus is on the immediate, or a micro set of interactions; the teacher designs an immediate set of learning experiences to achieve specific objectives.

Content and teaching strategies, when used in the classroom, are inseparable. However, for purposes of discussion, we need to look at each of these elements separately. In the previous section, we discussed the issues and criteria used in selecting content; in this section, we discuss issues related to and criteria for choosing teaching strategies or learning experiences—terms we use interchangeably.

Some teaching strategies are based on models of teaching that are rooted in various theoretical systems; others are not tied to any specific theoretical base. Saylor et al. (1966/1974/1981) define various types of teaching strategies:

- Lecture
- Discussion/questioning
- Community activities
- * Group investigation
- Independent learning
- * Inquiry learning
- Instructional system design
- * Jurisprudential
- Practice/drill
- * Programmed instruction
- * Role playing
- * Simulation
- * Synectics
- Viewing/listening

* Indicates a model of teaching (see Joyce & Weil, 1980).

In developing this list of strategies, Saylor et al. have relied in part on Joyce and Weil's (1980) work related to models of teaching. In our view, this list creates some confusion, because the teaching strategies that are models of teaching are rooted in specific theoretical systems, whereas other strategies, such as the lecture method, are not tied to any specific theoretical orientation.

## Models of Teaching

What is a *model of teaching*? According to Joyce and Weil (1980), "It is a plan or pattern that can be used to shape curriculum (long-term course of studies), to design instructional materials, and to guide instruction" (p. 1). A model is based on a particular concept of a learning environment (i.e., a particular orientation). In other words, each different model of teaching provides a different overall conception of curriculum. Although we have some reservations about some of the specific models, we think that the general concept of teaching models is congruent with the orientations approach.

Joyce and Weil argue that there is not one best approach to teaching; rather, there are several alternatives that are appropriate in different contexts; in *Models of Teaching* (1980), they describe 22 models, which they place within four families representing the Joyce–Weil conception of four orientations to curriculum:

1. Information processing models
2. Personal models
3. Social interaction models
4. Behavioral models.

These models are shown in Tables 8.3–8.6.
Joyce and Weil (1980) assert that there are six common components to each model.

   **1.** *Orientation.* This includes the goals, assumptions, and principles and concepts underlying the model. Orientation is the component that clearly separates a model of teaching from a simple teaching strategy such as a lecture.

   **2.** *Syntax.* This refers to the stages in the model. In other words, what steps does the teacher employ in using the model?

   **3.** *Social system.* This refers to the roles and relationships that teachers and students develop when the model is in use; the teacher plays a directive role in some models, and, in others, the teacher is more of a facilitator of inquiry. There are varying degrees of structure in the social system. In some models there is a great deal of structure, whereas in others the amount of structure is minimal.

   **4.** *Principles of reaction.* This refers specifically to teacher activity; in some models the teacher responds to students in a directive manner and in other models the teacher is an equal partner in inquiry.

   **5.** *Support system.* This refers to the human and technical resources that are essential to the use of the model. Some models require unique personal skills; others require appropriate learning materials.

   **6.** *Instructional and nurturant effects.* These effects include the direct (instructional) and indirect (nurturant) outcomes of instruction. The nurturant effects result from the student's presence in the learning environment; they arise, in part, from the "hidden curriculum" associated with the model. A curriculum worker or the teacher needs to examine both instructional and nurturant effects to determine whether a model is appropriate for his or her classroom.

   The concept of a teaching model is a useful one because it takes instruction beyond a collection of unrelated techniques to a level where

### TABLE 8.3   Information Processing Models: A Selection

| Model | Major theorist | Mission or goal |
|---|---|---|
| Inductive thinking and<br><br>Inquiry training | Hilda Taba<br><br>Richard Suchman | Designed primarily for development of inductive mental processes and academic reasoning or theory building, but these capacities are useful for personal and social goals as well. |
| Scientific inquiry | Joseph J. Schwab (also much of the curriculum re-form movement of the1960s) | Designed to teach the research system of a discipline, but also expected to have effects in other domains (sociological methods may be taught in order to increase social understanding and social problem-solving). |
| Concept attainment | Jerome Bruner | Designed primarily to develop inductive reasoning, but also for concept development and analysis. |
| Cognitive growth | Jean Piaget<br>Irving Sigel<br>Edmund Sullivan<br>Lawrence Kohlberg | Designed to increase general intellectual development, especially logical reasoning, but can be applied to social and moral development as well (see Kohlberg, 1976). |
| Advance organizer | David Ausubel | Designed to increase the efficiency of information-processing capacities to absorb and relate bodies of knowledge. |
| Memory | Harry Lorayne<br>Jerry Lucas | Designed to increase capacity to memorize. |

Bruce Joyce, Marsha Weil, *MODELS OF TEACHING*, 2nd Ed. © 1980, p. 10. Reprinted by permission of Prentice-Hall, Inc., Englewood Cliffs, N.J.


strategies are rooted in conceptual frameworks. In our view, however, many of the models identified by Joyce and Weil have become outdated and do not represent state-of-the-art work in the various orientations. This is particularly true of the information processing and the personal models.

The information processing models Joyce and Weil present do not

## TABLE 8.4   Behavioral Models: A Selection

| Model | Major theorist | Mission or goals |
|---|---|---|
| Contingency Management | B. F. Skinner | Facts, concepts, skills |
| Self-Control | B. F. Skinner | Social behavior/skills |
| Relaxation | Rimm & Masters, Wolpe | Personal goals (reduction of stress, anxiety) |
| Stress Reduction | Rimm & Masters, Wolpe | Substitution of relaxation for anxiety in social situation |
| Assertive Training | Wolpe, Lazarus, Salter | Direct, spontaneous expression of feelings in social situation |
| Desensitization | Wolpe | |
| Direct Training | Gagne, Smith and Smith | Pattern of behavior, skills |

Bruce Joyce, Marsha Weil, *MODELS OF TEACHING*, 2nd Ed. © 1980, p. 13. Reprinted by permission of Prentice-Hall, Inc., Englewood Cliffs, N.J.

## TABLE 8.5   Personal Models: A Selection

| Model | Major theorist | Mission or goals |
|---|---|---|
| Nondirective Teaching | Carl Rogers | Emphasis on building the capacity for personal development in terms of self-awareness, understanding, autonomy, and self-concept. |
| Awareness Training | Fritz Perls William Schutz | Increasing one's capacity for self-exploration and self-awareness. Much emphasis on development of interpersonal awareness and understanding as well as body and sensory awareness. |
| Synectics | William Gordon | Personal development of creativity and creative problem-solving. |
| Conceptual Systems | David Hunt | Designed to increase personal complexity and flexibility. |
| Classroom Meeting | William Glasser | Development of self-understanding and responsibility to oneself and one's social group. |

Bruce Joyce, Marsha Weil, *MODELS OF TEACHING*, 2nd Ed. © 1980, p. 11. Reprinted by permission of Prentice-Hall, Inc., Englewood Cliffs, N.J.

**TABLE 8.6   Social Interaction Models: A Selection**

| Model | Major theorist | Mission or goals |
| --- | --- | --- |
| Group Investigation | Herbert Thelen<br>John Dewey | Development of skills for participation in democratic social process through combined emphasis on interpersonal (group) skills and academic inquiry skills. Aspects of personal development are important outgrowths of this model. |
| Social Inquiry | Byron Massialas<br>Benjamin Cox | Social problem-solving, primarily through academic inquiry and logical reasoning. |
| Laboratory Method | National Training Laboratory (NTL), Bethel, Maine | Development of interpersonal and group skills and, through this, personal awareness and flexibility. |
| Jurisprudential | Donald Oliver<br>James P. Shaver | Designed primarily to teach the jurisprudential frame of reference as a way of thinking about and resolving social issues. |
| Role Playing | Fannie Shaftel<br>George Shaftel | Designed to induce students to inquire into personal and social values, with their own behavior and values becoming the source of their inquiry. |
| Social Simulation | Sarene Boocock<br>Harold Guetzkow | Designed to help students experience various social processes and realities and to examine their own reactions to them, also to acquire concepts and decision-making skills. |

Bruce Joyce, Marsha Weil, *MODELS OF TEACHING*, 2nd Ed. © 1980, p. 12. Reprinted by permission of Prentice-Hall, Inc., Englewood Cliffs, N.J.

reflect the latest research in cognitive processes. For example, they do not mention Posner's (1982) instructional model, which does reflect the most recent research in this area. Posner states that instruction occurs when the teacher presents a set of tasks to students together with appropriate resources and the students then interact with these tasks. His theory of instruction focuses on the research finding that students may bring inaccurate frames of reference to bear on the task. These student frameworks may run counter to concepts articulated by experts in the field. Therefore, he proposes that instructors need to identify these frames and then to use examples and analogies to point out to students discrepancies in their personal frameworks. Joyce and Weil also do not mention the work of other researchers who, like Posner, have developed instructional models to facilitate conceptual change (e.g., Driver & Erickson, 1983).

Posner's (1982) model is concerned essentially with inner cognitive processes related to goals and to operations.

> Goals (and, therefore, also learning outcomes) are not to be confused with behavioral objectives in the Mager/Popham sense. Goals refer to internal changes in the student which are not directly observable. These internal changes may be represented by the curriculum developer or researcher as lists, networks, or flowcharts.
>
> Similarly, the operations of a task are not to be confused with the traditional concept of instructional activities. The term 'operations' refers to internal actions presumably performed by students, typically their thought processes. I am more interested in how a student arrives at a problem solution than in the correctness of the answer. As a matter of fact, student mistakes are perhaps the most valuable but, for the most part, untapped source of useful information. If we could only learn enough about the relation between student thought processes and student mistakes, we might begin to focus our research and teaching more on mistakes, on tasks and less on achievement-test results. If we are to do this, we will need to develop the kinds of models of human thought processes currently under development in mathematics and physics. (p. 348)

Joyce and Weil's discussion of personal models also is somewhat dated. For example, they do not include Purkey and Novak's (1984) invitational learning model in their coverage of teaching models, even though it is more in use than some of the models they do mention; nor do they deal in a systematic way with models that focus on the transpersonal domain (e.g., Miller, 1981).

In summary, we advocate the use of teaching models because they are consistent with the orientations approach outlined in this text. However, we suggest that teachers and curriculum workers carefully examine all models before selecting one for use and be prepared to investigate new models.

## Criteria for Selecting Teaching Models

Criteria for selecting models include the following:

1. Models should be congruent with one's aims and developmental goals, one's overall purposes, and the predominant orientation(s) identified by the curriculum worker. Although teachers do not work from one single orientation, there should be a general match between one's position and the model selected. If a teacher is cognitively oriented, for example, a transpersonal model probably will be inappropriate.

2. Models should be congruent with the general environment of the school. In Chapter 11, we outline a model that describes institutional environments. In an institutional environment that is integrated and holistic, it is inappropriate to use a model that is highly behavioral in its orientation. However, this criterion does not mean that the teacher should avoid innovation if the environment is tradition bound. It only means that he or she needs to think carefully about how much room there is for innovation.

3. Models should be examined to see if they achieve mutiple goals. Mastery of a few models that achieve multiple goals is probably more productive than attempting to develop a large repertoire of models, each of which achieves only a few goals.

4. Models should be related to the student's framework or level of development. Some models are appropriate for students who can work in an unstructured setting, whereas other models are appropriate for students who prefer a structured learning environment.

In the list that follows, we link various criteria to the three major curriculum positions.

*Transmission Criteria*
- Models of teaching should contain clear, concise objectives.
- Models should be structured to enable the teacher to provide specific direction in the learning of content and skills.
- Models should allow for straightforward evaluation of instructional goals.
- Models should facilitate retention of content in traditional subject areas.
- Models should reinforce traditional values through instructional and nurturant effects.

*Transaction Criteria*
- Models should allow students to examine their own reasoning processes.
- Models should stimulate inquiry and investigation.

- Models should be based on a particular scheme of intellectual development.
- The role of the teacher in these models generally should be to stimulate probing by students and a process of mutual inquiry between student and teacher.

*Transformation Criteria*
- Models should involve students in social awareness and social change.
- Models should make connections between students' inner and outer worlds.
- Models should stimulate integration of subject areas.
- Models should focus on strategies that let students become aware of their own consciousness.
- Models should stress divergent thinking processes.
- Models should relate left-brain and right-brain thinking processes.

## ORGANIZING CONTENT AND TEACHING STRATEGIES

After the content and teaching strategies have been selected, the curriculum worker attempts to organize these elements. Stratemeyer, Forner, McKim, and Passow (1957) have outlined a number of questions that can be raised as one approaches this task:

### FUNDAMENTAL QUESTIONS IN CURRICULUM

1. How can balanced development be assured? What guarantees can there be that important areas of life in which students or teacher are insensitive to problems will not be neglected?
2. How can there be continuous growth from year to year without undesirable repetition or undesirable gaps in learning?
3. How can desirable depth of knowledge be assured? How is it possible to prevent learners from ending up with a smattering of superficial knowledge about many areas and little of the depth they need for genuine understanding?
4. How will the depth of command of special subject areas important to individual learners be assured? Where will the persons with specialized talents come from—the scientists, historians, linguists, artists, teachers, statesmen, philosophers of the future?
5. How can it be guaranteed that children and youth will become acquainted with the broad cultural resources which are part of our heritage and become skilled in drawing upon and using these resources in meeting life situations?
6. How can there be guarantees that choices of problems are not

trivial and do not represent transitory interests rather than basic concerns?

7. How can there be genuine group problems? Will there not actually be many times when extrinsic motivation will be needed if group study is desired? Does the point of view not logically lead to work that is completely individualized? (pp. 110–111)

Curriculum workers respond to these questions, in part, by focusing on scope and sequence. *Scope* refers to horizontal relationships in the curriculum and the attempt to maintain an appropriate balance in the curriculum. Scope raises the issue of whether subject matter is treated separately, or presented in an integrated manner. *Sequence* refers to vertical relationships in the curriculum. Zais (1976) claims that the main problem associated with sequence is the "difficulty of developing *cumulative and continuous* learning as students move through the curriculum" (p. 439). Taba (1962) argues that part of the difficulty with sequence is that it is linked only to content and ignores thinking skills that students learn in their interaction with content. We will now examine how the issues of scope and sequence are addressed by each of the major curriculum positions—transmission, transaction, and transformation.

## Scope

***Transmission Position.***   Transmission curricula are most often organized around subjects, disciplines, or broad fields. We discussed the advantages and disadvantages of subject organization in Chapter 3 (pp. 58–60); a complete discussion of the subject and the disciplines orientations is also found in *The Educational Spectrum* (Miller, 1983). A major problem with both subject and disciplines organization is fragmentation of learning materials. One attempt to respond to this problem is the broad-fields design, in which a number of subjects are combined into a broad field of study. In elementary school, reading, writing, spelling, and speaking are combined into language arts, and science, history, and geography are combined into environmental studies. It can be argued that, currently, the broad-fields design is the principal method of organizing curriculum at the elementary level, whereas organizers of secondary school curricula rely more on the subject design. However, Sizer (1984), in *Horace's Compromise,* argues that high school courses should be grouped into four broad fields: inquiry and expression, math and science, literature and the arts, philosophy and history. The National Commission on Excellence in Education's report, *A Nation at Risk* (1983), unlike Sizer, advocates a traditional subject approach to curriculum. This report recommends four years of English, three years of mathematics, three years of science, three years of social studies, a half-year of computer studies, and, for college-bound students, two years of a foreign language.

***Transaction Position.*** Curriculum developers working from a transaction perspective tend to move away from using subject matter as the basic mechanism for organizing the horizontal relationships in the curriculum. Instead, they turn to problem-centered designs for curriculum that focus on developing students' problem-solving skills. In the transaction curricula, however, the teacher and the school system select the problems that will be central to the curriculum; student interests are taken into account, but they do not override the views of the teacher and the school.

Metcalf and Hunt (1970) have proposed a curriculum that is built around critical social problems, specifically, the following four questions:

1. What kind of society now exists, and what are the dominant trends within it?
2. What kind of society is likely to emerge in the near future . . . if present trends continue?
3. What kind of society is preferable, given one's values?
4. If the likely and prognosticated society is different from the society that one prefers, what can the individual, alone or as a member of groups, do toward eliminating the discrepancy between prognostication and preference, between expectation and desire? (p. 360)

Other curricula that use problem-solving as a central focus for organizing the scope of curriculum include the Dewey-school model and a model recommended by Smith, Stanley, and Shores (1957).

***Transformation Position.*** From a transformation position, it is more difficult to identify a clear perspective on organizing the scope of a curriculum. Instead, several themes emerge. One theme is integration; for example, in Waldorf education the arts play a central role and language arts often are integrated with artistic activity. In confluent education, another transformation model, cognitive and affective experience are integrated. A second theme is the emphasis on learner choice and interest, which means the learner is allowed to define what will be studied. A third theme arises from the social change position, which places strong emphasis on having students identify issues that are socially relevant and encouraging them to work on problems that are vital to the community's interest. Thus, the scope of transformation curricula is linked with involvement in the community.

## Sequence

*Transmission Position.*   Generally, in transmission curricula sequencing, subject matter is ordered in a fixed hierarchy that often involves movement from simple to complex concepts. This type of movement is often used as an organizing principle in science. Chronology is another traditional ordering principle in transmission curricula. In history, for example, the traditional method of sequencing is to proceed from earlier times to the present day.

*Transaction Position.*   In transaction-oriented curricula, which tend to focus on the development of mental processes, various developmental theories have been used as organizers for sequencing. For example, the work of both Piaget and Kohlberg can be used as frameworks for linking learning experiences to stages of development. Similarly, Ross and Maynes's growth schema (see Chapter 5, pp. 104–107) represents another transaction perspective on sequencing.

*Transformation Position.*   It is difficult to identify a type of sequencing that is clearly representative of the transformation orientation. Humanistic educators tend to be suspicious of fixed hierarchies; instead, they are more concerned with horizontal relationships in the curriculum. However, the Wilber growth scheme (discussed in Chapter 6, pp. 129–132) can be viewed as a transformation approach to sequencing curriculum. Social change curricula, which focus on providing students with increasing responsibility in their social projects, also reflect the transformation approach. For example, Fred Newmann's social action curriculum (see Chapter 7, p. 159) has the student begin with study and research in the community before he or she becomes actively involved in a social action project.

Posner and Strike (1976) have developed a scheme for sequencing curricula in which learning experiences are grouped into five categories: (1) content-related sequences; (2) concept sequences; (3) inquiry-related sequences; (4) learning-related sequences; and (5) utilization-related sequences.

Content-related sequences relate content to phenomena and focus on space, time, and physical attributes. The space subcategory refers to bottom-to-top and closest-to-farthest sequences; the time subcategory refers to chronological sequencing of content and the principle of cause and effect; the physical-attributes subcategory (e.g., soft-to-hard) is often used in sequencing science content.

Concept sequences are based on class relations, sophistication, and logical prerequisites. In class-relations sequencing, the teacher introduces a general category (e.g., mammal) before teaching about its members (e.g., whale). In sequencing based on sophistication, the teacher moves from concrete to more abstract categories; for example, in science, the teacher would deal with Newtonian physics before moving to the theory of relativity. In logical-prerequisites sequencing, concepts are ordered according to some inherent logic in the concepts; in math, for example, the concept of set would be taught before the concept of number.

Inquiry-related sequences focus on principles for discovering or verifying knowledge, such as induction or deduction. With induction, the student studies specific instances before moving to generalizations; in deduction, the generalization is developed and then tested against specific cases.

Learning-related sequences are based on psychological principles of learning. For example, Piaget's, Kohlberg's, or Erikson's theories of developmental stages can be used to organize a sequence of learning experiences. Humanistic psychologists might use student interest as a principle for sequencing learning experiences; for example, the teacher would begin with activities that most interest students and move to those that are less interesting.

Utilization-related sequencing focuses on skill development and on practical applications of skills. In this type of sequencing, learning experiences might be organized on the basis of procedures; for example, a skill (e.g., swimming) will be taught in a manner that allows the student to learn the activity in the way it actually will be used.

Posner and Strike's sequencing scheme correlates in the following way with the three major curriculum positions: Transmission educators often focus on content- and utilization-related sequences; Transaction educators focus on concept-related, inquiry-related, and learning-related sequences; transformation educators focus on learning-related sequences based on student-interest criteria.

The main elements of curriculum—aims and objectives, content, teaching strategies, and organizational design—are outlined in the accompanying chart. The elements are summarized in relation to the major curriculum positions.

## REFERENCES

Ausubel, D. (1963). *The psychology of meaningful verbal learning.* New York: Grune & Stratton.

Bloom, B.S. (1956). *Taxonomy of educational objectives: Cognitive domain.* New York: McKay.

Bobbitt, F. (1924). *How to make a curriculum.* Boston: Houghton Mifflin.

Dewey, J. (1902). *The child and the curriculum.* Chicago: The University of Chicago Press.

Driver, R. & Erickson, G. (1983). Theories-in-action: Some theoretical and empirical issues in the study of students' conceptual frameworks in science. *Studies in Science Education, 10,* 37–60.

Florida Department of Education. (1972). *Goals for Education in Florida.* Tallahassee, FL: State Department of Education.

Joyce, B., & Weil, M. (1980). *Models of teaching.* Englewood Cliffs, NJ: Prentice-Hall.

Krathwohl, D.R., Bloom, B.S., Masia, B.B. (1964). *Taxonomy of education objectives, handbook II: Affective domain.* New York: McKay.

Mager, R. (1962). *Preparing instructional objectives.* Belmont, CA: Fearon Publishers.

Metcalf, L.E., & Hunt, M.P. (1970, March). Relevance and the curriculum. *Phi Delta Kappan.*

Miller, J. (1981). *The compassionate teacher.* Englewood Cliffs, NJ: Prentice-Hall.

———. (1983). *The educational spectrum: Orientations to curriculum.* New York: Longman.

National Commission on Excellence in Education. (1983). *A nation at risk.* Washington, DC: Government Printing Office.

Oliva, P. (1982). *Developing the curriculum.* Boston: Little, Brown.

Ontario Ministry of Education. (1984). *Ontario schools intermediate and senior divisions, Grades 7–12.* Toronto, Ontario: Ministry of Education.

Popham, W.J. (1969). Objectives and instruction. In Stake, R. (Ed.), *Instructional objectives.* Chicago: Rand McNally.

———. (1972). Must all objectives be behavioral? *Educational Leadership, 29,* 608.

Posner, G. (1982). A cognitive science conception of curriculum and instruction. *J. Curriculum Studies 14,* 343–351.

Posner, G., & Strike, K.A. (1976). A categorization scheme for principles of sequencing content. *Review of Education Research, 46*(4), 665–690.

Purkey, W.W., & Novak, J.M. (1984). *Inviting school success: A self-concept approach to teaching and learning.* Belmont, CA: Wadsworth.

Ross, J. & Maynes, F. (1982). *Teaching problem solving.* Toronto: Ontario Institute for Studies in Education.

Saylor, J.G., Alexander, W., & Lewis, A. (1981). *Curriculum planning for better teaching and learning* (4th ed.). New York: Holt, Rinehart and Winston.

Sizer, T. (1984). *Horace's compromise: The dilemma of the American high school.* Boston: Houghton Mifflin.

Smith, P.O., Stanley, W.O., & Shores, J.H. (1957). *Fundamentals of curriculum development.* New York: Harcourt, Brace & World.

Stratemeyer, F.B., Forner, H.L., McKim, M.G., & Passow, A.H. (1957). *Developing a curriculum for modern living* (2nd ed.). New York: Teachers College Press.

Taba, H. (1962). *Curriculum development: Theory and practice.* New York: Harcourt Brace Jovanovich.

Weinstein, G., & Fantini, M. (1970). *Toward humanistic education.* New York: Praeger.

Zais, R.S. (1976). *Curriculum: Principles and foundations.* New York: Harper & Row.

**SUMMARY CHART: Chapter 8**

| | *Transmission* | *Transaction* | *Transformation* |
|---|---|---|---|
| *Aims–Objectives* | Behavioral<br>Content-oriented | Complex intellectual skills | Integrated objectives (e.g., cognitive and affective) |
| *Content* | Knowledge viewed atomistically as "objective" and<br>Content should reinforce traditional values | Knowledge is related to mental processes and cognitive frameworks<br>Social content focuses on public policy questions | Personal knowledge is as important as public knowledge<br>Social content stresses identification and resolution of pressing social concerns |
| *Teaching Strategies* | Structured teaching approaches<br>Transmission of facts and values | Focus is on problem solving and analysis<br>Teaching strategies are matched to student developmental frameworks | Focus on connecting inner life of student to outer worlds<br>Divergent thinking is encouraged |
| *Organization* | Subject-centered<br>Hierarchical | Problem-centered<br>Developmental | Learner-centered<br>Integrative |

# CHAPTER 9 CURRICULUM DEVELOPMENT MODELS

In Chapter 8, we examined the key elements of curriculum, using the major curriculum positions to help analyze their applicability to curriculum design. In this chapter, we examine several models of curriculum development. Again, the major curriculum positions can help in our analyses of these models. For example, Gagne's (Gagne & Briggs, 1979) system, which is based on behavioral learning theory and is basically an atomistic view of curriculum development, is representative of the transmission position, whereas the Tyler (1949) rationale, perhaps the predominant curriculum paradigm (Tanner and Tanner, 1980), is a broadly based model that reflects both transmission and transaction influences. Two of the models discussed in this chapter lie clearly within the transaction position—the Taba (1962) model, which reflects a transaction-oriented conception of inquiry and thinking processes and the curriculum design model designed by Robinson, Ross, and White (1985), which is based on a transaction approach to cognition and problem solving. One model outlined in this chapter, developed by Weinstein and Fantini (1970), is representative of the transformation position; this model focuses on the needs and concerns of learners.

Finally, we outline in this chapter our own approach to curriculum development. In one sense, the major sections of this book (orientation, development, implementation, evaluation) represent the components of our model; we present our model here in relation to the three curriculum positions. Although this model reflects both transaction and transformation influences, it lies mostly within the latter position, because it links curriculum development with development of a clear awareness of one's social, philosophical, and psychological assumptions about curricula.

# A TRANSMISSION MODEL: GAGNE'S INSTRUCTIONAL-DESIGN SYSTEM

Competency-based education and instructional design theory are curriculum development models reflecting the transmission position. These models focus on reducing the curriculum components into elements that are clearly definable and measurable. Robert Gagne is one of the foremost proponents of instructional design systems. In *Principles of Instructional Design*, Gagne and Briggs (1979) describe a model based on educational technology. Educational technology is related to the following elements:

> (a) Interest in individual differences in learning, as seen in educa-.. tion and military research and development programs; in self-instructional devices such as those of Pressey (1950), and Crowder's (1959) branching programs; in computer applications to instruction; and in product-testing concepts for hardware; (b) behavioral science and learning theory, as seen in Skinner's emphasis upon contingencies of reinforcement and in his teaching machines (1968); and in Guthrie's contiguity theory (1935); and (c) physical science technology, as represented in motion-picture, television, and video-tape instruction; and in audio-visual devices to supplement printed media. (pp. 210–211)

Gagne advocates a "system approach" to the design of instruction that is based on "logical, systematic thinking" and "empirical test and fact finding." He claims that this approach to curriculum development is "closer to a science of education than other approaches to the design of instruction" (p. 214). According to Gagne, the main advantage of such an approach is that it provides a basis for an accountability system. Gagne's model includes 12 steps:

1. Needs analysis
2. Analysis of goals and objectives
3. Analysis of alternate ways to meet needs
4. Designing instructional components
5. Analysis of resources and constraints
6. Constraint-removal actions
7. Selecting or developing materials
8. Designing student-performance assessment
9. Field testing and formative evaluation
10. Adjustments, revisions, and further evaluation
11. Summative evaluation of systems
12. Operational installation

## Needs Analysis

The first step is to identify the need for course development. According to Gagne, perceived needs usually fall into three types: "(1) a need to conduct instruction more effectively and efficiently for some course which is already a part of the curriculum; (2) a need to revitalize both the content and the method for some existing course; or (3) a need to develop a new course" (p. 216). Gagne argues that as the tempo of change in society increases, educational needs should be reviewed more frequently, or else the lag between actual and needed curricula will widen rather than close.

## Analysis of Goals and Objectives

The next step in the process is to describe goals and objectives for the instructional system, working from general goals to specific objectives. If the curriculum moves in the opposite direction, from specific content to general goals, the teacher probably will repeat what has gone on before in the course. Gagne gives an example of one range of descending levels of specificity: "The K–12 curriculum; the K–12 science curriculum; the sixth grade science course; topic objectives within the sixth grade course; specific objectives within the lesson; subordinate capabilities for a specific objective; a particular communication in a lesson for one subordinate capability" (p. 217). In practical terms, the curriculum plan for a one-year course might include general goals, 3 unit objectives, and 20–30 specific objectives under the 3 units. The most specific level of objectives should be described in behavioral terms, so that measurement can take place.

## Analysis of Alternate Ways to Meet Needs

This step deals with what to teach and how to teach it. In the public school system, this step involves choosing the appropriate learning environment—e.g., classroom versus laboratory, large group versus small group, lecture versus individualized study, and choices among "problem-centered," "process-centered," or "content-centered" curricula. In Gagne's model, decisions about what should be taught are made according to transmission criteria such as those outlined in Chapter 8.

## Designing Instructional Components

Decisions at this point in the sequence involve the following procedures:

1. Planning the nature of materials for study
2. Specifying the method of studying the materials
3. Deciding between self-pacing and group-pacing of materials for presentation

4. Identifying the nature of the activities the learner is to engage in with respect to the materials, or with respect to the objectives
5. Planning how to keep track of student progress and how to direct such progress
6. Making explicit the role of the teacher in respect to materials and pupil progress
7. Scheduling group activities and the teaching methods to be employed
8. Deciding upon time limits for self-paced learning, or "open scheduling," if mastery rather than time is the scheduling constraint
9. Assessment of student performance
10. Devising "guidance" procedures, where options in objectives are offered, or where different "routes to the goal" are provided. (pp. 220–221)

## Analysis of Resources and Constraints

In this step, each component is examined in relation to available resources and constraints. For example, curriculum materials should be examined to ascertain whether commercial materials are appropriate or if system-based materials must be created. Other constraints also must be examined; for example, if the curriculum calls for students to go outside the school, the teacher must deal with legal and administrative constraints related to off-premise activities.

## Constraint-Removal Actions

Gagne claims that constraints arising from cost-effectiveness needs may be very difficult to remove; therefore, he argues, the price of "failure" (e.g., dropouts, delinquency, incompetent graduates) must be considered in any analysis of the cost effectiveness of educational programs. In his opinion, a few hardened criminals or a few dozen individuals on relief can cost more in taxes than it would cost to remove financial restraints in the educational system.

## Selecting or Developing Materials

In this step, the planner examines the relevant materials. This may involve both the purchase of instructional materials and the redesigning of materials that are currently in use. Gagne presents an example of this process:

> Suppose, for example, one is designing a course on "How to prevent future shock." A book on this topic could be examined to see if its

contents could help the learners achieve all or some of the specific objectives for the course. A search could be made to locate other relevant materials. One might need to design components of instruction in such a way that the teacher and the learners are shown how to use available materials to meet the objectives. (p. 223)

## Designing Student-Performance Assessment

The designer now turns to the development of assessment tools. Such tests enable the teacher to discover what a student has mastered and whether the student is ready to proceed to the next objective. Tests also allow the teacher to see if any student has failed on a small unit of study and, if so, to prescribe remedial instruction. If large numbers of students are not achieving in a particular area, the test will encourage the instructor to design new content or methodologies. The tests also assist in a summative evaluation of the curriculum.

## Field Testing and Formative Evaluation

Gagne suggests that the new system should first be tried with small groups of students or with a few individual learners in one-to-one situations. After these initial trials, the new system can be used in normal-sized classrooms. Data collected during field testing can be used for formative evaluation and program improvement, whereas summative evaluation occurs only after the program has been fully implemented.

## Adjustments, Revisions, and Further Evaluation

After the new program has been fully implemented, further refinements can be made. For example, after the system has been in use for several years, further feedback from teachers can be solicited. Gagne also encourages the use of what he calls *design objectives*; these are statements of objectives such as the following: "The new system will be considered satisfactory when 90 percent of students pass the minimum standard set for 90 percent of the objectives of the course, when the course is taught by regular teachers under normal conditions" (p. 226).

## Summative Evaluation of Systems

Summative evaluation is conducted after the new curriculum has been fully implemented, initial modifications have been made through formative evaluation, and the system has been in place for an extended period under normal conditions.

## Operational Installation

After the instructional system has been demonstrated to be effective through summative evaluation, the new curriculum is now ready for widespread use. Of course, adjustments must be made for each particular locale. For example, the new system may require adjustment to fit the time-scheduling pattern for a particular school.

The Gagne model, as well as other instructional-design systems, has received a great deal of attention in recent years. Many of the advantages and disadvantages of behavioral objectives, as discussed in Chapter 8 (pp. 183–84), also apply to instructional-design systems. In addition, several points pertaining specifically to instructional-design systems are worth noting here.

One problem is the claim that these systems are value-neutral. In Gagne's words, "It is pointed out that such an approach makes no pre-judgments about the nature of educational goals or about the objectives derived from them. Thus it encounters no difficulty in encompassing broad varieties of outcomes of learning" (p. 227). Clearly, this approach to curriculum development is primarily oriented to learning basic skills and mastering content. High-level cognitive skills and integrative curricula cannot easily be reduced to fit into Gagne's system; therefore, many transaction programs and most transformation programs could not be developed within this framework.

We also believe that Gagne's system does not provide adequately for curriculum implementation. He indicates that special training in the use of a new program would involve "workshops, or . . . arranging for the teachers to see demonstrations of the course conducted by a selected teacher who has been given special training in advance" (p. 225). The research on implementation, which is discussed in the Chapters 10 and 11, indicates that this type of limited approach to in-service training is inadequate. Programs that are much more comprehensive are needed to facilitate curriculum implementation.


## A MODEL COMBINING TRANSMISSION AND TRANSACTION PRINCIPLES: THE TYLER RATIONALE

In *Basic Principles of Curriculum and Instruction*, Tyler (1949) describes a model of curriculum development known as the *Tyler rationale*. This model deals with four basic questions:

1. What educational purposes should the school seek to attain?
2. What educational experiences can be provided that are likely to attain these purposes?

3. How can these educational experiences be effectively organized?
4. How can we determine whether these purposes are being attained? (pp. 1–2)

## What Educational Purposes Should the School Seek to Attain?

Tyler recommends that three sources be used for identifying objectives—the learner, the society, and the subject matter.

The learner is the first source of educational objectives. Tyler states that the learner's needs and interests should be identified. He focuses in particular on the needs of the learner, which he suggests can be identified through interviews, observation, tests, and questionnaires.

Study of contemporary life both in the local community and in society in general is the second source for deriving educational objectives. In a proposal similar to Bobbitt's (see Chapter 2, pp. 24–25), Tyler suggests that curriculum developers first classify life into various categories, such as religion, vocation, recreation, family, health, and consumption, and then develop a list of objectives relevant to each of these areas.

Tyler's third source is subject matter; the curriculum developer will expand his or her list of objectives by examining the various subjects to be taught and then creating lists of objectives that are derived from the content and the skills associated with the subjects.

After the curriculum group or the teacher has developed a list of objectives from the learner, the society, and the subject matter, Tyler suggests that the teacher use a screen drawn from philosophy and psychology in order to sort out the most important objectives. He points out that a school's philosophy can be an important factor in the process of screening objectives.

Tyler brings a number of factors into his model. In part, he was influenced by Dewey's work. This influence is reflected in Tyler's (1949) list of four values he believes schools should consider when formulating an educational philosophy.

> These four values are 1) the recognition of the importance of every individual human being as a human being regardless of his race, or national, social, or economic status; 2) opportunity for wide participation in all phases of activities in the social groups in the society; 3) encouragement of variability rather than demanding a single type of personality; 4) faith in intelligence as a method of dealing with important problems rather than depending upon the authority of an autocratic or aristocratic group. (p.22)

Tyler's model also draws on principles of learning as developed through research in educational psychology. In Tyler's (1949) view, "A psychology of learning not only includes specific and definite findings but it also involves a unified formulation of a theory of learning which helps to outline the nature of the learning process, how it takes place, under what conditions, what sort of mechanisms operate and the like" (p. 27). The curriculum developer's psychology of learning should be written down, so that its influence on the selection of educational objectives is clear. This statement then becomes part of the screen for selecting objectives.

The final step in developing a set of objectives is to state the objectives in a clear and concise way. Tyler (1949) contends that the real objective of education is to bring about "significant changes in the student's patterns of behavior" (p. 28). An objective should have two components—a behavioral component and a content component. Here are two examples of objectives that contain both of these components:

- To understand the basic principles of nutrition
- To analyze the causes that led to World War I and identify the most significant causes

Tyler (1949) stresses the importance of stating objectives in specific terms: "One can define an objective with sufficient clarity if he can describe or illustrate the kind of behavior the student is expected to acquire so that one could recognize such behavior if he saw it" (p. 38).

## What Educational Experiences Can Be Provided that Are Likely to Attain These Purposes?

After the objectives have been selected, student learning experiences need to be developed that will attain the stated objectives. Tyler defines a learning experience as the "interaction between the learner and the external conditions in the environment to which he can react" (p. 41). This statement, with its emphasis on interaction between the person and the environment, reflects a Deweyean influence. In Tyler's model a second major influence in regard to choice of learning experiences is behavioral psychology; this influence is evident in the way objectives are to be stated.

Tyler suggests that several criteria be used for selecting appropriate learning experiences. For example: learning experiences should allow the student to practice the behavior implied by the objective; students should obtain satisfaction from the learning experience; the learning experience should be appropriate to the student's background. Tyler outlines four general categories of possible learning experiences:

1. Development of thinking skills
2. Acquisition of information

**3.** Development of social attitudes

**4.** Development of student interests

## How Can These Educational Experiences Be Effectively Organized?

The third major element in the Tyler model is the organization of learning experiences for instruction. Tyler states that learning experiences can be organized according to continuity, sequence, and integration. *Continuity* refers to the vertical reiteration, or recurring opportunities to learn various skills. *Sequence* refers to student exposure to experiences that build upon each other. *Integration* refers to the horizontal relationships in curriculum materials—in other words, the relationships among different subjects in the curriculum. Interdisciplinary studies are an example of integration.

Tyler (1949) states that after general principles have been identified, curriculum development might proceed along the following lines:

> 1. Agreeing upon the general scheme of organization; that is, whether specific subjects, broad fields, or core programs are to be used. 2. Agreeing upon the general organizing principles to be followed within each of the fields decided on. This may mean, for example, that in mathematics the general scheme adopted involves an increasing abstraction of algebraic, arithmetic, and geometric elements which are treated together year after year in place of the principle of treating arithmetic elements first, then algebraic, and finally geometric. Or, it may mean an agreement in the social studies on the development of problems beginning with the community and moving out into the wider world, rather than the decision on the use of organizing principles based upon purely chronological considerations. 3. Agreeing upon the kind of low-level unit to be used, whether it shall be by daily lessons or by sequential topics or by teaching units. 4. Developing flexible plans or so-called "source units" which will be in the hands of each teacher as he works with a particular group. 5. Using pupil–teacher planning for the particular activities carried on by a particular class. This general operational procedure is increasingly used by various curriculum groups. (p. 66)

## How Can We Determine Whether These Purposes Are Being Attained?

The fourth and final step is to evaluate the effectiveness of the learning experience against the original objectives. Evaluation, Tyler states, should focus on changes in student behavior. Thus, pretests should be used, so that teachers can determine whether student performance improves in the designated areas. In the Tyler model, data is collected through tests, observation, interviews, questionnaires, and actual student products. Tyler insists that all evaluation procedures must relate to the original objectives.

Kliebard (1970) offers one of the most comprehensive analyses of the Tyler model. He states that one of the main problems with the model arises from the three sources it draws upon for educational objectives. Instead of attempting to integrate or relate the sources, this model simply lays them out side by side. Thus, in Kliebard's opinion, Tyler's model is eclectic, and is not integrative.

Kliebard also asserts that Tyler, in his presentation of subject matter as a source of objectives, does not make a distinction between content and objectives. Thus, there is confusion about the exact way in which subjects are to be sources of objectives. There are also difficulties in Tyler's conception of the needs of the learner. *Need* is an ambiguous term that inherently assumes a norm. However, in Kliebard's view, because Tyler is not specific regarding how needs should be derived from prior norms, "the concept of need turns out to be of no help insofar as avoiding central value decisions as the basis for the selection of objectives, and without that feature much of its appeal seems to disappear" (pp. 264–265).

Kliebard connects Tyler's use of studies of society as a source of educational objectives to the work of Bobbitt. However, he is very critical of Tyler's philosophic screen; in his opinion, Tyler implicitly avoids the difficulties of Bobbitt's cultural relativism by asserting that the philosophical screen will serve as a check on objectives derived from observation of society.

> We are urged only to make our educational objectives consistent with our educational philosophy, and this makes the choice of objectives precisely as arbitrary as the choice of philosophy. One may, therefore, express a philosophy that conceives of human beings as instruments of the state and the function of the schools as programming the youth of the nation to react in a fixed manner when appropriate stimuli are presented. As long as we derive a set of objectives consistent with this philosophy (and perhaps make a brief pass at the three sources), we have developed our objectives in line with the Tyler rationale. The point is that, given the notion of educational objectives and the necessity of stating them explicitly and consistently with a philosophy, it makes all the difference in the world what one's guiding philosophy is since that consistency can be as much a sin as a virtue. The rationale offers little by way of a guide for curriculum making because it excludes so little. (p. 267)

Kliebard also is critical of Tyler's approach to evaluation, because it ties evaluation so tightly to the original statement of objectives that there is no opportunity to identify unanticipated outcomes. In other words, Tyler's method of evaluation does not allow the teacher or evaluator to identify the overall effects of the course or curriculum. Instead, evaluation focuses on how the learning experiences fulfill the stated objectives.

Tanner and Tanner (1980) echo, in part, Kliebard's critique. They point out that Tyler presents the three sources of educational objectives as separate entities, and does not elaborate on possible interactions between these three sources. However, Tanner and Tanner generally are positive in their assessment of the Tyler model. They state that, by identifying the three sources of objectives, Tyler avoids the excesses of other curriculum theorists; as an example of such excesses, Tanner and Tanner cite the disciplines movement in the 1960s, which, in their opinion, would not have become so subject-oriented if it had kept the other two sources—the learner and the society—in perspective. Tanner and Tanner (1980) suggest that, despite the criticisms raised by Kliebard and others, the Tyler rationale remains the predominant curriculum paradigm (p. 96).

Several revisions of the Tyler rationale have been developed. Leyton Soto (1969) has collaborated with Tyler to produce a revision of the model in which the screen of philosophy and psychology precedes the three sources (e.g., subject matter, the learner, society). This is more in keeping with the model we outline in this book, because we believe that philosophy and psychology are parts of an overall metaorientation that forms the basis of one's curriculum position, which should precede selection of objectives. Leyton Soto argues that one's philosophical and psychological orientations can inform the examination of the three sources of objectives. Finally, unlike Tyler, Leyton Soto distinguishes between learning experiences and learning activities. Reflecting a behavioral influence, he says that learning experiences consist of behaviors that are written into the objectives, whereas learning activities are behaviors in which the learner engages, in order to achieve the particular objectives. In the Leyton Soto model, learning experiences are the terminal behaviors that are evaluated.

In sum, the Tyler model reflects two broad influences. First, Dewey's influence can be seen in Tyler's three broad sources of educational objectives. Second, the behavioral orientation of educators such as Bobbitt and Thorndike has influenced Tyler's conception that the purpose of education is to bring about change in student behavior. Tyler's model is eclectic; it spans a broad spectrum of educational perspectives reflecting both transmission and transaction influences. The fact that both transmission- and transaction-oriented educators can identify with various aspects of the model is one of the reasons this model has been so popular.

# TWO TRANSACTION MODELS: TABA AND ROBINSON

## The Taba Model

Taba (1962) argues for an inductive approach to curriculum development. She believes that teachers should develop curriculum and that curriculum should not be handed down from higher authorities. Her conception of the curriculum process is related to her conception of inquiry. In brief, she sees the process of developing curriculum as a logical sequence of steps that she calls "steps of inquiry in curriculum thinking and curriculum planning" (p. 347):

- Step 1: Diagnosis of needs
- Step 2: Formulation of objectives
- Step 3: Selection of content
- Step 4: Organization of content
- Step 5: Selection of learning experiences
- Step 6: Organization of learning experiences
- Step 7: Determination of what to evaluate and of the ways and means of doing it (p. 72)

There is an eighth step in Taba's model, which she calls "checking for balance and sequence."

Because Taba argues that curriculum work should begin with the design of units rather than a broad curriculum plan, her approach to developing a curriculum model is *inductive*. In the following section, we describe in detail Taba's model for developing a curriculum unit.

*Step 1: Diagnosis of Needs.*   In this step, the teacher identifies a number of needs that will form the basis of unit planning. How comprehensive this diagnosis is will depend on the nature of the unit.

*Step 2: Formulation of Objectives.*   Formulation of objectives should encompass the following areas:

1. Concepts or ideas to be learned
2. Attitudes, sensitivities, and feelings to be developed
3. Ways of thinking to be reinforced, strengthened, or initiated
4. Habits and skills to be mastered

Taba states that different units will place different degrees of emphasis on these four basic areas.

*Step 3: Selection of Content.*   The first two steps provide criteria for selecting content. State guidelines, as well as the "logic" of the subject matter, will also provide a framework for selecting content. Subject mat-

ter should be related to the grade level of the student. Thus, two important criteria for selecting content are the inherent logic of the subject
matter and the psychological or developmental level of the student. Selection of basic ideas also is important in the Taba scheme; fundamental
concepts of a subject or discipline are identified for the unit.

***Step 4: Organization of Content.***     Taba states that an "inductive logical
arrangement of the content and a psychological sequence for learning
experiences need to be established" (p. 359). In this step, the curriculum
is organized so that each succeeding idea or mental operation requires a
cumulative development of cognitive skills. At the center of this organizational structure is Taba's concept of thinking: "The very plan for the
unit is a method of teaching thinking" (p. 359).

In organizing content, Taba states that the first step is to determine
a topic and then to identify the basic ideas. For example, in a unit on
American peoples, topics were organized around the following basic
ideas:

1. The U.S. is a multiculture society; it is composed of many kinds
   of people, with many different backgrounds and styles of life.
2. These people came from many places, for many different reasons, and over a long period of time.
3. All people who move from one place to another have to make
   adjustments: they are not accepted at once, nor do they feel at
   home.
4. The wider the cultural distance of the home background from
   the new place, the more severe and difficult is the adjustment.
5. All people in the U.S. have contributed something to the shaping
   of the life, customs, strength, richness and well-being of this
   country. (Taba, 1962, p. 361)

In this unit, topics to be studied include various groups of people, such
as Germans, Poles, Irish, and so on.

The next step in organizing content is to establish the dimensions
of the topic; in the unit on American peoples, for instance, dimensions
include place of origin, time of arrival, place of settlement, reasons for
migration, nature of problems in adjustments, and the nature of contributions. The following questions represent these dimensions:

• Who came from which country?
• When?
• When settled?
• Why came?
• What problems and adjustments they had to meet?
• What contributions they made? (Taba, 1962, p. 361)

***Steps 5 and 6: Selection and Organization of Learning Experiences.*** To select learning experiences, Taba suggests that the teacher should ask a number of questions, for example: Is the experience appropriate for learning the main ideas? Does the experience promote "active learning"? Is the experience appropriate to the student's maturity level? Taba also feels that learning experiences should reflect a variety of experiences, including "reading, writing, observing, doing research, analyzing, discussing, tabulating, painting, constructing and dramatizing" (p. 364).

Taba (1962) outlines a sequence for organizing learning experiences: introduction, development, generalization, and application or summary. *Introduction* involves developing student interest and providing diagnostic evidence for the teacher. *Development,* or study, consists of learning activities that are designed to develop various aspects of the subject and to provide needed factual material. These activities include "reading, research, analysis of data, committee work, and study of various kinds." *Generalization* refers to students' attempts to put ideas together. According to Taba, this step can involve a good deal of comparing and contrasting and exploration of the reasons for similarities and differences. *Application* or *summary* is the stage at which the student applies generalizations to a larger framework.

This sequence for organizing learning experiences reflects Taba's conception of cognitive processes, particularly her emphasis on inductive inquiry.

***Step 7: Evaluation.*** The seventh step involves determining whether objectives have been met, diagnosis of the curriculum plan, and assessment of any changes in student behavior. Taba suggests a variety of formal and informal measures to assist in this assessment.

***Step 8: Checking for Balance and Sequence.*** In this step, a number of questions are asked, to assess the overall effectiveness of the unit:

> Are the ideas pertinent to the topic? Does the content outline match the logic of the core ideas? Is the sampling of detail as sharp as it could be? Do the learning activities provide a genuine opportunity for the development of the content ideas? Do the activities provide for the achievement of all the objectives as well as they might? Does the sequence of content and of learning experiences flow? Is there a proper cumulative progression? Is there a proper balance and alternation in the modes of learning: intake and synthesis and reformulation; reading, writing, oral work; research and analysis? (Taba, 1962, p. 378)

Taba recommends that the unit be tested after it has been completed. This allows teachers to assess the validity of the unit. The units can then be revised and modified as needed. Curriculum coordinators or supervisors may be involved in ensuring that the units adhere to basic principles and guidelines developed by the school system. This last step, then, leads to the development of a broad curriculum framework and a rationale that supports the overall direction of the material. Again, this is an inductive process, because the general principles and rationale for the curriculum are developed *after* the construction of specific units. Finally, Taba discusses strategies to implement the new curricula, many of which involve in-service training for teachers.

As mentioned previously, Taba's framework for curriculum and unit development reflects her cognitive-process orientation. In *The Educational Spectrum*, Miller (1983) discusses Taba's curriculum for social studies inquiry, which attempts to develop student thinking skills, particularly inductive thinking skills. For example, one of her classroom approaches calls for interpreting, inferring, and generalizing about data. This is similar to the sequence she suggests for developing a larger curriculum unit. In other words, her ideas about thinking, instruction, and curriculum development are closely interrelated. This interrelationship places her model of curriculum development clearly within the transaction position. We turn now to the Robinson model, which is also closely tied to a transaction view of cognitive processes.

## The Robinson Model

Robinson, Ross, and White's (1985) model of curriculum development is related to the inquiry and problem-solving model described in *The Educational Spectrum* (Miller, 1983) and in Chapter 5 of this text.

Robinson and his colleagues have focused on curriculum design, in order to ensure that their inquiry programs can be more easily integrated into the schools' existing curricula. The Robinson group's approach is to start with specific tasks that teachers and curriculum workers usually address when they are designing or revamping curricula. These tasks, which Robinson calls *surface tasks*, are as follows:

1. Developing goal statements
2. Developing defensible sets of objectives
3. Developing descriptions of growth (growth schemes)
4. Developing instructional objectives
5. Sequencing objectives
6. Devising growth schemes related to instruction and assessment methods
7. Developing written curriculum materials

The Robinson group found that most curriculum teams need assistance in clarifying the procedures associated with these tasks. For example, a teacher might generate a list of goals by simply writing down possible goals as they come to mind (e.g., brainstorming) or by recalling goals staements employed in the past. Robinson argues, however, that without more-detailed procedures for curriculum design, this type of activity will not have much of an impact on student growth. There are three key assumptions in the Robinson and Hedges (1982) model:

- Curriculum guidelines do not provide the teacher with much assistance in actually instructing students about complex intellectual tasks. Thus, for the teacher to achieve goals stated in the guidelines, curriculum guidelines and instructional materials must be made more explicit.
- The task of curriculum design involves matters of choice, such as the selection of objectives and intended learning outcomes. These choices can be broken down into manageable steps. The procedures for selecting objectives and outcomes should be grounded in "models of the problematic situation on the one hand and in practical results on the other" (p. 3).
- The goal of the curriculum developer is to make defensible choices that can be supported with reference to specific criteria.

The uniqueness of the Robinson model is its explication of detailed *procedures* for each of the surface tasks. These procedures are elaborated in two stages:

**1.** In the first step, each task is approached as a problem to be solved, so that the curriculum worker must identify the framework for each problem. This framework then will be used to clarify further procedures. For example, as a result of an analysis of Ontario Ministry of Education guidelines over a 50-year period, Robinson determined that goal statements in the guidelines have this form:

| *Educable qualities* | *Contexts in which guidelines are in evidence* | | | |
|---|---|---|---|---|
| | | | | |
| | | | | |
| | | | | |
| | | | | |

For example, one educable quality might be *attitudes,* and the context might be *minority groups,* in which case the objective would deal with attitudes toward minority groups. Robinson claims that this framework can be used as a systematic device for generating goal statements of higher quality than those found in common practice. Robinson calls this first step an *analytic task.*

  2. In the second step, an image of what is an *educated person* is used to develop the content of the matrix. Robinson calls this second step a *recovery task.* In this task, the dominant qualities of an educated person (e.g., the ability to solve problems) are listed across the top of the matrix and the dominant contexts in which these qualities are found are listed from top to bottom in the matrix. To develop the goals for a course, then, these dominant qualities and contexts are adapted to specific courses. For example, in the design for a history course, the "ability to solve problems" might become "ability to analyze past and contemporary issues."

  In the Robinson model, each surface task generates one or more analytic tasks and one or more recovery tasks. For the curriculum designer to go from major goal statements to specific instructional course objectives, he or she must do the following:

1. Develop an objectives-classification scheme
2. Develop "organizing sets" for each relevant category in this scheme
3. Adapt the material in the organizing sets to fit the particular curriculum space

The organizing sets allow the teacher to identify the knowledge and skills that are most important and can thus act as organizers for other concepts and skills in the curriculum. Organizing sets can be developed for knowledge, skills, and beliefs. Robinson acknowledges that the above process is arduous, but he claims that it is necessary if objectives are to move beyond low-level cognitive skill levels (e.g., knowledge recall).

  A key feature of the Robinson system is that it offers field-developed procedures for describing growth toward the attainment of educational objectives. Such descriptions of growth (which we discussed in Chapter 5 in relation to problem solving) are called *growth schemes.* There are five basic steps in developing a growth scheme for any objective:

1. Identify a task that calls for a behavior designated by the objective.
2. Administer the task to groups of increasingly greater maturity in respect to this behavior.
3. By comparing performances of groups of different maturity, identify major differences and articulate them as *dimensions* of growth.
4. Identify describable *levels* within each dimension (these also must meet several practical criteria).

**5.** Where necessary and useful, render this multidimensional growth scheme into a linear sequence.

As with other curriculum tasks, growth-scheme analysis can proceed at both the analysis and the recovery levels. At the most advanced (recovery) level, psychological models for the various types of outcomes are used to suggest significant dimensions of growth.

Robinson also has developed instructional procedures for moving students through the stages of the growth schemes. According to Robinson, the most effective procedure involves a highly interactive process in which students articulate and gradually incorporate rules for operating at the higher levels of the particular growth scheme.

Written curriculum materials, developed by Robinson and his associates, are related to this instructional process. These materials, of course, are most effective when integrated within the overall framework of the model. Robinson has studied how these written materials can be related to teacher behavior and teacher growth.

Robinson's model includes one of the most sophisticated curriculum systems that we know of. The uniqueness of this model is the powerful procedures it contains for developing and analyzing curriculum. These procedures are rooted in a clear conception of inquiry and problem solving. Because of its clear theoretical base, this model should be very appealing to curriculum workers who are concerned with teaching higher level cognitive skills.

Our concern about this model is that it is not easily accessible. Robinson himself acknowledges that some of these tasks are complex and arduous. In *Curriculum Development for Improved Instruction*, Robinson (1985) addresses the issue of accessibility. We believe this text should help a great deal in making the Robinson model more accessible and in assisting teachers and curriculum workers in the use of this model that is so conceptually sound.

## A TRANSFORMATION MODEL: WEINSTEIN AND FANTINI

Weinstein and Fantini (1970) have developed a model for what they call *identity education*. Central to this model is a process of curriculum development built around the concerns of the learner. The focus of this model is to ascertain and diagnose learner concerns and then to build lessons around those concerns. Weinstein and Fantini also attempt to integrate in their curriculum model the affective and cognitive spheres.

This curriculum model, which is based on several steps, is diagrammed in Figure 9.1.

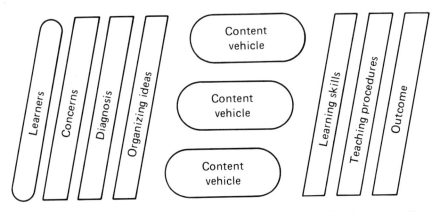

**Figure 9.1** The Weinstein-Fantini model of curriculum development. (*From Weinstein, G., and Fantini, M.* Toward Humanistic Education. *New York: Praeger, 1970. Reprinted with permission.*)

***Step 1.***   The first step is to identify the learners. This means assessing the students' characteristics, including "developmental (age), economic (lower, middle, or upper income), geographic (rural or urban), cultural and racial or ethnic characteristics" (Weinstein & Fantini, 1970, p. 35). In this first step, characteristics common to the group are identified, rather than characteristics that are unique to the individual students.

***Steps 2 and 3.***   The second and third steps are to ascertain the learners' concerns and to diagnose the reasons for these concerns. The word *concern* connotes an inner uneasiness for the individual and is deeper and more pervasive than a simple interest or feeling. Students' concerns often center around issues such as self-image and disconnectedness. Concerns can be identified through what learners say and write about themselves. Through diagnosis, the third step, the teacher attempts to develop ideas for teaching strategies that can meet those concerns. This means looking behind the student's statement. For instance, the statement, "It's no use trying, there's nothing you can do about it," made by a middle-class child, might mean that he lives in an overprotected situation, whereas the same statement, made by a lower-class student, could indicate a lack of protection and support. Thus, the same statement can lead to different teaching strategies, depending on the student who made the statement.

Weinstein and Fantini (1970) describe several activities that can facilitate the diagnostic process. "Faraway Island," for example, is designed to uncover students' self-perceptions and value systems. The following instructions are used to introduce this exercise to children:

> Assume that you have to spend the rest of your life on a remote island with just six people and no one else. Imagine that! None of

these six people can be anyone you already know, but you're allowed to specify what they should be like. What kinds of people would you pick to live the rest of your life with? You might think about how old they'd be, their sex, the things they'd like to do and the things they wouldn't like to do, their personalities, their looks, or any other qualities. Assume, also, that all your basic needs are taken care of, so you don't have to scrounge around for food, clothing, and shelter. All you have to do is describe as fully as you can what the people you'd choose to live with would be like. (pp. 123–124)

The responses of a racially mixed group of 15- and 16-year-olds enrolled in an Upward Bound project in New Jersey included the following:

| | |
|---|---|
| FIRST GIRL: | First I'd pick a doctor in case I get sick. It could be anybody, as long as they're nice and can be trusted. Just as long as I have the doctor first. |
| FIRST BOY: | I would like one or two people that's older than I. Can't be anybody I know. I would like a person like a college professor that's hip. He knows what's happening and all, and you know he's smart, and he could keep order in case anything happens, you know. Let's say two older people, two girls, in the same age bracket, understanding, and what not. And then another guy around my age. And I would like these to possess qualities and be able to do things. Maybe one is musically inclined and has talent and you could do this. And another one draws, you know, things that would keep you busy. |
| SECOND BOY: | I would like to have one older guy that's real smart. . . . He'd picka part and argue like mad. You couldn't put nothing over on him. And I'd like a guy and a girl around my age that I could talk with that would be good conversations. (pp. 124–125) |

Weinstein and Fantini found that the people these students tended to select are those who have the greatest amount of control over their own lives, which indicates that self-determination is a basic concern. They were concerned also with economic security and racial segregation issues. Diagnostic techniques such as the "Faraway Island" exercise, which generate data about students that are related to identity questions, can help the teacher "read" student needs more accurately and then shape activities to meet some of these needs.

***Step 4.*** Once the teacher has made a diagnosis, he or she should develop a set of desired outcomes aimed at meeting some of these concerns. For example, if a student's concern is to have a more positive self-image, the teachers would look for behavioral indicators showing that a more positive identity is developing. Sometimes students' statements can be indicative of change in self-concept.

***Step 5.*** This step involves developing a theme to organize the lesson. The organizing idea or theme gives direction and coherence to teaching. It is essential that the theme be relevant to student concerns. Weinstein and Fantini (1970) provide the following examples of organizing ideas:

1. You use people, things, and events to tell you who you are.
2. Some people, things, and events are more important to you than others.
3. The most important ones are those you use most often in judging yourself.
4. It is important to know what you are using to measure your own self-worth.
5. Certain things, people, and events are important to you because of (a) where you live and who else lives there, (b) what you think is good for people, and (c) the fact that you are you. (pp. 49–50)

***Step 6.*** After an organizing idea has been selected, the teacher selects content vehicles to achieve the desired outcomes. Several avenues are open to the teacher, including subject disciplines, various media, and excursions. The teacher should not overlook the students' concerns, feelings, and experiences as content vehicles, because these are part of identity education.

Learning skills—skills that the student needs in order to deal with the content vehicles—are also part of this model; some examples of learning skills are basic skills such as reading and writing, learning-to-learn skills such as problem-solving and other process skills needed to deal with information and concepts, and self-awareness skills that focus on the ability to be more in touch with oneself and more effective in communicating emotional states.

***Step 7.*** Teaching strategies are developed that are appropriate to the learning skills, content vehicles, organizing ideas, and outcomes. Weinstein and Fantini emphasize the importance of matching procedures to the learning styles of the students.

***Step 8.*** Finally, the teacher should attempt to evaluate the effect of the curriculum, asking questions such as these: "Has the children's behavior changed? Were the content vehicles the best that could have been employed? Were the cognitive skills and teacher procedures the most effective for achieving the affective goals?" (p. 58).

This model is similar to the Tyler model, particularly in the way it presents overall sequencing; for example, it proceeds from objectives to learning experiences to evaluation. The defining characteristic of this model is the emphasis it places on the needs and interests of the learner. The major thrust of not only this model, but, also, many other humanistic approaches to curriculum, is this learner-centered focus. Unlike the Tyler approach, in transformation models, the curriculum developer does not look to subject matter or to society as a source of learning objectives; instead, the primary source is the learner.

## THE MILLER–SELLER MODEL

In this section we outline our own curriculum model, which we have already discussed briefly in Chapter 1. Now we present it in somewhat more detail. Figure 9.2 illustrates this model.

### Orientations

We contend that curriculum work is based on the particular orientation of the curriculum worker. This orientation will reflect one's philosophy, one's view of psychology and learning theory, and one's view of society, which, in turn, are related to one's basic world view, or paradigm. For example, we have seen that the transmission orientation is rooted in an

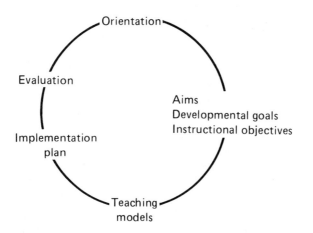

**Figure 9.2** The Miller-Seller curriculum model.

atomistic world view, the transaction position is based on the scientific method, and the transformation position is founded on a holistic and interdependent world view. In our model, the first step is for the curriculum worker to examine and clarify his or her basic orientation and the philosophical, psychological, and social roots of that position. This is not to say that one's position is fixed; as one immerses oneself in examining the orientations, movement can be expected. Nonetheless a curriculum plan should begin with a statement that sets forth its basic orientation(s). Examples of such statements can be found in Chapter 8 (pp. 178–79). An instrument for clarifying orientations can be found in *The Educational Spectrum* (Miller, 1983).

## Aims/Objectives

The next step, after clarifying the orientation(s) of the curriculum, is to develop aims, developmental goals, and specific objectives based on the orientations. *Aims,* the most general objectives, reflect a person's image of the educated person and an image of society. These images should be clearly articulated and should reflect one's orientation. We use the term *image* here to refer to mental imagery; we believe it would be useful for curriculum workers to use right-brain strategies for stimulating mental imagery—for example, visualization (Miller, 1981)—to evoke images that reflect their educational vision. In other words, curriculum workers should use their imagination to call forth images of the educated person. The Dutch futurist Fred Polak (1973) has shown that our images of the future play an important role in shaping the direction of society. He claims that positive images help maintain the vitality of society. For example, he has noted that the spiritual images of the Jewish people have helped them survive centuries of adversity. On the other hand, he claims that when the guiding images of the culture become weak, as in the case of the Roman Empire, this can contribute to the decline of the society. He concludes that visionary thinking is essential to effective social change. In line with Polak's thinking, we maintain that having a clear, visionary image of the educated person can help in planning and implementing educational programs.

After one has developed an image of an educated person, he or she should then articulate a concept of development that is congruent with the image. This process is somewhat similar to the stage in Robinson's conception of a growth scheme; however, in our model, this process is more general. Each broad aim might be broken down into programs that are designed to relate the aim to children at various levels of development. In other words, each aim can be broken down to correspond to the general growth pattern that has been selected as an organizing principle for the curriculum plan.

After this intermediate step, specific instructional objectives should be established. The level of specificity will vary with the instructional context. Some courses (e.g., driver education) may lend themselves to specific objectives; in other subjects, such as art, what Eisner (1972) calls *expressive objectives* tend to be more appropriate. We believe that objectives, even at this most specific level, should provide a rough map, not a straitjacket. They should help to guide our overall direction as teachers, but should not tie down the teacher to long lists of tasks that can hinder the spontaneity that is essential to curriculum activities such as creative thinking. Here are some examples of the three levels of objectives in our model:

1. *Aim:* Development of social responsibility.
2. *Developmental goal:* Student (age 17–18) will identify an area of social concern and participate in a community-oriented project that deals with that concern.
3. *Instructional objectives:* Student will develop skills in project organization.

## Learning Experiences/Teaching Strategies

At this stage in our model of the curriculum process, the curriculum worker should identify learning experiences and teaching strategies. For this purpose, we advocate the use of the models-of-teaching approach developed by Joyce and Weil (1980) (see Chapter 8, pp. 191–94). In our approach, the teaching models are selected according to major positions. In other words, teachers would select teaching models that are congruent with the position from which they are working. The list that follows shows some of the criteria that can be used for selecting models:

• Overall objectives of the model match its aims, developmental goals, and instructional objectives.
• The structure of the model is congruent with the student's need for structure (Hunt, 1970). For example, some students prefer a good deal of direction, others are more comfortable in a loosely structured environment.
• The teacher has received appropriate in-service training in and support for use of the model.
• Resources essential to implementation of the model are available.

Table 9.1 shows the three major positions and some of the teaching models that are congruent with each.
Curriculum workers also should investigate new models that reflect state-of-the-art thinking about curriculum, such as the models mentioned in

## TABLE 9.1 Congruence of Curriculum Orientations and Teaching Models

| TRANSMISSION MODELS | |
|---|---|
| *Model* | *Theorist* |
| Contingency management | Skinner |
| Direct training | Gagne |
| Stress reduction | Rimm and Masters |

| TRANSACTION MODELS | |
|---|---|
| *Model* | *Theorist* |
| Group investigation | Thelen |
| Social inquiry | Massialas |
| Scientific inquiry | Schwab; Driver; Posner |

| TRANSFORMATION MODELS | |
|---|---|
| *Model* | *Theorist* |
| Nondirective teaching | Rogers |
| Synectics | Gordon |
| Classroom meeting | Glasser |

Chapter 8 (e.g., Driver & Erickson, 1983; Miller, 1981; Posner, 1982; and Purkey & Novak, 1983).

## Implementation

Implementation involves adaptation of the curriculum so that new practices, materials, and beliefs are integrated into the teacher's repertoire. Implementation is best accomplished with a plan such as the one we describe in Chapter 12 (see pp. 276–93), which includes the following components:

- Study of program
- Identification of resources
- Roles
- Professional development
- Timeline
- Communication system
- Monitoring the implementation

## Evaluation

Evaluation procedures will reflect one's orientation. For example, highly standardized evaluation procedures generally are incongruent with

**SUMMARY CHART:   Chapter 9**

| TRANSMISSION | TRANSACTION | | TRANSFORMATION |
|---|---|---|---|
| *Gagne Model* | *Taba Model* | *Robinson Model* | *Miller-Seller Model* |
| Needs analysis<br>Analysis of goals<br>Analysis of ways to meet needs<br>Designing instructional components<br>Analysis of resources and constraints | Developing units<br>Diagnosis of needs<br>Objectives<br>Selection of content<br>Organization of content<br>Selection of learning Experiences<br>Organization of experiences<br>Evaluation<br>Balancing and sequencing | Developing goals<br>Developing defensible objectives<br>Developing growth schemes<br>Developing instructional objectives<br>Sequencing objectives | Clarifying orientations<br>Transmission<br>Transaction<br>Transformation<br>Developing aims, developmental goals and objectives<br>Identification of teaching model congruent with aims and orientation<br>Development of implementation plan |
| Constraint removal | Testing units | Developing instructional and evaluation methods related to growth schemes | Evaluation that is congruent with orientation |
| Selecting or developing materials<br>Designing student performance assessment<br>Field testing formative evaluation | Revising units<br>Developing a framework<br>Installing and disseminating units | Developing curriculum materials | |
| Adjustments and further evaluation | | | |
| Summative evaluation | | | |
| Operational installation | | | |

transformation curricula; in contrast, transmission curricula usually employ highly structured evaluation techniques to assess how well learning experiences and teaching strategies meet the aims and objectives. In Chapter 14, a flexible strategy for evaluation is described.

Some of the models discussed this chapter that are representative of the different curriculum positions are summarized in the accompanying chart.

## REFERENCES

Crowder, N.A. (1959). Automatic tutoring by means of intrinsic programming. In E. H. Galanter (Ed.), *Automatic Teaching: The State of the Art*, (pp. 109–116), New York: Wiley.

Driver, R., & Erickson, G. (1983). Theories-in-action: Some theoretical and empirical issues in the study of students' conceptual framework in science. *Studies in Science Education, 10*, 37–60.

Eisner, E. (1972). Emerging models for educational evaluation. *School Review*, 573–590.

Gagne, R.M., & Briggs, L. (1979). *Principles of instructional design*. New York: Holt, Rinehart.

Guthrie, E.R. (1935). *The Psychology of Learning*. New York: Harper & Row.

Hunt, D.E. (1970). A conceptual level-matching model for coordinating learner characteristics with educational approaches. *Interchange, 1*, 4.

Joyce, B., & Weil, M. (1980). *Models of teaching*. Englewood Cliffs, NJ: Prentice-Hall.

Kliebard, H.M. (1970). The Tyler rationale. *School Review*, 259–272.

Leyton Soto, M., & Tyler, R. (1969). *Planeamiento educacional*. Santiago, Chile: Editorial Universitaria.

Miller, J. (1981). *The compassionate teacher*. Englewood Cliffs, NJ: Prentice-Hall.

———. (1983). *The educational spectrum: Orientations to curriculum*. New York: Longman.

Polak, F. (1973). *The image of the future*. San Francisco: Josey-Bass.

Posner, G. (1982). A cognitive science conception of curriculum and instruction. *J. Curriculum Studies, 14*, 343–351.

Pressey, S.L. (1950). Development and appraisal of devices providing immediate automatic scoring of objective tests and concomitant self-instruction. *Journal of Psychology, 29*, 417–447.

Purkey, W., & Novak, J. (1983). *Inviting school success: A self-concept approach to teaching and learning*. Belmont, CA: Wadsworth.

Robinson, F., & Hedges, H.G. (1982). *Curriculum design for improved learning: A systematic approach*. St. Catharines, Ontario: Ontario Institute for Studies in Education, Niagara Centre–Curriculum Processes Centre.

Robinson, F., Ross, J, & White, F. (1985). *Curriculum development for improved instruction*. Toronto, Ontario: Ontario Institute for Studies in Education.

Skinner, B.F. (1968). *The technology of teaching*. New York: Appleton-Century-Crofts.

Taba, H. (1962). *Curriculum development: Theory and practice.* New York: Harcourt Brace Jovanovich.

Tanner, D., & Tanner, L.N. (1980). *Curriculum development: theory into practice* (2nd ed.). New York: Macmillan.

Tyler, R.W. (1949). *Basic principles of curriculum and instruction.* Chicago: University of Chicago Press.

Weinstein, G., & Fantini, M. (1970). *Toward humanistic education.* New York: Praeger.

# IMPLEMENTATION: A Personal and Social Process

In this chapter we focus on the nature of change. We analyze the individualistic nature of curriculum implementation, the key role of the teacher in this process, and the effect on change of the school as a social system.

The working world of the teacher contains realities that make the acceptance of change difficult. The teacher's world is characterized by time pressures and feelings of loneliness and uncertainty (Lortie, 1975). Many duties fill their day—they must teach, monitor student behavior, complete clerical tasks, and talk to parents. They do most of this in the confines of their classrooms, with little opportunity to interact with their colleagues.

Teachers also are members of a social system that exists in the school (Sarason, 1982). Within this social system there is a set of values that underpins the teachers' activities; certain behaviors are expected of members of this system and they are expected to play a number of roles, both explicit and implicit. These expectations, along with the extent to which a change is intended to alter classroom practice, and the amount of autonomy a teacher has in making this change, are factors that affect implementation.

## THE NATURE OF CHANGE

Change in organizations can occur in several ways. It can be slow and occur naturally over time, in which case alterations to existing practices happen in small stages; often, such changes are not noticed until a conscious comparison is made of present and past practice. This type of change comes as a result of growth, maturation, and learning. The infusion of new ideas, combined with accumulated experience, can produce subtle changes in practice. This kind of change is not mandated; it evolves.

Another type of change, which is more dramatic, comes as the result of new knowledge. For example, new knowledge about how students learn and develop (e.g., the work of Piaget) can change teachers' attitudes toward learning. There is also a growing body of knowledge about the stages of adult development and principles of adult learning. This information can affect professional development for teachers. Advances in health knowledge is another kind of new knowledge that is having an impact on schools—for example, new information about the psychological effects of artificial lighting, especially fluorescent lighting, is resulting in changes in the physical structure of some schools. Increased knowledge, therefore, is not limited to subject disciplines. New knowledge in many different areas may lead to changes in various aspects of school practice. This type of change occurs more rapidly than evolved change.

Planning for change in schools does not begin just because new knowledge emerges. There must also be a recognized need for a change. If teachers do not recognize this need, the intended change will be a nonevent. A number of different factors influence the decision to begin planning for a change. One such factor is the source of the new knowledge that triggers change.

University professors and curriculum consultants often are the source of ideas for change. The introduction of the new math, following the launching of Sputnik in 1957, is one example of a change that occurred as a result of new information derived from expert sources. However, as Fullan (1982) points out, there is no guarantee that quality will be associated with an innovation. Many new programs may not be practical for classroom application.

Funding agencies can also be a source of suggested changes. Departments of education can attempt to legislate change through the issuance of mandatory curriculum guidelines. Other governmental agencies and foundations can attempt to promote a change by providing special funding for schools that participate in the new program. In fact, governmental commissions and committees often are judged on the basis of the number of reforms they recommend, which can lead to the formation of what Fullan (1982) calls the "innovation establishment"—a segment of the educational world that has a vested interest in promoting change in schools.

Professional organizations, such as teachers' federations or unions, become part of the "innovation establishment" when, as often happens, ideas and suggestions for change are passed to local members, who then become internal sources of change in a school system.

Because the accumulation of knowledge that can affect school practice tends to take place outside of the school, a major problem for promoters of change is to have the new ideas accepted by local officials. Rogers (1962, pp. 125–128) identifies five major characteristics of a suggested change that will affect its adoption by others:

1. *Relative advantage:* The degree to which the change is perceived to be an improvement over present practice.
2. *Compatibility:* The congruity between the values implied by the change and those values present among the people who must implement the change.
3. *Complexity:* The ease with which the change can be understood and then applied.
4. *Divisibility:* Some programs can be implemented by breaking them into smaller units.
5. *Communicability:* The ease with which the effects of the change can be shared with others.

Even if the new program is sound and the decision makers decide to adopt a change, the ultimate responsibility for implementation rests with the teacher. Regardless of whether a change is to affect a whole school system or a single school, individual teachers often are expected to change their own classroom practice. Change at a personal level can evoke a number of common responses.

Marris (1974) argues that a need exists for stability and predictability in both our physical and our social worlds. We feel comfortable when the surroundings in which we work and our relationships with our workmates are consistent. When we have this sense of familiarity, we are confident about what is likely to happen. In this way, each of us builds a picture of reality, within which we perform our various tasks. However, the introduction of a change alters our picture of reality, and this requires us to act differently. In Marris's (1974) words, "We assimilate new experiences by placing them in the context of a familiar, reliable construction of reality. This structure in turn rests not only on the regularity of events themselves, but on the continuity of their meaning" (p. 6). Marris goes on to explain the importance to us of this reality structure when a change is suggested:

> We cannot act without some interpretation of what is going on about us, and to interpret it we must first match it with an experience which is familiar. . . . Hence, there is a deep-seated impulse in all of us to defend the validity of what we have learned, for without it, we would be helpless. (p. 8)

The first encounter with a change, therefore, elicits a defense of one's present practice. When a new program is introduced to teachers, often their first reaction is to describe what they are presently doing. This response, which Marris calls the "conservative response," is not necessarily an outright denial of the change; instead, this reaction helps the individual to consolidate his or her present position, so that the change can be understood. By explaining how the change is different from this present practice, the person introducing the change can help teachers to understand the new program.

The defense of one's present situation establishes the possibility that conflict over acceptance of the proposed change might arise. Marris (1974) maintains that this is an integral part of the adoption process, which must be played out: "Every attempt to pre-empt conflict, argument, protest by rational planning can only be abortive; however reasonable the proposed changes, the process of implementing them must still allow the impulse of rejection to play itself out" (p. 155). As part of this "playing out" processs, the teachers often will assess the new program in terms of their own framework or orientation.

The individual's need for meaning pervades the introduction of a change. Until this sense of meaning is achieved, the individual will feel a high level of ambivalence about the proposal, as he or she struggles to understand the reasons both for the change and for its effect on his or her actions. Attainment of meaning takes time.

Change is a very personal experience. Regardless of the extent of the proposed alterations, it can be the source of much anxiety and frustration. The greater the degree of change required, the longer the time needed for the adjustments. Information overload and uncertainty about new methods can further add to one's personal dilemma. Implementation is marked by passage through "zones of uncertainty" (Schon, 1971), which denote the successive stages of coping with the new information and assimilation of the ideas into one's own reality.

## THE SUBJECTIVE WORLD OF THE TEACHER

Ultimately, it is the teacher who implements a new program. However, as Lortie (1975) points out, there are many factors that affect the teacher's reactions to a proposed change.

> Teachers have a built-in resistance to change because they believe that their work environment has never permitted them to show what they can really do. Many proposals for change strike them as frivolous—they do not address issues of boundedness, psychic rewards, time scheduling, student disruption, interpersonal support, and so forth. (p. 235)

The work environment Lortie refers to is the day-to-day world of the classroom. The introduction of change takes place in this context. Fullan

(1982) also refers to the "subjective meaning of change" (p. 26). He states that each participant in implementation has his or her own subjective reality, which affects how he or she views the new program.

> The extent to which proposals for change are defined according to only one person's or one group's reality is the extent to which they will encounter problems in implementation. This is not to say that subjective realities should define what is to change, but only that they are powerful constraints to change or protections against undesirable or thoughtless change. (p. 29)

The subjective world of the teacher is not receptive to implementation. Lortie (1975) and Fullan (1982) describe the daily life of the teacher as one in which there is little opportunity for interaction with one's peers. This isolation is a result of the structure and organization of the school, because teachers are enclosed in classrooms with their students for most of the day. Sarason (1982) uses the analogy of a visitor from outer space to depict the actions of people in a school. He claims that, at the end of a year, this visitor could sum up its observations in this way:

1. During the course of the average day, the teachers spend almost all of the time with small children.
2. Leaving lunchtime aside, during the course of the average day, the amount of time teachers spend in face-to-face contact with eath other is extremely small. . . . It is unusual for these face-to-face contacts to exceed one minute.
3. During eating time in the teachers' room there is considerable variation in how much the different teachers talk, and in the degree to which any one teacher will talk to any other teacher.
4. It is extremely rare for a teacher to be physically alone. (p. 132)

Teachers, then, are isolated from their colleagues and from adults in general. This results in two psychological effects. First, teachers feel that, professionally, they are on their own; they must solve their own problems and learn to cope with the classroom by themselves. If a change is introduced into the program, implementation also is viewed as an individual activity. Sarason (1982) describes additional problems teachers might then encounter: "The psychological loneliness of teachers will contain a good deal of felt inadequacy as well as simmering hostility to administrators who seem insensitive to the teacher's plight" (p. 134).

Thus, the loneliness leads to the second effect of the isolation—feelings of inadequacy and uncertainty. Lacking contact with their colleagues, teachers may begin to doubt their ability to affect student learning. Lortie (1975) describes the "widespread feeling of uncertainty": "Teachers are not sure they can make all their students learn. They hope for widespread, or even universal effectiveness, but such aspirations receive too little reinforcement to yield assurance" (p. 132).

One result of this situation is a discrepancy in classroom practice from teacher to teacher. Their basic methodologies and the time they allot to individual subjects can vary widely. For example, as a part of a curriculum development project, the authors of this text surveyed the classroom practices for teaching reading in grades four through six in a small school system. They found that the time allotted for the teaching of reading varied from 30 minutes per day to 90 minutes per day. Although all of these teachers were teaching the same reading program, four different methodologies were in use. Similarly, the variety of teaching materials being used meant that different classes at the same grade level were receiving quite different instruction in reading. When presented with these findings, the teachers expressed concern, but not surprise. They explained that their working day did not provide them with the time necessary to discuss their concerns with their colleagues; each taught reading in his or her own way and hoped that their students would be able to cope when they moved into the next grade.

Noninstructional aspects of the teachers' daily world can add to their difficulties. For example, clerical tasks such as record-keeping or collecting money for various events take time away from instruction and program concerns; monitoring student behavior in the hallways and on the playground has a similar effect.

One reality of change, therefore, is that, to be effective, it must be introduced into the subjective world of the teacher. The criteria teachers use to assess a possible change reflect the immediate needs they perceive in their daily work. These criteria are listed by Fullan (1982):

1. Does the change potentially address a need? Will students be interested? Will they learn?
2. How clear is the change in terms of what the teacher will have to do?
3. How will it affect the teacher personally in terms of time, energy, new skill, sense of excitement and competence, and interference with existing priorities? (p. 113)

Another reality of change is that teachers have a need for an objective description of the innovation itself. The purpose of such a description is to clarify what is to actually change in practice. Too often, a teacher's initial view of a change is simplistic. For example, a new program may suggest that the best methodology to be used is an inquiry approach. A teacher working from a transmission position may view the change as "just" requiring the learning of new classroom instructional techniques. However, a closer inspection of the impact of the new program reveals the need for far deeper change. Old teaching materials (e.g., textbooks) may not be suitable to the new approach. Teachers who believe that children learn best when provided with direct instruction will resist the new transaction-oriented approach and will have a difficult time learning the new techniques, because they do not agree with the basic philosophy of the new program. Change, therefore, is multidimensional (Fullan, 1982). An alteration to one aspect of the teaching process will have repercussions on other aspects as well.

There are three basic dimensions to any significant educational change: teaching resources, methodologies, and beliefs (Fullan, 1982). For a teacher to introduce a new program, adjustments are often necessary in all three dimensions. However, as Fullan and Park (1981, p. 8) note, it is possible for a teacher to implement one, two, or all three dimensions of a new program. Resources can be used with minimal adjustments to methodology and a new methodology can be learned and used without an understanding or belief in the underlying principles. It is useful to describe a change in terms of the adjustment needed in each dimension. When a change is being contemplated, teachers and curriculum workers should be aware of these three aspects of change, in order to minimize implementation problems.

For example, a school system with which the authors worked developed a new mathematics program for grades one through six. A new textbook series was introduced with the program that was more consistent with the philosophy of the new program than with those texts formerly in use. The approach to mathematics taken in the new texts was a spiral approach. In this approach, a topic is introduced with a few examples, then put aside while another topic is introduced. Further on in the text, the original topics are picked up, expanded, and then put aside again. Also, the new texts did not have exercises for drilling the math skills. The teachers were accustomed to developing a topic in depth before moving on to a different one. Therefore, the new books (resources) required a new methodology, which, in turn, was based on a set of beliefs about how mathematics is learned. Thus, in this situation, the transmission-oriented teachers confronted a transaction-oriented program. The teachers had to make a greater adjustment than simply learning a different set of teaching strategies or getting used to a new textbook.

Resources are often the focus during implementation, because new textbooks or teaching materials are concrete and easily identified. Similarly, teaching methodologies can be addressed through professional development sessions, so they, too, receive early attention. Beliefs, or orientations, are the most difficult component in educational change, because they are less obvious and therefore not easily addressed during implementation. An objective description of an innovation may, in fact, reflect only the beliefs of the program developers, without taking into account the orientations of teachers. Beliefs develop over many years, and reasons to change must be very convincing to teachers.

Fullan (1982) points out that the dimensions of change are not entirely separate. During change, there is a dynamic interrelationship between them: "Beliefs guide and are informed by teaching strategies and activities; the effective use of materials depends on their articulation with beliefs and teaching approaches; and so on" (p. 33).

Individual teachers will implement a new program in ways that are consistent with their own beliefs and practices. For some, the interrelationship will be obvious and readily accepted. For others, the change will be agonizing and slow.

In our example of the new mathematics program, little attention was paid to the various dimensions of change. As a result, teachers coped with the implementation in various ways. Some teachers were familiar with the spiral approach and adapted their classroom style to it. Other teachers accepted the texts and continued teaching as they had always done; this meant that they would choose only the pages from the book related to the topic they were teaching (e.g., addition), a practice that both students and teachers found very confusing and frustrating. A third group of teachers attempted to teach from the new text as it was written. Because they did not understand the assumptions in this approach, they found teaching mathematics in the new way very frustrating; student achievement in these classrooms was disappointing to the teachers.

Implementation of a change does not guarantee that the change, in practice, is the one that was intended; nor does it guarantee that real change will occur. There are two forms of nonchange, which Fullan (1982) calls "false clarity" and "painful unclarity":

> False clarity occurs when people think that they have changed but have only assimilated the superficial trappings of the new practice. Painful unclarity is experienced when unclear innovations are attempted under conditions which do not support the development of the subjective meaning of the change. (p. 28)

In our mathematics example, the teachers who attempted to use the new text in the "old" way (i.e., skipped about the book picking out the pages relating to the topic being taught) were experiencing "painful unclarity." The way in which the change was introduced had not accounted for the necessary changes in methodology or in beliefs about the teaching of mathematics. The group of teachers who taught the topics in sequence without understanding assumptions of the approach evidenced the false clarity situation. They assumed they could use the new text in the same manner as they had used the old one (i.e., beginning at the front and working through to the end) without changing their teaching methodology.

To summarize, there are many personal factors that affect implementation of a change. Because the teacher is the ultimate implementor of a new program, the personal world of the teacher must be considered. This world, however, is enclosed in a broader setting—the collective reality of the school.

## THE SCHOOL AS A SOCIAL SYSTEM

As administrators, teachers, support staff, and students interact on a daily basis in the operation of a school, a social order develops that affects the actions of everyone involved. Hoy and Miskel (1982) describe this process:

> The school is a system of social interaction; it is an organized whole comprised of interacting personalities bound together in an organic relationship. As a social system, the school is characterized by an interdependence of parts, a clearly defined population, differentiation from its enviroment, a complex network of social relationships, and its own unique culture. (p. 51)

In practice, a teacher's actions and attitudes toward a proposed change are influenced by the social system within the school, where sets of values, norms, and roles are developed. Individual teachers must reconcile their personal beliefs with the values of the institution. For example, a teacher may believe that students should be allowed to talk with one another and move freely around the classroom while working. This teacher, working from a transaction position, can allow this practice only as long as other teachers do not complain of being disturbed. If student interaction is encouraged in the school, an individual teacher will not encounter a conflict between his or her values and the social system norms. However, if most of the staff have a basic transmission orientation and value quiet behavior from students, the teacher in our example will have to either alter the way in which students work (i.e., they will have to conform to accepted practice) or be prepared to live with sanctions imposed by the staff. The manner in which decisions are made, the according of status within the school, and the sanctions used on nonconforming members are all determined by the social system.

Both Joyce, Hersh, and McKibbin (1983) and Sarason (1982) explain how the social system can have a profound psychological effect on teachers. As described previously, the subjective world of the teacher is one of loneliness and uncertainty. The social system, through the climate it creates, may or may not help teachers to cope with these frustrations. For example, the way in which the school reacts to pressures to teach more courses (e.g., Family Life and Sex Education) or to assume more roles (e.g., student counselling) will affect the individual teacher. If the response is to mount a team effort, individuals will feel less isolated. However, a climate in which everybody is expected to fend for themselves can lead to increased frustration and teacher "burn out." As Joyce et al. (1983) point out:

> Some environments encourage extreme dependence, where others encourage autonomy. Some press us to conformity, others free us. Some are punitive and make us feel guilty, while others are supportive and reassure us. Some climates tear at self-confidence and others induce us to explore new things. (p. 110)

Within a school social system, a set of values develops. These values, which affect many different activities within the school, at times are evident in school goals or expectations. Expectations often focus on discipline (how students act in and around the school) and achievement (the importance of tests and other methods of demonstrating achievement). These values will also be manifested in a school in its set of beliefs about change. The willingness to explore new programs may or may not be important to the principal and teachers, or change may be viewed as a continuous attempt to improve the quality of the experiences provided for the students. All these values influence the behavior patterns that are acceptable within a school's social system.

Normative behavior for a school staff develops over time. From his study of teachers in Dade County, Florida, Lortie (1975) concludes that teachers learn about accepted behavior through a trial-and-error method. Because a teacher is expected to manage a classroom alone, regardless of how much experience he or she possesses, self-reliance develops early. Also, the social organization of a school does not allow frequent periods for consultation with colleagues. It is more likely that teachers will implement change individually, if they believe it is advantageous to their students. The reactions to the innovation by other staff members indicates the norm for such behavior. For example, encouragement from teachers and administration demonstrates that innovative behavior is valued by the staff.

All teachers do not uniformly adhere to these behavior expectations. Subgroups form within a staff. Teachers sharing a common orientation often associate with one another and develop their own behavior patterns. Within these subgroups, a teacher can sometimes find a more supportive climate for his or her preferred behavior. It is possible, therefore, within a school, to find a general climate of support for an implementation project although there also exists a group of teachers who avoid the change.

Within the norms for expected behavior in the social system, there are also a number of defined roles. Some roles are official and are built into the formal organization—for example, the role of the principal. Legislation often defines specific duties and responsibilities for these roles.

Unofficial roles also develop within the school's social setting. These roles may provide leadership positions to some members of the staff, who may promote or hinder implementation in a school. An opinion leader on a staff (a staff member who has earned the respect of many of the other teachers) can have a great deal of influence in this regard. Respect for the opinion leader may come from this person's personality, knowledge of educational practice, or competence in teaching. Whatever the source, other teachers will listen to an opinion leader and adjust their actions accordingly. If this person feels that a change is necessary and beneficial, there is a much better chance for its implementation. Similarly, a social system may have a gatekeeper. This person filters new ideas coming into the school. If a staff member has knowledge of a new program, the gatekeeper can either assist the teacher in supporting the program or discredit the person or program before it is seriously considered by the other teachers.

Within a school, therefore, a social system is formed which establishes a set of values, expected behaviors, and roles for the individuals within the system. Together, these elements make up the culture of the school. Sarason (1982) points out that the culture of a school is observable through the behavior of the people in it. The values underlying the goals of the school will be reflected more accurately in the activities undertaken to achieve them than in spoken or printed words. This is particularly true of the value teachers place on change in a school culture. Attitudes toward innovation can be more accurately assessed through observations of what changes actually occur than through what staff members *say* they are doing.

Knowledge of the culture of a school is important to anyone planning a change. Rosenblum and Louis (1981) identify collegiality and morale as key characteristics of the type of culture that can affect implementation. A spirit of collegiality and high morale can offer support to those using a new program. Rosenblum and Louis (1981) describe what can happen if these features are not present.

Unless there is a supportive school culture, planned innovations may be isolated in a limited number of classrooms or may involve a very small percentage of the normal school day. The innovations will not necessarily disappear, but they will be confined to those individual teachers who are willing to use them or will be minimized in terms of their impact upon the total teaching environment. (p. 158)

Sarason (1982) points out that the concept of a school is often limited to its physical boundaries; when planning an implementation, "this usual concept of a school system can be an effective barrier because it restricts the scope of what you will look at and consider" (p. 10). In other words, the possibility of significant change coming from outside the school is decreased. Viewing the school as isolated, when implementing a change, ignores another important characteristic of a social system—the fact that groups within the system develop links with other groups outside the school.

The school exists in an environment composed of many other systems, both formal and informal. Pressure for change in a school program may come from one of these "outside" systems. For example, a state or provincial department of education might produce a new curriculum guideline calling for the development and implementation of a school program, or a local P.T.A. might apply to the board of education to have certain books removed from a high-school English course. The reverse is also true: a change effected by a school may have an impact on other systems in its environment. For instance, the introduction of microcomputers into the elementary schools will alter the computer-awareness and skill level of students entering high school. In turn, this means that the computer courses at the secondary level will need to be revised.

Schools develop different ways of coping with outside agencies. The methods utilized determine the number and nature of the interactions individual teachers have with others (e.g., curriculum workers, parents). Although a school cannot operate in isolation, it can develop a more open or more closed approach to other systems or individuals. For example, a school staff with an open approach will encourage visits from parents and take time to explain to them school programs and practices, and curriculum workers will be made to feel welcome and comfortable in the school. How visitors are treated on their arrival, their treatment while in the building, and the ease with which they find what they are seeking are indicators of a school's attitude toward outside agencies.

The ecology of a school, which is determined by all of the factors we have mentioned, may either support or impede a climate conducive to mutual adaptation: Individual teachers may or may not be encouraged to adopt innovations; they may or may not receive assistance in their implementation attempts; time may or may not be made available to teachers to confer with colleagues about what they are doing in the classroom.

Sarason (1982) emphasizes the need to study the ecology of a school, rather than the activities of individual teachers. Reasons behind teacher behavior can be better understood when observed in the context of their interactions with others in the environment. This type of study of the overall environment often helps to explain why a change is, or is not, taking place. It can also provide valuable information when planning an implementation. For example, an ecological description of a school can indicate which individuals from outside the staff appear to have the greatest credibility with the teachers. This information can be of assistance in gaining acceptance for a change or in providing help to teachers during the implementation. When the relationships between the various elements within the social system and also between the system and outside agencies are stable, a state of equilibrium exists, within which significant change is unlikely to occur. Disequilibrium occurs when pressure is put on the school to change. Hoy and Miskel (1982) describe two alternatives that are available to the school when this happens: A change can be made in accordance with the pressure or a compromise can be reached. In either case, all groups in the environment will try to re-establish the equilibrium. This is illustrated in the following description of a parent's advisory group.

During the period of equilibrium, this advisory group worked in support of the school by raising money for various projects and assisting the school staff with supervision. At times, parents and teachers made presentations together to the school board concerning special program changes or improvements to the school grounds. At one point, however, the parents' group became quite unhappy with the open-area architecture of the school and began pressuring the staff to change their teaching methods (team teaching) and to treat the building as if it were divided into individual classrooms. Delegations of parents went to the school board without the teachers who they perceived as opposing the construction of walls in the school. A state of disequilibrium ensued. The school staff met a number of times—by themselves, with parents, and with school trustees. The teachers finally decided that the construction of walls would be acceptable. The school board provided some money for materials and parents provided the labor. The walls were built. Within a short period of time, a new equilibrium had been established. The new situation was similar to the old, but not identical, because relationships between the staff and the parents had changed.

## PERSPECTIVES ON CHANGE

Changes planned for schools vary in the extent to which they intend to alter classroom practice. Some changes, such as the introduction of an additional teaching aid, are relatively small-scale; this type of change in practice is minimal and easily incorporated into existing practice. Other changes, such as the development of a new course of studies, are far more extensive in their impact; thus, more difficult to implement. The extent to which the subjective world of the teacher, and the social system of the school, affect implementation is related to the scale of the proposed change.

For example, the characteristic isolation of the teacher can assist the implementation of a small-scale change, because this isolation makes it possible for an individual to incorporate a small change with a minimum disruption to existing practices. In this situation, the teacher is already teaching the program; there is less need to consult with other teachers about the change; the implementation of a small-scale change usually does not affect anything beyond what individual teachers do in their classrooms. For these reasons, there is less likelihood of interference from the school social system.

A large-scale change, such as the introduction of a new program, is more complex. In this situation, the change is much more visible and will receive more attention from teachers and administrators. Now the isolation works against the implementation, because there is a need for teachers to interact with one another as they learn new skills and try to apply them. This need is even more important if the innovation involves a change in orientation.

The expectations of the curriculum workers (e.g., developers) also will interact with the social system within the school. These expectations are summarized by Fullan (1982) in his description of two common perspectives on change, which he calls the "fidelity perspective" and the "mutual-adaptation or evolutionary perspective" (p. 31). The former approach assumes that the purpose of implementation is to get all teachers to use the innovation as intended by the developer. The latter approach allows much more freedom to the teacher during the implementation; this perspective assumes that those implementing a change will adapt the innovation to the actual situation, so that decisions about what to change and how to change it are made at the school or classroom level. The final change in practice that will result from this adaptation/decision-making process may not be exactly what was envisioned by the developer. Mutual adaptation is much more in tune with an ecological or interdependent perspective than the "fidelity perspective."

Various combinations of scale of change and perspective on change can affect the likelihood of implementation. On the one hand, the implementation of a large-scale change can be more difficult if it is implemented from a "fidelity perspective." Both the social system within the school and the working conditions of the teachers will be important factors in this kind of situation. On the other hand, a small-scale change from a "mutual-adaptation perspective" would probably create the fewest implementation difficulties.

## WHAT IS IMPLEMENTATION?

Throughout this chapter, the word *implementation* has been used without definition. Too often, this is precisely what happens during the development and introduction of a new program. Curriculum workers, teachers, and principals use the word *implementation,* and each assumes that everyone else has the same understanding of what this word means, although, in fact, there are many definitions.

For example, Fullan (1982), addressing the "subjective reality" of the teacher and the impact of a change on resources, methodologies, and beliefs, defines *implementation* as "the process of putting into practice an idea, program, or set of activities new to the people attempting or expected to change" (p. 54). This process results in a "change in practice on the part of teachers and students, which affects outcomes" (p. 55).

Leithwood (1982) also views implementation as a process. For him, "implementation involves reducing the differences between existing practices and practices suggested by the innovation" (p. 253). The process by which this is accomplished has certain definite characteristics. "Implementation is a process of behavioral change, in directions suggested by the innovation, occurring in stages, over time, if obstacles to such growth are overcome" (p. 254).

Other definitions of *implementation* are linked to the curriculum cycle. For example, Saylor and Alexander (1974) view the teaching process as implementation: "Instruction is . . . the implementation of the curriculum plan, usually, but not necessarily, involving teaching in the sense of student-teacher interaction in a school setting" (p. 245).

There are three common approaches to defining the word *implementation.* In the first, which is the oldest and is disappearing, *implementation* is defined as an event. This event occurs, as a professional-development activity, when a new program document is distributed to teachers. Explanations of the objectives of the program, descriptions of the new resources, and demonstrations of the new teaching methodologies may be provided at this session. According to this definition, the professional development session (or series of sessions) constitutes the implementation. When the session(s) have been completed, the teachers are then expected to teach the new program.

A second approach to implementation emphasizes the process of interaction between the curriculum developers and teachers (see Chapter 9). For example, if a new mathematics program is to be developed, the developers work with input from the teachers who will teach the new program, which may point to current problems with the mathematics program or provide detailed descriptions of current teaching methodologies. With this information, the developers design new approaches, examine new resources, or integrate new content into the existing program.

Teachers may be asked to try out these revisions. The developers then adjust the program based on the results of the field trials. When the final revision is completed on the new program, implementation is considered to be completed.

The third view of implementation recognizes it as a separate component in the curriculum cycle. Following the development and adoption of a new program, a plan for its introduction must be organized and carried out. This planning consists of more than one workshop. Because use of the new program will require changes in resources and teaching methodologies, planning requires careful examination of alternatives, resources, and strategies. Those best suited to the new program are first described and listed, and then presented to the teachers in document form (resource booklets to accompany the new program) and/or they may form the substance of introductory workshops. When this planning is finished, however, implementation is considered to be completed.

Although the preceding descriptions are simplified, they demonstrate a common problem associated with implementation. Too often, implementation is centered on *things*, such as textbooks, teaching aids, explanatory booklets. However, as illustrated by the definitions offered by Fullan and Leithwood, implementation is not as one-sided as it is often portrayed; rather, it is a process during which the teacher adapts the program to his or her subjective reality. The introduction of a change into the subjective world of the teacher is a human activity; the teacher is expected to teach a new program in the classroom while working within a complex social system. Thus, we define implementation as a process that leads to the shared ownership of the innovation. During this process, change will likely occur in an interactive way both in the teacher and in the innovation. The teacher acquires some ownership of the new program, and the developer relinquishes some control.

## CONCLUDING COMMENTS

Implementation does not affect individual teachers only. The school as a whole, parents' groups, and others interested in the innovation also may react to the change.

For example, suppose that a new science program is being introduced into an elementary school. We will assume that this program reflects a transaction position: it recommends the "inquiry approach" as the teaching methodology, and its content stresses ecology and the interdependence of different life systems. The school, as a unit, now has to come to grips with the new program. Previously, the school worked from a transmission position in its science program, relying on the use of lectures and textbooks as its primary instructional method. In such a situation, changes in the social norms would be required. Children in the school would now be doing different activities in science. These new activities might conflict with the previous norms, if, for instance, students now go on more field trips or they are allowed more time for "hands-on" activities in the classroom. Similarly, parents might have to adjust to the content of the new program, which may challenge their beliefs. For example, their beliefs may reflect a transmission position, if they think a science program should be the transference of a body of specific knowledge to their children, and the new program may be based on a transaction or transformation position.

In practice, the meaning of change extends beyond the individual classroom. It includes the school's social system and the individual parents as well. Everyone connected with a new program is affected in some way. If the teachers' perspective and the overall culture of the school are considered, implementation can be accomplished with systematic planning and an interdependent perspective.

## REFERENCES

Fullan, M. (1982). *The meaning of educational change.* Toronto: Ontario Institute for Studies in Education Press.

Fullan, M., & Park, P. (1981). *Curriculum implementation: A resource booklet.* Toronto: Ontario Ministry of Education.

Hoy, W.K., & Miskel, C.G. (1982). *Educational administration: Theory, research, and practice* (2nd ed.). New York: Random House.

Joyce, B.R., Hersh, R.H., & McKibbin, M. (1983). *The structure of school improvement.* New York: Longman.

Leithwood, K.A. (1982). Implementing curriculum innovations. In Leithwood, K.A. (Ed.), *Studies in curriculum decision making.* Toronto: Ontario Institute for Studies in Education Press.

Lortie, D.C. (1975). *Schoolteacher: A sociological study.* Chicago: University of Chicago Press.

Marris, P. (1974). *Loss and change.* New York: Pantheon Books.

Rogers, E. (1962). *Diffusion of innovations.* New York: The Free Press.

Rosenblum, S., & Louis, K.S. (1981). *Stability and change.* New York: Plenum.

Sarason, S.B. (1982) *The culture of the school and the problem of change,* (2nd ed.). Boston: Allyn and Bacon.

Saylor, J.G., & Alexander, W.M. (1974). *Planning curriculum for schools.* New York: Holt, Rinehart.

Schon, D. (1971). *Beyond the stable state.* New York: Norton.

# CHAPTER 11 CURRICULUM IMPLEMENTATION MODELS

In recent years, curriculum implementation models have been developed that address some of the issues raised in Chapter 10. These models allow curriculum workers to identify particular areas of difficulty in implementation and to develop strategies to deal with these difficulties.

One model, the Concerns-Based Adoption Model (CBAM), developed by Hall and Loucks (1978), identifies the various levels of teacher concern about an innovation and how the teacher is using the innovation in the classroom. It is primarily a descriptive model, although the descriptive data can help curriculum workers and teachers develop implementation strategies.

The Innovations Profile model, developed by Leithwood (1982), also focuses on the teacher. This model allows teachers and curriculum workers to develop a profile, of the obstacles for change, so that teachers can overcome these obstacles. Leithwood's model is not only descriptive, but also provides teachers with strategies to overcome implementation obstacles.

The Concerns-Based Adoption Model and the Innovations Profile can be applied to the implementation of programs having various orientations, although their most frequent use would probably be with the introduction of transaction curricula.

A third model, which is rooted in the transformation position and is most appropriate to addressing the implementation of programs from that orientation, is Gibb's (1978) TORI model. This model focuses on personal and social change. It provides a scale that helps teachers identify how receptive the school environment is toward implementing a particular innovation and provides some guidelines for facilitating change.

All of the models presented in this chapter are transaction or transformation oriented. In general, transmission educators have not been

concerned with implementation, because most schools already use transmission-oriented curricula, a fact that has been documented by Goodlad
(1984) in his major study of schools:

> No matter what the observational perspective, the same picture
> emerges. The two activities, involving the most students, were being
> lectured to and working on written assignments (and we have seen
> that much of this work was in the form of responding to directives
> in workbooks or on worksheets). When we add to the time spent in
> these learning modes the time spent on the routines of preparing
> for or following up instruction, the extraordinary degree of student
> passivity stands out. The amount of time spent in any other kind of
> activity (e.g., role playing, small group planning and problem solv-
> ing, constructing models) was miniscule—and does not add up to a
> great deal even when the totals for all such deviations are computed.
> Students were working alone most of the time, whether individually
> or in groups. That is, the student listened as one member of a class
> being lectured, or the student worked individually on a seat assign-
> ment. (p. 230)

For the transmission educator, the concern is not to change schools but
maintain the status quo.

## TWO TRANSACTION MODELS: CBAM AND
## INNOVATION PROFILES

### Concerns-based Adoption Model

Research on the implementation of innovations in schools and colleges,
conducted by the University of Texas Research and Development Center, has produced the Concerns-Based Adoption Model (see Hall,
George, & Rutherford, 1977; Hall & Loucks, 1978). This research has
concentrated on the use of innovations by teachers. The CBAM presents
two dimensions for describing change: 1) Stages of Concern about the
Innovation (SoC), which describes the feelings of the teacher toward the
change, and 2) Levels of Use of the Innovation (LoU), which describes
the performance of the teacher using a new program. In this model, *implementation* is defined as "the process of establishing the use of an innovation" (Loucks, 1978, p. 1). The model was developed to assist in the
description of teacher behavior during that process.

***Assumptions.*** A basic assumption of the CBAM is stated in Loucks's
definition of implementation. She states that change is a process; it is not

an event, that occurs when a new program is delivered to the teachers. A second assumption in this model is that the change process is a personal experience; each teacher experiences the change in a personal way. The result of a successful implementation is a change in the classroom practice of individual teachers.

This leads to the third assumption: Individuals within an institution must change before the institution itself will change. Planning for implementation would therefore require that initial activities be directed toward meeting the individual needs of teachers. The model is designed to assist in the identification of these needs.

The final assumption is related to how change occurs. Change is viewed as a developmental process that occurs in stages or through a series of steps. This process takes place in two areas—growth in the knowledge and use of skills, and the development of a set of feelings toward the innovation.

### *The Model.*

STAGES OF CONCERN   When confronted by a change, new teachers develop various reactions that are related to their feelings toward the change and their thoughts about its impact on their classroom. Hall et al. (1977) call the expression of these feelings and thoughts "concerns." The nature of the concerns will depend on the individual's personality and on his or her knowledge and experience relative to the specific change. Therefore, individual teachers may react in different ways to an innovation. For example, a new program may cause one teacher to feel overwhelmed by the perceived impact on the classroom; another teacher with little understanding about the program might feel indifferent; yet another teacher, who has already been exploring its use in the classroom, may feel excited about the prospects for its implementation.

Depending on the nature of their concerns, different teachers will approach a new program in different ways, to determine ways of using it and to identify the rewards or risks connected to its use. Similarly, the intensity of the teacher's concern can vary (Hall et al., 1977, p. 5). For example, the immediacy of the impending change can affect the intensity, as well as the type of concern. Thus, if a new program is scheduled for a year in the future, concerns are likely to be less intense and more centered on the need for general information. As the date approaches for use in the classroom, the concerns may become more intense and focus on management and training needs. The perceived impact on an individual's situation and his or her past experiences with similar changes are additional factors that affect the intensity and type of concerns expressed.

An individual may have more than one type of concern about a change at a given time. The type and the intensity of these concerns will vary and change as the implementation progresses. The CBAM defines the various types and levels of intensity of the concerns as *stages of concern* (see Figure 11.1).

Figure 11.1 shows the stages of development of the concerns, from a basic awareness stage, through full implementation of the change, to

---

**6** *Refocusing:* The focus is on exploration of more universal benefits from the innovation, including the possibility of major changes or replacement with a more powerful alternative. Individual has definite ideas about alternatives to the proposed or existing form of the innovation.

**5** *Collaboration:* The focus is on coordination and cooperation with others regarding use of the innovation.

**4** *Consequence:* Attention focuses on impact of the innovation on student in his/her immediate sphere of influence. The focus is on relevance of the innovation for students, evaluation of student outcomes, including performance and competencies, and changes needed to increase student outcomes.

**3** *Management:* Attention is focused on the processes and tasks of using the innovation and the best use of information and resources. Issues related to efficiency, organizing, managing, scheduling, and time demands are utmost.

**2** *Personal:* Individual is uncertain about the demands of the innovation, his/her inadequacy to meet those demands, and his/her role with the innovation. This includes analysis of his/her role in relation to the reward structure of the organization, decision making, and consideration of potential conflicts with existing structures or personal commitment. Financial or status implications of the program for self and colleagues may also be reflected.

**1** *Informational:* A general awareness of the innovation and interest in learning more detail about it is indicated. The person seems to be unworried about himself/herself in relation to the innovation. She/he is interested in substantive aspects of the innovation in a selfless manner such as general characteristics, effects, and requirements for use.

**0** *Awareness:* Little concern about or involvement with the innovation is indicated.

---

**Figure 11.1** Stages of concern about the innovation. (*From Hall, G.E., and Loucks, S.F. Teacher concerns as a basis for facilitating and personalizing staff development.* Teachers College Record, 80(1), 1978, p. 41. Reprinted with permission.)

global implications and possible alternatives. These stages may be grouped into four broader developmental stages:

**1.** Stages 0–1: Unrelated Concerns. Teachers at this level do not perceive a relationship between themselves and the proposed change. For example, if a school system is developing a new social studies program for grades one through six, a teacher at the unrelated concerns stage would simply be aware that the development is occurring. At Stage 1, this teacher would be interested in gaining more information, but would not be concerned about how the new program would affect his or her classroom.

**2.** Stage 2: Personal Concerns. At this stage, the individual considers the impact of the innovation in relation to his or her personal situation and is concerned about how the new program compares to present practice. In our social studies example, a teacher at this stage would express concerns about his or her ability to teach the new program. The degree to which the program is different from what is currently being taught might also be a concern. The teacher might raise questions concerning the amount of freedom he or she would have in choosing topics or adjusting the methodology.

**3.** Stage 3: Task-related Concerns. The use of the innovation in the classroom forms the basis of the concerns at this level. Returning to our social studies example, the teacher would now be concerned about the implementation of the program in his or her classroom. Length of time required to teach the units, the best way to organize the students for instruction, and acquiring familiarity with new textbooks would be typical concerns of the teacher at this level.

**4.** Stages 4–6: Impact-related Concerns. When a teacher reaches this level, his or her concerns extend beyond self to the impact of the change on others. Beginning with the consequences for students, these concerns expand to include other teachers and, finally, to the impact of the change on a more universal scale. At this stage, concerns have developed to the point where alternatives to the original innovation are conceived.

To use another example, a social studies teacher at Level 4 would express concerns about how students should be evaluated, expected levels of achievement and ways to help students improve their work. Level 5 concerns reflect interest in how other teachers are implementing the program and might also extend to the influence of the program on the skills and concepts to be taught in subsequent grades. Finally, teachers at Level 6 would reveal concerns about the future impact of the social studies program on the whole classroom program, which might result in exploration of ways to improve its integration with other programs.

Hall et al. (1977) suggest that, during an implementation, different concerns increase and decrease in intensity. These variations can be used to plot the progress of the implementation. For example, the concerns found at Levels 0,1, and 2 are most intense at the beginning of an implementation, whereas management concerns (Levels 4–6) become more intense as teachers begin to use the new program and the earlier concerns are resolved.

LEVELS OF USE    The LoU dimension of the Concerns-Based Adoption Model (see Figure 11.2) focuses on what teachers actually do with a new program; it does not attempt to explain causality (i.e., why a teacher is at a certain level). Eight levels of use are described, ranging from a level at which the teacher is not even aware of the existence of the change to a level that demonstrates sophisticated use. This chart also shows the decision points associated with each level of use. The decision point indicates what actions the teacher must take to move to the next higher level. Each level shown on the chart is further defined by the seven categories shown across the top of the chart. The categories describe the teacher's typical behaviors at each level of use of an innovation.

During the implementation of change, teachers will demonstrate various uses of the new program. The different levels of use will develop as the teacher's skill level increases. For example, before actually using the new program, a teacher requires information about it and familiarity with its application. This is the orienting stage. As teachers begin to use the innovation, they may need to learn new teaching techniques and make adjustments in their classroom (Sharing Level 0). When questioned, this teacher may report that he or she is still trying to assess the nature of the new program and what its impact will be on the current classroom mathematics program (Status Reporting Level 1).

It is possible for a teacher to show different levels of use in different categories. For example, a teacher faced with the need to implement a new mathematics program may display the following characteristics: He or she might show a high level in the knowledge category, if this teacher has learned about the new program's recommended text, organization of the content, and requirements of the classroom timetable (Knowledge Level 2). However, this same teacher may be at a lower level on the Sharing scale, if he or she is not talking about the new program with other teachers who are also attempting to use it. As teachers begin to use the innovation, they may need to learn new teaching techniques, make adjustments to their classroom organization, or incorporate new resources into their teaching. This is the managing stage. Once use of the innovation has become routine, teachers can then direct their attentions to increasing the benefits for their students. In the final stage, teachers integrate their use of the change with what others are doing.

*Applications.* The SoC and LoU dimensions of the Concerns-Based Adoption Model can be used to describe teacher positions in relation to the use of a new program. The knowledge gained from the application of this model can then be used to facilitate further implementation activities.

In order to obtain the relevant information, both the SoC and the LoU scales would need to be used. The SoC will assist in defining the reasons for those particular levels, and the LoU will describe the activities of the teachers.

Gathering this information requires skill and training. Hall et al. (1977) describe the format, use, and interpretation of a questionnaire and the open-ended questions used to determine the stages of concern. Loucks, Newlove, and Hall (1975) provide similar information about the interviewing techniques used to determine levels of use.

The information gathered might also indicate other factors that need to be addressed. For example, many personal concerns and low levels of use might indicate that the new program is not suited to local conditions. A revision of the proposed program may be needed before teachers can move to higher levels of use. Similarly, information about the difficulty of the skills required by teachers can be obtained. If the skills required are too difficult, progress beyond the levels at which teachers became stalled is not possible.

Using the information to plan ongoing implementation strategies is another specific application. Knowledge of the teachers' particular concerns makes it possible to design implementation activities to address those concerns. Similarly, knowing the levels of use makes it possible to provide support designed to assist teachers in moving to the next level.

Use of this model can also assist in long-range planning for an implementation. Goals designed to bring about desired levels of use can be established when planning the implementation timeline. Through observation, progress of the implementation can be charted and interim goals can be set by groups of teachers.

Although the assumptions of this model are transaction-oriented, it is suitable for assessing the use of most programs being implemented. This model provides for teachers to express their concerns, whether they are attempting to implement a transaction program with which they feel quite comfortable or a transformation program they are trying to understand.

## Innovation Profiles Model

For Leithwood and Montgomery (1980), implementation is the "process of reducing the gap between images and outcomes" (p. 3). The word *images* refers to the image held by society of an "educated person." Policy

**FIGURE 11.2  The LoU Chart**

## LEVELS OF USE

### Scale Point Definitions of the Levels of Use of the Innovation

Levels of Use are distinct states that represent observably different types of behavior and patterns of innovation use as exhibited by individuals and groups. These levels characterize a user's development in acquiring new skills and varying use of the innovation. Each level encompasses a range of behaviors, but is limited by a set of Identifiable Decision Points. For descriptive purposes, each level is defined by seven categories.

## CATEGORIES

### Knowledge

That which the user knows about characteristics of the innovation, how to use it, and consequences of its use. This is cognitive knowledge related to using the innovation, not feelings or attitudes.

### Acquiring Information

Solicits information about the innovation in a variety of ways, including questioning resource persons, corresponding with resource agencies, reviewing printed materials, and making visits.

### Sharing

Discusses the innovation with others. Shares plans, ideas, resources, outcomes, and problems related to use of the innovation.

| | Knowledge | | |
|---|---|---|---|
| **LEVEL 0**<br>NON-USE: State in which the user has little or no knowledge of the innovation, no involvement with the innovation, and is doing nothing toward becoming involved. | Knows nothing about this or similar innovations or has only very limited general knowledge of efforts to develop innovations in the area. | Takes little or no action to solicit information beyond reviewing descriptive information about this or similar innovations when it happens to come to personal attention. | Is not communicating with others about the innovation beyond possibly acknowledging that the innovation exists. |
| **DECISION POINT A** | *Takes action to learn more detailed information about the innovation.* | | |
| **LEVEL I**<br>ORIENTATION: State in which the user has acquired or is acquiring information about the innovation and/or has explored or is exploring its value orientation and its demands upon user and user system. | Knows general information about the innovation such as origin, characteristics, and implementation requirements. | Seeks descriptive material about the innovation. Seeks opinions and knowledge of others through discussions, visits, or workshops. | Discusses the innovation in general terms and/or exchanges descriptive information, materials, or ideas about the innovation and possible implications of its use. |
| **DECISION POINT B** | *Makes a decision to use the innovation by establishing a time to begin.* | | |
| **LEVEL II**<br>PREPARATION: State in which the user is preparing for first use of the innovation. | Knows logistical requirements, necessary resources and timing for initial use of the innovation, and details of initial experiences for clients. | Seeks information and resources specifically related to preparation for use of the innovation in own setting. | Discusses resources needed for initial use of the innovation. Joins others in pre-use training, and in planning for resources, logistics, schedules, etc., in preparation for first use. |

**FIGURE 11.2 The LoU Chart** *Continued.*

| DECISION POINT C | | | |
|---|---|---|---|
| **LEVEL III**<br>MECHANICAL USE: State in which the user focuses most effort on the short-term, day-to-day use of the innovation with little time for reflection. Changes in use are made more to meet user needs than client needs. The user is primarily engaged in a stepwise attempt to master the tasks required to use the innovation, often resulting in disjointed and superficial use. | *Begins first use of the innovation.*<br><br>Knows on a day-to-day basis the requirements for using the innovation. Is more knowledgeable on short-term activities and effects than long-range activities and effects of use of the innovation. | Solicits management information about such things as logistics, scheduling techniques, and ideas for reducing amount of time and work required of user. | Discusses management and logistical issues related to use of the innovation. Resources and materials are shared for purposes of reducing management, flow and logistical problems related to use of the innovation. |
| DECISION POINT D-1 | | | |
| **LEVEL IVA**<br>ROUTINE: Use of the innovation is stabilized. Few if any changes are being made in ongoing use. Little preparation or thought is being given to improving innovation use or its consequences. | *A routine pattern of use is established.*<br><br>Knows both short- and long-term requirements for use and how to use the innovation with minimum effort or stress. | Makes no special efforts to seek information as a part of ongoing use of the innovation. | Describes current use of the innovation with little or no reference to ways of changing use. |

258

| | | | |
|---|---|---|---|
| **DECISION POINT D-2** | *Changes use of the innovation based on formal or informal evaluation in order to increase client outcomes.* | | |
| **LEVEL IV B**<br>REFINEMENT: State in which the user varies the use of the innovation to increase the impact on clients within immediate sphere of influence. Variations are based on knowledge of both short- and long-term consequences for clients. | Knows cognitive and affective effects of the innovation on clients and ways for increasing impact on clients. | Solicits information and materials that focus specifically on changing use of the innovation to affect client outcomes. | Discusses own methods of modifying use of the innovation to change client outcomes. |
| **DECISION POINT E** | *Initiates changes in use of innovation based on input of and in coordination with what colleagues are doing.* | | |
| **LEVEL V**<br>INTEGRATION: State in which the user is combining own efforts to use the innovation with related activities of colleagues to achieve a collective impact on clients within their common sphere of influence. | Knows how to coordinate own use of the innovation with colleagues to provide a collective impact on clients. | Solicits information and opinions for the purpose of collaborating with others in use of the innovation. | Discusses efforts to increase client impact through collaboration with others on personal use of the innovation. |

## FIGURE 11.2 The LoU Chart Continued.

*Begins exploring alternatives to or major modifications of the innovation presently in use.*

| DECISION POINT F | | | |
|---|---|---|---|
| **LEVEL VI**<br>RENEWAL: State in which the user reevaluates the quality of use of the innovation, seeks major modifications of or alternatives to present innovation to achieve increased impact on clients, examines new developments in the field, and explores new goals for self and the system. | Knows of alternatives that could be used to change or replace the present innovation that would improve the quality of outcomes of its use. | Seeks information and materials about other innovations as alternatives to the present innovation or for making major adaptations in the innovation. | Focuses discussions on identification of major alternatives or replacements for the current innovation. |

### CATEGORIES

| Assessing | Planning | Status Reporting | Performing |
|---|---|---|---|
| Examines the potential or actual use of the innovation or some aspect of it. This can be a mental assessment or can involve actual collections and analysis of data. | Designs and outlines short- and/or long-range steps to be taken during process of innovation adoption, i.e., aligns resources, schedules activities, meets with others to organize and/or coordinate use of the innovation. | Describes personal stand at the present time in relation to use of the innovation. | Carries out the actions and activities entailed in operationalizing the innovation. |

| | | | |
|---|---|---|---|
| Takes no action to analyze the innovation, its characteristics, possible use, or consequences of use. | Schedules no time and specifies no steps for the study or use of the innovation. | Reports little or no personal involvement with the innovation. | Takes no discernible action toward learning about or using the innovation. The innovation and/or its accouterments are not present or in use. |
| Analyzes and compares materials, content, requirements for use, evaluation reports, potential outcomes, strengths and weaknesses for purpose of making a decision about use of the innovation. | Plans to gather necessary information and resources as needed to make a decision for or against use of the innovation. | Reports presently orienting self to what the innovation is and is not. | Explores the innovation and requirements for its use by talking to others about it, reviewing descriptive information and sample materials, attending orientation sessions, and observing others using it. |
| Analyzes detailed requirements and available resources for initial use of the innovation. | Identifies steps and procedures entailed in obtaining resources and organizing activities and events for initial use of the innovation. | Reports preparing self for initial use of the innovation. | Studies reference materials in depth, organizes resources and logistics, schedules and receives skill training in preparation for initial use. |

**FIGURE 11.2  The LoU Chart** Continued.

| | | | |
|---|---|---|---|
| Examines own use of the innovation with respect to problems of logistics, management, time, schedules, resources, and general reactions of clients. | Plans for organizing and managing resources, activities, and events related primarily to immediate ongoing use of the innovation. Planned-for changes address managerial or logistical issues with a short-term perspective. | Reports that logistics, time, management, resource organization, etc., are the focus of most personal efforts to use the innovation. | Manages innovation with varying degrees of efficiency. Often lacks anticipation of immediate consequences. The flow of actions in the user and clients is often disjointed, uneven and uncertain. When changes are made, they are primarily in response to logistical and organizational problems. |
| Limits evaluation activities to those administratively required, with little attention paid to findings for the purpose of changing use. | Plans intermediate and long-range actions with little projected variation in how the innovation will be used. Planning focuses on routine use of resources, personnel, etc. | Reports that personal use of the innovation is going along satisfactorily with few if any problems. | Uses the innovation smoothly with minimal management problems: over time, there is little variation in pattern of use. |

| Assesses use of the innovation for the purpose of changing current practices to improve client outcomes. | Develops intermediate and long-range plans that anticipate possible and needed steps, resources, and events designed to enhance client outcomes. | Reports varying use of the innovation in order to change client outcomes. | Explores and experiments with alternative combinations of the innovation with existing practices to maximize client involvement and to optimize client outcomes. |
|---|---|---|---|
| Appraises collaborative use of the innovation in terms of client outcomes and strengths and weaknesses of the integrated effort. | Plans specific actions to coordinate own use of the innovation with others to achieve increased impact on clients. | Reports spending time and energy collaborating with others about integrating own use of the innovation. | Collaborates with others in use of the innovation as a means for expanding the innovation's impact on clients. Changes in use are made in coordination with others. |
| Analyzes advantages and disadvantages of major modifications or alternatives to the present innovation. | Plans activities that involve pursuit of alternatives to enhance or replace the innovation. | Reports considering major modifications of or alternatives to present use of the innovation. | Explores other innovations that could be used in combination with or in place of the present innovation in an attempt to develop more effective means of achieving client outcomes. |

**Figure 11.2** The LoU chart. *(From Hall, G.E., Loucks, S.F., Rutherford, W.L., and Newlove, B.W. Levels of use of the innovation: A framework for analyzing innovation adoption. Journal of Teacher Education, 26(1), 1975, pp. 54–55. Reprinted with permission of the American Association of Colleges for Teacher Education.)*

statements or curriculum guidelines translate into school programs what society believes an educated person should know. The strategy developed by Leithwood and Montgomery (1980) and Leithwood (1982) for implementing a new program involves teachers changing their practices in accordance with the new program.

A gap is assumed to exist between societal goals and the achievements of the students. The purpose of introducing new programs into the schools is to provide the means of narrowing that gap. The attempts to accomplish this constitute implementation. With this definition of implementation, many activities are possible, for example, alterations to the organization of the school, or in-service training of teachers.

***Assumptions.***  Leithwood and Montgomery assume that implementation is a process of mutual adaptation; both the developer and the classroom teacher are free to make adjustments to the new program. This means that the classroom teacher has some degree of autonomy during the implementation period to make decisions about the use of a new program.

A further assumption is that all teachers will not be at the same level of readiness to use a new program. Due to their variations in curriculum skills, different teachers will have different needs during implementation. Thus, the size of the gap between existing practice, and the practice suggested by the innovation, will vary from teacher to teacher.

The strategy of this model for closing this gap is based on the assumption that the gap is not closed in one step, but, rather, that a number of steps will be taken to narrow the discrepancy. Individual teacher growth occurs in the movement from one step to the next. The number of steps involved varies with the complexity of the innovation. Generally, there are not as many steps required in learning to use a new textbook as there are in adopting a new teaching methodology.

Finally, this model assumes that growth is possible once the stages involved have been identified. Movement from stage to stage is accomplished by overcoming identifiable obstacles. Understanding what stimulates or inhibits this growth is the key to successful implementation.

***The Model.***  Figure 11.3 illustrates how the Innovations Profile model divides the process of implementation into six different tasks. The six prime tasks are subdivided into two phases: tasks 1–3 form the diagnostic phase and tasks 4–6 form the application phase. Two evaluation tasks are added to measure whether the strategies employed are successful.

DIAGNOSIS TASKS   In order to complete the three diagnostic tasks, a close study of the new program is necessary. To aid in the identification of the pertinent elements, the program should be described in relation

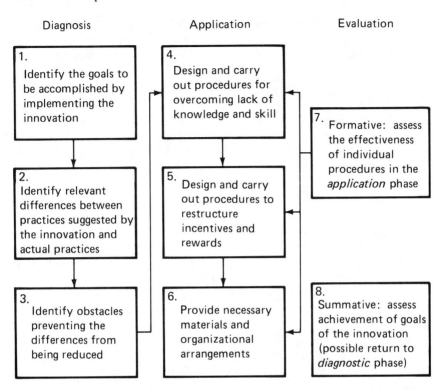

Diagnosis      Application      Evaluation

1.
Identify the goals to be accomplished by implementing the innovation

2.
Identify relevant differences between practices suggested by the innovation and actual practices

3.
Identify obstacles preventing the differences from being reduced

4.
Design and carry out procedures for overcoming lack of knowledge and skill

5.
Design and carry out procedures to restructure incentives and rewards

6.
Provide necessary materials and organizational arrangements

7.
Formative: assess the effectiveness of individual procedures in the *application* phase

8.
Summative: assess achievement of goals of the innovation (possible return to *diagnostic* phase)

**Figure 11.3** A strategy for implementing curriculum innovations. (*From Leithwood, K.A. (Ed.). Studies in curriculum decision making. Toronto: Ontario Institute for Studies in Education, 1982, p. 255. Reprinted with permission.*)

to a set of criteria. Leithwood (1982, p. 249) presents a set that he calls *curriculum dimensions*. Nine categories are included in the set:

1. Images or platform: The belief or orientations on which the program is based.
2. Objectives: The intended learning outcomes for the students.
3. Student entry behaviors: Expected student achievements before beginning the new program.
4. Content: The subject matter.
5. Instructional material: The resources to be used by the student.
6. Teaching strategies: Proposed teacher behavior to facilitate learning by the students.
7. Learning experiences: Student activities, mental or physical.
8. Time: The amount of time the student will spend on a given activity.
9. Assessment tools or procedures: The means to be used to assess student achievement.

It is not anticipated that all nine dimensions will be of equal importance in a new program. Upon examination, it may be found that a new program is different from current practice in a few dimensions only. For example, a school staff beginning the implementation of a new social and environmental studies program may find that the *images* dimension is quite important. This would be the case if the new program required combining previously separate subjects, such as social studies and science. To use another example, the implementation of a new physical education program might stress new *content* and *teaching strategies*. This would occur if the new program introduced into the existing program the use of noncompetitive games and activities.

A description of a classroom using the new program should be developed, so that implementation of the nine curriculum dimensions can be translated into appropriate activities. Steps representing stages for moving from nonuse to full implementation are developed for each dimension. A teacher who has fully implemented the new program will have taken action in all nine dimensions.

In the physical education example, full implementation in the *teaching strategies* dimension might entail use by the teacher of a problem-setting technique to encourage cooperative activities suitable for all students in the class. One intermediate stage might be the use of a form of classroom organization that involves the whole class instead of the traditional small groups. Another intermediate stage might involve setting problems for students, rather than supplying them with a set of rules to follow for an activity.

The combination of the description of the program with the desired behaviors broken down into stages of growth forms an Innovation Profile. The production of the profile is the purpose of the first diagnostic task.

The second diagnostic task identifies the gap between present practice and that required by the new program. To accomplish this comparison, a "user profile" is developed for each teacher, which presents the position of each teacher in relation to the stages of growth. The information may be gathered through interviews and observations. The gap between present and new practice can then be identified for each teacher. It is to be expected that the teachers within a school may be at various levels at the beginning of an implementation. In the physical education example, a teacher who had attended a summer course and received instruction in the use of noncompetitive games would not be at the same stage as a teacher who was not aware of the games.

The purpose of the third diagnostic task is to define specific obstacles to be overcome by the teachers. Figure 11.4 shows the obstacles in relation to the defined stages of growth. It is the presence of these obstacles that hinders the movement of teachers from one level to the next during the implementation of a new program.

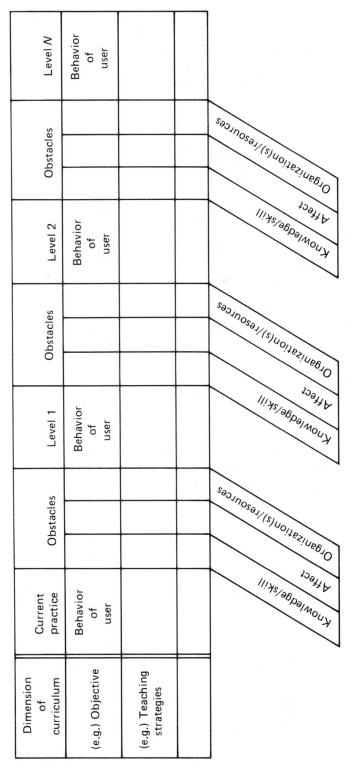

**Figure 11.4** A conception of curriculum implementation: A process of growth over time, in selected curriculum dimension, as successive obstacles to growth are identified and overcome. (*From Leithwood, K.A. (Ed.). Studies in curriculum decision making. Toronto: Ontario Institute for Studies in Education, 1982, p. 256. Reprinted with permission.*)

For example, insufficient knowledge of content can be one source of obstruction. Obstacles with an affect base can be more difficult to isolate, but should be carefully studied; feelings of inadequacy may develop from lack of knowledge or skill. Because changing a practice is a risk-taking activity, a supportive climate is necessary. The third type of obstacles are those related to the organizational structure and the necessary resources to support the move to the next stage.

Identification of obstacles will provide the information necessary to continue with the implementation. Professional development and resource needs for teachers can then be identified.

APPLICATION TASKS   When the initial examination and analysis of the innovation has been completed, the second set of implementation tasks begins. At this stage, the focus is on practices in the classroom. The purpose is to facilitate a changeover to practices suggested by the new program. Strategies to overcome the identified obstacles also need to be developed.

The process of developing and carrying out the strategies forms the substance of the three application tasks. Leithwood (1982) refers to this as "a curriculum the teachers must develop for themselves" (p. 264). The strategies used to overcome the obstacles will vary depending on the exact nature of the obstacles.

For the teachers involved with the physical education program in our earlier example, the application tasks might include a variety of strategies: attendance at workshops and observations in classes where the new program is being used might be planned; budget submissions might be prepared to ensure that the necessary equipment is available; if it is anticipated that student attitudes will be an obstacle, special classes might be planned to explain the purpose and operation of the new program. All these activities would be scheduled for appropriate times during the implementation period.

EVALUATION TASKS   The evaluative tasks are conducted on the basis of criteria developed in the previous tasks. The purpose of the formative evaluation in Task 7 is to see if the obstacles identified have been overcome. Task 8, a summative assessment of the innovation, is instituted when it is ascertained that most of the obstacles have been overcome.

*Applications.*   The Innovations Profile model is best used when the people involved in the implementation of a new program can meet together frequently, because the intensive nature of the planning and discussions required by the various tasks necessitates many meetings. The staff of an elementary school or a department in a high school are groups that might use this model effectively.

Although programs with any orientation could use this model, it is especially suitable for transaction-oriented curricula, because descriptions of teacher activities and the establishment of clear goals are crucial to its use. Suppose, for example, that a new social studies program is being introduced and that this new program represents a change from a content-oriented program to one which stresses the teaching of concepts and complex intellectual skills. The processes outlined in the Innovations Profile model would require descriptions of classrooms using this new program and a clear description of goals for the implementation. Teachers would have to understand both of these descriptions before "user profiles" could be developed; it is less likely that an implementation will continue if teacher expectations are unclear.

Because this model establishes a series of steps and identifies obstacles, it is applicable in situations when a detailed timeline for implementation is required. The overview of the anticipated steps needed can be used to determine the complexity of the implementation and to assist in establishing suitable timelines.

## TRANSFORMATION MODEL

### TORI Model

TORI, a method developed by Jack Gibb that focuses on personal and social change, is representative of the transformation position. It centers on how people in an organization such as a school system can assess change in the total organizational environment.

***Assumptions.*** Gibb (1978) explains the four processes that comprise the basic assumptions of the TORI model:

> To trust with fullness means that I *discover and create my own life.* The trusting life is an inter-flowing and inter-weaving of the processes of discovery and creation. These processes have four primary and highly interrelated elements:
> - discovering and creating who I am, tuning into my own uniqueness, being aware of my own essence, *trusting* me—*being who I am.* (**T**)
> - discovering and creating ways of opening and revealing myself to myself and to others, disclosing my essence, discovering yours, communing with you—*showing me.* (**O**)
> - discovering and creating my own paths, flows, and rhythms, creating my emerging and organizing nature, and becoming, actualizing, or realizing this nature—*doing what I want.* (**R**)

• discovering and creating with you our interbeing, the ways we can live together in *interdepending* community, in freedom and intimacy—*being with you.* (**I**) (p. 20)

***The Model.***    Gibb asserts that an organization can exist on different levels of what he calls *environmental quality* (see Figure 11.5).

Gibb claims that this scale of 10 states applies to the development of a person, the evolution of the race, the evolution of our myths and beliefs, and the development of our attempt to "manage" processes and people. At each level there is some kind of integration. Each new level brings a new set of needs, a new set of assumptions about people, and new problems. According to Gibb "a new level integrates these changes, gives wholeness to the system and helps to maintain a perceived rationality and order to the emerging processes" (p. 59).

Gibb offers the following guidelines for facilitating growth to higher levels of environmental quality.

**1.** *Freedom of flow:* The person is allowed to move in tune with his or her rhythms and inner harmony. Thus, there is a minimum of emphasis on specific procedures but more stress on how people can be "freed up" in an organization such as a school system.

**2.** *Trusting the process:* The organization allows people to trust their own inner processes. This allows a teacher to take risks in the classroom as opposed to developing highly structured learning environments.

**3.** *Creating vision and clarity:* In Gibb's view, it is important that each organization, such as a school, sets its own mission or sense of where it is going.

**4.** *Caring for the self and for the system's self:* Gibb asserts:

There are many ways of applying this self-care principle to our professional and organizational lives. If, for instance, I am the teacher in a classroom, my first consideration is: How can I make this an environment that turns me on, that I look forward to, in which I find daily love, and where I am doing what I want to do? When I can do this for myself, the environment cannot help but be a good one for students. There will be learning, growth, and community. (p. 123)

**5.** *Encouraging the open life and the open system:* Openness allows the person to unlock "blocked" behavior and to release energy consumed in the neurotic effort to cover up behavior, lessens our need to be defensive, and is helpful in reducing negativity. Gibb advocates "open spaces" in schools and classrooms and open agendas for meetings.

| Phase theme | Definitive nature of phase | Key function best nurtured |
|---|---|---|
| I Punitive | Punishment as a form of control and socialization | Reduces frightening chaos and apparent danger |
| II Autocratic | Power and authority used to maintain control and order | Provides order and structure |
| III Benevolent | Parental nurturing and caring as a primary theme | Provides security and affection |
| IV Advisory | Focus on consultative help and data collection | Expands the data base and enriches communication |
| V Participative | Focus on participation, consensual decision-making, and choice | Increases involvement, loyalty, and group strength |
| VI Emergent | Rise of group and community as new and leaderless level of reality and interaction | Reduces dependency, adds vitality and functional resources |
| VII Organic | Rise of major role of emphatic and intuitive modes of being and communicating | Taps intuitive and sublingual sources of creativity and being |
| VIII Holistic | Integration of unconscious, archetypical and latent processes into enriched living | Releases wellsprings of energy and creativity |
| IX Transcendent | Integration of altered and extra-sensory states into being and consciousness | Taps non-sensory sources of being and energy |
| X Cosmic | Focus on cosmic, universal, and nirvanic states of community and being | Taps into as-yet-little-known universal energy and being |

**Figure 11.5**   The development of environmental quality. (*From Gibb, J.R.* Trust: A new view of personal and organizational development. *Los Angeles, CA: Guild of Tutors Press, 1978, p. 51. Reprinted with permission of Omicron Press, La Jolla, California.*)

**6.** *Focusing energy:* People focus their energy on what they enjoy doing or what is intrinsically motivating. When people work at this level, they attain the deepest satisfaction from their effort.

**7.** *Reducing constraints:* Reducing constraints in an organization or classroom allows people to be who they are rather than responding to unreasonable external expectations.

**8.** *Focusing on environmental design:* An effective environmental design in which there are not hard boundaries separating student from teacher creates mutuality and flow within a school or classroom.

**9.** *Building community:* A deep sense of interpersonal connectedness in an organization or school is encouraged. The teachers feel responsible to one another.

**10.** *Sensing the cosmic all-in-all:* This involves an inner tranquility, a more encompassing perspective on life, an awareness of divinity in every being, an openness to experience, and a new appreciation for the nonrational and nonverbal.

Gibb discusses the classroom environment and argues that teachers often block learning through a number of behaviors:

**1.** Placing too many controls on the students
**2.** Getting too involved "in the evaluation process and draining energy into grade setting" (Gibb, 1978, p. 180)
**3.** Spending excessive amounts of work in planning rather than focusing on direct learning
**4.** Focusing too much on power and authority rather than learning
**5.** Repressing one's emotions and thus reducing opportunities for caring
**6.** Focusing excessively on gimmicks or techniques

According to Gibb, the application of TORI to education usually leads to the following results:

> When the TORI community is used as a medium for education, the essence of education becomes a process of creative, joint inquiry, learning of emergent knowledge and skills, rather than a teaching–learning process. The focus of thought, action, and responsibility is in the learner rather than in the teacher. The motivation to learn comes from sources inside the learner and the process, and from intrinsic rewards and punishments within the very processes of interaction. The curriculum comes from the learner and the requirements of the process of inquiry, rather than from sources external to the learner.
> Life in a learning community is a continuing, flowing process.

All activities justify themselves as enriching to the moment, the process and the goals. Classical education is seen as preparatory to later and more significant life, and thus requires constraint, goal-deferment, and discipline. In the learning community, the goals are set by the learners as they emerge from the process, rather than being set by role, authority, or system. Rewards and punishments are informal, emergent, and intrinsic to the process of joint inquiry and interaction; they are not prescribed, formalized, extrinsic, or used as controls. (p. 222)

*Applications.* In Gibb's TORI model, curriculum workers focus on personal and organizational development, which provides the necessary conditions for a positive change. The teacher or curriculum worker using this model would identify where they are on the environmental quality scale and where they would like to go as a class, school, or system. They then would apply the TORI guidelines in attempting to improve the environmental quality of the unit.

The strength of this model is Gibb's scale of environmental quality. He has developed an intriguing framework for analyzing the range of environments that we might find in a school. These environments mesh with the metaorientations presented in this text. The punitive, autocratic, and benevolent levels can be viewed as transmission environments. The advisory, participative, and emergent environments are linked to the transaction position. The organic, holistic, transcendent, and cosmic environments are within the transformation position. Thus, the environmental scale allows the curriculum worker to match the program and its orientation to local environment. For example, if a school system's environment were at the autocratic level, it would be extremely difficult to introduce a transformation program.

The weakness in this model is Gibb's guidelines for change. Basically, these are transformation guidelines and would not be applicable at the lower stages of the environmental-quality scale. Also, because Gibb's guidelines are very general, the average teacher or curriculum worker would be left with little specific guidance on how to provide an appropriate environment for change.

## CONCLUDING COMMENTS

Each innovation will have a unique impact on a school. The degree to which the change is different from existing practice and the number of new components it contains (e.g., methodologies, resources) will affect the way school personnel respond. The use of one implementation model for all changes in a school is not practical.

For example, if the mathematics program has been revised to introduce the spiral approach, one particular set of concerns needs to be addressed during the implementation. Another change, such as the introduction of a dramatics arts program to grades seven and eight, will raise different concerns. In the first case, a model such as the Concerns-Based Adoption Model might provide a process that can be used to plan the introduction of a new methodology. In the second situation, there is a need to study both the new document and the reactions of teachers to it; the implementation approach used in this case might be one that draws on a number of models, to combine document and teacher concerns. A guideline for the dramatic arts program may have been issued by the state department of education. If the local school district already has a course of studies for dramatic arts, the implementation might involve identifying discrepancies between the new curriculum and the existing programs. Following this analysis, the Concerns-Based Adoption Model may be employed to provide further direction to the implementation, at which point the use of the Innovation Profiles model might then be more appropriate. Finally, the TORI model could be used to assess the appropriateness of the environment for change.

The emphasis in this chapter on models makes it possible to overlook the student. However, the purpose of introducing a change in a school is to facilitate student growth. An implementation is not complete unless student growth is facilitated and the concerns, needs, and activities/achievements of students are addressed.

Parents and the community can play an important part in the implementation of a change in a school. Their support and understanding is required. The models do not address these people specifically, but modifications to the models can be made. For example, the stages of concern in the Concerns-Based Adoption Model could be modified to provide information about parents.

Implementation models facilitate the process of introducing a change and make the monitoring of its use in the classroom easier. Yet, as mentioned, some aspects of change are not addressed by these implementation models. To deal more completely with implementation, it is necessary to make the model part of a broader, more comprehensive, implementation plan.

A summary chart follows that outlines the major steps within each model discussed in this chapter.

## REFERENCES

Gibb, J.R. (1978). *Trust: A new view of personal and organizational development.* Los Angeles, CA: Guild of Tutors Press.

Goodlad, J. (1984). *A place called school.* New York: McGraw-Hill.

## SUMMARY CHART:  Chapter 11—Implementation Models

| TRANSACTION MODELS | | TRANSFORMATION MODEL |
|---|---|---|
| Hall–Loucks—Levels of Use | Leithwood—Innovations Profile | Gibb—Environmental-Quality Scale |
| 0  Nonuse | Diagnosis Phase | Punitive |
| 1  Orientation | Identify goals | Autocratic |
| 2  Preparation | Identify gaps between | Benevolent |
| 3  Mechanical use | practices and new | Advisory |
| | program | |
| | Identify obstacles | |
| 4a  Routine use | Application | Participative |
| 4b  Refinement | Design procedures to | Emergent |
| 5  Integration | overcome obstacles | Organic |
| 6  Renewal | Restructure incentives | Holistic |
| | Provide materials and | |
| | organizational | |
| | arrangements | |
| | Evaluation | Transcendent |
| | Assess procedures | Cosmic |
| | used in applica- | |
| | tion phase | |
| | Summative evaluation | |

Hall, G.E., & Loucks, S. (1978). Teacher concerns as a basis for facilitating and personalizing staff development. *Teachers College Record, 80*(1), 36–53.

Hall, G.E., George, A.A., & Rutherford, W.L. (1977). *Measuring stages of concern about the innovation: A manual for use of the SoC questionnaire.* Austin, TX: The University of Texas.

Leithwood, K.A. (1982). Implementing curriculum innovations. In Leithwood, K.A. (Ed.), *Studies in curriculum decision making.* Toronto: Ontario Institute for Studies in Education Press.

Leithwood, K.A., & Montgomery, D.J. (1980). *Assumptions and uses of a procedure for assessing program implementation.* Paper presented at the annual meeting of the American Educational Research Association, Boston.

Loucks, S.F. (1978). *Conceptualizing and measuring program implementation: A variable useful for planned change and evaluation.* Paper presented at the annual meeting of the American Educational Research Association, Toronto.

Loucks, S.F., Newlove, B.W., & Hall, G.E. (1975). *Measuring levels of use of the innovation: A manual for trainers, interviewers, and raters.* Austin, TX: The University of Texas.

# CHAPTER 12 PLANNING IMPLEMENTATION

The models presented in Chapter 11 provide frameworks for assessing whether implementation has occurred. The procedures and strategies suggested in each model provide a focus for implementation activities and information gathering. In order to decide on the most appropriate model and to apply it to an actual implementation, a plan must be developed. Poor planning is often a leading cause for failure to bring about change. In this chapter, we outline the main components of an implementation plan. This plan can be utilized to identify potential difficulties and to deal with the problems, because even the most conscientious anticipation is not likely to identify all the difficulties to be encountered.

Problems can begin with the proposal of change itself. More than a superficial examination of the new program is required, so that subsequent planning is relevant to the teachers. Other barriers to the adoption of the change can also be anticipated. Identification of barriers to successful implementation makes it possible to specify key elements in an implementation plan and to devise methods of dealing with the barriers as well as accomplishing effective implementation. One crucial element, professional development, is the most important element of the implementation plan and thus receives particular attention in this chapter.

There are seven primary components of an implementation plan:

1. A study of the new program
2. Identification of resources
3. Role definition
4. Professional development
5. Timelines
6. Communications system
7. Monitoring the implementation

## BARRIERS TO IMPLEMENTATION

When implementation is considered to be an event, rather than a process, it is assumed the presence of a new program results in its use. Research has shown us, however, that not all innovations are actually implemented. Berman and McLaughlin (1975) report a relatively low success rate with the implementation of various federally sponsored Title programs and the Right-to-Read program. Although Crandall and his associates (1982) report a higher success rate in their study entitled *Dissemination Efforts Supporting School Improvement* (DESSI), they also report varying degrees of success and some failures. Between the development of a new program and its use in classroom, the complex interactions between people, the innovation, and the organization can produce barriers that hamper, or even halt, the implementation process.

Potential obstacles can begin to appear when teachers, administrators, and curriculum workers are first introduced to the new program. The Concerns-Based Adoption Model discussed in Chapter 11 identifies a number of concerns people might have with regard to a new program:

- Beliefs rooted in a particular metaorientation about the purpose and impact of the curriculum
- Role expectations
- Responsibilities
- Skills required
- The implementation process

Questions and concerns that are inadequately addressed can become the barriers on which implementation founders.

Fullan and Park (1981) have identified 12 factors that affect an implementation (see Table 12.1). These factors hinder or facilitate the use of a new program. Fullan and Park indicate that careful planning of the implementation is necessary to avoid potential barriers. Discussions between teachers, administrators, and curriculum workers during the planning sessions can clarify the issues and identify solutions.

Fullan (1982) points out one reason why planning for change often fails:

> One of the basic reasons why planning fails is that planners or decision-makers of change are unaware of the situations which potential implementers are facing. They introduce changes without providing a means to identify and confront the situational constraints, and without attempting to understand the values, ideas, and experiences of those who are essential for implementing any change. (p. 83)

## TABLE 12.1  Factors Affecting Implementation

---

### A.  Characteristics of the Innovation or Revision

---

1. Need for the change
2. Clarity, complexity of the change
3. Quality and availability of materials

### B.  Characteristics at the School System Level

---

4. History of innovative attempts
5. Expectations and training for principals
6. Teacher input and professional development (in-service, technical assistance)
7. Board and community support
8. Time line and monitoring
9. Overload

### C.  Characteristics at the School Level

---

10. Principals' actions
11. Teacher/teacher relations and actions

### D.  Factors External to the School System

---

12. Role of the Ministry of Education and other educational agencies

---

From Fullan, M., and Park, P. *Curriculum Implementation: A Resource Booklet.* Toronto: Ontario Ministry of Education, 1981, p. 14. Reprinted with permission.

To assist in ensuring that situational barriers are avoided, planning for different roles is required. Clarification of responsibilities of teachers, administrators, and curriculum workers can facilitate the interdependence of those involved in implementation. This also aids in clarifying the expectations teachers may have of principals and curriculum workers. For example, teachers should know who will provide in-service support.

Other barriers may occur if the appropriate skills and resources are not available. These skills relate to both teachers (e.g., new teaching methodologies) and principals (e.g., curriculum leadership skills). Professional development and budget planning are essential.

Communications can be another barrier. In Dow and Whitehead's (1981) summary of the most common barriers identified by teachers, principals, and consultants, communications was high on all lists. The existence of an effective communications system cannot be taken for granted in an organization. When a teacher has a problem, he or she should know who to talk to. Similarly, if there is need for a revision in the new program, clear communication routes are required. Provision for the interaction of everyone involved is vital to the implementation process. This emphasis on interaction and communication is in keeping with an interdependent perspective.

Certain characteristics of the organization should also be examined for potential obstructions. A change in the curriculum may entail changes in the organization itself (timetable changes, or additional personnel, for example). Shipman (1973), reporting on the relationship between the organization of schools and the persistence of change, points out the need for an organization to remain flexible. Another important consideration during implementation is the organizational relationships among staff members (i.e., positions of responsibility, length of time on staff, etc.).

In summary, the formation of an implementation plan requires a careful scrutiny of both the proposed innovation and many aspects of the existing organizational structure, including the roles people play. As the plan develops, it must also be examined for possible barriers. In the final form, the plan should anticipate problems and offer alternative solutions. In order to accomplish this, the planning should involve teachers and address their needs first.

## COMPONENTS OF AN IMPLEMENTATION PLAN

Implementation plans will vary in different school systems, depending on their organizational structure (e.g., the number of supervisory personnel, the availability of program consultants, the nature of established curriculum procedures, etc.) and their intended scope (i.e., whether the plan is to serve an entire school system, a family of schools, or a single school).

An implementation plan should be based on a long-term curriculum plan that outlines the programs to be reviewed, revised, or implemented over a period of time (we have found five years to be a common time period). Long-term plans are used in order to avoid overlap and to pace curriculum activities within a district. We turn now to the components of the plan.

### A Study of the New Program

The initial planning for implementation requires a study of the new program for possible sources of barriers. This study can take place at the district level and be conducted by a committee planning the introduction of a new program, or it can take place at the school level. One factor requiring early consideration is whether the origin of the program is internal or external to the system.

An internally generated change may come from a locally identified need for program revision. In this situation, the change is likely to be more widely accepted, because it is a response to a need identified by teachers within the system. The implementation of this type of change, which would be anticipated by the staff, could reduce the number of preimplementation activities. When a change is imposed from an external source, a different set of circumstances arise. The issuance of a new curriculum guideline by a state or provincial department of education requires preliminary study to determine exactly what the change implies for the local system. An implementation plan should identify who will translate the guideline into classroom practice. It also will be necessary to determine the differences between present practices in the schools and practices called for by the new guideline.

It is necessary to examine the new program to identify the specific impact that is anticipated. The need for the change, as perceived by teachers, consultants, and principals, will determine the degree of commitment to the implementation process and the amount of energy required for implementation activities. A strategy should be developed to elicit the views of the personnel who will be involved in the change, to ensure that the implementation plan reflects the real concerns of school personnel.

The study of the new program also should identify its potential impact on teacher beliefs, methodologies, and resources. This kind of analysis is facilitated if the goals of the innovation are clearly stated. School staffs can be encouraged to study the rationale of the new program and discuss their perceptions of what methodologies should be used and what resources will be required. Clear goals make it possible to outline the dimensions of the change and to identify discrepancies between the present practice and that called for by the new program. On the basis of this information, subsequent planning can be carried out.

It is necessary to examine both the explicit and implicit changes that will result from an innovation. If the new program implies many changes in what teachers will teach or how they will teach, major changes can be anticipated in the school and its social environment, whereas a new program that is similar to present practice will result only in minor changes. The degree of change can vary from school to school. Each staff should be encouraged to conduct its own examination; at the same time, a central committee may take the information produced from the schools and combine it into a strategy for district-wide implementation.

For example, a school system in which the authors worked decided to develop a new outline for its reading program in grades one through three. The main difference in the revised program was that it required a greater degree of specificity of skills for decoding words and reading comprehension. The old program had been vague and open to wide interpretation.

In this situation, the implementation plan emphasized how the new program could be used for planning lessons, as well as which resources would be most useful for teaching the specific skills. Because the teachers already were in general agreement with the basic position of the program (transmission-oriented with some developmental influences), there was no need to plan sessions designed to explain the program rationale (its orientation) or teaching methodologies.

On the other hand, another school system did change its basic orientation when it developed a new social studies program. The old elementary school program, which focused on the factual content in history and geography, reflected a transmission position. Each teacher had laid claim to specific topics (e.g., grade three teachers taught Eskimos and grade five teachers taught Vikings). Textbooks and other resources were geared both to the grade levels and the topics. The curriculum committee developed a new program that placed a greater emphasis on thinking skills, reflecting a shift to the transaction position.

Because it required a number of basic changes from the teachers, they had to examine their beliefs about the new social studies program. For many, this required adjustments in what they had believed and how they had taught. Methods for evaluation of student achievement, and the curriculum resources, are two other factors teachers had to examine. An implementation plan that did not address all of these factors and did not allow sufficient time for them to be incorporated into the new practice would assure continued discontent and the absence of any real use of the new program.

Although the preceding examples illustrate curriculum innovations developed at the local level, it is equally important to examine changes put forward at the state or provincial level. Curriculum guidelines published at this level to provide direction to local school jurisdictions can portend far-reaching changes. What is being reflected by the curriculum guidelines put out by departments of education—the wishes of society or the most recent thinking of academics—is not always clear. Because these guidelines reflect a broader social base and affect a much wider audience (a whole state or province rather than a single school system), the implementation plan is more complex. Parents and other interest groups in the community are more likely to express their concerns with an innovation that has received wide media coverage, particularly when they perceive it as a radical departure from what schools currently are doing.

Although there is an implied responsibility for higher levels of government to help in such implementation tasks, there is still the need for school boards and individual schools to ensure that their own plans meet the needs of local interest groups. Board personnel, then, are held accountable for the "fit" between community concerns and local programs. Should the new guideline include a change in curriculum orientation, the question of local interpretation assumes an even greater importance.

In the early 1970s, the Ontario Ministry of Education introduced a new guideline for elementary schools in that province. Prior to the new guideline, expectations of both schools and teachers for each subject were quite specifically explained. The new guideline, entitled *The Formative Years*, reflecting the work of Piaget and other developmentalists, took an entirely different approach to both the organization and delivery of programs at the elementary level. The guideline currently in use was based on the transmission position; the new provincial guideline, which assumed a transaction position, stressed cognitive processes and democratic citizenship. Teachers and principals were not sure of what should be taught. Parents also were confused. Local school systems were assigned the task of developing programs based on the new guideline. Ten years later, many school systems were still working at implementing *The Formative Years*. Parents, not particularly happy with the new thrust, called for a return to the basics.

In all of the preceding situations, the innovations themselves held the clues to what could be expected during the implementation period. An implementation plan must include, as an initial step, the study of the innovation itself. The balance of the plan depends on this analysis for its detail.

## Identification of Resources

Resource identification encompasses three areas: 1) print and audiovisual resources (e.g., textbooks, teaching materials), 2) people resources (e.g., consultants), and 3) financial resources. Identification involves ascertaining both availability and quality of the resource.

Prior to implementing a new program in the classroom, teachers should be given opportunities to examine resource materials and make recommendations about their suitability. This ensures that the teachers have studied the applicability of the resources to the new program. This activity also implies that complete classroom application of the new program will not be expected before the new materials are available.

Careful selection of support personnel for teachers is another area of resource identification. Specific needs of the teachers must be matched to skills possessed by particular individuals. Often, this requires locating consultants from outside the school district. Although such people can be very helpful, McLaughlin and Marsh (1978) point out that information gathered by the Rand Change Agent Study shows the importance of choosing consultants of high quality:

> It was better for projects to use no outside consultants than to use poor ones—and much better than to use poor ones often. Good consultants helped by providing concrete practical advice to project teachers—showing them how to adapt project methods or materials

to their own situation. Good consultants assisted teachers in learning how to solve problems for themselves, rather than by solving
problems for them. Ineffective consultants often furnished advice
that was too abstract to be useful. (p. 78)

The costs of implementation include the price of new textbooks,
new teaching materials, and the possible expenses involved in obtaining
the services of consultants. Additional expenses can arise from the need
to release teachers for professional development activities. Anticipation
of all possible expenses is an integral part of the resource identification
component of the implementation plan.

The purpose of the resource identification component is to identify
particular needs. These will vary with the nature of the program and the
degree of change. For example, a new program with a transmission orientation may involve the incorporation of a new text and other teaching
materials into the classroom, while allowing the teaching methodology to
remain the same, whereas a new program with a transaction orientation
could require a new teaching methodology and different ways of organizing the classroom.

## Role Definition

Role descriptions can help ensure that important tasks are not overlooked. For example, a person in the central office might be assigned the
job of ordering sufficient textbooks or other required resources. Principals might be given the task of distributing certain questionnaires concerning the progress of the implementation. Other responsibilities, such
as the coordination of implementation activities between schools and
planning professional development activities, would also have to be assigned to specific individuals.

Although the teacher is the actual implementor of a new program,
the roles of the principal, consultant, and superintendent as support to
the teachers are equally important. The DESSI Study (Crandall et al.,
1982) indicates that implementation success can depend a great deal on
the overt signs of support for the new program given by principals and
superintendents, for example, budgetary actions, comments made in
public, and personal interest shown in the progress of the implementation. Principals who frequently discuss the implementation with their
staff at meetings, who personally talk with individual teachers about the
new program and assist them in solving problems show a greater success
in implementation in their schools than principals who do not engage in
these activities. Principals also can show support through their use of
timetables and other organizational factors that make it easier for teachers to meet and discuss the implementation.

The teacher's role as implementor is complex. In the classroom, the teacher's role may be to remain relatively stable, as is the case in the implementation of a transmission-oriented program, or it may call upon the teacher to be more flexible, for example, in the interactive climate of a transformation classroom program. Teachers also support one another in the implementation outside the classroom. Discussions among themselves and sharing of common problems provide psychological support to teachers as they attempt to use the new program. To accomplish this, teachers need to know both what is expected of them and what they may expect of others during the implementation. Clearly outlined responsibilities for everyone involved can assist in this process.

## Professional Development

Many professional development needs of the teachers of a new program will become apparent as the previous components of the planning are completed. The program orientation will provide a basic indication of the nature of the professional development that is required.

For a transmission-oriented program, professional development needs may center on organizing new course content. Teachers also may require help in using resources such as textbooks. A transaction-oriented program might produce a need to help teachers learn a new teaching methodology. In a transformation-oriented program, the focus of professional development might be on helping teachers to understand the rationale of the program and to incorporate it into the total school program.

In their discussion of the results of the Rand Corporation's Change Agent Study, McLaughlin and Marsh (1978) point out the importance of in-service training:

> Local planners had considerable discretion in selecting project implementation strategies ... The most important of those local choices were those that determined the ways in which the school staff would be assisted in acquiring the new skills and information necessary to project implementation—staff development strategies.
>
> Project strategies that fostered staff learning and change had two complementary elements: (1) staff training activities; and (2) training support activities. The study found that well conducted staff training and staff training support activities improved project implementation, promoted student gains, fostered teacher change, and enhanced the continuation of project methods and materials. (p. 76)

McLaughlin and Marsh (1978) also point out that not all of the specific details of the professional development program need to or can be planned before the implementation begins.

> Even a carefully planned staff training program usually cannot anticipate the nature or the timing of project staff assistance requirements, especially as they relate to particular classroom problems. Likewise, staff often cannot perceive what they need to know until the need arises. For both reasons, the needs of project staff are not always predictable or synchronized with scheduled training sessions. (p. 78)

Detailed planning might be done for initial activities, such as the introduction of the new program to the teachers, whereas less detailed plans might be made for anticipated needs that will arise at a later time.

Research has yielded a number of characteristics of an effective professional development program. These are summarized by Burrello and Orbaugh (1982).

1. In-service education programs should be designed so that programs are integrated into and supported by the organization within which they function.
2. In-service education programs should be designed to result in collaborative programs.
3. In-service education programs should be grounded in the needs of the participants.
4. In-service education programs should be responsive to changing needs.
5. In-service education programs should be accessible.
6. In-service activities should be evaluated over time and be compatible with the underlying philosophy and approach of the district. (pp. 385–386)

The needs of the teachers, principals, and curriculm workers can be addressed in two stages. During the first stage, which begins with the initial introduction of the new program, there is a need for information and for time to become familiar with the innovation. A new program that is not understood and does not have the commitment of the teachers is doomed to failure. Teachers need ample time to explore the ramifications of the new program for their classrooms and also need to examine its effect on their teaching style and their orientation. Orientations change slowly. If the orientation of the new program clashes with the teacher's orientation, resistance is inevitable. Workshops and a proliferation of guest speakers will not overcome this resistance. Opportunities should be provided to allow teachers to interact with each other about the change. Values clarification, consciousness raising, and group-process experiences can facilitate this interaction.

The second stage in a professional development program, which begins when the new program is being used in the classroom, encompasses a different set of needs. During this stage, questions may arise that were not anticipated in earlier phases. Problem solving assistance, explanations, and support must be available, if the teachers are to persist in their implementation activities. At this point, professional development becomes more closely related to individual teacher needs.

Other factors that can affect professional development programs are the nature of the social system within a school, the relationship between the school and its community, and the leadership style of the school principal. It is in this second phase that the in-service program must display its flexibility and adaptability.

Joyce, Hersh, and McKibbon (1983, pp. 139–142) identify five components of a professional development program:

1. Presentation of theory
2. Modeling or demonstration
3. Practice under simulated conditions
4. Structured feedback
5. Coaching for application

Although each component helps the teacher learn about the new program, the effect of each component is different. A study of the theory behind a new program can raise the level of the teacher's awareness of the change and help the teacher understand the rationale of the program. This initial step usually does not result in change in classroom practice, because there is little opportunity for the teacher to learn the necessary skills.

If the teacher has an opportunity to see a demonstration of the new skills required, his or her understanding of the theory can be increased. When the demonstrated skill is a refinement of something the teacher already does, the theory and modeling components of the implementation plan might result in new classroom practices for some teachers. However, if the required skills are more complex and are new to the teacher, further professional development is required.

The number of teachers who will begin to use the new program can be increased by providing opportunities for teachers to practice the new skills required by the program. Such practice can be most effective if it occurs in simulated conditions, where the teacher does not have to be concerned about the effects of mistakes on his or her students. The teacher's learning and skill level can be enhanced if feedback is provided to assist the teacher in learning how effective he or she is in managing the applications of the new program.

Even after they have studied the theory, observed demonstrations, practiced the skills, and received feedback, there still may be some teachers who will be unable to use the new program in their classrooms. The coaching component can help these teachers determine how to change their classroom practice to implement the new program.

A two-stage process for the application of these five components of an implementation plan applied yields a number of alternatives for the long-term professional development program.

Presentation of theory, and modeling or demonstration clearly belong in stage-one, which is the stage at which explanations, rationale, and methodologies are required. At this stage, needs are general in nature, which allows participation of a broader audience. Presentations by guest speakers and curriculum developers and large-scale workshops can be conducted at district-wide professional activity days. A series of activities can be planned, in order to avoid numerous presentations of the same information to individual staffs. Once the basic information has been delivered and teachers have had an opportunity to study its possible impact on their own classroom, the scope of the professional development activities can be shifted to smaller units (e.g., families of schools, individual schools, or particular groups of teachers). Specific needs of other groups involved in the change also can be addressed; for example, principals and consultants can be provided with information they will need to facilitate implementation.

The second stage of the professional development program requires different techniques than those used in stage one and a different location. The stage-two components of the implementation plan are practice, feedback, and coaching; these are individual activities that allow teachers to personalize the use of the new program. During practice sessions, teachers can make mistakes without jeopardizing student achievement. The feedback they receive on the applications of the new program provides teachers with information on which they can reflect and which they can use to plan for future use in their own classroom. These activities are best conducted in schools.

Coaching further personalizes the implementation program. A teacher or curriculum worker (the coach) works closely with a classroom teacher (the partner) who is using the new program. The coach helps the partner plan the use of the new program in his or her classroom and provides support on several levels. The partner receives psychological support when attempting to use new techniques. Problems are addressed as they arise. In this respect, the teacher also finds companionship from someone who understands the difficulties in using the program. The teacher can thereby feel less alone in his or her attempts to use a new program.

A model developed by Seller (1984) outlines a five-part coaching process:

**1.** *Analysis:* Analysis assists the coach in understanding the circumstances present within the partner's classroom. The coach also determines how the partner perceives the new program. The coach gauges the partner's level of knowledge of the new program as well as any training in its use the partner has received.

**2.** *Observation 1:* Following the analysis, the coach visits the partner's classroom to become familiar with the setting and to make some preliminary observations. These observations focus on items agreed upon by the coach and the partner prior to the visit. The coach develops an understanding of the present situation as described by the partner during the analysis.

**3.** *Planning:* Planning begins with the development of what Seller calls an *end view*—an understanding of what the partner's classroom will be like when the new program is fully implemented. This end view may include descriptions of what the teacher will be doing (teaching methodologies), what the students will be doing (learning experiences), and what resources will be in use. The coach and the partner should ensure that they share the same view of the final goals.

The gap between the present situation and the final goals is identified. Appropriate *steps* are outlined by which the partner will reduce and ultimately eliminate the gap. It is the partner's responsibility to establish steps that are realistic. The coach acts as an advisor to ensure that important aspects of the new program are not omitted. The coach also assists as a problem solver, drawing on his or her experience with the new program to suggest specific steps to help close the gap.

During the planning session(s), a timeline is established that outlines the sequence of events to be followed while the coach and partner are working together.

**4.** *Observation 2:* Two options are available for these observations: 1) the partner may observe the coach while he or she is teaching the program, by visiting the coach's classroom or by having the coach teach a lesson in the partner's classroom, or 2) the coach may observe the partner as he or she teaches the new program. The coach observes the technical aspects of the partner's implementation of the new program and other mutually agreed upon items.

**5.** *Feedback:* The coach and the partner meet to discuss the observation(s). Perceptions about what took place are shared and reasons for the partner's success or failure are explored. At this point, a decision is made to either continue working on the step under discussion or to move on to the next step that was outlined during the planning session.

When agreement has been reached on what is to occur next, the cycle moves back to component three. Criteria are established for the next set of actions by the coach and partner and for the next observation(s). Steps 3 through 5 are repeated until all intermediate goals have been accomplished and the partner is using the new program.

As the partner integrates the new program into the classroom, each of these five steps is used by the coach and partner to direct their activities. The coach assists the partner in planning the use of the new program or solving problems; he or she may make suggestions, but the partner decides what to try and how to alter actual practice. The partner accepts responsibility for what is done and for the adaptations made for his or her classroom.

The following example illustrates the use of this five-step coaching process. In a project conducted by Seller involving teachers in grades seven to ten, a change was proposed in the way students are grouped for instruction. The traditional use of achievement levels was perceived to be too restrictive. Two workshops presented the theory behind alternative grouping procedures. The purposes of the new method of grouping, criteria for assembling the new groups, and information sources for the criteria were presented in a planning guide. Alternative roles for teachers and students in each of the different groups to be formed also were outlined. In the workshops, participants applied the new approach to their own situations and received feedback from other teachers.

Following the workshops, the teachers planned how they would use the new method of grouping in their own classrooms. The workshop leader, in a coach's role, visited the classroom while the teacher used the new grouping technique. After the visitation, the coach provided feedback to the teacher on the observations made during the visit.

Teacher reaction to this method of professional development was positive. Its strengths, as listed by teachers, were as follows:

- The practicality of the theory workshops, which addressed their particular concerns
- The opportunity to work with the innovation with their peers and to talk about how they might apply it
- The in-class support of the coach as they attempted to use the innovation
- The nonjudgmental feedback from the coach about the observations made by the coach in their classrooms

An additional benefit was the reaction to the coaching process of other staff members not directly involved with the project. As they observed the interaction between the coach and the teachers in the school, they began to express interest in participating in the project. Thus, the impact of the innovation extended beyond the original group.

Seller's coaching process model demonstrates that it is possible to provide theory, demonstration, practice, feedback, and coaching in a manner that responds to the needs of the teachers.

## Timelines

An implementation schedule, or timeline, sets intermediate goals as benchmarks against which the progress of the implementation can be assessed. Time for the examination of necessary curriculum materials, for allowing people to feel comfortable with the change, for trying out the new program and revising it if necessary, and for settling into new teaching methodologies must all be accommodated. These requirements are identified on the timeline by the specification of dates for activities (e.g., professional development activities) and for interim progress reports. For example, if the new program has a transmission orientation, these reports might discuss the number of units taught and suggestions for changes. For a program with a transformation orientation, the timeline might specify meeting dates to discuss teacher reactions to new methodology and their perceptions of student adaptation to the new program. In the authors' experience, full implementation of a new program can take three years or longer. The time element, more than anything else, reveals that implementation is a process, not an event.

Other purposes of the timeline are that it facilitates a proper sequencing of events and it allows for the allocation of adequate time to accomplish the necessary tasks. The timeline makes role expectations explicit in terms of when particular functions are to be completed. Flexibility will allow alterations when necessary, but a well-planned timeline can offer protection against administrative pressure to speed up the implementation process.

An established schedule of events pertaining to implementing new programs can help avoid overload caused by too many initiatives. The presence of one implementation project will not likely cause all other curriculum work to be suspended, but a timeline can indicate the most propitious points for other activities to take place (e.g., development, evaluation).

Planning the timeline for an implementation requires careful analysis of the new program and the needs of the teachers implementing it. The timeline will be most effective if it reflects the discussions between all the groups involved. Accurate estimates of how much professional development activity will be needed and of reasonable time periods for each stage of the implementation can be best provided by teachers who will be using the new program.

## Communications System

Both the Rand Change Agent Study (Berman and McLaughlin, 1975) and the DESSI Study (Crandall et al., 1982) indicate that a key to successful implementation is frequent discussion about the new program among teachers, principals, and curriculum workers. A well-defined communications system facilitates these discussions by providing information about the new program and notice of when the discussions will take place.

The information flow and the contacts provided by a communication system can help in reducing feelings of isolation during the implementation. For teachers, opportunities to talk to others about the new program can be a reminder that they are not alone in the implementation, that problems and suggestions can be shared. By keeping principals and curriculum workers informed about classroom activities, the communications system can reduce their feelings of isolation as well.

The communications system can provide support to teachers. Assistance from others can be arranged by the principal when a teacher indicates a need for help. Through the communications system, a high profile is maintained for the new program. This can provide psychological support for the teachers. Also, this profile, reinforced by a professional development program, can emphasize the school board's commitment to the innovation.

Planning the communications system begins with the identification of what information will be required, who will use this information, and when it will be needed. Teachers will need to know about planned professional development activities, proposed changes to the existing program, and the progress of the implementation generally. Principals and curriculum workers will need to know about problems being encountered by teachers and the general progress of the implementation.

The communications system usually has two parts. One part is formal routing system to ensure that essential information is passed between teachers and central committees. Such routes assist everyone in knowing who to contact for specific information. The other, more important, part of the communications system involves networks. These networks consist of groups of teachers and principals and/or curriculum workers who regularly share experiences, form joint problem-solving groups, and otherwise circulate information about the implementation of the new program.

## Monitoring the Implementation

The purpose of monitoring is to gather information related to the implementation and to use this information to facilitate and support the efforts of the teachers.

The flow of the information, supported by the communications system, will provide a continuous picture of the progress of the implementation. Through monitoring, decisions can be made about activities necessary to support the implementation and about possible changes in the new program. The degree to which the new program has been implemented is also determined through the monitoring process.

Planning an implementation includes determining what decisions need to be made during the implementation and what information will be collected. For example, to determine whether changes are needed in the timeline, information is needed about the degree to which the new program has been implemented in the classroom. Similarly, to make decisions about possible changes in the new program, information is needed from teachers about difficulties encountered in the implementation and the suitability of the program for their classes. To make decisions about in-service activities, it is necessary to know what needs have been identified by teachers.

Various models for organizing information about an innovation and presenting an analysis of it were described in Chapter 11 (e.g., the Concerns-Based Adaptation Model and the Innovation Profiles Model). Developing the monitoring component of the implementation plan involves deciding which models will best serve the needs of the particular program implementation. This decision, and the decision about how the information needed for monitoring is gathered, will be influenced by various factors.

One factor is the orientation of the new program. A program with a transmission orientation might be monitored, in large part, through the use of teacher questionnaires about the suitability of content to particular grades. Evaluation forms indicating the usefulness and applicability of individual units might also be used. Transaction- or transformation-oriented programs, with an accent on classroom organization and climate, may require observations in the classroom, self-assessments on the use of specific techniques, or studies of the students to gauge the level of implementation. The role descriptions for the implementation will indicate who will collect the information and who will analyze it. The communications system will form the medium through which much of the information needed for monitoring is gathered and distributed.

Although monitoring constitutes a formative evaluation of the implementation, more formal evaluation procedures occur later in the process; these are discussed in subsequent chapters.

## CONCLUDING COMMENTS

An implementation plan should facilitate interactions between teachers, so that mutual adaptation of a new program can occur. In our view, it is unrealistic to expect that a program will be implemented exactly as the developers intended. As Goodlad et al. (1974) point out, the program's use in the classroom occurs within the confines of the teacher's perspective. In a sense, a sound implementation plan should provide bridges between curriculum workers and teachers so that teachers involved in implementing new programs do not work in isolation. To build such bridges, people in curriculum leadership positions must take the initiative, but in such a way that teachers can feel free to respond to new programs.

If curriculum leaders work from a transmission position, then there is little chance for mutual adaptation or, in fact, for teachers to play any role in the implementation of new programs. The transmission position, when applied to implementation, does not acknowledge the subjective reality of the teacher; instead, it assumes that the teacher will be a tool in implementing a new program.

From the transaction position, mutual adaptation can occur. Teachers and curriculum workers can exchange their perceptions of the new program, which can lead to possible revisions of the new curriculum and its eventual use in schools.

Implementation from a transformation perspective is more difficult. At this level, the curriculum workers and teachers interact in a holistic way; that is, interaction is not just cognitive (as it is in the transaction position), but occurs within a number of interrelated dimensions (emotional, aesthetic, and moral). Planning implementation from a transformation persepctive requires that curriculum workers be aware of these dimensions as well as the school environment. Thus, the transformation perspective requires the curriculum worker to be aware of the complexity of change. If the curriculum worker and teacher can take this complexity into account, change will not be limited to superficial change but can be integrated into the life of the classroom in a more complete way.

We close this chapter with a chart that summarizes how curriculum workers from each of the major positions would develop an implementation plan.

## REFERENCES

Berman, P., & McLaughlin, M.W. (1975). *Federal programs supporting educational change: Vol. IV. Summary.* Santa Monica, CA: Rand Corporation.

Burello, L.C., & Orbaugh, T. (1982). Reducing the discrepancy between the

**Summary Chart:   Chapter 12**

| | *Transmission* | *Transaction* | *Transformation* |
|---|---|---|---|
| *Study of New Programs* | Focus on content | Focus on how teaching methodologies affect cognitive processes | Focus on how program affects the whole child |
| *Resources* | Textbooks | Variety of resources to stimulate mental processes | Human resources are stressed; personal growth of teachers is central |
| *Roles* | Roles fixed within system hierarchy | Roles more flexible, which allows for interaction among teachers | Roles very flexible with emphasis on I–thou relationship among teachers |
| *Professional development* | General professional development sessions that focus on information transmission | More individualized professional development, with stress on practice, feedback, and coaching | Individualized professional development, with emphasis on coaching and personal growth for teachers |
| *Timeline* | Short timeline; implementation seen as event, not process | Reasonable, flexible timeline; implementation seen as process, not event | Long, flexible timeline; implementation seen as holistic process |
| *Communication system* | One-way, top-down communication | Two-way, interactive communication | Two-way interactive communication, that goes beyond cognitive elements |
| *Monitoring system* | Focus on accountability through use of tests | Variety of methods used to monitor progress | Informal methods are used, particularly teacher feedback |

known and the unknown in in-service education. *Phi Delta Kappan* 63(6), 385–388.

Crandall, D.P., and Associates. (1982). *People, policy and practices: Examining the chain of school improvement.* Andover, MA: The NETWORK Inc.

Dow, I.I., & Whitehead, R.Y. (1981). *New perspectives of curriculum implementation.* Toronto: Ontario Public School Men Teachers' Federation.

Fullan, M. (1982). *The meaning of educational change.* Toronto: Ontario Institute for Studies in Education Press.

Fullan, M., & Park, P. (1981). *Curriculum implementation: A resource booklet.* Toronto: Ontario Ministry of Education.

Goodlad, J.J., Klein, M. Frances, and Associates. (1974). *Looking behind the classroom door.* Worthington, OH: Charles A. Jones.

Joyce, B., Hersh, R., & McKibbin, M. (1983). *The structure of school improvement.* New York: Longman.

McLaughlin, M.W., & Marsh, D.D. (1978). Staff development and school change. *Teachers College Record 80*(1), 69–94.

Ontario Ministry of Education. (1975). *The Formative Years.* Toronto, Ontario.

Seller, W. (1984). The use of coaching in curriculum implementation. Ontario Institute for Studies in Education, *Field Development Newsletter, 14*(4).

Shipman, M.D. (1973). The Impact of a Curriculum Project. *Journal of Curriculum Studies, 5*(1), 47–54.

# CHAPTER 13

# THE SEARCH FOR A CURRICULUM EVALUATION BASE

Defining a base for curriculum evaluation involves identifying what role curriculum evaluation should play in the curriculum process, the purposes to be served by evaluation, and the approaches to be used. A clear base helps determine what information is sought and how the data are to be gathered.

Identifying an evaluation base is complex because the base must provide for evaluation of change in curriculum evaluation practices as well as for changes in the school curricula. Thus far in the twentieth century, there have been three distinct eras in the development of curriculum evaluation.

In the first era, which is associated with the work of Bobbitt (1918) and Charters (1923), evaluation concentrated on measuring student achievement. The curriculum work of these two educators was used as a basis to determine specific student-achievement objectives; evaluation focused on measuring whether these objectives were achieved.

This type of evaluation reflected a growing interest in the behavioral sciences. Psychological and intelligence testing was used to determine aptitude for learning and to find explanations for why students had difficulties when learning. When students failed to achieve stated objectives, the fault was assumed to lie with the student, not the curriculum.

Borich and Jemelka (1982) explain another influence that also was at work at this time:

> The empiricist movement of the eighteenth and nineteenth centuries heavily shaped what was to become the social sciences (and subsequently, evaluation). The scientific method, which emanated from the work and writings of Descartes, proved an invaluable heuristic that did much to make possible the many startling discoveries

of the day. It is not surprising that when human behavior came within the purview of scientists, they applied their tried-and-true methods for understanding and controlling the world. (p. 36)

One of the main results of the influence of the physical sciences and the scientific method was the drive to make evaluation as precise as possible. This led to the development of standardized tests and the use of the results of these tests to compare individuals against a set of norms.

The second era in evaluation practices began in the 1940s with the work of the Commission on the Relation of School and College (also known as the *Eight-Year Study*). Ralph Tyler and a group of his associates developed a philosophy of evaluation that emphasized higher-order cognitive and affective objectives. They also demonstrated that such objectives could be subjected to measurement (Smith & Tyler, 1941).

Along with this new philosophy of evaluation, there was a movement toward development of classroom programs at a local level, so that evaluation was based more in the classroom. This meant that teachers would construct their own tests, which were used to evaluate locally developed curricula. These tests might also be used to provide information to individual students concerning their strengths and weaknesses. The way was now opened for a broader range of roles for curriculum evaluation: evaluation results could provide a measure of student achievement; they could be used to help a teacher alter the classroom program; individual teachers and schools could use evaluation to measure the achievement of their goals, and then revise their programs when weaknesses were identified.

The launching of Sputnik in 1957 marked the beginning of the third era. The content of the curriculum (especially in mathematics and science) came into question. As Lewy (1977) points out, educators began to ask other questions also:

Existing educational programs were criticized not only from the point of view of their content, but also from the point of view of the mode of instruction. Although educational research had called attention to the fact that memorizing factual information contributes little to the intellectual development of the learner and does little to improve his ability to solve problems, most textbooks were still crammed mainly with factual information that students were required to memorize. (p. 3)

Changes in many areas occurred during this period. Inquiry learning, discovery approaches, problem-solving skills, and other methodological variations were combined with new curricula. The result, during the 1960s, was a great deal of curriculum development with little attention to evaluation.

During the 1970s however, the situation began to change. Although large expenditures for the development of new programs resulted in calls for accountability, the methods of evaluation in use at that time, which stressed measurement of student achievement, did not fit the new curricula. In other words, these methods did not suit the transaction-oriented programs that had been developed.

Cronbach led the call for reform in the curriculum evaluation field. The new evaluation paradigms, which focused on program improvement, had to be able to measure more than cognitive learning. Cronbach outlines some of the requirements of the new evaluation methods:

> Insofar as possible, evaluation should be used to understand how the course produces its effects and what parameters influence its effectiveness. . . . Hopefully, evaluation studies will go beyond reporting on this or that course and help us to understand educational learning. Such insight will, in the end, contribute to the development of all courses rather than just the course under test. (Cronbach, quoted in Taylor & Cowley, 1972, p. 13)

Cronbach does not ignore the importance of evaluating the results of instruction.

> Course evaluation should ascertain what changes a course produces and should identify aspects of the course that need revision. The outcomes observed should include general outcomes ranging far beyond the content of the curriculum itself—attitudes, career choices, general understandings and intellectual powers, and aptitude for further learning in the field. (Cronbach, quoted in Taylor & Cowley, 1972, p. 18)

As a result of the emergence of these new approaches to evaluation, we are now faced with a pool of information that includes much more than student achievement data. It is important, then, to establish a base that clearly defines the purpose and approach of each curriculum evaluation. We begin our search with an examination of the role of curriculum evaluation.

## THE ROLE OF CURRICULUM EVALUATION

Evaluation is often considered to be the final step in an overall process. Students are evaluated at the end of a course. Teachers are evaluated at the end of a probationary period, to determine whether they will be tenured. Curricula are evaluated after they have been implemented, to determine whether their stated goals have been achieved.

In practice, however, evaluation has a more ubiquitous nature. Students often are tested to identify problem areas. Teachers receive interim reports on their effectiveness. Curricula can be field tested during development to ascertain the appropriateness for specific grade levels of the skills and content they are designed to teach.

Scriven (1967) has made the distinction between summative and formative evaluation. When studying curriculum evaluation, it is helpful to distinguish between these two types of evaluation. In summative evaluation, the function of evaluation is to provide an overall assessment of a program. This involves judging the overall value of a particular program in relation to its contribution to the total school curriculum. According to Scriven, summative evaluation does not seek to determine causes, only the overall worth of a program, whereas formative evaluation involves making judgments and attempting to determine specific causes. The information gathered in formative evaluation contributes to the revision of program; it allows curriculum developers to make changes and to improve the curriculum before it assumes its final form.

It is not always easy to distinguish between summative and formative evaluation. For example, a summative evaluation might indicate that a program is not achieving its goals. As a result, a decision might be made to revise the program. In this sense, the evaluation could be considered formative in nature. However, the basic difference between these two types of evaluation involve how an evaluation will be conducted, what will be evaluated, and how the results will be used.

## THE PURPOSE OF CURRICULUM EVALUATION

As indicated by Scriven (1967, p. 42), summative evaluation focuses on the outcomes of a completed program. It can originate within the school or school system or from a source outside of the school.

Figure 13.1 illustrates summative evaluation that originates within a school or a school system; we call this a *closed system*. In this case, the program has been developed according to procedures established for the entire school district and probably reflects a particular metaorientation. Implementation has been directed by an implementation plan and the program is now being used in the schools. The prescribed curriculum procedures call for an evaluation of a program after a certain period of time. This often involves a cyclic review process by which all programs are studied on a regular basis. This summative curriculum evaluation is designed to proceed according to a predetermined timeline and is estab-

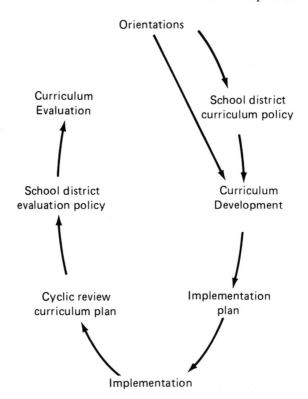

**Figure 13.1** Summative evaluation in a closed system.

lished through school system policies. Tyler's (1949) approach to evaluation resembles this type of summative evaluation. He states:

> It is important to make a more inclusive check as to whether these plans for learning experiences actually function to guide the teacher in producing the sort of outcomes desired. This is the purpose for evaluation and the reason why a process of evaluation is necessary after the plans themselves are developed. (p. 105)

Cronbach (1982), who favors a more formative type of curriculum evaluation, argues that summative evaluation procedures that are used consistently become ineffective. Once teachers and schools adopt a program and feel confident that they are able to achieve desired outcomes, there is less chance that an evaluation will persuade them to change: "Established programs are comparatively immune to serious evaluation, save as proposed modifications lead to a new study of prototypes" (p. 3).

A summative evaluation might also be precipitated by developments outside of the school or school system; we call this a *breached system*. For instance, a program said to be more effective might be introduced, or community pressure to change a program might become apparent through parent groups' demands to a school board. Summative evaluation in a breached system is depicted in Figure 13.2.

In a breached system, the purpose of curriculum evaluation often is to conduct a comparison. The current program might be compared to a new set of goals espoused by a parent group, or the current program might be compared to another program being considered for adoption in the school district. When such comparisons are conducted, the need to specify the basis of the comparison is paramount. It may be necessary to begin with a comparison of the orientations of the current and the proposed practices, in order to ensure that the objectives, outcomes, and methodologies are comparable.

In both closed and breached curriculum systems, the purpose of summative evaluations usually is to provide information for decision making. These decisions might involve continuing or terminating a program, or making a choice between different programs. A further type of decision could entail revising the current program. For Stufflebeam et al. (1971), the prime purpose of curriculum evaluation is to provide information to decision makers, or for use in the "process of delineating, obtaining, and providing useful information for judging decision alternatives" (p. 40).

The curriculum evaluation model developed by Stufflebeam et al.

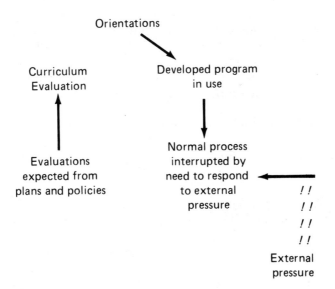

**Figure 13.2**  Summative evaluation in a breached system.

(1971), called the Context-Input-Process-Product (CIPP) model, is described in the Chapter 14. This model acknowledges the need for both summative evaluation (the second *P* in C.I.P.P. stands for "product" evaluation) and formative evaluation. In many cases, summative evaluation either resembles formative evaluation (e.g., suggests areas where the program is weak) or leads to formative evaluation (e.g., recommends further study to decide how the present program can be revised).

Cronbach, also, sees curriculum evaluation as a component in the decision making process: "We may define 'evaluation' broadly as the collection and use of information to make decisions about an educational program" (Quoted in Taylor & Cowley, 1972, p. 11). Cronbach also suggests that another purpose of evaluation is program improvement. Lewy (1977) provides us with a more specific view of how evaluation can be formative in the curriculum process.

> Evaluation essentially is the provision of information for the sake of facilitating decision making at various stages of curriculum development. This information may pertain to the program as a complete entity or only to some of its components. Evaluation also implies the selection of criteria, the collection of data, and data analysis. (p. 30)

The expansion of this definition, shown in Figure 13.3, indicates the stages of curriculum development at which formative evaluation might occur, the components that might be studied, and the criteria that might be used. Each of the possible paths might serve different purposes. For example, an evaluation during the planning stage of a teacher's guide can determine its degree of congruence with a set of identified standards; evaluation during the implementation stage can determine the use teachers were making of the guide and how it might be improved.

Eisner (1979) identifies five purposes for evaluation.

> Of the functions of evaluation in education, five seem especially important:
> 1. To diagnose
> 2. To revise curricula
> 3. To compare
> 4. To anticipate educational needs
> 5. To determine if objectives have been achieved. (p. 168)

He argues that these purposes can be applied to the curriculum itself, to teaching, and to the student. In Eisner's opinion, curriculum evaluation serves a formative purpose: "The use of evaluation to revise the curriculum is . . . one of the central functions of evaluation" (p. 171).

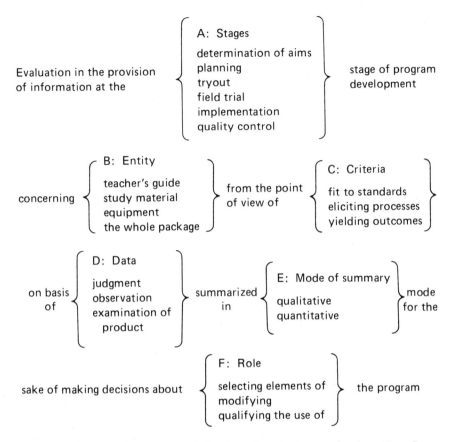

**Figure 13.3** Mapping sentence definition of curriculum evaluation. (*From Lewy, Arieh*. Handbook of Curriculum Evaluation. *White Plains, NY: Longman Inc., p. 30. Reprinted with permission.*)

The preceding views of evaluation as a formative activity indicate the diverse nature of the evaluation process and the wide variety of purposes it might serve. It is important that decision makers and evaluators agree upon the purpose of evaluation. Reporting on a study of 10 applied research studies, Weiss (1973) describes the consequences of failure to establish the purpose before beginning an evaluation: "Disagreement over purpose had several unfortunate consequences. When administrators expected 'formative' evaluation to aid ongoing program development and evaluators designed 'summative' studies to render judgment on the program after its conclusion, administrators lost interest and withdrew support" (p. 2).

## APPROACHES TO CURRICULUM EVALUATION

The various approaches to curriculum evaluation provide a means of addressing the questions the evaluation asks. The approach that is used affects the choice of criteria to be used and which sources of data are used.

Although a specific approach may indicate how information should be collected, it does not predetermine a particular methodology. The specific questions asked by an evaluation, the conditions under which an evaluation is to be conducted, and the particular program being evaluated may indicate the appropriateness of one approach over another.

Cronbach (1982) identifies two basic approaches: the *scientistic ideals approach* and the *humanistic ideals approach*. He suggests that these two approaches represent opposite extremes on an evaluation continuum: "I overdramatize only slightly when I contrast a scientistic school of evaluators with a humanistic one. Writers at one pole prize experiments; those at the opposite extreme find evaluative experiments misinformative" (p. 23).

The extreme positions suggested above may be rare among curriculum evaluators, but characteristics of each approach can be identified. Cronbach (1982) describes the scientistic ideal:

> A true experiment, as described in the literature on evaluation, concentrates on outcome or impact and embodies three procedures; (1) Two or more conditions are in place, at least one of them being the consequence of deliberative intervention. (2) Persons or institutions are assigned to conditions in a way that creates equivalent groups. (3) All participants are assessed on the same outcome measure(s). (p. 24)

Curriculum evaluations conducted from a scientistic approach tend to concentrate on the learner. Test scores form an important part of the data collected. These data are used to compare the achievement of students in different situations, with each situation controlled as much as possible. Most of the information collected is quantitative, so that it can be statistically analyzed. Decisions about the program(s) are made on the basis of the comparative information provided by the evaluation.

As described by Cronbach (1982), the humanistic ideal provides a distinctly different approach:

> Writers at the humanistic extreme find experiments unacceptable. For them, naturalistic case studies are the panacea. A humanist would study a program already in place, not one imposed by the evaluator. If persons are assigned to a treatment, that is because the policy under study calls for assignment; assignments are not made

for the sake of research. The program is to be seen through the eyes of its developers and clients. Naturalistic investigators would ask different questions of different programs. Benefits are to be described, not reduced to a quantity. Observations are to be opportunistic and responsive to the local scene, not prestructured. (p. 25)

In their discussion of a naturalistic approach to curriculum evaluation, Borich and Jemelka (1982) offer a similar description or the humanistic ideal:

In theory, a naturalistic study consists of a series of observations that are directed alternately at discovery and verification. This process supposedly leads to successive reorientations on the part of the investigator towards the phenomena being observed and to further discovery. Unlike formal evaluation models, the naturalistic inquirer approaches data collection with a minimum of preconceived categories or notions of what will be seen, as though the behavioral phenomena were being observed for the first time. Any effort to manipulate any part of the program setting prior to observation or to constrain the behavior of those being observed reduces the "naturalism" of the method. (p. 70)

Data collected from a naturalistic evaluation are analyzed in a different way than data resulting from a scientistic evaluation. Naturalistic data will be more qualitative than quantitative in nature, which means that it may represent the evaluator's impressions of what was observed as well as a description of actual incidents occurring during the observations. Interview data might be included, discussion of relationships and patterns among various observations will form much of the analysis. In practice, curriculum evaluation usually employs an approach somewhere between the two extremes described above.

One reason for taking a more eclectic approach concerns the relationship between curriculum evaluation and decision making. As discussed previously, a common purpose for curriculum evaluation is to provide information to curriculum decision makers; however, establishing this link creates problems in the selection of a basic approach for an evaluation.

The first problem is to identify the real audience of an evaluation report—that is, who the decision maker is. Cronbach (1982) describes this difficulty as a conflict between our assumptions and the reality of the situation; he suggests that one assumption in education is that the "context of command" (p. 6) prevails, although, in reality, education practices tend to be determined by a policy-shaping community in which a "context of accommodation" prevails (p. 6). The difficulty for the evaluator is often that he or she works with a person in a position of authority, but knows that that person has a limited ability to affect practices because the "context of accommodation" must be taken into account.

The approach chosen may reflect the evaluator's perception of the way subsequent program decisions will be made. For example, if the perception is that a "context of command" is present, a more scientistic approach may be taken, to provide the decision maker with the facts and the numbers required for the decision. The specific facts and numbers would probably be discussed with the decision maker. The perception of the presence of a "context of accommodation," however, may lead to a more humanistic approach, because, to reach a decision, the evaluator requires a number of viewpoints about the issues.

The relationship between curriculum evaluation and decision making creates a further problem related to approach. This problem centers on the question of whether an evaluation should provide a description of or a judgment about the program being studied.

The scientific evaluation presents a description. It usually presents statistical results of tests as well as comparative data and allows the reader to judge the best course of action. The humanistic approach acknowledges subjectivity in reporting results. The evaluator in this situation is more likely to make subjective judgments about what was observed.

Scriven (1967) argues that evaluation must be part of decision making, and that there is no evaluation until judgment has been passed. He further argues that the evaluator is the best person to pass judgment. Stake (1967) supports Scriven's stand and calls for both approaches.

> Curriculum evaluation requires collection, processing, and interpretation of data pertaining to an educational program. For a complete evaluation, two main kinds of data are collected: (1) objective descriptions of goals, environments, personnel, methods and content, and outcomes; and (2) personal judgments as to the quality and appropriateness of those goals, environments, etc. (p. 5)

In order to accomplish an evaluation, as suggested by Scriven and Stake, a balance of approaches is required. Description derived from scientistic activities can be used along with data from other sources to help judge merit. At the same time, naturalistic observations can describe and help judge the effectiveness of a program's less measurable objectives and unintended outcomes.

## CONCLUDING COMMENTS

Evaluation, like curriculum itself, is based on a set of beliefs about what should be done and what can be accomplished. Establishing a base for evaluation clarifies these underlying beliefs and provides direction for subsequent evaluation activities.

The orientation of the program to be evaluated and the philosophy of the school district in which the program is being used will influence the purpose and approach taken during an evaluation. For instance, a program with a transmission orientation in a district where school administrators are primarily interested in the achievement levels of students requires a scientistic approach to evaluation, whereas a combination of approaches can be used to evaluate a transaction-oriented program. Scientistic evaluation methods can provide information about some student outcomes, whereas naturalistic observations can be used to judge the success of the methodologies being employed. Both student and teacher reactions can be studied through naturalistic approaches. If a program has a transformation orientation, humanistic approaches will be most appropriate. Like the transformation orientation, the humanistic approach recognizes the wholeness of learning. This involves evaluating a program holistically in its environment, not piecemeal in artificially established segments.

The need to establish a base for evaluation is apparent when studying specific models of evaluation, which provide the methods for conducting evaluations. We examine some of these models in Chapter 14.

## REFERENCES

Bobbitt, F. (1918). *The curriculum.* Boston: Houghton Mifflin.

Borich, G.D., & Jemelka, R.P. (1982). *Programs and systems: An evaluation perspective.* New York: Academic Press.

Charters, W.W. (1923). *Curriculum construction.* New York: Macmillan.

Cronbach, L.J. (1963). Course improvement through evaluation. *Teachers College Record, 64*(8), 672–683.

―――. (1982). *Designing evaluations of educational and social programs.* San Francisco: Jossey-Bass.

Eisner, E.W. (1979). *The educational imagination: On the design and evaluation of school programs.* New York: Macmillan.

Lewy, A. (1977). The Nature of Curriculum Evaluation. In Lewy, A. (Ed.), *Handbook of curriculum evaluation* (pp. 3–33). New York: Longman.

Scriven, M. (1967). The Methodology of Evaluation. In Tyler, R.W., Gagne, R.M., & Scriven, M. (Eds.), *Perspectives on curriculum evaluation* (A.E.R.A. Monograph Series on Curriculum Evaluation, No. 1) (pp. 29–83). Chicago: Rand McNally.

Smith, E.R., & Tyler, R. W. (1941). *Appraising and recording student progress.* New York: Harper & Row.

Stake, R.E. (1967). Toward a technology for the evaluation of educational programs. In Tyler, R.W., Gagne, R.M., & Scriven, M. (Eds.), *Perspectives on curriculum evaluation* (A.E.R.A. Monograph Series on Curriculum Evaluation, No. 1). (pp. 1–12). Chicago: Rand McNally.

Stufflebeam, D.L., Foley, H.J., Gephart, W.J., Guba, E.G., Hammond, H.D., Merriman, H.O., & Provus, M.M. (1971). *Educational evaluation and decision making*. Itasca, IL.: Peacock.

Taylor, P.A., & Cowley, D.M. (Eds.). (1972). *Readings in curriculum evaluation*. Dubuque, IA: Wm. C. Brown.

Tyler, R.W. (1949). *Basic principles of curriculum and instruction*. Chicago: University of Chicago Press.

Weiss, C.H. (1973, December). Between the Cup and the Lip. *Evaluation Comment*, *4*(3), 1–6.

# CHAPTER 14

# CURRICULUM EVALUATION MODELS

In this chapter, we examine a number of curriculum evaluation models. Inherent in each model is a set of values and beliefs about curriculum; these are reflected in the aspects of the curriculum chosen for study, the nature of the information gathered, and the method by which the data are analyzed. Each of the models presented reflects a different orientation to curriculum and evaluation.

What is an evaluation model? In response to this question Brickell (1981) states:

> Every evaluation model is an abstraction based on an abstraction, a generalized plan for assessing a generalized program. The strength of every model is in its grasp of the general, the common; the weakness of every model is in its missing of the particular, the uncommon. (p. 97)

As abstractions, each of the following models provides a different way to conceptualize curriculum evaluation. The Discrepancy Evaluation Model developed by Provus (1972) reflects a transmission orientation to evaluation; the language of this model demonstrates a behavioral and technological approach to curriculum. Two models discussed in the chapter are transaction oriented. Stake (1967) uses the intentions of the teacher as a focus in the Contingency-Congruence Model; he suggests that an evaluation should examine the consistency between what is intended and what actually occurs in the classroom. The CIPP model developed by Stufflebeam et al. (1971) places the emphasis on curriculum decision making; the purpose of evaluation changes as the types of decision making changes. The transformation position is represented by the work of Eisner (1979). Curriculum criticism, as described by Eisner

looks to less concrete factors for curriculum evaluation. The climate surrounding classroom practice as well as unintended outcomes are central
to this approach.

Models such as those outlined above are conceptual in nature and
sometimes it can be difficult to adapt these models to educational problems. A strategy developed by Leithwood et al. (n.d.) presents a process
that could be used to adapting these models to practical problems. This
strategy illustrates the specific tasks of conducting an evaluation from in-
ception to completion. The Leithwood strategy should assist the nonspecialist in conducting program evaluation.

## A TRANSMISSION MODEL: THE DISCREPANCY
## EVALUATION MODEL

This model, developed by Provus (1972), combines evaluation with management theory, reflecting Provus's assumption that program evaluation
fills two purposes: It provides a process for program development and it
also provides a means of assessing the merits of a program.

The information that is gathered through evaluation is intended for
decision makers at two different levels: 1) program personnel responsible
for the development and implementation of school programs and 2) personnel at the policy-making or administrative level. Provus (1972) describes the relationship between the two levels in this way: "Evaluation is
the handmaiden of program development and quiet counselor to administrators—but it operates in accordance with its own set of rules and on
an authority independent of the program unit" (p. 118).

In this model, evaluation involves a comparison of actual performance with an established standard. Figure 14.1 shows five such comparisons made in this model. Provus calls the difference between the
performance and the standard a *discrepancy*. Evaluation provides information about the discrepancy, so that decision makers can act.

*Stage 1.* The standards are established within the program being evaluated. The first stage, therefore, involves a comparison of the program
design with an established set of design criteria. Figure 14.2 illustrates the
criteria for design suggested by Provus (1972). These criteria require that
the program describe its various components in three areas—inputs, or
beginning conditions; process, or planned activities for both staff and
students; and outputs, or the objectives. In addition to providing adequate descriptions of each of these performance elements, the program
also should indicate criteria for standards by which to judge the success
of the program.

Provus (1972) suggests that in this first comparison, the program
should be viewed as a series of paired elements. A pair includes an input

| Stage | Performance | Standard |
|---|---|---|
| I | Program Design<br>Input Dimension<br>Process Dimension<br>Output Dimension | Design Criteria |
| II | Program Operation | Program Design<br>Input Dimension<br>Process Dimension |
| III | Program Interim Products | Program Design<br>Process Dimension<br>Output Dimension |
| IV | Program Terminal<br>Products | Program Design<br>Output Dimension |
| V | Program Cost | Cost of Other Programs<br>with Same Product |

**Figure 14.1** Provus's sentence definition of curriculum evaluation. (*From Provus, M. The discrepancy evaluation model. In Taylor, P., and Cowley, D.M. (Eds.). Readings in curriculum evaluation. Dubuque, IA: Wm. C. Brown, 1972.*)

and an output. Along with this input–output pair, there also occurs a process of bringing about the change from input to output.

The Stage 1 comparison is designed to answer two questons: (1) "Is there specific and complete information for each element of the program design?" and (2) "Is the information in useable form?" (Provus, 1972, p. 120). The internal consistency of the program is examined to determine if it is basically sound. The adequacy of resources for teaching and professional development are checked, the probability of the planned processes bringing about the desired changes is examined, and other aspects of the program design are studied. External consistency also is examined. This involves a study of the compatibility of the new program with other programs taught in the school system. This study is done at the first stage so that any apparent conflicts between programs can be identified and, also, to ensure that the new program is consistent with the apparent values of the whole system.

After Stage 1, the evaluator identifies the discrepancies between the criteria and the program design. These are reported to the decision maker(s), who must decide whether the discrepancies are acceptable, or if the program design must be altered. These decisions must be made at this point, because the program design becomes the standard against which subsequent comparisons are made.

| Inputs | Process | Outputs |
|---|---|---|
| I. Variables—the things the program is attempting to change | Variables—those activities that change inputs into desired outputs | Variables—the changes that have come about |
| A. Student Variables<br>B. Staff Variables<br>C. Other Variables | A. Student Activities<br>B. Staff Activities | A. Student Variables<br>B. Staff Variables<br>C. Other Variables |
|  | 1. Functions and Duties<br>2. Communication<br>  a. Intra-staff<br>  b. With Others |  |
| II. Preconditions—the things that are prerequisite to program operation yet remain constant throughout the program<br>Student Conditions<br>Staff Qualifications<br>Administrative Support<br>Media<br>Facilities<br>Time |  | Preconditions—same throughout the program |
| III. Criteria must be specified for each input variable and precondition above. The criteria specified for student variables and preconditions constitute the selection criteria of the program. | Criteria must be specified for each of the process variables. | Criteria are specified on the variables to define the goals of the program. The participant is released from the program if he achieves the goal of the program or if he violates a precondition. |

**Figure 14.2** Design criteria. (*From Provus, M. The discrepancy evaluation model. In Taylor, P., and Cowley, D.M. (Eds.).* Readings in curriculum evaluation. *Dubuque, IA: Wm. C. Brown, 1972, p. 119.*)

***Stage 2.***   Stage 2 begins the comparison between the actual operation of the program and its design. The conditions present in the classrooms are compared to those outlined in the program design. The use of the process elements also is observed. Discrepancies noted between the program design and classroom practice are reported to the appropriate decision maker. Provus leaves the judgment of whether the discrepancies are detrimental to the success of the program to the decision maker. The evaluator's task is to report on the practice and to identify the discrepancies.

Any alterations to the program are then made and time is allowed for them to become part of the practice before the evaluation proceeds. This might involve professional development activities to assist teachers in learning new teaching methodologies (processes).

***Stage 3.***   Provus calls Stage 3 the *microlevel evaluation*. Specific processes and outcomes are studied to determine cause-and-effect relationships. If the processes are not producing the desired results, they should now be refined. At Stage 3, the evaluator is also expected to provide reasons for any problems that are detected.

***Stage 4.***   Stage 4 represents what Provus calls the *macrolevel evaluation* of cause and effect. The effect of the program as a whole in terms of changing student behavior is examined. The question of whether the program has achieved its goals is addressed. The knowledge gained from Stages 2 and 3 will assist in making the evaluation at Stage 4 more appropriate to the actual use of the program. Provus differentiates his model from other evaluation practices by claiming that many of the other models begin at what is Stage 4 in his own model.

***Stage 5.***   Stage 5 is not clearly outlined by Provus. He suggests that once all of the above data are collected, it should be possible to compare the program being evaluated with others designed to accomplish the same goals. The purpose of this comparison would be to see if the present program is providing the best value for the money. However, the methods of establishing a cost–benefit analysis of this type are not explained in the model.

## TWO TRANSACTION MODELS: CONTINGENCY–CONGRUENCE AND CIPP

### Contingency–Congruence Model

Stake's (1967, p. 373) stated purpose for this model is to provide the framework for the development of an evaluation plan. His main concern

is the purpose of the evaluation and the subsequent decisions about the
nature of the data collected. Stake (1967) sees a discrepancy between the
expectations of evaluators and those of teachers.

> The countenance of evaluation beheld by the educator is not the
> same one beheld by the specialist in evaluation. The specialist sees
> himself as a "describer," one who describes aptitudes and environ-
> ments and accomplishments. The teacher and school administrator,
> on the other hand, expect an evaluator to grade something or some-
> one as to merit. Moreover, they expect that he will judge things
> against external standards, on criteria perhaps little related to the
> local school's resources and goals. (p. 374)

The model, therefore, is designed to ensure that all the data is collected
and then processed to provide relevant information to the recipients.
This means that complete descriptive information must be gathered, including information about student achievement and descriptions of instructional practices and the relationships between these two factors. It
also means that judgment data must be collected. What Stake means by
*judgment data* are the opinions held by various local groups as well as the
opinions of experts in the particular subject fields. From these opinions,
standards can be extracted and the curriculum can be evaluated against
them.

The matrices shown in Figure 14.3 are used to organize the information gathered and also to ensure that the information is complete. The
first box is for the rationale, which is a statement of the basic purposes of
the program and its orientation. The rest of the data is classified as either
Description or Judgment. Data within the description matrix are of two
types: 1) intents (the purposes, as expressed by the program and/or the
teachers, in relation to student achievement, teaching strategies, and resources) and 2) observations (records of what actually occurs in the classroom).

The judgment matrix also has two categories: 1) standards (acceptable levels of participation, achievement, or understanding), which are
gathered from various sources (e.g., the teacher, students, parents, or
other interested groups may be asked to present their views), and 2) judgments (statements about how the performance, as described in the observations, compares to the standards established).

To assist in the organization and analysis of the information, the
data are gathered into three groups, as shown in Figure 14.3. Antecedents are any conditions existing prior to the teaching of the program;
these data may refer to previous learnings by the students or to the availability of specified resources. Transactions are the dynamics of the teach-
ing/learning process; the numerous interactions among the students,

Rationale

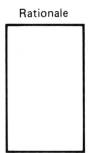

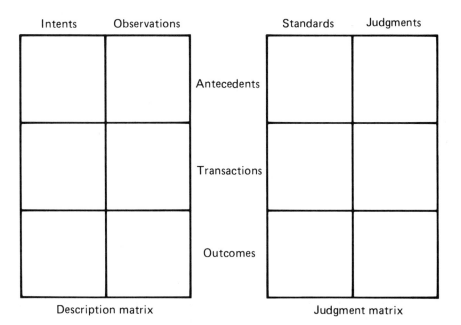

Intents    Observations                          Standards    Judgments

Antecedents

Transactions

Outcomes

Description matrix                              Judgment matrix

**Figure 14.3**   A layout of statements and data to be collected by the evaluator of
an educational program. (*From Stake, R. The countenance of educational evaluation.*
Teachers College Record, 68(7), 1967, p. 529. *Reprinted with permission.*)

teachers, and parents comprise this type of data. Outcomes are the results
of the teaching/learning process, including student growth in knowledge,
skills, and attitudes and the effects of the program on teachers and administrators. Because Stake stresses the need to consider both short- and
long-term results, he includes transfer of knowledge and skills in this section.

    Different processing methods are used for each of the matrices. Fig-
ure 14.4 illustrates the method of processing the descriptive data.

Descriptive Data

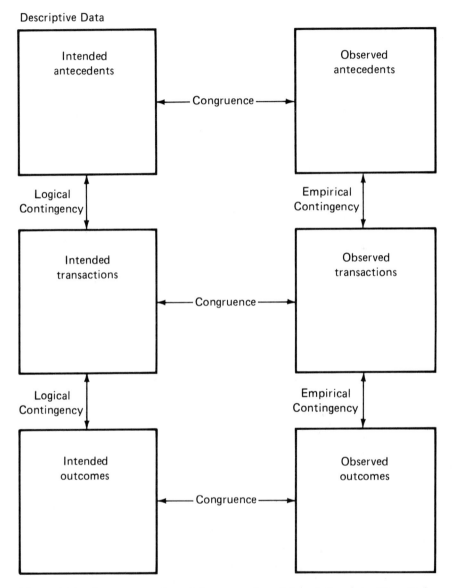

**Figure 14.4** A representation of the processing of descriptive data. (*From Stake, R. The countenance of educational evaluation.* Teachers College Record, 68(7), 1967, *p. 532. Reprinted with permission.*)

Two processes are used. The first process determines the congruence between the two bodies of information—intents and observations. Congruence exists if what was intended actually occurred.

Within the intents and the observations columns, the relationships between the antecedents, transactions, and outcomes also are studied. Ideally, it can be shown that the outcomes result from the antecedents and the transactions. If it can be demonstrated that the transactions are logical activities based on the prior conditions (antecedents), the transactions are logically contingent on the antecedents. Similarly, if the outcomes are logical expectations from the transactions, contingency exists.

For the intents data, the criterion used to evaluate contingency is logic, whereas for observation data, empirical evidence of contingency is required. The evaluator may gather such evidence from the program being evaluated and from existing research results.

Data from the judgment matrix are processed as illustrated in Figure 14.5. The sets of standards, gathered from various sources, are used as criteria to study the program. The standards are applied to the antecedents, transactions, and outcomes. The degree to which the standards are being met is assessed. One of the main tasks of the evaluator, is to ascertain the standards held by those involved. This is what Stake calls the absolute comparison.

The relative comparison occurs when the program is compared to other programs. Again, the evaluator determines which characteristics to compare and which programs to use in the comparison.

Stake's model, with its emphasis on classroom process or "transactions," lies within the transaction orientation. Stake (1967, p. 97) also argues that objectives do not have to be behavioral; they can represent a wide range of outcomes, including those that are taxonomic and humanistic. Since he developed this model, Stake also has explored some unusual approaches to evaluation that reflect a transformation orientation. For example, he has suggested that some evaluations be conveyed through artistic media in order to convey the uniqueness of the curriculum being evaluated.

## CIPP (Context-Input-Process-Product) Model

This model was developed by the Study Committee on Evaluation (Stufflebeam et al., 1971), which was created by the Phi Delta Kappa Research Advisory Committee. The model is established on the premise that the purpose of program evaluation is to assist in the improvement of curricula within a school system. This purpose is served when evaluation data are used in the curriculum decision-making process. The accent, therefore, is on formative rather than summative evaluation.

Four types of curriculum decisions are identified. The first type,

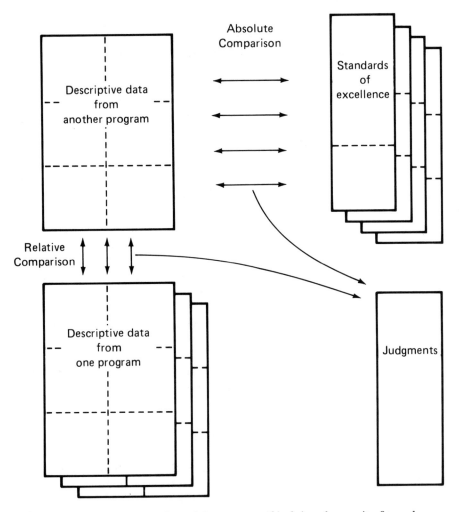

**Figure 14.5** A representation of the process of judging the merit of an educational program. (*From Stake, R. The countenance of educational evaluation.* Teachers College Record, 68(7), 1967, p. 537. *Reprinted with permission.*)

planning decisions, may involve discontinuing, changing, or maintaining the program. If a planning decision requires a curriculum change, then there is a need for the second type of decision—structuring decisions—which involve activity that will bring about the change. The third type of decision—implementing decisions—are made during the implementation of the change. These decisions rest on whether actual practices coincide with desired practices and whether modifications of the implementation procedures are required. Finally, recycling decisions are made after the effectiveness of the change has been determined. These decisions specify whether the change is to be incorporated into the curriculum or modified and tried again.

There are four components to program evaluation in this model—context evaluation, input evaluation, process evaluation, and product evaluation. Each component is associated with a particular type of curriculum decision. Figure 14.6 summarizes the purpose of each evaluation component and illustrates the relationship between the evaluation components and the types of decisions.

Context evaluation, the initial part of the program evaluation, involves a study of the environment in which that program is run. Stufflebeam et al. (1971, p. 219) suggest that the context be studied from two perspectives. First, a contingency study of the environment identifies those forces outside of the school system that can affect the curriculum, for example, the attitudes of the community or the policies of agencies such as the state or federal governments. The second aspect of the context evaluation is a congruency study. Here, actual and intended performance is compared to determine the apparent success of present practice. All aspects of the environment in which the program operates (e.g., cost, roles played, and timelines) are examined. Comparisons are made between how the program is being conducted, and the expectations as expressed in policy statements.

Planning decisions focus on two alternatives. One possible decision, to not change the program, results in the end of the evaluation. If the decision is made to change the program in some manner, input evaluation begins.

During the input evaluation, alternative implementation strategies are studied. From this examination, the most effective and economical course of action is to be determined. It is possible, with this model, if there is a great deal of information available about the proposed changes and their effects, for the evaluation to end at this point, and for implementation to proceed. In such situations, the alterations are usually modest and easily accessible. The evaluation ends because the modified program easily becomes the new, accepted practice. However, the change may require practices the effects of which are known only in principle. In this situation, field testing is required before the final format for the new program can be established. When this occurs, the two final evaluation components are used.

Process and product evaluations may be conducted concurrently. They both occur during the field trial period, but they examine different aspects of the new program. Process evaluation is used to determine the congruency between the planned and actual activities called for by the program. Implementation procedures, teaching methodologies, and student activities are included in process evaluation.

|  | Context evaluation | Input evaluation | Process evaluation | Product evaluation |
|---|---|---|---|---|
| Objective | To define the operational context, to identify and assess needs in the context, and to identify and delineate problems underlying the needs | To identify and assess system capabilities, available input strategies, and designs for implementing the strategies | To identify or predict, in process, defects in the procedural design or its implementation, and to maintain a record of procedural events and activities | To relate outcome information to objectives and to context, input, and process information |
| Method | By describing individually and in relevant perspectives the major subsystems of the context; by comparing actual and intended inputs and outputs of the subsystems; and by analyzing possible causes and discrepancies between actualities and intentions | By describing and analyzing available human and material resources, solution strategies, and procedural designs for relevance, feasibility and economy in the course of action to be taken | By monitoring the activity's potential procedural barriers and remaining alert to unanticipated ones | By defining operationally and measuring criteria associated with the objectives; by comparing these measurements with predetermined standards, and by interpreting the outcome in terms of recorded input and process information |

| Relation to decision making in the change process | For deciding upon the setting to be served, the goals associated with meeting needs and the objectives associated with solving problems (i.e., for planning needed changes) | For selecting sources of support, solution strategies, and procedural designs (i.e., for programming change activities) | For implementing and refining the program design and procedure (i.e., for effecting process control) | For deciding to continue, terminate, modify or refocus a change activity, and for linking the activity to other major phases of the change process (i.e., for evolving changes activities) |
|---|---|---|---|---|

[1]From Stufflebeam et al. (1971). (Used with permission of Peacock Press.)

**Figure 14.6** The CIPP evaluation model. *(From Borich, G.D., and Jemelka, R.P.* Programs and systems: An evaluation perspective. *New York: Academic Press, 1982, p. 11. Reprinted with permission.)*

Product evaluation examines the outcomes of the program during the field tests and compares them to the expected outcomes. Criteria for this comparison are drawn from the program objectives as well as from information gained from the context, input, and process evaluations.

Data from the process and product evaluations are used to make recycling decisions. For example, the field trial results might suggest that the new program can be incorporated into the school system in the form resulting from the trial. If this is the decision, the evaluation procedure for this program is finished. A second possible decision is that the program should be modified further and subjected to another field trial.

## A TRANSFORMATION MODEL: CURRICULUM CRITICISM

Eisner (1979) claims that curriculum criticism is analogous to art criticism. The task of the art critic is to assist others in clarifying their perceptions of the work of art. To accomplish this, the critic uses an approach that addresses the qualities of the work and presents them in a language that helps others achieve a deeper understanding of the work. As Eisner (1979) explains it,

> The critic's task is to function as a midwife to perception, to so talk about the qualities constituting the work of art that others, lacking the critic's connoisseurship, will be able to perceive the work more comprehensively. (p. 191)

This approach, therefore, requires that the data collected during an evaluation be qualitative rather than quantitative in nature. When evaluating a school program, such data are likely to focus on the activities children engage in, the character of the school day, or the classroom atmosphere. The data collected for a curriculum criticism usually are not revealed by standardized tests, interviews, or checklists.

Educational connoisseurship is another aspect of this approach. Eisner (1979) describes the general aspects of connoisseurship:

> The ability to see, to perceive what is subtle, complex, and important, is its first necessary condition. The act of knowledgeable perceptions is, in the arts, referred to as connoisseurship. To be a connoisseur is to know how to look, to see, and to appreciate. (p. 193)

In the educational context, the connoisseur must be able to distinguish what is significant about what is observed in schools. The connoisseur also must be able to recognize how the individual aspects of classroom life form the overall structure within which the teacher and students work. Finally, to assist in understanding both what and how the students are learning, the connoisseur must be able to deduce the "rules" at work in a classroom.

Proponents of curriculum criticism (Eisner, 1979; Mann, 1968–69) do not suggest that this approach be used to replace the traditional quantitative approaches. The two approaches are viewed as complementary. Both qualitative and quantitative methods have particular strengths to be used in specific curriculum evaluation situations.

Although there is not a recommended structure for conducting curriculum criticism, there are three phases to the process. The first is the descriptive phase, during which the critic describes qualities of life in a classroom. This description attends not only to particular factors (e.g., student activities), but to relationships among the factors. Thus, a description might describe student activities as well as teacher's manner when organizing the activities. The degree of enthusiasm, the nature of the student interactions, and other factors might also be included.

The factors or details chosen for description depend on the critic's knowledge and experience in classrooms, the purpose of the evaluation, and the critic's degree of connoisseurship. The description should convey a feeling of what life in the classroom is like. The results are similar to a literary description.

During the second or interpretive phase, the critic interprets the events described in phase one. Explanations are provided for the actions, reactions, and interactions observed. For Eisner (1979) and Mann (1968–69), the prime function of curriculum criticism is the disclosure of meaning. Mann (1968–69) suggests that the critic accomplishes this by applying what he calls *disclosure models* to the situation.

> The models are to be regarded as grounded and entailed in personal knowledge of ethical reality. That is to say that the models employed to disclose meanings in phenomena are not the results of operations upon data, but are rather the result of extensions, transformations, and deployments of intuitively held personal knowledge. (p. 10)

This personal knowledge will include theoretical knowledge (e.g., how children learn, effective teaching methodologies) as well as practical knowledge.

The culmination of a curriculum criticism is the evaluative phase. Besides describing and interpreting, the curriculum critic also renders a judgment. For Eisner (1979), "the point of educational criticism is to improve the educational process" (p. 209). Mann (1968–69), also, indicates that the critic has an obligation to assist in the decision-making process: "The meanings the curriculum critic discloses, then, are meanings about which he believes ethical judgments are to be made" (p. 11).

The criteria on which the judgments are made will be based on the personal values of the critic. It is possible, therefore, that different critics would arrive at different conclusions when observing the same classroom. According to Eisner and Mann, this is a strength of this approach. This acceptance of pluralistic viewpoints places this model within a transformation framework.

> Acknowledgment of different points of view about the effectiveness of a curriculum provides more alternatives to the decision makers. Proponents argue that the curriculum criticism approach, rather than oversimplifying the situation by limiting decisions to one set of criteria, acknowledges the complexity of classroom life. This implies that more than one point of view should be sought when evaluating a curriculum.

Because this approach relies heavily on the selected observations and judgments of the critic, there is concern over the validity of the criticism. Eisner (1979) suggests that two particular processes can be used to address this problem during the evaluation.

> These two processes, structural collaboration and referential adequacy, are the two major procedures with which to determine the validity of educational criticism. Structural collaboration seeks to determine the extent to which criticism forms a coherent, persuasive whole. It seeks to determine if the pieces of the critical story hold together, make sense, provide a telling interpretation of the events. Referential adequacy is the process of testing the criticism against the phenomena it seeks to describe, interpret, and evaluate. Referential adequacy is the empirical check of critical disclosure. (p. 218)

## AN EVALUATION STRATEGY

For many school systems, program evaluation is a desirable, but difficult, curriculum task. Although there are an abundance of evaluation models, there is a shortage of personnel with the necessary skills to conduct evaluations.

The models presented in the first part of this chapter are representative of the theoretical knowledge available. It is apparent from a study of these models that the evaluator requires a high level of knowledge about evaluation and research methods. The authors of many of these models (e.g., Stake, 1967, Stufflebeam et al. 1971) assume that personnel with such qualifications are available to a school system to conduct the evaluations. A literal application of some of these models, such as the one proposed by Provus, would require the establishment of an evaluation department in a school system to carry out the evaluations.

A strategy developed by Leithwood et al. (n.d.) is designed for the nonspecialist. This strategy outlines a process that makes it possible for school systems that do not have resident evaluation experts to conduct an effective evaluation. This process can be followed by teachers, principals, or superintendents.

It is assumed, however, that the person conducting the evaluation would have developed a personal model for evaluation that enables him or her to identify important tasks to be carried out. The ability to establish procedures for the evaluation also is needed. These requirements reflect the need for the evaluator to use the evaluation literature to develop the details for the project being undertaken. Models, such as those presented in this chapter, may present the theoretical basis for the evaluation, but they usually require the evaluator to develop more specific procedures.

The strategy we present here addresses the roles in the evaluation process of three groups: (1) primary decision makers (e.g., superintendent), who usually are the ones who initiate the evaluation and are most interested in the results; (2) principals and other school personnel who are interested in the results of the evaluation and will likely use the results in some way; and (3) evaluators, who will do the actual work of carrying out the evaluation.

These three groups assist in the task of program evaluation: "In our view [Leithwood et al.] the central task of program evaluation is the judgment of value or worth and the central purpose is to assist in improving both the process and outcome of program decision making" (p. 12).

Figure 14.7 illustrates the five sequential steps in the Leithwood et al. evaluation strategy.

**1.** In Phase I, the evaluator determines the nature of the information to be sought. This is accomplished by identifying the rationale for the evaluation and by clarifying the decisions to be made from the final results. The primary decision maker and others who will use the results usually provide this information. The relative importance of the information is determined by rank ordering the potential decisions to be made. Decision rules provide the basis for decision making. A decision rule states that under specified conditions, a certain decision will be made. For example, during the evaluation of a mathematics program, a potential decision might be to revise the content of the program. A decision rule might be that the content will be revised if more than 10% of the students cannot achieve a satisfactory level and a majority of the teachers indicate that the content is not suitable to their respective grade levels. Thus, decision rules also provide the criteria that decision makers will use to follow up an evaluation.

Phase I: Defining the Evaluation Problem

1.1 Record initial statement of the problem
1.2 Identify other users of the results of
      the evaluation
1.3 Identify potential decisions to be made
1.4 Generate a list of rank-ordered decisions
1.5 Develop general decision rules

Phase II: Choosing an Appropriate Methodology

2.1 Identify the specific questions
2.2 Identify the best sources of information
2.3 Identify the best ways of collecting information
      from each source
2.4 Identify the best design
2.5 Choose the best type and size of sample for each
      source of information
2.6 Select the best forms of data and methods of
      analysis for each question
2.7 Prepare a methodological package

Phase III: Planning for Data Collection, Analysis, and Reporting

3.1 Identify the major tasks
3.2 Identify the subtasks
3.3 Identify responsibilities
3.4 Plot the subtasks in chronological order in a timeline

Phase IV: Collecting and Compiling Data

4.1 Establish relationships
4.2 Select instruments
4.3 Develop instruments
4.4 Prepare instruments for use
4.5 Select samples
4.6 Schedule the data collection
4.7 Collect the data
4.8 Compile the data

Phase V: Analyzing and Reporting the Data

5.1 Summarize the data
5.2 Refine the decision rules
5.3 Apply the decision rules
5.4 Report the results

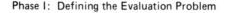

**Figure 14.7** Overview of the evaluation strategy. (*From Leithwood, K.A., Montgomery, D., Wilson, R., Marshall, A.R., and Connock, L. A handbook and practical strategy for evaluating educational programs. Unpublished paper, n.d., p. 19.*)

One purpose of Phase I, often overlooked by the nonspecialist, is to help ensure that the information gathered during the evaluation is pertinent to decision making. The second purpose of this phase is to increase the commitment of the decision makers to the use of the results after the evaluation is completed.

**2.** In Phase II, specific questions are formulated. These questions are based on the possible decisions that might be made and usually will reflect a particular orientation. Following the formulation of the questions, a number of decisions are then required of the evaluator, as shown in Figure 14.7, steps 2.2 through 2.6. The evaluator's knowledge and skill regarding evaluation procedures, as well as his or her personal model of evaluation, are used extensively in this phase. When all the methodological decisions have been made, they are combined into an overview of the evaluation, called the methodological package.

**3.** Phase III continues the planning in greater detail. The tasks are identified and timelines are established. The responsibilities of everyone involved in the evaluation process are clearly outlined. This step also assists the evaluator in taking a final look at the proposed evaluation. It now becomes clear whether it is feasible to carry on as planned or whether alterations are required. If alterations are suggested, the evaluator still has time to discuss them with the decision makers before the data-gathering process begins.

**4.** In Phase IV, the plan developed in Phase III is carried out. Selection of questionnaires and interview formats to be developed is completed. Again, the type of instrument will reflect a particular curriculum position. The evaluator also ensures that principals and teachers are aware of their roles and solicits their cooperation. Finally, the data are actually collected and compiled. It is the work done in this phase that nonspecialists often attempt to do too soon.

**5.** Phase V requires that the evaluator apply the data collected to the criteria of the decision rules developed in Phase I. The results are then reported to the decision maker so that action can be taken.

## CONCLUDING COMMENTS

The basic purpose of the curriculum evaluation models presented in this chapter is to gather information for curriculum decision making. Improved curriculum should result from these decisions.

Before selecting a particular evaluation model, further refinement of the model's purpose is needed. Clarification of the purpose should indicate where, in the curriculum cycle, the information is to be gathered and the decisions made. A model such as Stufflebeam et al.'s CIPP Model might be most suitable if the purpose is to make evaluation an integral part of the whole curriculum cycle. Data from this model provide information for decisions about the aims of the program, the development of the program, and the implementation process. However, this model is complex and its use requires many human and financial resources. Provus' Discrepancy Evaluation Model might be more suitable in situations where curriculum decisions are related primarily to the implementation process. With this model, however, the accent is on the design of the program and appears to be less concerned with the educational environment.

A refinement of the purpose of the evaluation also will help to identify the criteria to be used in the evaluation. Stake's Contingency–Congruence Model provides a method for studying a variety of standards when evaluating a program. The specificity of the information gathered for the antecedent, transaction, and outcome segments might make this model more suitable for a school-based, rather than a systemwide, evaluation. Similarly, the curriculum criticism approach, which is also applicable to the classroom, offers alternative sets of criteria on which to judge a program.

Too often, measurement of student achievement is considered to be the sole purpose of curriculum evaluation. However, the models presented in this chapter have demonstrated that student evaluation is only a small segment in curriculum evaluation. Classroom climate (Eisner), teaching methodology (Stake), program design (Provus), and the social and cultural environment (Stufflebeam) are a few of the factors that curriculum evaluation can assess. Because school programs are part of an environment that includes many other activities and groups, the partic-

## SUMMARY CHART:   Chapter 14

| TRANSMISSION | TRANSACTION | TRANSFORMATION |
|---|---|---|
| *Discrepancy Evaluation Model* | *CIPP Model* | *Curriculum Criticism Model* |
| Program design<br>Program operation<br>Program interim<br>  products<br>Program terminal<br>  products<br>Program cost | Context evaluation<br>Input evaluation<br>Process evaluation<br><br>Product evaluation | Descriptive phase<br>Interpretive phase<br>Evaluative phase |

ular combination of elements to be included in an evaluation will vary. A determination of the most important elements will affect which model or combination of models should be used.

Curriculum evaluation provides the information necessary to bring about improvements in schools. To do this, it is necessary to gather the proper information and to present it in a useful manner. In choosing a model for evaluation, as in choosing models for the other components of the curriculum cycle, the orientation of the model and its overall purpose should be clarified. The model should be congruent with the orientations of the educators who are developing and implementing the curriculum.

## REFERENCES

Borich, G.D., & Jemelka, R.P. (1982). *Programs and systems: An evaluation perspective*. New York: Academic Press.

Brickell, H.M. (1981). Groping for the elephant. In Brandt, R. S. (Ed.), *Applied strategies for curriculum evaluation*. Alexandria, VA: Association for Supervision and Curriculum Development.

Eisner, E.W. (1979). *The educational imagination: On the design and evaluation of school programs*. New York: Macmillan.

Leithwood, K.A., Montgomery, D., Wilson, R., Marshall, A.R., & Connock, L. (n.d.). *A handbook and practical strategy for evaluating educational programs*. Unpublished paper.

Mann, J.S. (1968–69, winter). Curriculum criticism. *Curriculum theory network, 2*, 2–14.

Provus, M.M. (1972). The discrepancy evaluation model. In Taylor, P.A., & Cowley, D.M. (Eds.), *Readings in curriculum evaluation*. Dubuque, IA: Wm. C. Brown.

Stake, R.E. (1967). The countenance of educational evaluation. *Teachers College Record, 68*(7), 523–540.

Stufflebeam, D.L., Foley, W.J., Gephart, W.J., Guba, E.G., Hammond, H.D., Merriman, H.O., & Provus, M.M. (1971). *Educational evaluation and decision making*. Itasca, IL: Peacock Press.

# CHAPTER 15 CURRICULUM: The Decades Ahead

The children going to school now will live most of their lives in the twenty-first century. Educators are just beginning to grapple with what this might mean. In this chapter we examine the future from two perspectives. First, we identify major issues for the future and analyze the impact of these issues on education. Second, we look at how social groups will attempt to influence the future and examine these influences in relation to the major curriculum positions and the social movements associated with them.

## AN AGENDA FOR THE FUTURE

Predicting the future is tricky business. For instance, one recent book that examines future trends—Toffler's (1980), *The Third Wave*—contains material that is already out of date. Toffler's book reflects the period in the 1970s when the Organization of Petroleum Exporting Countries (OPEC) was dominant and oil prices were skyrocketing. Shortly after *The Third Wave* was published, oil prices headed downward and OPEC began to lose its stranglehold on oil prices. This is one example of how political and economic trends can change very quickly, making any attempts to extrapolate from these trends treacherous work.

Like Toffler, Naisbitt (1982), in his book *Megatrends*, presents a picture of a future characterized by decentralization, participatory democracy, a benevolent technology under human control, and a global economy. Our view is not so optimistic. Instead of clear trends, we see the future mostly in terms of tensions that will continue for the next few decades. The following issues will often be at the core of these tensions:

- Globalism versus regionalism
- Decentralization versus centralization
- Human technology versus an autonomous technology

We also examine two issues that are likely to be central in the next few decades:

- Family structure/the role of women
- The effects of an aging society

## Globalism versus Regionalism

The move to globalism has been facilitated by advances in technology and communication. Naisbitt claims that the development of communication satellites has had a very important impact on the speed with which information is conveyed in society. He uses the term *information float* to describe the gap between the occurrence of an event and the time when people find out about the event. Satellite technology has reduced this gap.

Naisbitt (1982) points out that technology has also led to greater economic interdependence, as the following comment shows:

> An American architectural-engineering firm is building three hotels in Saudi Arabia. The room modules for the hotels—right down to the soap dishes in the bathrooms—will be made in Brazil. The labor to build the hotels is coming from South Korea, and we Americans are doing the construction management, the information side. That's a model we will see a lot in the future. (p. 67)

At the same time that we are witnessing global interdependence, we also are seeing intense identification with ethnic and cultural groups. For example, Russia is concerned about the large number of ethnic groups within the Communist bloc that are threatening to assert their own identities; in Europe, a number of groups are challenging the national consensus in countries such as Spain (e.g., Basques) and Belgium (Walloons); In North America, the French threaten separatism in Quebec, and Spanish-speaking groups in the United States demand bilingualism.

Curriculum developers will have to deal with these tensions in their work. Some programs will move toward an increased recognition of global interdependence and will provide more coverage of Third World problems. At the same time, students will learn languages that reflect ethnic assertiveness (e.g., French in Canada, and Spanish in the United States). Some transmission-oriented educators will fight these changes and stress programs that reinforce traditional images of national unity.

## Decentralization versus Centralization

In *1984,* Orwell predicts the ultimate centralized society where Big Brother controls almost every aspect of the citizens' lives. Some futurists claim that many aspects of Orwell's nightmare are already part of our society. Goodman (1978), for example, has made a study of *1984* in which he identifies 137 predictions and claims that over 100 of these predictions have come true. He concludes that almost all the scientific and techno- logical predictions have come true and that many of the grim social pre- dictions *could* happen through "a single triggering incident."

This view is challenged to some extent by the work of Toffler (1980/ 1981) and Naisbitt (1982), who see movement toward decentralization in many aspects of life. We will now examine the tensions between central- ization and decentralization in politics, economics/corporate life, and ed- ucation.

*Politics.*    Centralized political decision making is still predominant in many countries. Most Third World countries have found it difficult to sustain democratic processes; in the West, the political Right has fre- quently allied itself with a conservative nationalism that often is adverse to pluralistic alternatives. In both the Third World and the United States, religious fundamentalism has been exerting political power. This trend toward political, economic, and religious conservatism is often accom- panied by an emphasis on military preparedness, censorship, and pa- triotic values.

Counter to this trend is the move toward decentralized political de- cision making. Local groups are asserting themselves against federal and state authorities. Naisbitt (1982) cites a few examples of this trend:

- A Chicago coalition of 100 neighborhood associations took to the streets for a day-long street drama protesting that more money is being spent on downtown projects than on housing.
- New England's Section 8 Coalition set up a tent in downtown Provi- dence to protest the "unjust distribution of federal rent subsidies."
- Residents of Bordentown, New Jersey, have organized a group called HOPE (Help Our Polluted Environment) to oppose a Love Canal-type plan being considered by the state.
- Local opposition in Minnesota forced the state to return a $3.7 million federal grant for a toxic-waste landfill and chemical-disposal facility. (p. 115)

The move toward decentralization is even more apparent in Can- ada. For example, Quebec elected a government pledged to separatism in 1976. Although the vote on separation was defeated in 1980, separatism will be a continuing theme in Quebec politics. It is also a continuing issue in Western Canadian politics.

In *The Nine Nations of North America*, Garreau (1981) argues that Mexico, the United States, and Canada are actually composed of nine distinct geographical and economic units. For example, Garreau claims that MexAmerica (Mexico, Southern California, and the Southwestern United States) will replace the Foundry (the industrial area around the Great Lakes) as the dominant and most populous region in the twenty-first century.

***Economics/Corporate Life.***   The tension between centralization and decentralization was described in Chapter 4 in relation to Galbraith's work. He sees two economies—one is made up of small businesses and the other is the technostructure, which is composed of large corporations and the government. However, a movement toward decentralization that exists within some large corporations has led, for example, to the use of quality circles (small groups of workers who make decisions on work-related problems). Another example is Hewlett Packard's institution of a management system where managers report to their own peers. Toffler (1980/1981) describes his visit to a Hewlett Packard "factory":

> My old friends' shrewd eyes would take in much that is new and sharply different from the classical factories they knew. They would notice, for example, that instead of all the H-P employees arriving at once, punching the clock, and racing to their work stations, they are able, within limits, to choose their own individual working hours. Instead of being forced to stay in one work location, they are able to move about as they wish. My old friends would marvel at the freedom of the H-P employees, again within limits, to set their own work pace. To talk to managers or engineers without worrying about status or hierarchy. To dress as they wish. In short, to be individuals. In fact, my old companions in their heavy steel-tipped shoes, dirty overalls, and working-men's caps would find it hard, I believe, to think of the place as a factory at all. (pp. 180–181)

Of course, it is possible to extrapolate the vision of decentralization to almost comic proportions. Consider Helprin's (1983) description in *Winter's Tale* of a newspaper company named The Ghost:

> So, as of next Monday, The Ghost parent corporation will be recast into clusters, macroclusters, microclusters, pods, micropods, minipods, macropods, macronuggets, supernuggets, bulboaggregates, and pings. Some departments will tie into other clusters, pods, nuggets, bulboaggregates, and pings, and some will remain essentially

stable. For example, a secretary in what is now the secretarial pool of the real estate section of the classified department, will henceforth be referred to as a ping in the secretarial cluster of the real estate pod in the classified macronugget. This, of course, is in turn a bulbo-aggregate of the revenue-generating supernugget. (p. 397)

***Education.***   In education, there has been tension between federal control of educational programs and the move toward educational programs that reflect local initiatives. Many parents have taken an activist stance in their desire to exert an influence over their children's education. Private schools have seen increased enrollments as a result of parents' attempts to exert more control over what is happening in schools. Naisbitt (1982) provides some examples of these activities:

• The National Committee for Citizens in Education proposed creating a citizen/parent office in what was then to be the new Department of Education. The National Committee passes out wallet-sized cards informing parents of their rights in the education system.
• In New Jersey, a group sued the local school board for "effectively excluding" parents from the educational goal-setting process.
• Parents in Palo Alto, California, pushed for a role in collective bargaining between teachers and the school board. (p. 143)

Overall, it appears that curriculum planners will be confronted with these kinds of tensions in their work. They will be called upon to develop programs that reflect, on the one hand, a concern for a national consensus and, on the other hand, a need to respond to local initiatives. Planners working from a transformation position will lean toward decentralized decision making. Curriculum workers having a transmission orientation will be more concerned with making sure the curriculum reflects their image of a national consensus. Michael Apple (1983) asserts that textbook publishers can have a strong impact on curriculum decisions.

As decision-making power coalesces at the state level, publishers will tailor their textbooks increasingly to the values of those states that encourage statewide textbook adoptions—generally through reimbursements to local school districts for some portion of the cost if they select their instructional materials from an approved list. For publishers, getting materials placed on such lists is quite important, since it nearly guarantees high sales and profits. Given this economic fact, states such as Texas and California, which have state textbook adoption policies, will have disproportionate power to determine which textbooks and resources will be available throughout the U.S. Hence we will see even greater standardization of the curriculum. The curriculum will become "safer," less controversial, less likely to alienate any powerful interest group. (p. 323)

## Human Technology versus Autonomous Technology

One of the main theses of Ellul's *The Technological Society* is that technology has a life of its own that is independent of our efforts to control it. Ellul (1967) states:

> The one best way: so runs the formula to which our technique corresponds. When everything has been measured and calculated mathematically so that the method which has been decided upon is satisfactory from the rational point of view, and when from the practical point of view, the method is manifestly the most efficient of all those hitherto employed or those in competition with it, then the technical movement becomes self-directing. I call this process *automatism.*
>
> There is no personal choice. In respect to magnitude, between, say 3 and 4, 4 is greater than 3; this is a fact which has no personal reference. . . . Technique itself, ipso facto and without indulgence or possible discussion, selects among the means to be employed. The human being is no longer in a sense the agent of choice. (pp. 79–80)

Counter to this view is the concept that technology is an extension of our human consciousness and is something with which we can interact in an intelligent manner. This latter theme is predominant in the Toffler–Naisbitt vision of the future, in which the microcomputer will be at the center of a number of positive trends, including the following:

- The development of a high-tech economy—often referred to as the *information society*—based on the production and exchange of information. Naisbitt (1982) predicts that the rate of increase in scientific and technical information, which currently is increasing at the rate of approximately 13% per year, will soon jump to 40% and that manufacturing also will be subject to increasing automation and computerization.
- The increased use of the home computer, which, in Toffler's view, will lead to what he calls the *electronic cottage,* or more people working and learning at home. Naisbitt challenges this view, arguing that the high-tech society will be accompanied by "high-touch"; people will still go out of their homes to work because they will continue to seek interpersonal contact.
- Computers will facilitate networking. As a result, people from different

geographic locations will be able to communicate about their specific interests.

- Computers will play an increasing role in education. They will assist the student in learning various literacy skills (e.g., math and reading) and will lead to widespread computer literacy.

Although Smith (1981) acknowledges some of these positive trends, he has also pointed out some of the possible dangers of the computer:

- Degradation of work. In some instances, the use of computers has led to work becoming more regimented. Smith gives one example:

  Workers become adjuncts to the needs and capabilities of the machine rather than the reverse. (In some Bell operating companies, for example, computerized monitoring of terminal activity for "productivity" purposes means that the operators cannot even go to the bathroom, let alone walk around, unless there is someone to take their place, because the moment a terminal is closed, the computer rings a bell alerting the supervisor.) (p. 30)

- Unemployment. The effects of computers are of great concern to blue collar workers. Robotics is moving gradually into factories and the long-term consequences of this change could be a significant increase in unemployment.

- Transborder data flow. Smith describes a scenario in which "global computer networks could be profoundly subversive of national borders" (p. 30). He also suggests that countries in the West will be "information rich," whereas countries in the Third World will remain "information poor," a situation that will maintain or lengthen the gap between these two areas of the world. In Smith's words, "Coupled with this 'information gap' is the threat of a new form of imperialism, in which the developed countries export their manufacturing industries (and pollution) to the Third World, but retain and expand the knowledge industries" (p. 30).

- Who will control data access? This is one of the main questions in the information age. Who decides which of the many thousands of publications printed each year should become resource material in the data base? Who controls the cross indexing of computerized information? Librarians and cataloguers will possibly play a key role in screening non-mainstream material from the data bases.

The implications of the microcomputer for education are not clear. However, it may be helpful to use the major curriculum positions as a framework for analysis of the future use of the computer. For instance, transmission-oriented educators probably will focus on using the microcomputer for learning basic skills and subject content. The computer would be allied with competency-based education and mastery-learning programs to make learning more individualized and efficient. Transaction educators probably will emphasize computer programming and the ways in which computers can facilitate logical thinking and problem solving. Computers will be integrated with information-processing teaching models, which will enable students to analyze mental processes. It might be argued that programs developed for computers represent thinking made visible on the computer screen. Teachers working from a transformation position will be concerned with the interactive aspect of computers, in other words, how they can be used to access various data bases. Computers also will be used to enhance creativity. For example, students might be encouraged to use computers to develop graphic arts or music programs.

## Family Structure/The Role of Women

In a study conducted by Miller, Taylor, & Walker (1982), one of the prominent factors identified by teachers was the increasing impact on students of single-parent families. The teachers noted that their role often shifts to one of social worker, where the major concern is the child's social and emotional development. Ravitch (1983) claims that schools also will have to deal with the increase in the number of working women:

> Today about half of all females are in the workforce, a trend that seems likely to continue in the years ahead. This means that our society will need, more than ever, good institutions designed to nurture and to supervise young children during most of the day. This is and will continue to be one of the important roles of the school. (p. 320)

Today, only a small percentage of families qualify as the traditional nuclear family in which the husband works and the mother stays at home. In a study of the family conducted by the Joint Center of Urban Studies of MIT and Harvard, the following findings were predicted for the year 1990:

- Husband-and-wife homes with only one working spouse will account for 14% of households, as compared with 43% in 1960.
- Approximately 13 separate types of households will replace the traditional nuclear family, including categories such as "female head, widowed with children" and "male head, previously married with children."
- Approximately one-third of the children will have spent part of their childhood living with a single parent.

In response to the question, *"What other changes in values have you seen coming into the mainstream?"*, Naisbitt (1983) discusses the emerging role of women:

> One of the biggest—which isn't in the book [*Megatrends*], so I call it "The Eleventh Megatrend"—is the shift from a machismo society to an androgynous society. In our very best law schools, not to mention med schools, architectural schools, and other professional programs, a large proportion of students are now women. When you think of how macho and adversarial law has been, and how women often tend to work situations out in a more positive, conciliatory way, you can see that there will be profound effects. It's not that everything was run by male patriarchs and now will be run by women; it's that we're struggling for a balance between male and feminine values. (p. 96)

What are the implications for schools of the changing role of the family? To some extent, as students increasingly will turn to teachers for emotional support, schools will increasingly fulfill expectations that previously were fulfilled by parents. Programs in affective education, values education, and personal development will continue to be in demand. Conservative profamily groups will fight this trend and argue that schools should not deal with the child's emotional life.

## The Effects of an Aging Society

Another prominent trend in today's society, which has received little attention from futurists such as Toffler and Naisbitt, is the anticipated increase in the percentage of older people in our society. As the baby boom generation ages, it will tend to dominate social priorities. Just as schools were being built in the 1960s to accommodate the baby boomers, they are being closed in the 1980s. One of the implications of this trend is that we can look forward to a stable, aging teaching force in school systems. With few opportunities for mobility or promotions, school systems will have to examine alternative mechanisms for stimulating teacher growth.

Teachers in their late thirties and early forties are making crucial decisions about career advancement. Some of the decisions are coincident with what Daniel Levinson (1978) calls the *mid-life transition*. It is clear that opportunities for educational leaves and for transfers to other schools are important alternatives for teachers. A leave allows the person to work through a particular area of interest and return to teaching with renewed commitment. Some boards have developed plans that permit teachers to defer part of their salary toward a leave of absence. This type of option is an important alternative, particularly for teachers from 35 to

45 years old, for whom opportunities for advancement are extremely limited, because it allows teachers to redefine their career aspirations.

The present time is also a time of rising aspirations for women, particularly women in the age range of 35 to 40. Because, in the past, women teachers were not encouraged to move into administrative or supervisory positions beyond the classroom, some school boards now are moving toward affirmative action programs for women. As Levinson (1978) notes, involving women in positions of responsibility can benefit both men and women.

> The freer participation of women in the work world is an important step toward the liberation of men from their one-sided masculinity and their anxiety about the feminine. Men need women as colleagues, bosses and mentors. These relationships enable them to form richer identities, to live out more aspects of the self, and to reduce the burdens created by the excessive feminization of parenting and by the discrimination that restricts their participation in most of our institutions. (p. 381)

## THE CURRICULUM POSITIONS IN THE FUTURE: THREE SCENARIOS

We turn now to a discussion of how each of the major positions may evolve over the next few decades. In the coming years, each of the positions will compete with the other viewpoints for influence in school practices.

### Transmission Scenario

The transmission scenario will coincide with a political scene that will continue to be dominated by conservatism. Federal initiatives will continue to diminish as decision making is turned over to states and to local education authorities. People will demand that schools prepare students for the workforce by teaching literacy and computational skills. Competency-based education will remain in the forefront. Mastery learning also may be advocated as a means to teaching the basics. Testing will receive a great deal of attention as states attempt to ensure that students graduate with certain skills.

In general, in this scenario, schools as we know them will not change very much. In elementary schools, students will be taught language and math through traditional methods in the morning and in the afternoon they will study social studies, science, art, music, and physical education. Of course, educators working from other perspectives will attempt to change the curriculum, but the traditional barriers to change (finances, the structure of the school, teacher unions) will continue to blunt these efforts. One innovation that will crack these barriers is the computer. Schools will use the computer to assist in the teaching of basic skills and content mastery. Gifted students will use computers in a more creative manner in special classes.

The affective dimension of learning will not receive much attention in this scenario. Most transmission educators argue that schools can only accomplish so much and that many affective education programs are an invasion of student privacy.

In secondary schools, there will be a tightening of both curriculum and discipline. A standard core curriculum will be offered, with only a few electives. Students will be "tracked" into various streams that clearly indicate whether a student is college bound or is focusing on vocational skills that will lead to employment directly after graduation. Business will have a strong influence on the curriculum.

In general, the curriculum will continue to be dominated by the textbook. State review boards will approve what texts are to be used in the schools; therefore, very little controversial material will be introduced into the curriculum. Teachers will build their curriculum, with little deviation, around these texts.

## Transaction Scenario

In this scenario, there is a revival of liberalism. Unemployment will have become so intolerable that the voters turn to politicians who emphasize job programs. This liberalism, however, will not be a Keynesian liberalism, but will center around creating a national strategy for industrial growth. Government will play a strong role in determining what industries should receive help, thus strengthening the ability of the United States to compete with other countries. Employment programs geared to this industrial strategy thus will not be mere make-work programs. The overall political/economic strategy will focus on developing the high-tech industries.

Cognitive psychology will have a major role in school reform, as new discoveries about mental processes exert a strong impact on the curriculum. This impact will be most heavily felt in math and science programs in the schools. Teachers will focus on teaching problem-solving skills in these disciplines. The focus on math and science in this scenario also is congruent with its high-tech industrial strategy. This emphasis will be most pronounced in secondary schools. Computers will play a central role in the reform of curriculum. The computer will not just be used for learning basic skills, but will also be used to teach students computer literacy and programming skills. Computer studies will become a requirement in the secondary school curriculum.

Problem-solving skills will also be taught in elementary schools. Teachers will focus on making students aware of their own thinking processes. Computers will be used at the elementary level to teach thinking skills. Elaborate software programs will be developed that allow students to develop at their own rate in acquiring problem-solving competencies.

The transaction scenario is characterized by some degree of emphasis on applying problem-solving skills to social dilemmas. Students will discuss various problems that confront society at different levels (e.g., international, national, state, local). The emphasis in these discussions will be on identifying rational solutions to problems. Beyond an emphasis on social analysis, the affective domain does not receive much emphasis in this scenario.

Research on implementation will be used to bring about the transaction scenario. Unlike the 1960s, when similar efforts to change the curriculum failed, this effort will be more successful because educators will not be as naive about the difficulties involved in bringing about change. Strong support systems will be developed to accompany the new programs. Because these changes will be congruent with the liberal industrial strategy, funding for them will be available at the federal level.

## Transformation Scenario

In this scenario, many of the social changes predicted by Toffler and Naisbitt occur. In general, there will be a move toward decentralization and demassification of society. The economy will be characterized by the growth of human-scale businesses. Because even large corporations will be decentralized, workers in these corporations will have a say in what goes on. People will tend to be more sensitive to global concerns and, also, more likely to participate in local politics. Technology will speed this process along, as interactive computers allow people to register their viewpoint. The political process will move from representative government to participative decision making.

Elementary schools will focus on an integrated approach to learning. Language study, for example, will often be linked with the arts. Drama will be frequently used and students will be encouraged to use visual images to express their thinking. Movement also will be part of the curriculum, allowing students to express their emotions and thoughts through physical activity. By connecting thought, feeling, and movement, a sense of wholeness will be developed within the student. A certain portion of the curriculum will focus on developing the student's inner life. There will be short periods of silent meditation so that students can become more aware of their internal images and thoughts. Students will be encouraged to record these thoughts and images in a daily journal.

In secondary schools, in the first two years the emphasis will be on subjects such as English, math, science, and the social studies. However, in the last two years of high school, there will be a strong emphasis on social-action learning. In the first two years, students will learn to analyze society from a critical perspective. In the last two years, they will attempt to apply this perspective to various social-action projects. These projects will involve various efforts to improve the quality of life in the community. For example, students might work with elderly persons in a variety of activities that range from collecting oral history to improving the atmosphere in nursing homes.

The computer will have a role in the transformation school. It will be used to help students communicate with various data bases and to encourage creative thinking. The computer also will be used at home, as some students and parents will decide to carry out part of the child's education at home. However, many of these students also will spend a portion of their time in school, in order to learn social skills.

In this scenario, there will be a number of alternative schools that represent local initiatives. Some parents, of course, will still demand traditional programs in schools, but these demands will decrease as a result of social and technological changes that will make traditional programs increasingly inappropriate.

## CONCLUDING COMMENTS

It is unlikely that any one position will become totally dominant, thereby excluding the other positions. Instead, we will witness tension between the various positions in their efforts to influence the school curriculum. Again the relative impact of each position on the schools' curriculum will be closely linked to the general social climate. For example, a conservative social climate would mean that the transmission position would continue to be influential. On the other hand, if the Toffler–Naisbitt scenario unfolds we could witness a rise in transformation-oriented programs.

## REFERENCES

Apple, M.W. (1983, January). Curriculum in the year 2000: Tensions and possibilities. *Phi Delta Kappan*, 321–326.

Ellul, J. (1967). *The technological society*. New York: Alfred A. Knopf.

Garreau, J. (1981). *The nine nations of North America*. Boston: Houghton Mifflin.

Goodman, D. (1978). Countdown to 1984: Big Brother may be right on schedule. *The Futurist, 12*, 345–355.

Helprin, M. (1983). *Winter's tale*. New York: Harcourt Brace Jovanovich.

Joint Center for Urban Studies of MIT and Harvard. (1980, June 9). The nation's families 1960–1990. *Behavior Today*.

Levinson, D. (1978). *A season of man's life*. New York: Albert A. Knopf.

Miller, J., Taylor, G., & Walker, K. (1982). *Teachers in transition: Study of an aging teaching force.* Toronto: The Ontario Institute for Studies in Education.

Naisbitt, J. (1982). *Megatrends.* New York: Warner Books.

———. (1983, October). Interview: The world according to John Naisbitt. *New Age Journal,* 30–38, 93–96.

Orwell, G. (1949). *1984.* London: Lecker and Warburg.

Ravitch, D. (1983). *The troubled crusade: American education 1945–1980.* New York: Basic Books.

Smith, C. (1981, September). Visions of tomorrow: Life in the information age. *New Age Journal,* 22–32, 68–69.

Toffler, A. (1980). *The third wave.* New York: William Morrow. 1980. (Reprinted 1981, Bantam Books).

# Index